Social Capital, Diversity, and the Welfare State

Equality
Security
Community

The Equality, Security, and Community (ESC) project, conducted during a six-year period, was conceived as a multidisciplinary collaborative research project. Its objectives were concisely described in its subtitle: "Explaining and Improving the Distribution of Well-Being in Canada." *Explaining the distribution of well-being* requires a concerted multidisciplinary effort that considers the interplay among market behaviour, political and community participation, and policy formation. *Improving the distribution* requires effective and durable policies, which, in turn, must be based on sound theoretical and empirical foundations. Using a wide range of research methodologies, the ESC project sheds light on these complex issues, while it advances our ability to steer public policies toward improved outcomes.

Numerous journal articles and book chapters have resulted from the ESC project. Another major product is a unique national longitudinal survey of Canadians that covers the economic, political, cultural, and attitudinal bases of inequality. This database was analyzed by project co-investigators and has been posted for research by others (on the website of York University's Institute for Social Research).

Social Capital, Diversity, and the Welfare State is one of three edited volumes stemming from the ESC project. The other two volumes are:

Racing to the Bottom? Provincial Interdependence in the Canadian Federation
Edited Kathryn Harrison

Dimensions of Inequality in Canada
Edited by David A. Green and Jonathan R. Kesselman

All three volumes are published by UBC Press.

Social Capital, Diversity, and the Welfare State

...... Edited by Fiona M. Kay
and Richard Johnston

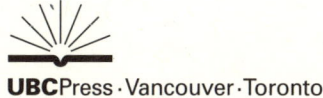
UBCPress · Vancouver · Toronto

© UBC Press 2007

All rights reserved. No part of this publication may be reproduced, stored in a retrieval system, or transmitted, in any form or by any means, without prior written permission of the publisher, or, in Canada, in the case of photocopying or other reprographic copying, a licence from Access Copyright (Canadian Copyright Licensing Agency), www.accesscopyright.ca.

15 14 13 12 11 10 09 08 07   5 4 3 2 1

Printed in Canada on ancient-forest-free paper (100 percent post-consumer recycled) that is processed chlorine- and acid-free, with vegetable-based inks.

Library and Archives Canada Cataloguing in Publication

Social capital, diversity, and the welfare state / edited by Fiona M. Kay and Richard Johnston.

(Equality, security, community 1715-8117)
Includes bibliographical references and index.
ISBN 978-0-7748-1309-9 (bound); ISBN 978-0-7748-1310-5 (pbk.)

1. Social capital (Sociology) – Canada. 2. Pluralism (Social sciences) – Canada. 3. Trust – Social aspects – Canada. 4. Canada – Social policy. I. Johnston, Richard, 1948- II. Kay, Fiona. III. Series.

HM708.S67 2006   302   C2006-905376-6

Canadä

UBC Press gratefully acknowledges the financial support for our publishing program of the Government of Canada through the Book Publishing Industry Development Program (BPIDP), and of the Canada Council for the Arts, and the British Columbia Arts Council.

The authors acknowledge, with thanks, the financial support of the Social Sciences and Humanities Research Council of Canada through a Major Collaborative Research Initiatives grant (#412-97-0003).

This book has been published with the help of a grant from the Canadian Federation for the Humanities and Social Sciences, through the Aid to Scholarly Publications Programme, using funds provided by the Social Sciences and Humanities Research Council of Canada, and with the help of the K.D. Srivastava Fund.

UBC Press
The University of British Columbia
2029 West Mall
Vancouver, BC V6T 1Z2
604-822-5959 / Fax: 604-822-6083
www.ubcpress.ca

Contents

Figures and Tables   vii

1 Introduction   1
FIONA M. KAY AND RICHARD JOHNSTON

Part 1: Theoretical Overview

2 Ubiquity and Disciplinary Contrasts of Social Capital   17
FIONA M. KAY AND RICHARD JOHNSTON

3 The Dynamics of Social Capital: Who Wants to Stay In If Nobody Is Out?   41
FIONA M. KAY AND PAUL BERNARD

4 Equality, Trust, and Multiculturalism   67
AVIGAIL EISENBERG

Part 2: Studies of Social Capital and Determinants of Social Capital

5 Measuring and Modelling Interpersonal Trust   95
STUART N. SOROKA, JOHN F. HELLIWELL, AND RICHARD JOHNSTON

6 Gender, Early Experiences with "Social Capital," and Adult Community Participation   133
JAMES CURTIS AND THOMAS PERKS

7   Ethnicity and Social Capital in Canada   169
    AMANDA AIZLEWOOD AND RAVI PENDAKUR

8   Social Capital and Political Struggles of Immigrants:
    Sri Lankan Tamils and Black Caribbean Peoples in
    Toronto   199
    SARA ABRAHAM

**Part 3: Consequences of Social Capital:
Policy and Government Programs**

9   Social Capital and Intergenerational Coresidence:
    How Ethnic Communities and Families Shape
    Transitions to Adulthood   219
    BARBARA A. MITCHELL

10 Social Capital and Health in Canada: (Compositional)
    Effects of Trust, Participation in Networks, and Civic
    Activity on Self-Rated Health   251
    GERRY VEENSTRA

11 Ethnicity, Trust, and the Welfare State   279
    STUART N. SOROKA, RICHARD JOHNSTON,
    AND KEITH BANTING

    Works Cited   305

    Contributors   335

    Index   341

Figures and Tables

FIGURES

1.1	The theoretical and empirical bases of social capital analyses in this book	5
3.1	Typology of social capital: processes of distribution and reproduction	47
5.1	The effects of ethnicity on trust	117
9.1	Living arrangement by ethnic group	231
9.2	Reason for (first) home-leaving by ethnic group	232

TABLES

5.1	Trust questions in the ESC survey	98
5.2	Relationships between generalized trust and wallet questions	101
5.3	Responses to general trust questions	102
5.4	Responses to wallet questions	110
5.5	Summary of wallets measure	112
5A.1	Descriptives	123
5B.1	Factor analysis of associational memberships	125
5B.2	Sources of associational memberships (ethnic, religious, and other)	126
5B.3	Sources of associational memberships (service clubs and recreation, political, youth, cultural, and help groups)	128
6.1	Participation in community voluntary activities as a youth, by gender, as reported by adult Canadians: national sample, 1997	143
6.2	Participation in community voluntary activities as a youth, by gender, for age cohorts among adult respondents	143

6.3	Levels of current participation in community activities, by gender, among adult respondents	145
6.4	Current participation in selected community activities, by gender, for age cohorts among adult Canadians	147
6.5	Zero-order correlations of participation in community voluntary activities as a youth (Index II) and current participation in community activities, by gender	149
6.6	Relative effects (betas from MCA/ANOVA) for participation in community activities as a youth (Index II) and seven other social background factors as predictors of current participation in community activities, for females and males	151
6.7	Levels of current participation in community activities (deviations from the grand mean), by gender, with statistical controls (MCA) for youth activities and seven social background factors	155
6A.1	Zero-order correlations of participation in community voluntary activities as a youth (Index II) and current participation in community activities, by gender and age cohorts	166
7.1	Characteristics of social capital measures	181
7.2	Comparisons of means for social capital measures according to employment equity categories and immigrant status	182
7.3	Basic model	183
7.4	Broad model	186
7.5	Full model	189
7A.1	Descriptives	196
9.1	Final survival analyses model for staying at home	235
9.2	Final survival analysis model for returning home	239
9A.1	Frequency distribution for home-leaving and home-returning analysis	247
10.1	Social capital and health: individual-level findings	256
10.2	Social capital and health: ecological findings	260
10.3	Social capital and health: multi-level findings	264
10.4	Multivariate logistic regression: basic demographic predictors of fair or poor self-rated health status	267

10.5	Multivariate logistic regression: sociodemographic predictors of fair or poor self-rated health status	267
10.6	Multivariate logistic regression: sociodemographic predictors of fair or poor self-rated health status, parsimonious version	268
10.7	Multivariate logistic regression: sociodemographic and social capital predictors of fair or poor self-rated health status	271
11.1	Modelling trust	287
11.2	Modelling support for social programs: EI/Welfare	291
11.3	Modelling support for social programs: health care	292
11.4	Modelling support for social programs: pensions	293
11A.1	Descriptives	299

Social Capital, Diversity, and the Welfare State

1
Introduction

Fiona M. Kay and Richard Johnston

Social capital is arguably the most critical concept to emerge in the social sciences in the last twenty years (Portes 1998, 2). Not only does it transcend disciplinary boundaries, it enlivens public discourse. Social capital speaks of the importance of social networks, of communication, and of an exchange of resources that strengthens community. Practically speaking, all aspects of people's lives are embedded in social networks, networks in which people invest time and energy and which influence their lives in manifold ways (Flap 1999, 6). Aspects of the concept are found in the phrase, "no man is an island" (Flap 1995), and of the commonplace, "who you know is as important as what you know" (Granovetter 1985). The emphasis on social involvement, investment, and resources embedded in social structure provides a link to community well-being that extends beyond individual utilitarianism and self-interest. At the same time, social capital speaks of the social-psychological orientations that emerge from networks, in particular, of bonds of trust.

Social capital has been invoked to explain an array of social consequences. At the individual level, for example, social capital facilitates employment (Granovetter 1986), social mobility (Forsé 1999; Friedman and Krackhardt 1997; Gabbay and Zuckerman 1998; Lin, Ensel, and Vaughn 1981; Wegener 1991), and entrepreneurial ventures (Burt 1998). Other individual-level behaviours explained by social capital include migration and assimilation (Liang 1994), educational attainment among immigrants and ethnic minorities (Teachman, Paasch, and Carver 1997; Watkins 1984; White and Kaufman 1997), language facility (Parcel and Geschwender 1995), mathematical abilities and truancy (Marjoribanks 1991; McNeal 1999; Morgan and Sørensen 1999), family structure (Mitchell 1994; Mitchell and Gee 1996), and criminality (Arnold and Kay 1995; Hagan 1993; Macmillan 1995; McCarthy and Hagan 2001; Nagin and Paternoster 1994). Social capital also has been aggregated to provide community-level impacts through studies of financial elites and cohesive subgroups (Frank and Yasumoto 1998), communities of place (Flora 1998; Hofferth and Iceland 1998), associational memberships (Eastis 1998; Putnam 1995a; Stolle and Rochon 1998), collective action (Macy 1991; Smith 1998), and economic development (Fukuyama 1989; Helliwell 1996; Helliwell and Putnam 1995; Woolcock 1998). Policy analysts and students of government decision making consider social capital to offer potential policy leverage, for example, perhaps harnessing social capital for the good of individuals and society (Fox 1997; Lin, Cook, and Burt 2001).

The concept has gained widespread currency across a number of academic disciplines, notably sociology, political science, and economics, and has motivated ambitious interdisciplinary research ventures. The different disciplinary treatments of social capital exhibit strong convergence: all see parallels between social capital and other forms of capital, most notably, human capital; all emphasize its fungibility; all distinguish between "bridging" and "bonding" social capital, although not always in so many words; all are alert to the distributional inequalities that social capital creates; and all assert the centrality of trust.

With only a handful of exceptions, positive evaluations vastly outweigh negative ones. The standard claim takes the form: interaction breeds trust, and trust makes other good things happen. On this reading, the task for policy makers or institutional designers is to get robust interaction going. But the general interaction-trust link is compatible with a wide range of *un*desirable outcomes. Social capital can produce durable social inequality. If social capital is an indicator of inclusion, so must it also mark exclusion. If a group is engaged in antisocial action, trust among its members may make the antisocial outcome even more dire. Honour among thieves does not make theft honourable or society better off. Some observers detect antisocial tendencies in the very agenda of social capital research. They worry that the real objective is to smooth the path of privatization or to compromise the boundary between church and state.

Bridging Disciplinary Divergences

This conceptual and evaluative confusion reflects divergences that go unrecognized because of disciplinary parochialism and the particular theoretical perspectives of individual authors (Wall, Ferrazzi, and Schryer 1998, 300). Some work concentrates on individuals and households, while other work focuses on collectivities; different units of analysis produce quite different perspectives and, commonly, quite different moral tones. Some work focuses on the structure of social relations, while other work emphasizes the content of interaction, especially the psychological implications of different structural forms. Roughly speaking, sociologists tend to speak of networks, to focus on their utility to individuals and families, and to emphasize the inequality and exclusion that results. Economists tend to focus on trust, especially of the interpersonal type, to focus on aggregates, such as whole economies, and to emphasize positive externalities. Political scientists talk about both networks and trust, the tendency of the former to produce the latter, the generalizability of trust orientations from the personal to the political (and vice versa), and the beneficial consequences of networks and trust for policy, indeed for democracy.

As a result, the literature is shot through with definitional dilemmas and explanations riddled by tautology. At this point in its intellectual evolution, the concept is suspiciously protean. It requires careful bounding, both to distinguish it from neighbouring concepts and to unpack its internal confusion. Unpacking is the necessary preliminary to identifying – rather than merely supposing – causal links within the domain.

To this end, it is critical to bring scholars from different backgrounds together. This was the central aim of the "Equality, Security, and Community" (ESC) Major Collaborative Research Initiative, of which this book is a product. The initiative drew twenty-three economists, political scientists, and sociologists from across Canada into a common research network, promoted a common discourse, and – we hope – built bonds of interdisciplinary trust. True to certain tenets in the social capital literature, the most powerful piece of bridging required personal bonding.

Much of this took place in the design phase of the central ESC product, a massive, two-wave sample survey. Representatives from each discipline took joint responsibility for the key elements: instrumentation, sample design, and analysis. To the best of our knowledge, no other survey gives as rich an inventory of variables of common interest to these three disciplines. The first wave of the survey was conducted in 2000 and 2001, and this is the version of the data represented here. The largest component of the study is a national probability sample, stratified by province and comprising 4,101 respondents. Supplementing the national sample is a "metropolitan over-sample," from Montreal, Toronto, and Vancouver and drawn disproportionately from census tracts with a high percentage of "visible minority" residents, as defined by the Census of Canada. This component comprises 1,051 respondents. A third component is the British Columbia Resource Community Sample, with 1,427 respondents from seven different towns in the Georgia Basin. These samples were merged for several analyses reported in this book.

Each sample uses the same survey instrument, which includes items on: (1) household composition, based mainly on the Canadian census; (2) income, based mainly on the *Survey of Labour and Income Dynamics* (Statistics Canada); (3) employment, based mainly on the *Labour Force Survey* (Statistics Canada); (4) well-being and perceptions of risk; (5) party identification and electoral behaviour; (6) policy opinion and perceptions, mainly on the welfare state; (7) links to family, neighbourhood, and secondary associations; (8) media and computer use; (9) ethnic attitudes and perceptions; and (10) trust in institutions and in other persons. The data set also includes geocodes that facilitate linkage to respondents' neighbourhood contexts. These codes enable the cross-level analysis, for example, on the effects of neighbourhood diversity on interpersonal trust. The ESC survey underpins over half the empirical chapters in this book.

The book originated in a conference hosted at Green College, University of British Columbia, in November 2001. Certain chapters were also aired at conferences at Nuffield College, Oxford, at Queen's University, and at the 2002 Annual Meeting of the Canadian Political Science Association. The original texts have undergone two complete rounds of editorial comment and revision, each of which also included exchange of mutually relevant papers.

The Book: A Conceptual Roadmap

This book considers the alternative *meanings* of social capital, its causal *foundations*, and its *consequences* in the realm of policy. Some chapters are devoted to theory and others to the presentation and analysis of data. Most of the latter deploy the ESC survey – sometimes linked to census data – while others use entirely separate data sets. Figure 1.1 locates each chapter jointly in terms of its theoretical focus, its empirical basis, and the aspect of social capital of central concern. Many chapters touch on more than one aspect.

The Centrality of Trust

Trust appears as a common theme in the social capital literature. Trust is often treated as the "message" embedded in networks of communication. Through investments in social relations, individuals earn and give their trust to others, facilitating new exchanges of resources and information. In the

FIGURE 1.1

The theoretical and empirical bases of social capital analyses in this book

Aspect of social capital	Theoretical	Empirical sources of data — ESC survey	Other
TYPE/NATURE			
Trust	Eisenberg (CHAPTER 4)	Soroka, Helliwell, and Johnston (CHAPTER 5); Aizlewood and Pendakur (CHAPTER 7); Veenstra (CHAPTER 10); Soroka, Johnston, and Banting (CHAPTER 11)	
Networks	Kay and Bernard (CHAPTER 3)	Soroka, Helliwell, and Johnston (CHAPTER 5); Aizlewood and Pendakur (CHAPTER 7)	Abraham (CHAPTER 8); Mitchell (CHAPTER 9)
FOUNDATIONS			
Social inequality	Kay and Johnston (CHAPTER 2)	Soroka, Helliwell, and Johnston (CHAPTER 5); Aizlewood and Pendakur (CHAPTER 7)	Mitchell (CHAPTER 9)
Bridging/ Bonding	Kay and Bernard (CHAPTER 3)	Soroka, Helliwell, and Johnston (CHAPTER 5); Soroka, Johnston, and Banting (CHAPTER 11)	Abraham (CHAPTER 8); Mitchell (CHAPTER 9)
Fungibility		Soroka, Helliwell, and Johnston (CHAPTER 5); Soroka, Johnston, and Banting (CHAPTER 11)	Curtis and Perks (CHAPTER 6)
CONSEQUENCES			
Life chances	Kay and Johnston (CHAPTER 2)		Mitchell (CHAPTER 9)
Health		Veenstra (CHAPTER 10)	
Opinions on policy		Soroka, Johnston, and Banting (CHAPTER 11)	

literature, trust is at times treated as collective (trust of a community or trust felt toward government) (Paxton 1999; Putnam 1993a), and at other times as interpersonal (individual investments within organizations) (Burt 2005; Coleman 1988; Portes 1998; Sandefur and Laumann 1998). For some scholars, trust acts as a lubricant for the growth of social capital (Light and Bonacich 1988), yet, for others, trust is itself an element of social capital, a resource in its own right (Flap 1999; Paxton 1999; Putnam 2000). For others still, trust is neither a conduit nor a form of social capital, but the product of social capital once activated (Granovetter 1985; Woolcock 1998). In this book, several chapters concern themselves with trust at least in passing, but it is a conceptual preoccupation for Chapters 2, 3, and 4.

Avigail Eisenberg (Chapter 4) focuses on the psychological element of trust in the social capital complex. She questions the adequacy of conceptions of trust that originate in interpersonal relations for understanding more impersonal dimensions of social life, including politics. Not only is interpersonal trust empirically misleading for the social and political variants, but it may also even be inappropriate, ethically speaking. More convincing, in her view, is work that starts with notions of trust (or its lack) expressed toward political and government actors. This work is a better guide to understanding trust among strangers than is work among intimates. In the social and political realm, the key is the relative equality of the players. This equality is assumed in analytic modelling of trust relations but is too often forgotten in empirical work. Of particular relevance to Canada is the role of multicultural policies in fostering social and political trust, specifically, as they address inequality. Far from promoting ghettoization – a critique that finds some inspiration in one part of the social capital literature – multicultural policies promote social integration and trust.

Stuart Soroka, John Helliwell, and Richard Johnston (Chapter 5) use the ESC survey to examine interpersonal trust, particularly as trust connects to immigration (with comparisons to Rice and Feldman's 1997 US study of civic attitudes among immigrants) and cultural diversity. They begin with the question of whether the standard measurement of interpersonal trust, which is so critical to comparison over time and across countries, really captures how much trust individuals *actually* repose in others, as opposed to how much they think they *should* repose. The pith of their investigation is a comparison of the traditional question with a new one predicated on the perceived probability of cooperative behaviour in a classic situation of pure trust: a lost wallet. Although trust measured by this set of questions clearly overlaps that indicated by response to the classic question, divergences are also sharp.

The chapter by Stuart Soroka, Richard Johnston, and Keith Banting (Chapter 11), which looks at the ultimate implications of diversity and trust on welfare policy attitudes, begins by distinguishing political trust from interpersonal trust. Unsurprisingly, interpersonal trust and political trust are related. The primary causal direction in the relationship remains contested (Brehm and Rahn 1997), but a strong case can be made that political trust is not so much a consequence of interpersonal trust as a precondition for it. No less striking, however, is the looseness of the link between the domains.

Networks: Insiders and Outsiders

Common to discussions of social capital is the proposition that social capital may present a double-edged sword: it may bridge, facilitating inclusion and integration of newcomers, even as it bonds, excluding undesirable outsiders (Putnam 2000; Tilly 1998). Fiona Kay and Paul Bernard (Chapter 3) explicitly link the aggregate and distributive sides and the inclusionary and exclusionary sides, and urge us to see the negative implications as true concomitants of the positive ones. Social capital must be seen as part of a system that produces and reproduces insiders and outsiders, winners and losers. The authors present a typology of social capital that is characterized by two dimensions: distribution and reproduction, two processes that explain how social capital enables the formation of coalitions and community enhancement, while simultaneously breeding disenfranchisement and ghettoization of the disadvantaged. On one level, this is a reassertion of the sociological origins of the concept and a brief against its sanitization. At another level, it pulls the divergent treatments in sociology, political science, and economics together, with an emphasis on the centrality of social inequality.

Foundations: Ethnic Diversity and Social Inequality

Canada is particularly well-suited to the exploration of the dynamics of ethnic diversity and social capital, both for its high level of and high variance in multicultural incidence. The contrast between the major cities and the rest of the country is very sharp. Canada has a long tradition as a society of immigrants, with one of the highest proportions among OECD countries of citizens born outside the country. No less critical is that Canada also harbours critically situated "national minorities" (Kymlicka 1995), notably francophones and First Nations. At the same time, many millions of Canadians have little or no practical experience of diversity – or they think they don't.

What, for instance, is the dispersion, or variance, of social capital across communities? Beyond mean levels of social capital, there is the potential for unequal distribution, and even the shrinking or expansion of social capital within certain communities (Paxton 1999; Putnam 2000; Wuthnow 1997). How is social capital distributed across various cultural communities, geographic regions, and the two official languages of Canada? Amanda Aizlewood and Ravi Pendakur (Chapter 7) use the ESC survey to construct a detailed picture of the ethnic foundations of social capital in Canada. Strikingly, those foundations are very modest. Although individual groups stand out for particular forms of affiliation or orientation, much more striking is the *lack* of ethnic differentiation. Rather, what stands out is the distinctiveness of metropolitan places, places where (to quote the authors) "myriad world-views, languages and cultures meet." Where most people are strangers, strangers may be more threatening. Affiliation and, with it, trust follow self-selected lines, based on pre-existing networks. The good news is that the ethnic diversification of Canada's cities does not by itself undermine the country's stock of social capital.

Barbara Mitchell (Chapter 9) deploys the *Culture and Coresidence Study*, a four-ethnic-group matched-sample survey drawn from Greater Vancouver, to examine a specific and potentially powerful network: the family. She finds that cultural groups create and reproduce their own social capital, which generates distinctive "social timetables." In particular, she finds sharp differences among ethnic groups in coresidence, the continued presence of adult offspring in the household. Coresidence lasts longer for Asian families than for those with British or Southern European backgrounds. For the latter, a norm of independence drives exit decisions, but exit on these terms may be premature and disadvantageous. The incidence of "boomerang" coresidence, the return of adults to the origin household, is higher among early leavers. The chapter is a powerful reminder of the social structuring of intergenerational ties. As the social safety net weakens, differences among groups in intergenerational social capital transfer will become only more important to the structuring of social inequality.

Foundations: Bridging and Bonding

Sara Abraham (Chapter 8) takes an ethnographic turn with a detailed comparison of political organization in two "visible minority" communities concentrated in the Greater Toronto area: Sri Lankan Tamils and Caribbean Blacks. The two groups share a common legacy of racial marginalization in Canada but diverge in their home-country legacies. Both groups exhibit a striking depth of organization, although many Caribbean organizations founded in the 1960s and 1970s have since folded. One line of feminist explanation for this organizational richness emphasizes pre-political organization around childrearing issues, but Abraham deftly shows the limitations of this claim. In both groups, the key to political organization is *politics* itself, specifically, nationalist politics. For Caribbean groups, the nationalist ideology is Pan-African, reflecting the dominant modes of black organization in the period of US Civil Rights struggles and of decolonization. Sri Lankans organized around home-country ethnic conflict, and Sri Lankan organization in Canada benefits from an international network for political mobilization. In each group, the depth of organization also reflects the very experience of marginalization, an ironic twist on a recurring social capital theme.

Soroka, Helliwell, and Johnston (Chapter 5), in their exploration of alternative indicators of interpersonal trust in the ESC study, examine both diverse groups and diversity as such (as indicated by census data on respondents' neighbourhoods) as factors in trust. They find significant levels of distrust, particularly toward police officers, among visible minorities. This is especially the case where visible-minority numbers are few. Conversely, "majority" individuals exhibit increased distrust as communities become more ethnically diverse. All this is generally consistent with the literature on the "contact hypothesis" (Forbes 1997). They also find that forms of affiliation that bring like into contact with like do little to promote interpersonal trust among strangers. All this raises deep anxieties for the future of the welfare state (Miller 1995). That said, Soroka, Johnston, and Banting (Chapter 11) find that *political* trust is not adversely affected by racial minority status or by community diversity. Much more important for political trust are the older divides in Canadian life, those among national minorities.

Foundations: Fungibility

Parallels are often drawn between social capital and other forms of capital, particularly to human capital (Burt 2001; Coleman 1988, 1990b; Flap 1999; Putnam 1995a; Wall et al. 1998). More intriguing is the idea that different forms of capital are fungible, that is, that they can be brokered for each other (Bourdieu 1986; Portes 2000b), enabling new opportunities and increased profits of social capital (Burt 1992). Fungibility claims concern both networks and trust.

James Curtis and Thomas Perks (Chapter 6) consider the extent to which adolescent experiences of group involvement cash out in adult equivalents, with data from the *National Survey of Giving, Volunteering and Participating*. Continuity from adolescence to adulthood is considerable, a finding with obvious policy implications. In both pre-adult and adult years, women are more participative than men, especially when characteristics indicating restraints on women's ability to participate are controlled. Only in sports do males dominate. Adolescent-adult continuity is also higher for females than for males. The chapter casts doubt on the applicability of Putnam's *Bowling Alone* thesis (2000) to Canada: younger adults claim more involvement for their adolescent years than older ones do.

In the realm of trust, Soroka, Helliwell, and Johnston (Chapter 5) show the strengths and limits of translation among forms of interpersonal trust, or at least among the indicators of each form. They assert that, if necessary, the classic indicator of interpersonal trust stands adequately for all subdomains of the property. Nonetheless, considerable slippage appears, and it is not just measurement error. "Generalized" trust appears to reflect socialization, including conformity pressures. Formal education, for instance, is a critical predictor. A particularly striking source is the cultural pattern in the country of origin outside Canada. For new Canadians and their children, memories of the home country are reflected in group differences within Canada. (No less strikingly, and in contrast to the situation in the United States, origin-country differences do not persist past the second generation.) But the radius of trust in the "wallet" measure is not much affected by conformity-driven cultural forces. Rather, this more strategic form of trust seems to reflect individualized experiences, especially of neighbourhoods' ethnic and economic diversity. Similarly, Soroka, Johnston, and Banting (Chapter 11) show the limits of fungibility across the interpersonal/political divide. If there is a tendency among political scientists to assume that one type of trust readily generalizes to the other, Soroka and his co-authors suggest that this assumption may be premature and naïve.

CONSEQUENCES

In their review chapter, Fiona Kay and Richard Johnston (Chapter 2) flag an issue that requires close further study. They emphasize a parallel between social capital and other forms of capital in the relationship between the society-wide aggregate and the within-society distribution. Does an accumulation of social capital that may, on balance, create external benefits for society at large (including a Rawlsian benefit for those at the bottom) also, and almost inevitably, increase the overall level of inequality? This concern seems especially compelling for social capital conceived as networks.

That social capital is a critical mediating factor between sociodemographic characteristics, networks (family, friends, community service clubs), civic participation, and health outcomes for individuals seems highly plausible. Gerry Veenstra (Chapter 10) explores individual-level relationships among trust, social engagement, civic participation, and self-rated health status with data from the ESC survey. Veenstra's work builds on a growing but contested literature on links among these variables and takes advantage of the depth of coverage of all the relevant controls and indicators in the ESC survey instrument. It turns out that social capital in both its dimensions – trusting orientations and certain network connections at least – is conducive to health. As Veenstra puts it, "people who are open to interactions with others, [who] believe in the inherent good will of others" reap a reward in personal health. Actual links to the larger world – informal networking with neighbours, membership in recreational groups, and watching television news – also promote health. In this domain, at least, more social capital always seems to be better.

Finally, Soroka, Johnston, and Banting (Chapter 11) carry the theme of ethnic diversity and dispersion of social capital through to public policy, in particular, to support for the welfare state. Soroka and his colleagues use the ESC survey to address a cross-national theme at a subnational level. Students of the welfare state ask whether the increasing ethnic and racial diversity of the rich, industrial societies is undermining the moral and political foundation of their welfare states. The fear is that diversity undermines the presumption of trust that arguably underpins a willingness to pool risk and redistribute income. Canada is a compelling case both as it has become more diverse and as it has resisted pressure for welfare cutbacks more than most societies. Analysis in the chapter exploits variation in diversity experiences within Canada. It does seem to be the case that interpersonal trust, as captured by the "wallet" measure described in Chapter 5 (Soroka, Helliwell, and Johnston) and Chapter 7 (Aizlewood and Pendakur), declines as the ethnic diversity of a neighbourhood increases. But *political* trust is not similarly affected, and this dimension of trust is also critical to welfare-state support: if one does not trust the political class to administer public programs, one is unlikely to support the programs themselves. Both forms of trust affect support for the welfare state, but the links along the causal chain are such that there is virtually no relationship between ethnic context and support for social insurance and redistribution. This leaves a question on the table: Is there something distinctive about the Canadian pattern of immigration and settlement?

The Book in Outline

Chapters are ordered, roughly, by two principles. The first puts the general before the particular. So chapters that focus on theory come first, and the theoretical chapters with the broadest reach precede the ones with a narrower compass. Empirical chapters follow. Almost all empirical chapters touch on many facets of social capital, but each chapter appears in the section that roughly corresponds to its place in a causal scheme stretching from the most basic foundations to the most remote consequences. The final three chapters say much about foundations, and even say much about conceptualization, but all focus on consequences.

Kay and Johnston (Chapter 2) begin with an overview of the entire field, networks and trust, conceptualization, foundations, and consequences. Their point is to portray both the reach of the concept and its limitations and to argue for the very exploration in depth that this book provides. Kay and Bernard (Chapter 3) don their sociological caps to address an interdisciplinary audience. Although social capital as a concept originates in sociology, political science and economics have hijacked the idea, as it were. In doing so, political scientists and economists have tended to downplay the role of social capital in inequality and exclusion, so Kay and Bernard enter a plea for righting the balance. Eisenberg (Chapter 4) presents an essay in political theory, and takes her fellow political scientists to task for their overemphasis on face-to-face interaction. This distracts them from the real challenge for complicated, diverse societies, of fostering trust among strangers.

Soroka, Helliwell, and Johnston (Chapter 5) devote care and attention to the sources of interpersonal trust but do so in a way that brings out slippage among alternative conceptualizations within the domain of the interpersonal. Along the way, they tell a complicated story about Canadian diversity and about the integrative power of well-conceived multicultural policy. This chapter is the first to introduce analysis of the ESC survey. Curtis and Perks (Chapter 6) show the continuity of adolescent-to-adult affiliation patterns, and indicate an abiding source of gender differences. Aizlewood and Pendakur (Chapter 7) use the ESC survey to explore the ethnic foundations of affiliation and trust at an unprecedented level of comparative detail. Abraham (Chapter 8) goes into even more detail, thanks to her ethnographic focus, as she compares Tamils with persons of Caribbean origin in Toronto.

Mitchell (Chapter 9) looks at ethnic differences in intergenerational coresidence as a source of variation in life prospects. Early departure from the home may foster an illusory independence, one that is unsustainable in the face of urban employment and housing pressure. Veenstra (Chapter 10) looks at health outcomes of both network affiliation and trust. Finally, Soroka, Johnston, and Banting (Chapter 11) look all the way down the road to redistributive politics, as they consider whether diversity is compatible with a generous welfare state.

Part 1
Theoretical Overview

2
Ubiquity and Disciplinary Contrasts of Social Capital

Fiona M. Kay and Richard Johnston

As a concept, social capital is both centrally important and disturbingly open-ended. Social capital is probably the single most ubiquitous social science concept currently in circulation. It is ubiquitous because it is fertile, but its fertility stems in part from the fact that it is also protean; it seems to promise something for everyone, which is also to say that it means different things to different people. This is a prescription for confusion. Is it about individuals and families or is it about aggregates, such as whole communities or nations? Does it describe networks of affiliation, or the psychosocial orientations that allegedly stem from affiliation, or both? Is it mainly about inclusion or about exclusion, or can one aspect not be discussed without the other? Is more social capital, however defined, always better? The answers to these questions differ according to personal predilection and disciplinary background. This chapter draws the various strands together, both to show why the idea is truly so fertile but also why it needs further pruning.

The Ubiquity of the Concept

SOCIOLOGICAL FOUNDATIONS

For sociologists, the core of the concept of "social capital" lies in the density and quality of ties among persons and households. Pierre Bourdieu (1980b, 1986) and James Coleman (1988, 1993) centred attention on the individual or the small group as their unit of analysis. Both scholars focused on the benefits accruing to individuals or families by virtue of their ties with others. Bourdieu (1986, 248) provides a concise definition: "Social capital is the aggregate of the actual or potential resources which are linked to possession of a durable network of more or less institutionalized relationships of mutual acquaintance and recognition – or in other words, to membership in a group." The volume of social capital possessed by an individual depends on both the size of the network of connections he or she can mobilize and on the volume of capital (e.g., economic or cultural capital) possessed by each person to whom he or she is connected (ibid., 249). For Bourdieu, this network of relationships is a product of investment strategies, either individual or collective, aimed at establishing or reproducing social relationships that are usable in the future (ibid.).

Coleman's view (1988, S98) of social capital illustrates how the social structure of a group can function as a resource for the individuals within that group. He argues that social capital "inheres in the structure of relations between actors and among actors" (ibid.). Coleman maintains that social capital exists in several forms: as obligations and expectations, information channels, and social norms (1988, S95; 1990b, 312). Two elements are critical to this form of social capital: the level of trustworthiness of the social environment (which means that obligations will be repaid) and the actual extent of obligations held. Each of these is a feature of social structure that also provides social capital as a resource for the individuals of the group (Paxton 1999, 92). For Coleman (1990c), community ties were important for the benefits they yielded to individuals, including greater safety on the streets, reduced crime, better access to education, and improved health.

Thus, sociologists typically consider social capital, in the form of networks of association and involvement in social activities (clubs, professional associations, religion, family networks), as pivotal to accomplishing goals. The most common use of social capital has been invoked in the field of stratification (Portes 1998). Social capital is invoked as determinant of access to employment (Smith 2005; Watkins 1984), mobility through occupational ladders (Erickson 1996; Granfield and Koenig 1992b; Kay and Hagan 1995; Wegener 1991), and income (Langton and Pfeffer 1993, 1994; Meyerson 1994). Sociologists have also employed the concept of social capital to explain reductions in secondary school dropout rates (Coleman 1988), academic achievement (Stanton-Salazar and Dornbusch 1995), and familial support for children (Gold 1995; Hagan et al. 1996; Mitchell 1994). The role of social capital also figures in studies of ethnic business enclaves. Studies of New York's Chinatown (Zhou 1992), Miami's Little Havana (Portes 1987; Portes and Stepnick 1993), and Los Angeles' Koreatown (Light and Bonacich 1988) demonstrate the role of community networks in providing resources for these firms. Resources include start-up capital, information about business opportunities, access to new markets, and a pliant labour force.

Political Science and the Community

Across other disciplines, the concept is transformed to become an attribute of the community itself. Portes (2000b, 3) observes that "in this new garb, its benefits accrued not so much to individuals as to the collectivity as a whole in the form of reduced crime rates, lower official corruption, and better governance."

Political scientist Robert Putnam (1993a, 1995a) is responsible for the conceptual extension that made it possible to speak of the "stock" of social capital possessed by communities, cities, and even nations, as well as its structural effects on their development. In 1995, Putnam first made the claim that America's social capital is in decline, a claim extended in his magisterial 2000 volume, *Bowling Alone: The Collapse and Revival of American Community*. He cited decreasing voter turnout and declining membership in groups such as bowling leagues and the PTA as evidence of a general decline in the ties connecting Americans to each other and to the political system. The result, Putnam contends, is a threat to the successful maintenance of democracy. Putnam (1995a, 66) eloquently argues: "The quality of governance was determined by longstanding traditions of civic engagement (or its absence). Voter turnout, newspaper readership, membership in choral societies and football clubs – these were the hallmarks of a successful region. In fact, historical analysis suggested that these networks of organized reciprocity and civic solidarity, far from being epiphenomena of socioeconomic modernization, were a precondition for it."

For political scientists, social capital represents interpersonal trust as well as political trust and indicates how each form of trust relates to support for public policies. More precisely, social capital refers "to features of social organization such as networks, norms, and social trust that facilitate coordination and cooperation for mutual benefit" (Putnam 1995a, 67). Political scientists are concerned with aggregate levels of interpersonal trust and view trust at this level as a gateway for trust in the political community. And trust in government may be a precondition for collective action, where the latter is necessary to effecting citizen preferences. If citizens value some collective good but, because of distrust, are unwilling to give the political class the necessary resources to deliver the good, the citizenry is impoverished. If the collective good is also a precondition for proper functioning of markets, the aggregate shortfall is all the greater. Social capital is, in short, the solution to the problems of *dis*trust and collective *in*action.

Political scientists mirror sociologists' concern for individual or household differences: private networks facilitate participation in public processes, and participation is normally a precondition for extracting benefits from the system. Several studies demonstrate that membership in voluntary associations stimulates political participation (Verba, Schlozman, and Brady 1995; Wolfinger and Rosenstone 1980). More generally, ties to the community increase the likelihood of individual political participation (Guest and Oropesa 1986). Political scientists extend the analysis from political participation to democratic vitality. For example, Inglehart's (1988, 1990) research examined the relationship between civic culture and countries' years of democracy. Putnam's research (1993a) on Italy considered the relationship between social capital and democratic governmental performance. He found a measure of "civic community" (which included association memberships) to be highly correlated with democratic institutional performance. Numerous studies have followed this tradition to explore the impact of social capital stocks on the maintenance of democracy (Halpern 2005; Muller and Seligson 1994; Paxton 1999; Peterson, Saporta and Seidel 2000; Rice and Sumberg 1997).

Social capital can be simultaneously a "private good" and a "public good." As Putnam (2000, 20) observes: "Some of the benefit from an investment in social capital goes to bystanders, while some of the benefit redounds in the immediate interest of the person making the investment." Networks of civic engagement foster a host of positive yields to participating individuals and to the larger community. Putnam (1995a, 67) describes several positive outcomes to communities rich with social capital:

> Life is easier in a community blessed with a substantial stock of social capital. In the first place, networks of civic engagement foster sturdy norms of generalized reciprocity and encourage the emergence of social trust. Such networks facilitate coordination and communication, amplify reputations, and thus allow dilemmas of collective action to be resolved. When economic and political negotiation is embedded in dense networks of social interaction, incentives for opportunism are reduced. At the same time, networks of civic engagement embody past success at collaboration, which can serve as a cultural template for future collaboration. Finally, dense networks of interaction probably broaden the participants' sense of self, developing the "I" into the

"we," or (in the language of rational-choice theorists) enhancing the participants' "taste" for collective benefits.

The two disciplines, sociology and political science, have tended to explore social capital at two different levels of analysis. Although individual and collective benefits derived from ties of involvement are not incompatible, important differences exist. As Portes (2000b, 3) observes: "Social capital as a property of cities or nations is qualitatively distinct from its individual version, a fact that explains why the respective literatures have diverged."

Economic Performance, Governance, and Civic Culture

Economists are like political scientists, only more so: focused on aggregate stocks of social capital and more likely to emphasize the attitudinal consequence of interpersonal ties than the ties themselves (Adler and Kwon 2000, 95). Dense, high-quality links among persons and households, often through neighbourhood or community organizations, enhance interpersonal trust among the units so linked. In the aggregate, economic regions characterized by high levels of interpersonal trust may outperform those in which relations are, on average, mutually distrustful. Helliwell (1996) extends to North America the analysis by Helliwell and Putnam (1995) that links regional growth and social capital in Italian regions. Helliwell examines the extent and nature of interprovincial, interstate, and international differences in social capital in Canada and the United States. In a similar vein, Fukuyama (1995a) outlines the benefits of social capital for national economic efficiency. According to Fukuyama (1995b), the centrality of the family in Chinese culture explains why China has a mercantile history but has been unable to develop large, economically successful corporations. In contrast, the Japanese have typically developed close ties beyond the family, and these ties help to build the social capital required for industrial capitalism.

This approach naturally leads to an investigation of the aggregate sources of community integration. Political trust is of most direct relevance to the demand for public programs or intervention in markets, but interpersonal trust may be a precondition for political trust. These issues have been investigated in other contexts under the "social capital" rubric (Helliwell and Putnam 1995; Knack and Keefer 1997; Putnam 1993b, 1995b, 2000; Whiteley 2000). Economists have examined the extent to which interpersonal trust and participation in voluntary associations, described as measures of social capital or civic culture, are linked to citizens' satisfaction with the efficiency of their regional governments (Helliwell 1996). Civic community as an index of social capital has been measured through newspaper readership, availability of sports and cultural associations, turnout in referenda, and the incidence of preference voting (Helliwell and Putnam 1995). Overlapping trust indicators are measures of sentiment about particular groups, such as the poor and the young. As citizens construct their positions on policy, they can bring both ideas and feelings to bear, and this mix can vary by level of cognitive awareness (Sniderman et al. 1991). Individuals' sentiments about various groups can also reflect their own memberships, and, through these channels, the changing ethnocultural, age, and family composition of Canadian society may influence social policy.

Common Themes

Parallels to Other Forms of Capital

A common premise is that there is a parallel between social capital and human capital. If human capital can be defined as the array of valuable skills and knowledge a person has accumulated over time, then social capital is the array of valuable relationships a person has accumulated over time (Burt 2001). Putnam (1995b, 667) acknowledges this parallel: "Human capital and social capital are closely related, for education has a very powerful effect on trust and associational membership, as well as many other forms of social and political participation."

Like human capital, social capital is productive; it makes possible the achievement of goals that in its absence could not be attained (Coleman 1988, S98). Social capital parallels human capital in its vulnerability to depreciation over time. Like human capital, social capital depreciates if it is not renewed. Coleman (1990b, 321) notes that "social relationships die out if not maintained; expectations and obligations wither over time; and norms depend on regular communication." Therefore, social capital can both increase with use and diminish with disuse, allowing for "either virtuous or vicious cycles" (Wall et al. 1998, 311).

And like human capital, social capital has multiple dimensions (Flap 1999, 14). Constituents of social capital include for some researchers the ties themselves and, for others, the resources exchanged through these ties. For those emphasizing ties or networks, the focus lies on the strength, density, quantity, and other qualities of these ties as well as the assembly of ties defining structural embeddedness and hierarchy (Burt 2001; Erickson 2001; Lin 2001b). Others emphasize the accessible resources accumulated through participation in social networks, particularly trust, control, and information (Cook and Hardin 2001; Wellman and Frank 2001). As Flap (1999, 15) observes: "Social capital is not a one-dimensional all-purpose resource, but has distinguishable components with different effects. Some kinds of social capital may be generally useful, while other kinds are goal-specific."

In contrast to human capital research, however, research on social capital has yet to clearly define the core concept. Can social capital meaningfully encapsulate such diverse entities as trust, information, norms, and networks? Can distinct forms of social capital be identified empirically? If so, how are they related to one another? How do the effects of social capital depend on its composition? And as Woolcock (1998, 161) asks: "If there are benefits and costs associated with possessing certain forms of social capital, how does the calculus of these change under different conditions and over time?" Further development of social capital theory may benefit from the analogy to human capital (Becker 1996; Flap 1999), calling attention to investments, rates of return, opportunity costs, investing and disinvesting, discounting, portfolios of different forms of capitals, substitution, and the ability to appropriate the returns from investment of social capital (Flap 1999, 20).[1]

Fungibility

Forms of capital are fungible, that is, they can be exchanged for each other and actually require such trades for their development (Portes 1998, 2). This exchange of capitals was perhaps first noted by Pierre Bourdieu (1986, 253): The convertibility of the different types of capital is the basis of the strategies aimed at ensuring the reproduction of capital (and the position occupied in social space) by means of the conversions least costly in terms of the conversion work and of the losses inherent in the conversion itself (in a given state of social power relations). The different types of capital can be distinguished according to their reproducibility or, more precisely, according to how easily they are transmitted.

According to Burt (1992), a network is not only a device for receiving resources but also a device for creating resources, such as other networks, which, in turn, create new resources and opportunities. Therefore, one's social capital offers opportunities to turn a profit from the exercise of human capital (ibid.). Portes specifies the primacy of other capitals, human and material, in the development of social capital. He observes that "social capital of any significance can seldom be acquired, for example, without the investment of some material resources and the possession of some cultural knowledge, enabling the individual to establish relations with others" (2000b, 2).

Although scholars acknowledge the fungibility of capital, they have yet to map out clearly how social capital interacts with other forms of capital. How do the effects of different forms of capital add up and interact? Can social capital act as a substitute for human capital? Under what circumstances does social capital enhance the return on human capital? Do individuals and groups invest in social and other types of capital with an eye to the larger repertoire of different types of resources they already have at their disposal? What is the role of other types of capital in the production of social capital (Flap 1999, 16)?

Bridging and Bonding

Another common proposition is the distinction between bridging (inclusion) and bonding (exclusion). This is perhaps the most important dimension along which forms of social capital can vary. Different forms of social capital have the potential to promote community solidarity and reciprocity among its members, while other forms offer a springboard to outside communities and a sharing of diverse resources. Putnam (2000, 22) observes these tendencies when he states: "Bonding social capital is good for undergirding specific reciprocity and mobilizing solidarity ... Bridging networks, by contrast, are better for linkage to external assets and for information diffusion." Putnam's insight has obvious affinities to Granovetter's (1973) insight about the strength of weak ties.

Some forms of social capital appear to be inward-looking and tend to reinforce exclusive, even elitist, identities and homogeneity of membership. Bonding social capital bolsters "our narrow selves" (Putnam 2000, 23) and encourages "hoarding opportunities" (Tilly 1998, 155). Putnam (2000) suggests that examples of bonding social capital include ethnic fraternal organizations, church-based women's reading groups, and fashionable country clubs. Bridging social capital is outward-gazing and links people across diverse social circles. It can generate reciprocity across social cleavages and foster broader identities (Putnam 2000, 23). Putnam suggests that examples of bridging social capital include the civil rights movement, youth service groups, and "ecumenical religious organizations" (ibid., 22). Research is beginning to explore how the ties that are fundamental to social capital have a tendency to remain within certain social groups defined by social status, religion, and ethnicity (Lopez and Stack 2001) and also to show the extent of and conditions for the cross-cutting ties that bridge communities (Tilly 1998). Can social capital be simultaneously bridging and bonding, including the elite few while excluding the many disadvantaged? Can social capital that offers benefits through bridging among smaller communities prove bonding or limiting in larger units such as cities or nations?

The Level, Distribution, and Generation of Social Capital

Aggregate assessments of social capital typically focus on variation in the *level* of social capital. But the *dispersion*, or variance, of social capital within a collectivity is also critical. The mean level of social capital in a collectivity may remain constant, but the dispersion may grow or shrink. To understand shifts in social capital over time, therefore, researchers need to investigate changes in both the level and dispersion of social capital (Paxton 1999, 90-91). The key question becomes: How is social capital distributed over the general population and over time? Recent research has assessed differences in the amount of social capital held by different segments of the population and how that distribution has changed over time (Paxton 1999; Putnam 2000; Wuthnow 1997). Wuthnow (1997) notes that the widely remarked decline in the associational component of social capital is not evenly spread among the population but is instead concentrated among "marginalized" segments of the population. Paxton's (1999) analysis, in contrast, shows no general change in the dispersion of social capital over time in the United States over a twenty-year period.

The multi-dimensional nature of social capital also encourages questions about the impact of uneven distribution of social capital. If social capital is unequally distributed, what else, especially in terms of economic well-being, flows from this distribution? Does the distribution compound, offset, or merely add another dimension to other social inequalities? Flap (1999) asks whether the deployment of social capital is a compensatory mechanism for elites threatened by downward mobility. Also, to what extent is the constitution of social capital, its operation and its effect, different across various social groups (Flap 1991)? What factors contribute to these variations? The level of social capital can also depend on the social distribution of other goods. This is so, at least, for social capital conceived as trust. Uslaner (2002) strongly asserts that the distribution of income in a place is critical to the overall level of trust exhibited by its inhabitants. Where incomes vary widely, both the well-off and the poorly off are distrustful.

At the core of this exploration is the question: How is social capital created, maintained, and fostered? When and how much do people invest in social capital? What are the costs involved? Even if the creation and functioning of social capital may be viewed as delayed or generalized reciprocity (Flap 1999, 16), not all stocks of social capital are the result of conscious investment. Some of it is endowed through family or obtained as a by-product of joining a group. Social capital can also be generated as a by-product of social interaction that has other goals. For example, individuals may join soccer leagues or children's play groups as pleasurable activities in themselves, yet the most important product may be public goods, such as enhanced community relations and improved health of children (Campbell 2000; Helliwell 2006; James, Schulz, and van Olphen 2001). Hence, the question posed by Flap: "How large are the contributions to the creation of social capital of endowment, of creation as a by-product of other activities, and of purposive investment?" (1999, 15-16). More important, as a policy issue, how can we harness social capital for community well-being? Further research is needed before we can understand what determines social capital (e.g., Brehm and Rahn 1997; Wuthnow 1997) and whether social capital can be transferred or infused from regions or groups with high levels of social capital to groups with low levels. Ultimately the question becomes: How can we "protect and enrich our stock of social capital to ensure a healthy society for the future" (Paxton 1999, 124)?

Trust as a Unifying Theme?

A final common theme in the social capital literature is the importance of trust. Some researchers speak of a collective trust (e.g., community trust or trust in government) (Paxton 1999; Putnam 1993b; Stolle 2003; Uslaner 2003), while others address interpersonal trust (dyads and ties within organizations) (Arnold and Kay 1995; Portes 1998; Sandefur and Laumann 1998). For some, trust is a social lubricant that facilitates the exchange of resources. Coleman (1988, S107) speaks of the "trustworthiness of social structures that allows the proliferation of obligations and expectations." In a rational-choice frame of mind, he argues that "an actor choosing to keep trust or not (or choosing whether to devote resources to an attempt to keep trust) is doing so on the basis of costs and benefits he himself will experience. That his trustworthiness will facilitate others' actions or that his lack of trustworthiness will inhibit others' actions does not enter into his decision" (S117). For scholars following Coleman's lead, social capital derives from the trust that each participant has in the community or network. Without such trust, no one will contribute and each will be deprived of the benefits of mutual participation (Light and Bonacich 1988; Portes 1998, 13).

For others, trust is more than a lubricant for or a vehicle that enables social capital to prosper. Trust is a component of social capital, a resource in itself (Flap 1999, 15). Putnam (2000, 134-37) views trustworthiness, or a generalized reciprocity, as a touchstone of social capital. Similarly, Paxton (1999) focuses on trust as a measure of aggregated social capital. She contends that "an emphasis on trust, over other types of ties, is prevalent in the literature, as it is difficult to measure positive emotions or the extent of reciprocity at the national level. Most theory is driven by discussions of trust, and trust is highly associated with generalized reciprocity, so trust remains a good proxy for positive, reciprocal ties in general" (98).

Finally, for other researchers, trust is neither a conduit nor a form of social capital, but rather the *product* of effective social capital. Granovetter (1985) argues that concrete personal relations and networks of relations, termed "embeddedness," are important to generating trust, establishing expectations, and enforcing norms. Trust is the outcome of social capital once it is engaged. This argument is stated most effectively by Michael Woolcock (1998, 185): "Trust and norms of reciprocity, fairness and cooperation are 'benefits' that are nurtured in and by particular combinations of social relationships; they are undeniably important for facilitating and reinforcing efficient institutional performance, but they do not exist independently of social relationships. In short, 'consequences' may be one indicator of the types and combinations of social capital that are present, but they are not to be confused with social capital itself."

Across these varying conceptions, trust remains essential to social capital research.

Divergent Conceptions

It should be obvious by now that social capital research embodies *two* contrasts, and these contrasts map roughly onto specific disciplines. One contrast is in the level of analysis. On one side is research that focuses on ties among *individuals* or households. On the other side is research that focuses on the larger social structure and its implications for *community*. This contrast is essentially one of the micro versus the macro of social relations, individual gains versus collective goods. The second contrast is between the *content* of social relations (e.g., resources of trust, norms, and information) and the *structure* of associations (e.g., avenues for and organization of communication). This contrast essentially asks: is social capital the message or the medium? Is social capital the *relations* that bring information and other valuable resources, or is it the *benefits* accrued through these relations?

LEVEL OF ANALYSIS

Sociologists typically operate at the individual or household level and treat the core of the concept as the density and quality of ties among persons and households. Sociologists use social capital to identify the importance of concrete personal relations and networks of relations in generating trust, in establishing expectations, and in creating and enforcing norms. Granovetter (1985) terms this the "embeddedness" of economic transactions in social relations. For the individual, social capital represents a fund of social connections and respectability (Bourdieu 1990; Coleman 1990b). Accumulating social capital is associated with the nature of the relations (e.g., between employers and employees, or citizens and government) that constitute the social organization of trust (Shapiro 1987). People use social networks to accomplish their goals, particularly job attainment and occupational mobility (Bourdieu and Boltanski 1978; Erickson 2001; Granovetter 1974; Marsden 2001; Snijders 1999; Watkins 1984).

Lin (1982, 1989, 2001), for example, shows that individuals act instrumentally, employing their social ties (especially more extended or "weak" ties) to gain occupational mobility. The strength-of-weak-ties argument was originally formulated by Granovetter (1974). It claims that news is more quickly communicated through strong ties, but strong ties rarely bring news that is truly new, because friends of friends tend be friends (ibid.). The "weak ties" approach exemplifies the egocentric perspective on social networks and the resources to which they give access. As Sandefur and Laumann (1998, 484) observe: "An individual's social capital is characterized by her direct relationships with others and by the other people and relationships that she can reach through those to whom she is directly tied."

The *structure* of a network can be relevant to its social capital properties for individuals within it. Sociocentric approaches in network analysis examine patterns of relationships within a social system. Perhaps best illustrative of this approach is Burt's (1992) "structural hole" work. Burt stresses that an individual has a comparative advantage in competitive situations if those who are connected to her/him do not have ties to each other. In his view, it is the relative absence of ties, absences he called "structural holes," that facilitates individual mobility (such as promotional ladders among managers). This is so because dense networks tend to convey redundant information, while weaker ties can be more extensive and can provide new knowledge and resources. Opinions and behaviour are more homogeneous within than between groups, so people connected across groups gain familiarity with alternative ways of thinking and behaving (Burt 2004). These well-positioned individuals have a minimum of redundancy between their relations and can play them off each other. The advantage of the autonomy (and freedom from control) that ensues from being in a network with structural holes is that it will offer a higher exchange rate for the focal actor (Burt 1992, 2004, 2005; see also Flap 1999, 10). If this approach focuses on an emergent, aggregate property of the network, the focus is still on implications for individual well-being and mobility.

That said, the structural approach also points toward the benefits of network density for the larger collective or community. For example, Coleman (1990b) emphasizes that a cohesive, all-connected network is a resource to its members because it promotes the willingness to cooperate and provide help to others. This aggregate emphasis is especially prominent in political science and, even more, in economics. Putnam's research (1993, 1995a, 1995b, 2000) suggests that civic engagement materially promotes community prosperity and well-being (see also Fukuyama 1989; Helliwell 1996; Woolcock 1998).

The embeddedness of relations in the social environment implies third-party effects on exchanges going on in each relation (Snijders 1999, 30). Putnam suggests that high levels of these types of social participation are indicative of a density of interaction that is instrumental in building mutual trust and commitment (1993b; see also Uehara 1990). Individuals residing in communities characterized by such patterns of social participation are said to benefit through various types of social support, such as confidence that unrelated adults will watch over children and neighbourhood safety (Sampson 2001).

Structure versus Content

The contrast between the content and the structure of social relations overlaps the contrast between individuals and collectivities. The structural focus is on the strength and other distinctive qualities of ties to others, the resources possessed by contacts, and the structural features of the network in which an individual is embedded, features that include cohesiveness and hierarchy (Flap 1999, 14; Granovetter 1974). As Coleman (1988, S98) states, social capital "is not a single entity but a variety of different entities, with two elements in common: they all consist of some aspect of social structures, and they facilitate certain actions of actors – whether persons or corporate actors – within the structure." The basic constituents of social capital are the persons in an individual's network, their resources, and the extent to which they are prepared (better yet, obliged) to help when called upon (Bourdieu 1980b, 2; 1986, 248; Coleman 1988, S95; de Graaf and Flap 1988, 453; Portes 1998, 3-4).

If the structural approach hints at the resources to be gained through these associations, the "content" approach focuses specifically on those resources. Individuals and families build up their "stock" of social capital by investing in others. This investment is not unlike investment in financial or human capital, in which investment yields returns (Bourdieu 1983). Assistance to others creates diffuse obligations (Coleman 1988; Portes 1998). Social capital is most useful if you can call upon it when you are in need rather than when the other person wishes to reciprocate (Blau 1994). In this sense, social capital can be thought of as the number of outstanding credit slips on which an individual can draw at any time (Coleman 1988, S103). Social capital is, therefore, an accumulation of resources possessed by others that are available to an individual through association with these endowed persons (Flap 1999, 10). Boissevain (1974) aptly called these "second-order" resources (see also Sandefur and Laumann 1998).

In political science and economics, the focus on content is even more explicit. And, as suggested earlier, second-order benefits accrue to collectivities. According to Putnam's (1993b) account of Italian regional government, the ultimate factor in policy outcomes is variation across provinces in diffuse trust in persons and institutions. For Putnam, this trust helps solve what is otherwise an endemic collective action dilemma. Economists see trust as a solution to market failure, an elixir that reduces transaction costs and liberates commitments, including capital investment, for the long-term.

Criticisms

Measurement

A thorough discussion of social capital must take into account the limitations and criticisms of the core concept. Much of the controversy surrounding social capital concerns its application to different types of problems and its use in theories involving different units of analysis (Portes 2000b, 2). The multifaceted nature of social capital has resulted in a bewildering array of definitions and measurements. In the last decade, the term "social capital" has been applied to so many events and in so many different contexts as to risk its losing any distinct meaning (Portes 1998, 2). Previous studies provide little rationale for how their measures of social capital connect to the theoretical definition of the concept. The lack of an obvious link between theory and measurement has, in some cases, led to questionable indicators (Paxton 1999, 90). These indiscriminate applications of social and other "capitals" are part of what Baron and Hannan (1994) disparagingly refer to as the recent emergence of "a plethora of capitals" (1122), such that scholars "have begun referring to virtually every feature of social life as a form of capital" (1124).

Measurements are not only inconsistent but also are commonly very narrow. Assessments of social capital often rely on single indicators, notwithstanding the complexity of the general concept. Also, with a single indicator, researchers cannot account for measurement error (Paxton 1999, 90). Progress in the area requires innovative measures that both capture the multiple dimensions of social capital and promote standardization of indicators (Flap 1999, 10). Attention to measurement should force clarification of the concept.

Conceptual Proliferation and Circular Explanation

The tremendous range of applications has prompted confusion about the meaning of social capital and controversy over its alleged effects (Portes 2000a; Skocpol 1996; Tarrow 1996). Coleman's rather vague definition of the concept (1988) is partly to blame for later researchers' labelling a number of different and even contradictory processes as social capital. As Portes (1998, 5) points out, "Coleman himself started that proliferation by including under the term some of the mechanisms that generated social capital (such as reciprocity expectations and group enforcement of norms); the consequences of its possession (such as privileged access to information); and the 'appropriable' social organization that provided the context for both sources and effects to materialize." Following Coleman's lead, Sandefur and Laumann (1998, 482) describe relationships as "characterized by both their structural form and the content that inheres in them, and aspects of both their form and their content will condition their productivity as social capital."

As social capital has been interpreted to mean at once the relations, networks, and obligations existing in social situations as well as the product of those interactions, it should not be surprising that confusion has arisen over measurement (Portes and Landolt 1996a; Wall et al. 1998). Some definitions focus on the benefits of social capital (e.g., Sandefur and Laumann 1998), but defining social capital functionally makes it impossible to distinguish "what it is from what it does" (Foley and Edwards 1997, 1999). The distinction between the sources of social capital and the benefits derived from them remains ambiguous (Lévesque and White 1999, 26).

The failure to disentangle causes and effects of social capital has given rise to circular reasoning. Bourdieu and his successors prevented this from happening to the individual version of the concept by focusing on a person's networks, including those explicitly constructed for that purpose, and by positing effects that are tangible and informational (McLanahan and Sandefur 1994; Hagan et al. 1996). Some effects are clearly separate and distinct from the social structures that produce them (Portes 2000a, 4). However, collective social capital or "civicness" lacks this distinct separation. As a property of cities and nations, stocks of social capital are said to encourage better governance and more effective policies. But its existence is simultaneously inferred from the same outcomes.[2] Portes (1998, 19) contends that "as a property of communities and nations rather than individuals, social capital is simultaneously a cause and an effect. It leads to positive outcomes, such as economic development and less crime, and its existence is inferred from the same outcomes. Cities that are well governed and moving ahead economically do so because they have high social capital; poorer cities lack in this civic virtue."

Two strategies can remedy this conceptual problem. First, researchers using the concept need to distinguish carefully between indicators that reflect the level of social capital (e.g., a rise or fall in participation rates for voluntary associations) and the determinants of such a measure (e.g., the strengthening or weakening of friendship obligations). As Wall and colleagues observe: "Too often, the indicators are so closely linked that distinctions are blurred, making rigorous empirical analysis difficult" (1998, 316). Second, circular reasoning can be avoided by observing certain logical cautions: (1) separate the definition of the concept, both theoretically and empirically, from its alleged effects (Flap 1999, 14); (2) establish controls for directionality so that the presence of social capital is demonstrably prior to its effects (Paxton 1999, 101); (3) control for the presence of extraneous factors that account for both social capital and its alleged effects (Portes 2000a, 5); and (4) identify the historical origins of community social capital (Portes 1998, 20-21).

Overemphasis on the Positive

Problems of measurement and logic contribute to a third problem: the tendency to see social capital exclusively as a "public good" (Coleman 1993). Strictly speaking, the emphasis in this expression should be on the "public" component, on its non-rivalness and non-excludability. Public goods can carry negative value; they can be public "bads." But the concept has tended to become synonymous with all things positive in social life (Field 2003, 71; Portes 2000a, 3).[3] Putnam (2000, 10) cautions against this tendency: "The key point of this analysis is that the ready attribution of positive effects of social capital, be it in its individual garb as social networks or in its collective one as civic spirit, is premature because observed effects may be spurious or because they are incompatible with alternative explanations arising from different theoretical quarters. There is a need for both logical clarity and analytic rigor in the study of these processes, lest we turn social capital into an unmitigated celebration of community."

The possibility that social networks mobilized by some groups or individuals might be dysfunctional is often left out of the equation (Portes and Landolt 1996a; Wall et al. 1998). At least three generic forms of dysfunction have been identified: (1) exclusion of outsiders; (2) devotion of social capital to perverse goals, generating parasitic negative externalities for the "host" community; and (3) debilitating claims on insiders (Portes 1998, 15-17).

Emphasis on bonds internal to a community also implies exclusion of outsiders. The same strong ties that benefit members of a group commonly enable it to bar others from access (Portes 1998, 15). An example is ethnic niches that emerge when a group is able to colonize a particular sector of employment in such a way that members have privileged access to new jobs, while restricting that of outsiders. Numerous examples from factories and government agencies as well as emergency services have been documented in this literature (Waters 1994; Waldinger 1996; Stepick 1989). The power of networks is such that access to entry-level positions is restricted to kin and friends in remote foreign locations and no opportunities arise for local workers (Sassen 1995).

Social capital, just like any other form of capital, can be directed toward purposes that are outright malevolent and antisocial (Putnam 2000, 22). As Portes (1998, 15) notes, "the same mechanisms appropriable by individuals and groups as social capital can have other, less desirable consequences." That is, "the potential energy created by an individual group could be used for nefarious purposes" (Paxton 1999, 96). Gambetta (1988, 214) suggests, for example, that there are instances of high social capital among robbers and murderers. This point has also been made in research on civil society (Foley and Edwards 1998; Edwards and Foley 1998) and trust (Gambetta 1988, 214) and, more recently, with regard to other forms of social capital (Foley and Edwards 1997; Portes 1998; Portes and Sensenbrenner 1993).

Social solidarity can become a liability for those who experience it from the inside. The solidarity that leads to effective social control in a community can also stifle innovation and impede individual mobility by "restricting the scope of individual expression and the extent of extracommunity contact" (Portes and Sensenbrenner 1993, 1341). Group or community closure may hamper the success of business initiatives by members. Cozy intergroup relations typical of high solidarity communities can restrict high achievers. Supporting free-riders reduces opportunities for entrepreneurial success (Portes 1998, 16).[4] Community or group participation tends to create demands for conformity, and high levels of social control can restrict personal privacy and autonomy (Portes 1998, 16-17; Portes and Sensenbrenner 1993). Strong, longstanding civic groups may inhibit individual economic gain by placing heavy personal obligations on members, in particular obligations that prevent members from participating in broader social networks (Portes and Landolt 1996a; Woolcock 1998). Group solidarity cemented by a common experience of adversity can be threatened by success stories of individuals. The result is a downward-levelling norm that keeps members of a downtrodden group in place and compels the more ambitious to escape the community (Portes 1998, 17). One example is that of youths who are embedded in criminal contexts, such as youth gangs, and who become isolated from opportunities to achieve legitimate adult employment (Hagan and McCarthy 1998). As Portes (1998, 18) observes: "Whereas bounded solidarity and trust provide the sources for socio-economic ascent and entrepreneurial development among some groups, among others they have exactly the opposite effect. Sociability cuts both ways."

Advancing a Social Capital Research Agenda

Social capital holds tremendous potential as a conceptual tool for the social sciences. The concept has already been used extensively to study economic development, political participation, education, family, employment, and other aspects of the overall health of communities. In this chapter, we have outlined competing conceptions of social capital across disciplinary boundaries of the social sciences, with particular attention to different emphases in conceptualization and common assumptions about the operation of social capital. We have also examined criticisms levelled against the concept. In this final section, we explore avenues for resolving measurement issues, the potential contribution of social capital to theory development, and strategies for data collection that are needed if social capital research is to advance.

Refinement of Measures: Conceptualization and Standardization

As social capital research has accumulated, methods of measuring the concept are beginning to take shape. Early empirical work suffered from measurements of social capital that were made in rather ad hoc, pragmatic, and unsystematic ways (Flap 1999, 19). In recent years more effective, reliable, and parsimonious strategies for the measurement of social capital are beginning to take hold. Gradually, comparative and international studies are taking place (Bian 1997; Helliwell and Putnam 1995; Helliwell 1996; Lin, Fu, and Hsung 2001; Putnam 2000). These studies yield standardized as well as flexible instruments for measuring social capital, which assure greater data quality and the possibility of deriving reliability measures. This does not imply a definitive measurement instrument that is easily transferable between different societies, but, rather, the development of common measures that can be adapted to (or restricted to) certain communities or life cycles (Snijders 1999, 38).

Two avenues predominate in the quest for reliable measures. The first focuses on *forms* of social capital, defined as obligations, information channels, trust, norms, and effective sanctions grounded in networks characterized by closure and multiplex ties (Burt 1992; Coleman 1990c; Portes 1998; Woolcock 1998). This measurement strategy has proven insightful, providing the groundwork for studies of employment (Erickson 2001; Fernandez and Castilla 2001), careers (Flap and Boxman 2001), development of firms (Arnold and Kay 1995), and industry expansion (Walker, Kogut, and Shan 1997), among many other topics.

The second measurement strategy defines social capital by its *function* (Coleman 1990b, 305). Coleman suggests the utility of the concept by presenting vignettes that illuminate trust, norms, and voluntary organizations (1988, 1990b, 1990c). A focus on benefits is characteristic of successful attempts to quantify an individual's, community's, or nation's stock of social capital (Evans 1996; Kenworthy 1997; Levi 1996; Putnam 2000; Sandefur and Laumann 1998; Woolcock 1998). For example, Sandefur and Laumann (1998) emphasize three important benefits of social capital: information, influence and control, and social solidarity. Yet, their research is careful to specify theoretical linkages between forms and benefits of social capital:

> (ii) A given form of social capital may confer benefits useful for a single goal of an actor, or the productive capacity of a form of social capital may generalize to aid in the attainment of many kinds of goals. That is, forms of social capital vary in the *effective specificity* of the benefits they confer.
>
> (iii) At the same time that a form of social capital may confer benefits useful for one or more purposes, it can confer liabilities as well. A form of social capital acquired to aid in one type of action may hinder other actions; thus, forms of social capital may be said to have *valence*, contingent upon the goals which the actor wishes to attain. (Ibid., 483)

In the scheme outlined by Sandefur and Laumann (ibid., 485), social capital's productive capacity ensues from three potential benefits: its ability to facilitate or hinder the flow of information, its ability to control others' and one's own autonomy, and the potential it provides for social solidarity.

Theory Development

If social capital has already had a significant impact on the development of social theory, many would still argue that the theory is underdeveloped in comparison to its use in research (Foley and Edwards 1999; Levi 1996; Portes 1998; Sandefur and Laumann 1998; Wall et al. 1998). Coleman claimed that a first stage of social capital research signals that "something of value has been produced for those actors who have this resource available and that the value depends on social organization" (1988, S101). Research is now entering a second stage of analysis in which the focus is to unpack the concept and to delineate components of social organization that determine the value produced (ibid.). While early research glossed over "social-structural details," more recent work engages in systematic analysis of the mechanisms through which social capital has its effects (see, e.g., Sandefur and Laumann 1998). Recent systematic treatments of the concept distinguish among: (a) the possessors of social capital (those making claims); (b) the sources of social capital (those agreeing to the demands); and (c) the resources themselves. Following Coleman, these three elements are often mixed in discussions of the concept, thus setting the stage for confusion in the uses and scope of the term (Portes 1998, 6).

This book, together with other new research (see, e.g., Baron, Field, and Schuller 2000; Saegart, Thompson, and Warren 2001; Stolle and Hooghe 2003), bridges interdisciplinary lines and engages in the challenging exploration of how social capital may be harnessed at different levels of analysis. For instance, what forms does social capital take when it exists at the levels of individuals, of communities, and even of nations? How does social capital at the level of individuals contribute to the aggregate holdings of social capital for the larger community (Eastis 1998; Hofferth and Iceland 1998; Stolle and Rochon 1998)? This engagement speaks to the public good aspect of social capital in the sense that relations between pairs of persons have external effects on others. Some fruits of social resources in a community are there for all members of the community, irrespective of whether or not they are personally implicated in the relations that constitute the social resources (Flap 1999, 17). Does social capital possessed by individuals sometimes undermine greater "stocks" of community social capital? For instance, the right connections allow certain individuals to gain access to profitable public contracts and bypass regulations binding on others. Yet, "individual" social capital in such instances consists precisely in the ability to undermine "collective" social capital – that is, a civic spirit founded on the assumption of impartial application of law (Portes 2000a, 4).

To the extent that social capital takes several different forms and is communicated through an array of interpersonal relationships, the question then becomes: What is the ideal empirical balance between cohesion and closure that will maximize access to diverse sources of information and influence? Sandefur and Laumann (1998, 491) discuss social capital held by individuals and argue that the "ideal balance may well be different depending on where the individual is in the hierarchy of the social system, whether the context is characterized more by cooperation or competition, and, in competitive settings, on whether team competition or individual competition is the operative game." This question of balance may also be posed between bridging and bonding social capital, between inclusion and exclusion, and between individuals and communities or nations. This theoretical question of balance or equilibrium of social capital also raises the issue of property rights (Flap 1999, 17). To what extent does an individual have rights to another's resources, as second-order resources, through obligation and former investments? Coleman (1990b) described this as a "credit slip" to be redeemed at some later date. In practice, how tenuous are property rights or credit slips on social capital?

Data Innovations

These advancements in social capital measurement and theory demand creative approaches to research design and data collection. We have seen that many different measures have been posited as indicators of social capital. But, in the absence of strong ties to theory, researchers are left to flounder among many different pieces of data that provide contrary pictures of the level of social capital within nations. Measures have also been drawn from a variety of different sources, rendering assessment difficult because of incomparability in sampling designs and question wording (Wuthnow 1997). New work is devoted to building flexible yet standardized measures of social capital, measures that are being replicated across different surveys (such as the World Values Survey) in different countries (Putnam 2000). In order to study whether there is a trend toward the erosion of social capital, longitudinal studies of networks in the general public are being initiated. These sorts of studies bring standardized international comparative studies of community involvement, participation, and cohesion within reach (Flap 1999, 21-22). This book builds on these data innovation efforts through refining standardized measures, introducing a national survey of social capital in Canada, and analyzing longitudinal, ethnographic, and metropolitan survey data.

Problems in untangling causation among social capital and employment, income, and health outcomes are especially acute. There is considerable evidence that healthy people have higher productivity and higher incomes and, conversely, that those with more interesting and challenging jobs also tend to have better health (Evans, Barer, and Marmor 1994). People with higher incomes and educational levels are also more inclined to contribute to maintaining the social capital of their communities, both through their willingness to trust others and their contributions of time to associations that facilitate social interactions. What is not clear is how to sort out the three-way interactions among social capital, health status, and economic performance. A core enterprise of this book is to reveal important distinctions between determinants of social capital (Part 2) and consequences of social capital (Part 3), with specific attention to community, economic, political, and health outcomes.

Conclusion

Our discussion of the common themes, divergent conceptions, and criticisms in the social capital literature reveals rich opportunities for the advancement of social capital theory and research. The authors assembled in this volume undertake numerous innovative approaches in order to successfully harness these opportunities. To sum up, we argue that the exploitation of these opportunities requires:

1 scholarship that bridges disciplinary cleavages
2 refinement of the conceptualization and measurement of the core concepts
3 development of programs of research that incorporate national social surveys, longitudinal in design, using standardized measures to allow rigorous comparative analyses
4 ethnographies, interviews and case studies to unpack the sources and scope of social capital's textured fabric
5 theoretical models that distinguish between lenders and receivers, that differentiate the various forms of social capital, and that identify the relationships between individuals' shares and communities' stocks of social capital
6 insights into the distribution and consequences, both beneficial and harmful, of social capital for individuals and the communities in which they live.

ACKNOWLEDGMENTS

We thank Tara Carnochan for research assistance. The research reported here was supported by a grant through the Major Collaborative Research Initiative program of the Social Sciences and Humanities Research Council of Canada (Grant #412-1997-0003). Please direct correspondence to Fiona M. Kay, Department of Sociology, Queen's University, Kingston, Ontario, Canada K7L 3N6; e-mail: kayf@post.queensu.ca.

NOTES

1 In recent years, Becker (1996) expanded his treatment of human capital to include other forms of capital such as personal capital, imagination capital, and social capital. Becker views an individual's social capital as part of his/her total stock of human capital. For Becker, social capital consists of past actions of others

in an individual's social network that affect current or future utilities. This approach emphasizes the impact of others' choices on the total amount of social capital available to an individual.

2   Portes argues that the theoretical problems in the formulation of the concept have been partially compensated for by subsequent efforts at measuring it empirically. Because collective social capital cannot be measured by its consequences, alternative indicators were developed. In later publications, Putnam suggested newspaper reading, expressions of trust in survey questionnaires, and participation in nonpolitical associations as plausible indicators (Putnam 1996). As a result, the truism was transformed into noncircular propositions and predictions that are testable (Portes 1998).

3   Portes is particularly critical of this tendency to attribute all things positive to social capital. He claims: "First, the transition of the concept from an individual asset to a community or national resource was never explicitly theorized, giving rise to the present state of confusion about the meaning of the term. In one sentence, social capital is an asset of children in intact families; in the next, it is an attribute of networks of traders; and in the following, it becomes the explanation of why entire cities are well governed and economically flourishing while others are not. The heuristic value of the concept suffers accordingly as it risks becoming synonymous with each and all things that are positive in social life" (2000a, 3).

4   This is ironic because one claim for social capital is that it reduces the incidence of free-riding.

3
The Dynamics of Social Capital: Who Wants to Stay In If Nobody Is Out?

Fiona M. Kay and Paul Bernard

During the past two decades, "social capital" has emerged as one of the most influential concepts in the social sciences (Lin 2001b, 3; Portes 1998, 2; Sandefur and Laumann 1998, 481). Since Bourdieu's initial treatment of the concept (1980), emphasizing various resources appropriable through social relationships, and Coleman's (1988, 1990a) theoretical elaboration on rational actors operating within social structures in pursuit of their interests, the concept of "social capital" has virtually exploded across disciplinary boundaries.[1] Social capital has been invoked to explain a host of individual behaviours: academic achievement (Hallinan and Kubitschek 1999; McNeal 1999; Marjoribanks 1991; Parcel and Geschwender 1995; Teachman et al. 1997), employment (Bourdieu and Boltanski 1978; Fratoe 1988; Granovetter 1986; Lin 1982; Meyerson 1994; Seron and Ferris 1995; Watkins 1984), career advancement (Bian 1997; Fernandez et al. 2000; Wegener 1991), earnings (Langton and Pfeffer 1993, 1994), and migration (Hagan et al. 1996; Liang 1994). Scholarly interest in the development of social capital is further motivated by the linkage between levels of social capital and collective outcomes, including: social cooperation (Jenson 1998; Lévesque and White 1999), social movements (Smith 1998), collective action (Flora 1998), economic development (Dasgupta 2000; Fukuyama 1995b; Helliwell 1996; Helliwell and Putnam 1995), trust and the efficacy of political institutions (Putnam 2000), health and the well-being of communities (House et al. 1988; Putnam 1995a, 1995b, 2001; Veenstra 2001), and reduced crime rates (Hagan et al. 1995; Macmillan 1995; Sampson and Laub 1993). Yet, the meaning of social capital and its heuristic value are being put to the test through increasingly diverse applications (Portes 1998, 2).[2]

We argue that too much commentary on social capital focuses on its beneficial consequences at the community or national level while ignoring the downsides. Moreover, these downsides arise from the very logic of the concept: they derive primarily from the exclusionary aspects of social capital, which lead to inequality of access to social resources among individuals and to ghettoization among collectivities. As well, some kinds of inclusion go so far as to heavily restrict the liberties of the group's own members. We shift the discussion of social capital to acknowledge both its strengths and its liabilities.

We address four key criticisms levelled against social capital. First is that the multifaceted nature of social capital has yielded a bewildering array of definitions and inconsistent measurements of the concept (Flap 1999, 10). For example, some scholars view social capital as the combination of ties and norms binding individuals within a larger social structure (Coleman 1990b), while others regard social capital as a "moral resource," as "trust" (Fukuyama 1995b; Gambetta 1988), or as a cultural mechanism used to discern and fortify boundaries of particular status groups (Bourdieu 1986). Indiscriminate applications of social capital are part of what Baron and Hannan (1994, 1122) disparagingly refer to as "a plethora of capitals." They lament the fact that scholars "have begun referring to virtually every feature of social life as a form of capital" (ibid., 1124). Social capital has become too vast, including too many elements at different levels of analysis, to be empirically specified apart from human capital and economic resources (Lin 1995, 687). This lack of measurement precision leads Woolcock to contend that social capital "risks trying to explain too much with too little" (1998, 155).

A second criticism concerns a tautology resulting from the tendency to equate social capital with the resources acquired through it (Lévesque and White 1999, 24; Paxton 1999, 90; Portes 1998, 5). For example, some studies emphasize the benefits of social capital (Coleman 1988; Sandefur and Laumann 1998) and the content of beneficial resources, such as trust, norms, and information (Gambetta 1988; Laumann and Knoke 1987; Putnam 2000); others contend that social capital, as a relational asset, must be distinguished from collective assets and goods such as culture, norms, and trust (Lin 2001a, 10). As Woolcock (1998, 156) observes: "This leaves unresolved whether social capital is the infrastructure or the content of social relations, the 'medium,' as it were, or the 'message.' Is it both?"[3]

A third controversy arises around the issue of social networks. Some scholars argue that social networks, the interpersonal ties that render valuable resources available, are central to a theory of social capital (Angelusz and Tardos 2001; Burt 1997a, 1997b; Diani 1997; Lin 1999, 2001a; Marsden 2001; Wellman and Frank 2001). As Lin (2001a, 9) argues: "Divorced from its roots in individual interactions and networking, social capital becomes merely another trendy term to employ or deploy in the broad context of improving or building social integration and solidarity." Meanwhile, other scholars caution against an "over-networked" conception of social capital (Foley and Edwards 1999). Overemphasis on networks can lead one to lose sight of the expectations, norms of reciprocity, and shared values embedded within these relations. Networks are of interest not merely as "contacts" but also for the mutual obligations, expectations, and rules of conduct implied and sustained through these relations (Liang 1994, 412; Putnam 2000, 20).

A fourth criticism raised in the literature is of the dominantly optimistic view of social capital as an asset, or public good. Social scientists have tended to see sociability as intrinsically favourable, failing to see the exclusionary practices of social capital (Portes 1998) and the consequent reproduction along class lines (Bourdieu 1990; Schulman and Anderson 1999). A more encompassing way of expressing this criticism is to say that a great majority of empirical research employing the concept of social capital has been theoretically unreflective. Instead, the concept has been invoked largely as a metaphor to include already well-established sociological insights (Sandefur and Laumann 1998, 481). Political scientists and economists need to be reminded of the mainly inegalitarian focus of the initial work on social capital, which was mostly undertaken by sociologists (Bourdieu 1983; Coleman 1988). As other disciplines appropriated the concept, they have further distorted it.

Our chapter addresses these challenges. First, we provide a definitional framework intended to clarify the boundaries and dynamics of social capital. Our work follows the lead of Coleman (1988) and Sandefur and Laumann (1998), focusing on the dynamics of social capital and the consequences for individuals and collectivities. Our dynamic approach to social capital shows how people access and use resources through social relations, and how the activation of these social relations, or networks, further builds social capital and shapes social structure.

Second, we attempt to address the tautological argument that equates social capital with the resources acquired through it. We distinguish between social capital itself and the initial resources used to procure subsequent resources. Social networks constitute the entry point to valued resources. However, once one has obtained resources, especially new social contacts, these resources provide the individual with enhanced volumes of social capital, better equipping one for the next round of life's challenges. In other words, individuals use social capital to attain resources (e.g., wealth, access to jobs, information, new contacts in business), and these resources can, in turn, lead to enhanced positioning for access to future pools of valued goods. In essence, resources entail social capital in the making. Rather than viewing this process as circular, we define it as a social network that, when activated, reinforces and even alters itself over time. The process is fundamentally interactive and, on occasion, transformative. Our starting point, however, is with one's initial stock of social networks and information channels.

Third, we acknowledge the important contribution of social networks to social capital theory, but we argue that, in empirical terms, one cannot dissociate linkages from norms. Norms imply and sustain relations. The thrust of our argument is that norms are crucial to determining who is "in" and who is "out." This process of structuring involves putting in place norms and building up normative structures. These normative structures produce expectations for future interaction and become the social context in which future transactions and interpersonal ties are negotiated (see Coleman 1990a, 1990b, 1990c).

Fourth, in response to criticisms of depictions of social capital as an overly beneficial public good, we propose a typology that explicitly recognizes both the inclusionary and the exclusionary dynamics inherent to social capital. Social capital does not necessarily lead to improved social integration and cohesion. We contend that social capital can also lead to the inclusion of privileged individuals with shared characteristics while simultaneously, or in close sequence, *ex*cluding disadvantaged "outsiders." Once social capital is structured, it becomes difficult to reshape. Durable inequalities are then manifested according to distinctions in characteristics, in common opportunity structures, and in bounded networks of association (see Tilly 1998, 91). The structure of social relations among individuals and collectives gains resilience as these relations are exercised. The point is that social capital maintains its value through the regular activation of networks, the flow of information, and the enforcement of norms. This makes social capital not unlike electrical current flowing through a network of power lines – social capital involves the transmission of information (e.g., active communication, exchange of valued knowledge, emergence of trust) and is inherently fungible (e.g., enabling, under the proper conditions, conversion to financial, human, and other forms of capital).

In order to capture the various dynamics just sketched, we propose a typology in the following pages, and then demonstrate its contribution as we employ it to cast light on empirical examples.

A Typology of the Dynamics of Social Capital

Central to social capital theory is the structure of social relations, the networks of opportunities offered through associations with others. As Coleman (1988, S100-1) remarks: "If physical capital is wholly tangible, being embodied in observable material form, and human capital is less tangible, being embodied in the skills and knowledge acquired by an individual, social capital is less tangible yet, for it exists in the relations among persons." But social capital is not a homogeneous good. As Flap (1999, 14) notes: "A person's social resources have many constituents: his ties to others, the strength, content, and other qualities of these ties, the resources of these others, structural features of the network in which he is embedded (cohesiveness, hierarchy, etc.)." Our typology emphasizes these networks of relations and the activation of these social ties in the accumulation of these "secondary-order resources."

Also fundamental to our typology is a dynamic approach to the processes of activating one's social capital and the consequences of these processes. Social structure, the networks central to this process, become social capital when appropriated by actors to further their goals (Coleman 1990b, 302-5).[4] Social capital is the sharing of resources through networks of social relations, with their attendant norms. As Bourdieu notes, social capital is "the aggregate of the actual or potential resources which are linked to possession of a durable network, or more or less institutionalized relationships of mutual acquaintance and recognition – in other words, to membership in a group – which provides each of its members with the backing of the collectivity-owned capital, a 'credential' which entitles them to credit, in the various senses of the word" (Bourdieu 1986, 248-49). This emphasis on the productivity, or benefits, of social capital is consistent with prior groundbreaking work attempting to devise a theory of social capital (Coleman 1990b, 305; Sandefur and Laumann 1998, 482). As Coleman (1988, S98) observes: "Social capital is defined by its function. It is not a single entity but a variety of different entities, with two elements in common: they all consist of some aspect of social structures, and they facilitate certain actions of actors – whether persons or corporate actors – within the structure."

Two axes define our typology. The first axis in our typology specifies *distribution dynamics*, emphasizing consequences of various patterns of social interaction. Many scholars (e.g., Coleman 1993; Dasgupta 2000; Flora 1998; Fukuyama 1995b; Helliwell 1996; House et al., 1998; Macmillan 1995; Muller and Seligson 1994; Sampson and Laub 1993; Sandefur and Laumann 1998;

Smith 1998) have focused attention on benefits in their attempts to quantify individuals' stocks of social capital.[5] We have chosen to focus on a broader understanding of outcomes, both beneficial and disadvantageous. Two dynamics are defined by distribution. One dynamic is that of *inclusion*, a building up of interpersonal coalitions and availability of resources through linkages, as well as a building up of community cohesion and integration. Another dynamic is that of *exclusion*, characterized by a closing out of those disadvantaged through a dearth of valuable associations. Note that distribution does not characterize social capital per se, but, rather, the benefits that social capital produces (some are inclusive, others exclusive).

The second axis examines *reproduction processes*. This axis emphasizes the fact that communications that take place through social networks create productive opportunities and shape social structure. These communications rest on *operating processes* at the micro-level of individuals and *structuring processes* at the meso- or macro-level of communities, institutions, and societies. The dynamics of networks of social relations lead to relatively permanent linkages among actors and to expectations of reciprocity. Such dynamics thereby contribute to building structure, specifically through the integration of actors within communities that serve to build social cohesion and fortify boundaries against others. Thus, operating processes reproduce and alter social structure while, at the same time, they are constrained by that very structure. These two axes of the typology are cross-tabulated in Figure 3.1. We next explore the intersection of these axes in greater depth.

Distribution Processes: Inclusion versus Exclusion

Inclusion

Distribution describes patterns of social interaction that can be characterized as embracing of newcomers or, conversely, as exclusive by virtue of resilient borders. The first distribution process is that of *inclusion*. Inclusion roots social capital in the relationships between individuals or between an individual and a group. The focus is directed to the potential benefits accruing to individuals through their involvement in networks or broader social structures (Portes 1998, 18). This essentially amounts to "knowing the right people and how 'to get a foot in the door'" (Passeron 1979, 52). Mark Granovetter's (1973) study of job searches is a clear illustration of this mechanism. His work demonstrates that "weak ties," such as friend-of-friend relations, are more useful to job searches than are "strong ties," such as close friends and

FIGURE 3.1

Typology of social capital: processes of distribution and reproduction

		Distribution processes	
Reproduction processes	Characteristics	Inclusion (association): building up ties	Exclusion (dissociation): closing out others
Operating social networks	Linkages at the micro-level: expectations of reciprocity; "counting your marbles"; emulation and adaptation (Tilly 1998)	Interpersonal linkages and coalescence Ties "add up"	Peripheral outsiders and disenfranchisement People are "subtracted" from ties
Structuring social networks	Integration at the meso/macro level: building structure; reproduction and opportunity hoarding (Tilly 1998)	Social cohesion and community enhancement Reach is "multiplied"	Boundary creation and ghettoization Social "division"

family relatives. In the case of "strong ties," the individual is likely to encounter the same information as those in his or her own social circle. However, "weak ties" offer connections to people who are more likely to move in different social circles and, therefore, provide opportunities to learn about job opportunities outside the knowledge of one's immediate social circle. The "weak ties" approach illustrates an instrumental perspective on social networks and the resources accessible through these networks. Here, social capital consists of an individual's direct relationships with others, and the resources and further relationships that are attainable through these proximate contacts (Sandefur and Laumann 1998, 484).[6] Deroy-Pineau and Bernard (2001), studying the mobilization of resources by Marie de l'Incarnation as she prepared to establish the first school for girls in New France, provide an interesting example of how, over time, strong and weak ties can buttress one another when networks are used to facilitate an innovative project.

Yet, inclusion is not solely a beneficial consequence. At times, inclusion can be stifling for those within networks or communities. Portes and Sensenbrenner (1993), for example, recognize that social capital is not always instrumental, but, rather, becomes a constraint on individuals' actions and choices (see also Portes and Landolt 1996a). Communities may impose heavy obligations on individual members, which require individuals to surrender resources to other members. For example, members of a small ethnic enclave may feel pressured to hire, lend money, provide accommodation, share privileged knowledge with others in their community, or forgo their own opportunities (education, jobs, migration) to remain within an impoverished ghetto. As Woolcock (1998, 165) observes: "A high level of social capital can be 'positive' in that it gives group members access to privileged, 'flexible' resources and psychological support while lowering the risks of malfeasance and transactions costs, but may be 'negative' in that it also places high particularistic demands on group members, thereby restricting individual expression and advancement; permits free riding on community resources; and negates, in those groups with a long history of marginalization through coercive non-market mechanisms, the belief in the possibility of advancement through individual effort."

EXCLUSION

The second dimension of distribution is that of *exclusion*. When Bourdieu (1986, 248) speaks of social capital as a "credential" that grants one access to circles of power and influence, he acknowledges, the simultaneous existence of those deficient in social capital, who are excluded from entry. Bourdieu's focus on reproduction of class through social and cultural capital makes clear these exclusionary properties of social capital. Accumulation of social capital leads to fortification of boundaries and exclusion of outsiders, as Goodin (1996) has shown.

The idea that social capital also holds liabilities is not entirely novel. Like any other form of capital, social capital can be directed toward malevolent, antisocial purposes (Putnam 2000, 22). Portes observes several negative consequences of social capital, including exclusion of outsiders, excess claims on group members, restrictions on individual freedoms, and downward-levelling norms (1998, 15). The very forms of social capital may confer different gains and losses. As Sandefur and Laumann (1998, 483) point out: "A form of social capital acquired to aid in one type of action may hinder other actions; thus, forms of social capital may be said to have *valence*, contingent upon the goals that the actor wishes to attain." Certain types of exclusionary benefits of social capital may play an instrumental role. For instance, minority groups struggling for their rights may need group membership that offers selective advantages to them until they attain equal status within society. Such distinct communities can provide resources to members who are establishing their presence within mainstream society. These communities can also lobby effectively for rights and special protections, such as affirmative action, pay equity, education admissions, and hiring quotas. Yet, at a more macro-level, the growth of social capital within privileged groups may also become obstructive. As Woolcock notes, "longstanding civil groups may stifle macroeconomic growth by securing a disproportionate share of national resources or inhibiting individual economic advancement by placing heavy personal obligations on members that prevent them from participating in broader social networks" (1998, 158; see also Portes and Landolt 1996a).

Reproduction Processes: Operating versus Structuring

Operating Processes

The second axis of our typology, termed processes of reproduction, focuses on communication and exchange of resources at the micro-level of individuals and at the meso/macro-level of collectivities. We begin with the former. *Operating processes* refer to the individual, or micro-level, of social exchange, highlighting the person-to-person interactions embedded in social capital theory. The emphasis is squarely on the importance of exercising one's social networks in the acquisition of valuable resources. Three elements are important to an operating process: resources, networks, and activation of networks (e.g., communications) in securing resources (De Graaf and Flap 1988, 453; Flap 1999, 10). We explore each of these elements in turn.

Operating processes refer to the importance of resources that, although possessed by others, are available to a given individual through his or her social relations with others. Boissevain (1974) aptly called them "second-order" resources. Nan Lin argues (1995, 687) that social resources constitute the central element of social capital. A theory of social resources concentrates on the resources that inhere in social networks and the strategies through which accessing and utilizing these resources benefits individual action (Lin 1982, 1995). Similarly, Snijders contends that it is not the number of persons to whom one is tied but the diversity of resources to which one has access that is the major determinant of the "quantity" of social capital (Snijders 1999, 41). Three resources were identified as crucial by Coleman (1998, S95): obligations and expectations, information channels, and social norms.[7] At the individual level, "embeddedness" in networks rich with resources is important to generating trust and establishing expectations (Coleman 1988, 1990b, 1990c).

Relationships, or *social networks*, are also fundamental to the operating processes of social capital. Social capital stands for the ability of actors to secure resources by virtue of membership in social networks or other social structures (Portes 1998, 6).[8] Bourdieu makes this clear when he defines social capital as "the aggregate of the actual or potential resources which are linked to possession of a durable network or more or less institutionalized relationships of mutual acquaintance or recognition" (1985, 248).[9] Networks offer an opportunity to borrow or access resources through connections to others.[10] As Flap (1999, 8) notes: "Those with more social capital will be better able to realize their goals or defend their interests. Social capital is a relational resource, having ties to others enables one to have access to their resources, to borrow them, so to speak." Therefore, a network is a device not only for receiving resources but also for creating resources such as other networks, which in turn create new resources and opportunities (Burt 1992). Sandefur and Laumann (1998, 484) clearly summarize the importance of social networks to understanding the basis of social capital: "An individual's potential stock of social capital consists of the collection and pattern of relationships in which she is involved and to which she has access, and further to the location and patterning of her associations in larger social space. That is, her potential social capital is both the contacts she herself holds and the ways in which those contacts link her to other patterns of relations."

Social networks can be *egocentric*. For example, a sizable body of research demonstrates how people use social networks in accomplishing their goals, particularly in career attainment (Bourdieu and Boltanski 1978; Granovetter 1974; Watkins 1984). Lin (1982, 1988), for example, shows that individuals act instrumentally, employing their social ties (especially more extended or "weak" ties) to gain occupational mobility. Yet, social networks can also be *sociocentric*, with an emphasis on community and social structure. Involvement in social networks can build social structure, enhancing community integration (Flora 1998; Putnam 2000; Woolley 1998) or hoarding resources for the reproduction of social status of privileged groups (Bourdieu 1983, 1986; Watkins 1984). Whether egocentric or sociocentric, networks remain vital to the essence of social capital.

Finally, *activation* of networks is essential to the operating processes of social capital. The reference to a dynamic process means that, just like other forms of capital, social capital is productive; its activation makes possible the accomplishment of goals that are unattainable otherwise (Coleman 1988, S98; 1990b, 300-3; Sandefur and Laumann 1998, 485).[11] Coleman (1988,

S98) begins with a theory of rational action in which "each actor has control over certain resources and interests in certain resources and events." A theory of social action further emphasizes the dynamic of activating one's social capital. The day-to-day functioning of social capital entails building expectations of reciprocity and, in essence, "counting your marbles" at opportune moments. Of course, the dynamic element in social capital theory is made most apparent by the observation that social capital represents a form of capital that depreciates over time if it is not renewed. Coleman notes that "social relationships die out if not maintained; expectations and obligations wither over time; and norms depend on regular communication" (1990b, 321). Thus, activation renders social capital not only accessible (at the individual level) but potentially expanding (at the community level), and, conversely, disuse can lead to a withering of linkages (at the individual level) or social disintegration (at the community level). As Wall and colleagues contend: "Social capital can increase with use and diminish with disuse, allowing for either virtuous or vicious cycles" (1998, 311).

STRUCTURING PROCESSES
Activation of social capital also involves *structuring processes* at the meso- or macro-level of groups, communities, institutions, and societies. The distinction between operating and structuring social networks is rooted in whether the level of analysis is at the individual or collective level. Where operating processes are the focus, it is the individual who operates the networks. In structuring processes, the collective plays the key role in becoming a structured network that fosters opportunities, mutual trust, and a context in which individuals can play their available networks. These two processes, operating and structuring, are not necessarily distinct phases, yet they are analytically distinct: as the individual plays her networks, she simultaneously lends structural weight to those networks, fortifying and consolidating these relations as elements of social structure. These principles move us away from a potentially "over-networked" conceptualization that equates social capital with access alone (Foley and Edwards 1999). Structuring implies that activation of social capital serves to renew withered associations, to build resilient trust and establish norms, and ultimately, to increase the rigidity of social inequality.

Social networks themselves constitute and build social structure. Sociocentric approaches network analysis explore patterns of relationships within a social system. For example, Burt's study (1992, 1995) of a large US high technology firm explores the effects of network constraints on the probability of early promotion for managers at the mid-level of the firm hierarchy. Burt demonstrates the benefits and costs of positions situated within a topography of interpersonal contacts. An individual's social capital is a by-product of how his or her relationships are located in the larger pattern of relationships within the system. Thus, for instance, similar behaviour is predicted for individuals located in the same social positions – individuals who are "structurally equivalent" – regardless of the conduct of their close associates (Burt 1987, 1998). Burt (1992) stresses that an individual has a competitive advantage in situations in which those who are connected to him or her do not have ties to each other. It is the relative absence of ties, labelled "structural holes," that facilitates individual mobility. This is the case because dense networks tend to convey redundant information, while weaker ties offer sources of new knowledge and diverse resources (see also Gabbay and Zuckerman 1998). The influence and control benefits provided by social capital are, in a sense, opposite sides of the same coin: the ability to influence others (Coleman 1990b) and the ability to be free from others' influence (Burt 1993, 1997a).

It is also possible to examine social capital as a structural property of larger aggregates. Coleman (1990b) emphasizes that a cohesive, well-connected network constitutes a resource to its members in the sense that it promotes cooperation and mutual support. There are benefits yielded through effective social associations: information, influence and control, and social solidarity (Sandefur and Laumann 1998, 485). Norms and trust are also valuable returns from such effective associations. As Coleman (1998, S104) notes: "When a norm exists and is effective, it constitutes a powerful, though sometimes fragile, form of social capital. Effectively, norms that inhibit crime make it possible to walk freely outside at night in a city and enable old persons to leave their houses without fear for their safety. Norms in a community that support and provide effective rewards for high achievement in school greatly facilitate the school's task."

Political scientists introduced an interesting conceptual turn by equating social capital with the level of "civicness" in communities such as towns, cities, and even countries. Social capital's role in supporting democratic vitality and active citizenship represents a concern with factors that affect social capital at the level of the social system. A stock of social capital is equated with the level of association involvement and participatory behaviour in a community and is measured by such indicators as newspaper reading, membership in voluntary associations, and participation in soccer and bowling leagues. Putnam suggests that high levels of various forms of social participation are indicative of a certain density of interaction that is instrumental to building mutual trust and commitment (Putnam 1993a).[12] Economists have further examined the extent to which interpersonal trust and participation in voluntary associations, described as measures of social capital or civic culture, are linked to citizens' satisfaction with the efficacy of their regional government (Helliwell 1996).[13]

However, an emphasis on collective social capital has generously viewed social capital as a "public good," a community resource that is of benefit to all members. Both Coleman and Putnam treat social capital as a public good and community resource that tends to be undervalued (Coleman 1990b, 311; Putnam 1993a, 176). The possibility that social networks mobilized by some groups or individuals may be dysfunctional is often omitted from the equation (Portes and Landolt 1996a; Wall et al. 1998). Yet, sociability has a downside. As Portes (1998, 18) observes: "Whereas bounded solidarity and trust provide the sources for socioeconomic ascent and entrepreneurial development among some groups, among others they have exactly the opposite effect. Sociability cuts both ways." Social capital can be a source of celebrated public goods, including trust, social cohesion, and community integration. It can also lead to less socially desirable ends, or "public bads" (ibid.), for instance, in the form of organized crime, gambling rings, and youth gangs (Stolle and Rochon 1998); these obviously are loci of social cohesion and inclusion, but of the sort that deviates from society-wide social trust and social good.

The existence of deviant groups also illustrates another downside of social capital. One factor contributing to their emergence is that some individuals who are excluded from mainstream, legitimate social networks react by forging their own instruments for access to alternative resources. Structuring processes, in other words, entail social inequality and exclusion, as the subtitle of our chapter suggests; many people who cannot access closed networks simply suffer the attendant hardships, but others react by forming or joining alternative networks (Portes and Landolt 1996a; Tilly 1998; Woolcock 1998).

Applications of the Theoretical Typology

In sum, our proposed typology examines two intersecting sets of processes. The first, *distribution*, emphasizes interpersonal exchanges, how association with others leads to inclusion and a sense of community and, often parallel to this, exclusion of outsiders and reinforcement of boundaries. A second process, *reproduction*, highlights how social capital is activated at the level of individual behaviour, which, in turn, leads to reproducing and structuring social relations, including new norms and enhanced social trust, at the level of communities. The intersection of the dynamics of distribution (characterized by properties of inclusion and exclusion) and reproduction (involving both operating and structuring process) constitutes the core of our typology. The latter yields four ideal types: coalescence, disenfranchisement, community enhancement, and ghettoization. We argue that the cross-cutting aspects of this typology are useful heuristic devices for developing a dynamic understanding of the full potential of a theory of social capital.

We note that these four processes (inclusion, exclusion, operating, and structuring) and the resulting typology are purely analytical distinctions. Obviously, when applied to real world situations, all of these processes, in principle, are present. Each example illustrates at once inclusion and exclusion as well as operating and structuring of the networks. The four cells of our typology and the associated examples strongly illustrate one of the processes, yet each example is destined to contain elements of all four processes. We next provide a detailed explanation of the core of the typology, strategically illustrating these ideal types with several empirical studies of social capital.

Coalescence

The first type of dynamics, coalescence, is the result of social capital put into operation with inclusive tendencies of distribution, leading to an *additive* model (see Figure 3.1). In this ideal type, social capital leads to the development of interpersonal coalitions, networks that are both cumulative and productive, which add to one's resources. Associations can take various forms. Coleman (1990b) emphasizes the social capital that develops in the close, stable, reciprocal relations found in families, intimate friendships, and informal organizations; this form of social capital is often characterized as "bonding" (Tilly 1998, Chapter 1). In contrast, Granovetter (1985) draws attention to less intimate associations and their capacity for providing information and new connections; the emphasis is on building "bridges" between individuals or groups (Gittell and Vidal 1998, 8). Bridging social capital can generate broader identities and reciprocity while encouraging linkages to external assets and diffusion of information (Putnam 2000, 22-23). And, of course, these two forms of linkages can be used in conjunction (Deroy-Pineau and Bernard 2001).

Numerous studies have demonstrated how social capital fosters inclusion with a building up of resources. For example, research by Stantan-Salazar and Dornbush (1995) demonstrates the relationship between outside social networks and academic achievement and aspirations among Mexican high school students in the San Francisco area. The most common demonstrations of the inclusionary consequences of social capital are in the study of stratification and mobility, where social capital is invoked to explain hiring and promotional practices. For example, Wegener's (1991) study highlights the role of social ties in job mobility among German workers, while Erickson's (1996) study of the security service industry in Canada reveals the importance of network variety to workplace relations and mobility within companies. Also, the idea that connections are instrumental in furthering individual mobility is central to Kay and Hagan's analysis (1995, 1998) of partnerships in law firms and to Granfield and Koenig's (1992b) exploration of pathways to elite law firms.

Studies of families clearly reveal the resources available for achieving diverse ends. For example, families characterized by close interpersonal relations and effective communication can facilitate academic achievement. Parents who interact with their children, and with their children's schools, have children who are likely to remain in school rather than dropping out during their teen years (Teachman et al. 1997, 1356). Hofferth and Iceland's comparative study of rural and urban communities in the United States demonstrates that rural families are more likely than are urban families to receive financial help from kin. "However, it is clear that although rural families benefit from the strong ties of kinship, they may suffer from a lack of weak ties that create social capital and permit upward mobility" (Hofferth and Iceland 1998, 596). Parallel studies by Hagan et al. (1996) and Gold (1995) suggest that immigrant families compensate for the absence of social capital in the form of outside networks with an emphasis on social capital in the form of familial support, including preservation of cultural orientations of their homelands.

A study of migration to the United States by Palloni and colleagues (2001) demonstrates the benefits of interpersonal ties connecting new and earlier migrants, founded on kinship, friendship, and shared community origin. These associations increase the likelihood of international migration by lowering the costs and risks of movement and augmenting the gains of migration. These ties to people who have already migrated provide social capital that new migrants can draw upon to access wider networks of employment, from which to earn high foreign wages, accumulate savings, and send remittances to family at home (Palloni et al. 2001, 1264). Similarly, Liang's (1994) study reveals that, in the case of naturalization, immigrants who have family members or friends already in the country can acquire information about naturalization (e.g., about procedures and benefits). Social capital operates to influence naturalization of other immigrant members of the family through two mechanisms. The first is informational: naturalized citizens are knowledgeable about the benefits and procedures of naturalization, and they impart this knowledge to alleviate immigrants' fears about US Immigration and Naturalization Services. The second mechanism is marital: marriage to a citizen reduces the residential requirements of naturalization, thereby accelerating the naturalization process.

Research in the area of criminality reveals that social capital also plays a role in illegal successes (Arnold and Kay 1995; McCarthy and Hagan 2001; Macmillan 1995; Nagin and Paternoster 1994). McCarthy and Hagan (2001) suggest that criminal social capital, arising from associations with skilled offenders and their knowledge of specialized skills and opportunities in regard to offending, contributes to greater success at drug dealing than does conventional capital that consists of family ties and level of education. These connections serve to foster the successful pursuit of illegal profits in settings where legitimate opportunities are very limited. At the same time, social capital can also be mobilized to deter crime. Studies of professional misconduct among lawyers reveal lower rates of professional offences (both charges and convictions) among lawyers in large law firms than among lawyers operating solo practices (Carlin 1966, 1994). Arnold and Kay (1995) contend that an increased volume and quality of social capital in large firms is readily available to firm lawyers through their organizational ties. Compared with sole practitioners, lawyers in firms are more effectively socialized to adhere to ethical standards, and their subsequent behaviours are closely monitored and sanctioned by colleagues. Moreover, lawyers working in firms have access to organizational (that is, internal to the firm) mechanisms preventing complaints from escalating to external authorities (e.g., law society or bar association) and, possibly, ties to others who might collude to conceal their misconduct and buffer them from professional sanctions.

Disenfranchisement

The second cell of our typology, disenfranchisement, reveals the consequences of social capital when it leads to exclusionary dynamics of distribution in a *subtractive* model. Here, social capital reveals its downside, leading to the disenfranchisement of outsiders, a closing out of those lacking the prerequisite credentials or associations for access to resources. Every time an advantage accrues to an individual because of a favourable positioning in a social network, other individuals who compete for scarce resources, but without the benefit of network connections, are likely to be denied access to these resources. It is useful to examine this flip side and the social characteristics of individuals who are typically excluded from the benefits of social capital.

Differential access to social capital, as a result of structural positions within the larger social structure (Tilly 1998), means that women and ethnic minority members may possess fewer opportunities to mobilize social resources to gain employment or advance careers (Lin 1999, 483).[14] A study by Peterson, Saporta, and Seidel (2000) of hiring processes in a mid-size high technology organization over a ten-year period found that ethnic minorities lacked access to social networks that lead to high success in securing employment. For them, job-getting is only partly meritocratic, with social networks, both personal and professional, taking on a significant weight: personal and professional networks accounted for 60 percent of the applications submitted and 81 percent of the job offers received over the course of this study (ibid., 810). This finding is consistent with research in the United States that demonstrates a significant portion of the gap between blacks and whites can be attributed to differences in access to, or in efficacy of, information channels (Granovetter 1995, 151). The most vulnerable to social exclusion are the chronically jobless, whose personal networks have collapsed. In contrast, although the recently jobless will have lost some of their contacts, they can still depend on support from their immediate network of friends and family members (Forsé 1999, 75); in these cases, strong ties seem to outlive the weak ones.

In a similar vein, Friedman and Krackhardt (1997) examined the social conditions experienced by Asian employees in the US workforce, focusing on the lower returns to education that have been documented for both immigrant and US-born Asians. Social capital appears to be the mechanism that transforms education into workplace gains. In their study of a computer services division of a major US investment bank, Friedman and Krackhardt found that Asian employees were disadvantaged in the networks (or centrality) of coworkers whom they could approach for advice about work-related matters or whom they could ask for feedback about their performance on the job. This reduced "centrality" of advice and feedback leads to Asian/European

American differences in supervisors' perceptions of employee potential. Similarly, Fratoe (1988) reveals that black business owners have less access than Asian, Hispanic, or non-minority male business owners to entrepreneurial role models and valuable training in firms run by close relatives. They are also disadvantaged by an inability to rely on friends or relatives for business loans. Black owners were the least likely to be married, thereby experiencing diminished access to business-supporting resources afforded through extended families. However, black entrepreneurs possessed greater availability of social capital in some other aspects: their firms were more likely to sell to minority customers and hire minority employees.

Community Enhancement
In the third cell, termed community enhancement, social capital is engaged in structuring activities at meso- or macro-levels that are characterized by inclusionary properties of distribution. Social capital builds up community, social cohesion, and social solidarity and is fundamentally *multiplicative* in the benefits yielded. Social capital can be both an individual or private asset, as revealed with coalescence, and a group-level or community good, as shown with community enhancement. Individuals not only profit from their associations, which serve as resources for achieving desired ends, but they also profit from social capital accumulated within their communities (McCarthy and Hagan 2001, 1038).[15] This model moves us from a focus on individual transactions (coalescence and disenfranchisement) to an understanding of social structures (Tilly 1998, 41). The effects of social capital, at the aggregate level, offer the potential to increase efficiency and productivity across a number of aggregate outcomes (Paxton 1999, 102). For example, networks, reciprocity, and trust are community-level resources that can facilitate collective action (Flora 1998), reduce high school dropout rates (Coleman 1988; see also Teachman et al. 1997; White and Kaufman 1997), increase government efficiency (Putnam 1993b), and boost national economic performance (Fukuyama 1995a).

Social capital multiplies a community's productive potential in several ways (Putnam 1993b). It promotes "business networking, shared leads, equipment and services, joint ventures, faster information flows and more agile transactions" (Wilson 1995, 1997). Furthermore, social capital fosters an atmosphere conducive to economic activity and cooperation to solve community problems (Wilson, 1997). Social capital builds organizational infrastructures that encourage citizens to take direct action and prosper through collaborative efforts. Thus, various associations, social clubs, civic groups, churches, mosques, synagogues, and grassroots groups often meet social and economic needs that increase the productive capacity of community members (Wilson 1997). In other words, social networks are not only private goods that individuals use but also public goods (in the economists' sense) that result from and multiply through the activation of networks. These goods then become widely available, though not to everyone – as we shall see in the final section, where we examine ghettoization.

Some of the most ambitious examples of the community enhancement model are to be found in economics and political science. Researchers working in these disciplines have examined the extent to which interpersonal trust and participation in voluntary associations, described as measures of social capital or civic culture, are linked to citizens' satisfaction with the efficacy of their regional governments (Helliwell 1996). Civic community as an index of social capital has been measured through newspaper readership, availability of sports and cultural associations, turnout in referenda, and the incidence of preference voting (Helliwell and Putnam 1995). Helliwell and Putnam (ibid., 304) confirm a strong convergence of per capita incomes among the Italian regions during the 1960s and 1970s, and this convergence is more rapid, and equilibrium income levels are greater, in regions possessing higher levels of social capital.[16]

Ghettoization

The fourth type of dynamics, ghettoization, is social capital at its worst. Structuring activities are characterized by the exclusionary consequences of distribution, resulting in the fortification of boundaries, further disempowerment of already disadvantaged groups, and the undermining of access and mobility (as well as hampering the flow of information and social trust) between communities. Social capital is highly *divisive* under these conditions. Organizations, such as firms or clans, intensify bonds and closure by drawing complete boundaries around their communities and then monitoring information flows across these boundaries (Tilly 1998, 17). Social capital thus manifests itself as oppressive inclusion, as social closure with limited access to external networks of knowledge (see Portes 1998). Under these conditions, social capital becomes "inward-looking" and reinforces exclusive identities and homogenous groups (Putnam 2000, 22). Further, the divisive character of this model often leads to exploitation and opportunity hoarding (Tilly 1998, 10) or even to pure and simple exclusion of those deemed to be outsiders.

Fortification of boundaries with exclusionary properties is evident in studies of elite communities. Watkins' study (1984), for example, demonstrates the importance of private school ties in fostering business opportunities. Those lacking the credential of attendance at a privileged private academy are excluded from the inner circles of business dealings. This exclusionary function is also illustrated in Anheier, Gerhards and Romo's (1995) use of block modelling techniques to map social ties among artists and intellectuals in the German city of Cologne. Their analysis shows very strong networks among core members of the city's intellectual elite, along with more restricted access to those networks among those in peripheral and commercial pursuits. These exclusionary consequences often correspond to ethnic niches. They emerge when a group is able to colonize a particular sector of employment so that members have privileged access to new jobs, and outsiders have restricted opportunities (Portes 2000a). Exclusionary properties have been signalled in numerous studies of ethnic niches in activities, ranging from restaurant work, garment factories, and civil service to fire departments (Stepick 1989; Waldinger 1996; Waters 1994). These network chains cause entry-level openings to be filled by contacting kin and friends in distant foreign locations rather than tapping available local workers (Sassen 1995).

Exclusion also takes place through the ghettoization of disadvantaged communities. This represents a closing out of "undesirables." It is most apparent in studies of ethnic business enclaves. Enclaves are dense concentrations of immigrant or ethnic firms that employ a significant proportion of the co-ethnic labour force. Studies of New York's Chinatown (Zhou 1992), of Miami's Little Havana (Portes 1987; Portes and Stepnick 1993), and of Los Angeles' Koreatown (Light and Bonacich 1988) demonstrate the role of community networks as a source of resources for these firms. While these ethnic enclaves are marginalized, they offer vital resources within the parameters of their community, including start-up capital, access to markets, tips about upcoming business opportunities, and a pliant labour force. In Chapter 11 of this volume, Soroka, Johnston and Banting examine linkages between geographic clustering of ethnic groups, levels of affiliation, interpersonal trust, and support for government social welfare programs. Their work has important implications for expansive immigration policies and provides support for social welfare programs across ethnic boundaries.

Another exclusionary dynamic that is characteristic of ghettoization prevails where there is a dearth of social connections in impoverished communities. Wilson (1987, 1996) shows that poor urban communities often lack ties beyond their neighbourhood, which deprives them of employment information elsewhere and of contacts to attain outside positions. Combined with the departure of industrial employment and middle-class families from African-American inner city neighbourhoods, this means that the remaining population is deprived of valuable social capital. This situation of abandonment leads to high levels of unemployment and welfare dependency (Wacquant and Wilson 1989; see also Sullivan 1989). Similarly, Fernandez-Kelly (1995) observes how dense but truncated networks of inner city black families deprive members of information external to the community about employment, while simultaneously encouraging alternative cultural styles that render access to mainstream employment even more precarious.

Conclusion

The concept of social capital is used extensively nowadays in the social sciences, in spite (and partly because) of the fact that it is poorly defined. We have proposed a view of social capital that brings into a coherent scheme the elements that have proven useful across a spectrum of analyses inspired by the work of James Coleman (1988): social capital involves networks, together with their attendant norms of reciprocity, which procure to insiders (as opposed to outsiders) resources for attaining goals. We also take inspiration from Charles Tilly's study of durable inequalities (1998) in arguing that two major dimensions are necessary for capturing the role and the consequences of social capital: distribution processes, with their two opposite sides of inclusion and exclusion, and reproduction processes, because social capital structures access to resources while it also reshapes, through time and practice, social capital itself.

We conclude that analyses of social capital remain incomplete without attention to four sets of consequences that flow from the exercise of social capital: the formation of coalitions (the enacting of inclusion that adds to one's resources), disenfranchisement (the enacting of exclusion that subtracts from one's resources), community enhancement (the structuring of inclusion that multiplies one's opportunities for further access to resources and networks), and finally ghettoization (the structuring of exclusion that divides members of societies into separate opportunity categories for further access to resources). These ideal types illuminate the processes by which social capital enables (and may disable) the attainment of various ends, from family support to health, employment, economic prosperity, community trust, cooperation, and political efficacy.

Our main contribution to clarifying the notion of social capital has been to insist that its dynamics significantly revolve around social inequality: social capital both includes and excludes social actors; it unites and divides them. Any type of social capital can be seen to have benefits to some and disadvantages to others, and there is almost no type of social capital that can be analyzed without this insight. A recent report published by the OECD (2001) devotes a full chapter to social capital and to its importance for the development of advanced societies. It admirably symbolizes the ambiguities of current uses of the notion of social capital, ambiguities, which originate, we contend, in the lack of attention paid to the social inequality inherent in social capital, especially as it becomes reproduced and structured over time.

A few quotes from the OECD report (2001) illustrate this profound ambiguity. It is first recognized that "social capital has 'social' and 'capital' dimensions since it resides in relations rather than individuals, being also a resource that can generate a stream of benefits for society over time. However, it can also lead to dysfunction when used by one group against others" (39). On one hand, "social capital allows individuals, groups and communities to resolve collective problems more easily. Norms of reciprocity and networks help ensure compliance with collectively desirable behaviour" (41). But, on the other hand, "although strong bonding ties give particular communities or groups a sense of identity and common purpose, without 'bridging' ties that transcend various social divides (e.g., religion, ethnicity, socioeconomic status), bonding ties can become a basis for the pursuit of narrow interests, and can actively exclude outsiders" (42). Moreover, "some forms of exclusive bonding can then be a barrier to social cohesion and personal development" (42). And "an exclusive focus on group interests to the neglect of wider public interests can promote socially destructive 'rent-seeking' activities" (42).

These quotes hint at the themes we have sketched here. But the conceptual analysis ends on the highly optimistic, *and largely undemonstrated*, following statement: "Some forms of exclusive social bridging at the national or regional level may have socially destructive consequences. These examples do not undermine the potential of human or social capital in other cases to generate benefits for all or most members of society. The benefits from most types of social bonding and bridging generally greatly outweigh the negative consequences" (OECD 2001, 42-43).

In fact, it is often assumed that, as far as social capital is concerned, "the more, the merrier." But things are not necessarily so. The problem, as we have shown, is not only that social capital is sometimes good and sometimes bad, at times inclusive and other times divisive. If that were so, we would only have to determine what sorts of social capital are welcome, and which should be avoided. But this is an impossible task, because social capital is often, in the same dynamic, simultaneously inclusionary and exclusionary. This is why, we argue, analysis of social capital cannot be undertaken without constant reference to the attendant social inequality. Social inequality precedes and shapes the use of social networks; it is reproduced and transformed as these networks are used, as they add up, as they multiply, and as they divide people into differentially endowed relation sets.

Several questions emerge from our typology of the dynamics of social capital. How can positive consequences of social capital, such as cooperation, trust, and organizational efficacy, be maximized while negative manifestations in the forms of ethnocentrism and corruption are minimized (Putnam 2000, 22)? More generally, how is social capital distributed over the general population and comparatively across nations (McNeal 1999, 137)? How can social capital be transferred or "infused" from advantaged groups, endowed with high social capital, to disadvantaged groups with low social capital (Paxton 1999, 123)? Our chapter suggests that social capital is both a source and a consequence of association. Further work needs to examine how social capital is produced and nurtured within groups, parlayed to other groups in reciprocal exchanges, and, on occasion, converted into other forms of capital (e.g., financial, human, and cultural).

ACKNOWLEDGMENTS

We wish to thank Ryan Causton and Joanna Kim for valuable research assistance. An earlier version of this chapter was presented in November 2001 at the Equality, Security, and Community Project annual meeting in Vancouver, British Columbia. The research reported here was supported by a grant through the multi-collaborative research initiative program of the Social Sciences and Humanities Research Council of Canada (Grant #412-1997-0003). Please direct correspondence to Fiona M. Kay, Department of Sociology, Queen's University, Kingston, Ontario, Canada K7L 3N6; e-mail: kayf@post.queensu.ca.

NOTES

1 The concept of social capital has gained wide use and acceptance most notably in the disciplines of sociology (see, e.g., Arnold and Kay 1995; Bourdieu 1986; Burt 1992, 1997b; Coleman 1988; Erickson 1996, 2001; Fernandez and Castilla 2001; Lesser, 2000; Lin 1995; Lin et al. 2001; Portes and Sensenbrenner 1993; Sandefur and Laumann 1998; Seron and Ferris 1995; Zukin and DiMaggio 1990), economics (Fukuyama 1995; Helliwell 1996; Helliwell and Putnam 1995), and political science (Putnam 1993a, 2000; Woolcock 1998). Our electronic search of the *Social Sciences Citation Index* of articles published from 1986 to 2001 reveals a total of 238 articles using the term "social capital" in their titles.

2 Wall et al. (1998, 318) argue that "social capital theory is underdeveloped compared to its use in research. Such lags are to be expected and, in part welcomed in the evolution of sociological knowledge."

3 Lévesque and White (1999) also argue that scholars need to distinguish the nature of social capital from the sources or conditions that produce social capital: "Cette confusion repose habituellement sur les deux aspects interreliés, soit les lieux de production du capital social et la nature de ce dernier. Cette situation n'est pas sans poser certains problèmes ... il n'est pas possible de cerner ce qu'on entend par capital social sans identifier l'espace dans lequel la réalité qu'il décrit prend form et agit" (ibid., 24).

4 Coleman contends: "The function identified by the concept 'social capital' is the value of these aspects of social structure to actors as resources that they can use to achieve their interests" (1988, S101).

5 In their theoretically insightful article, Sandefur and Laumann (1998, 482) recast social capital theory to focus on benefits rather than forms. They argue that a focus on benefits has been characteristic of successful attempts to measure individuals' stocks of social capital.

6 As Sandefur and Laumann (1998, 491) point out: "One can imagine each individual's relationships having an ideal empirical balance between cohesion and closure, and to access to diverse sources of information and influence. The ideal balance may well be different depending on where the individual is in the hierarchy of the social system, whether the context is characterized more by cooperation or competition, and, in comparative settings, on whether team competition or individual is the operative game. Here again, we see how the goals for which a form of social capital is activated condition its value."

7 Information channels have received close attention in the research literature. The information benefits of social capital arise from the relevance, timeliness (Burt 1992) and trustworthiness (Laumann and Knoke 1987) of the information provided (Sandefur and Laumann 1998, 485).

8 A growing body of literature focuses on social networks in the analysis of social capital (see, e.g., Berkman and Syme 1979; Burt 1997b; Diani 1997; Erickson

1996; Granovetter 1986; Gummer 1998; House 1987; Lin 1999; Popielarz 1999; Wellman 1992, 1999b).

9   Some scholars refer to the idea of "credit" or expectations of reciprocity embedded within networks of social relations. For example, Bourdieu argues that "membership in a group ... provides each of its members with the backing of the collectively-owned capital, a 'credential' which entitles them to credit, in the various senses of the word" (1986, 248). Coleman also refers to the idea of credit when he states: "Individual actors in a social system also differ in the number of credit slips outstanding on which they can draw at any time" (1988, S103).

10 Bourdieu emphasizes the centrality of social networks in the following passage: "Le capital social est l'ensemble des ressources actuelles ou potentielles qui sont liées à la possession d'un *réseau durable de relations* plus ou moins institutionnalisées d'interconnaissance et d'inter-reconnaissance; ou, en d'autres termes, à *l'appartenance à un groupe*, comme ensemble d'agents qui ne sont pas seulement dotés de propriétés communes ... mais sont aussi unis par des *liaisons* permanentes et utiles" (1980, 2).

11 The activation of social capital and its potential for productivity is expressed by James Coleman: "Social capital is defined by its function. It is not a single entity but a variety of different entities, with two elements in common: they all consist of some aspect of social structures, and they facilitate certain actions of actors – whether persons or corporate actors – with the structure. Like other forms of capital, social capital is productive, making possible the achievement of certain ends that in its absence would not be possible" (1988, S98).

12 It should be acknowledged that numerous critiques have been levelled against the work of Putnam. Critics have focused on the question of whether voluntarism and civic spirit have, in fact, declined in America and on the unacknowledged bias in Putnam's thesis (Skocpol 1996, 25). Another criticism of Putnam's argument is its logical circularity (Portes 1998, 19), which is illustrated in the following passage: "Some regions of Italy ... have many active community organizations ... These 'civic communities' value solidarity, civic participation, and integrity. And here democracy works. At the other end are 'uncivic' regions, like Calabria and Sicily, aptly characterized by the French term *incivisme*. The very concept of citizenship is stunted here" (Putnam 1993a, 36). The tautology results from two analytic decisions; "first, starting with the effect (i.e., successful versus unsuccessful cities) and working retroactively to find out what distinguishes them," second, trying to explain all of the observed differences" (Portes 1998, 20).

13 Civic community as an index of social capital has been measured through newspaper readership, availability of sports and cultural associations, turnout in referenda, and the incidence of preference voting (Helliwell and Putnam 1995).

14 The disadvantaged must engage in strategic behaviours to access resources beyond their usual social circles. For example, women may need to employ connections

with men or join clubs dominated by men (Beggs and Hurlbert 1997); Mexican-origin high school students may need to use ties to students of non-Mexican origin to establish ties with individuals in positions of authority, such as teachers and counsellors (Stanton-Salazar and Dornbusch 1995).

15 Paxton (1998, 96), however, notes that, while social capital within a particular group may hold positive effects for the members of that group, this need not "spill over" into positive gains for the community's social capital.

16 Helliwell and Putnam (1995) employ three measures of social capital: an index of the extent of civic community, an index consisting of various direct measures of the effectiveness of regional government, and surveys of citizen satisfaction with their regional governments.

4
Equality, Trust, and Multiculturalism

Avigail Eisenberg

An important objection to multiculturalism is that it erodes social solidarity and fragments community in a way that jeopardizes the advancement of egalitarian policies. This objection has been recently developed in a way that highlights the putative connections between ethnic diversity and the decline of social solidarity, trust, and the welfare state. The suggestion is that ethnically diverse societies tend to have weaker welfare states – a conclusion that is reached via a three-part explanation: (1) ethnic diversity may weaken the bonds within communities, especially bonds that give rise to the sort of trust that obtains between members of the same society; (2) trust is considered to be a foundation of social solidarity and, therefore, crucial to social and political relations; and (3) the social cooperation and solidarity that trust helps to sustain is putatively necessary to garner support for policies that redistribute wealth on a societal scale. In other words, the welfare state requires high levels of social trust. Voters support redistributive policies (e.g., public education, socialized healthcare, and social assistance) partly because they feel a sense of social solidarity with those who require assistance and partly because they trust that those who receive these benefits are, in principle, willing to give similar assistance to others if they were in the position to offer it. Where trust is present, cooperation and sharing come easily. Where trust is absent, cooperation and the policies that rely on cooperation, such as those that affect redistribution, become difficult to secure and costly to implement.

Although many studies suggest that ethnic diversity may impede the welfare state, few provide a focused and systematic examination of this suggestion. Of the studies that provide some empirical insight, none concludes that the relevant link exists. For instance, Soroka, Johnston, and Banting (Chapter 11) conclude, in a study that focuses on Canada and uses first wave data from the Equality, Security, and Community (ESC) study, that, while ethnic diversity affects levels of interpersonal trust, and while levels of trust have a strong impact on support for redistributive programs, a strong, consistent relationship between ethnic context and the health of the welfare state does not exist. Similarly, Aizlewood and Pendakur (Chapter 7) show that, with few exceptions, minority groups in Canada display attitudes that are similar to the majority in areas of trust and participation and, thus, that social diversity is not a factor significant to high or low levels of social capital. Banting and Kymlicka add a comparative dimension to the research by examining several welfare state programs and multicultural policy contexts and by providing an especially detailed comparison of Canada and Belgium. They conclude that "there is no evidence that countries that have adopted strong MCPs [multicultural policies] have seen an erosion in their welfare states relative to countries that have resisted such programs" (2003, 39).

This chapter complements these recent empirical studies by examining the ways in which the key concepts employed in these debates inform the empirical research and, especially, the analyses of social capital. The effectiveness and clarity of these analyses crucially turn on how they employ concepts such as multiculturalism, social solidarity, and trust. My aim is also to draw attention to the fact that many of the conclusions that follow from social capital studies are suspicious of ethnic diversity and implicitly (or sometimes explicitly) critical of programs like multiculturalism, which heighten the salience of diversity. But, after reviewing many of these studies, I argue that these suspicions are ill-founded and under-theorized. While ethnic diversity might indeed pose obstacles to social solidarity, trust, and the welfare state, social capital studies are unable verify that these obstacles exist because they have framed the challenges of ethnic diversity in misleading ways. Here, I focus on three sets of concepts that frequently contribute to misleading conclusions within these studies: (1) ethnic diversity/multiculturalism; (2) ethnic insularity/social solidarity as they are related to bridging/bonding; and (3) trust. The aim here is not to provide a definitive account of each concept (which would be impossible in any case) but rather to identify some challenges that need to be met to improve how each set of concepts is understood and used.

Ethnic Diversity and Multiculturalism
Ethnic diversity refers to a demographic characteristic of most, if not all, nation-states in the world. While some societies are more ethnically diverse than others, all nation-states are not only pluralistic on the basis of ethnicity, religion, and language, but most states contain within their borders minority

nations that seek rights and status distinct from the majority (Kymlicka 1995, 1). These factors potentially have dramatic impacts on redistributive programs, as numerous empirical studies of the welfare state have suggested. Within this literature, ethnic diversity, *not multiculturalism*, is often viewed as potentially contributing to a decline of or weakness in redistributive programs. Soroka, Johnston, and Banting (Chapter 11), as well as Aizlewood and Pendakur (Chapter 7), cite several such studies that show, for instance, that ethnically diverse states and cities spend less on income transfer programs, spend more on private education, and generally fail to sustain high levels of redistribution. In addition, ethnically diverse societies (including cities and states) putatively experience more income inequality and have weaker labour organizations than culturally homogeneous states such as Sweden, Norway, and Denmark (Stephens 1979).

In contrast to ethnic diversity, multiculturalism usually refers to the set of ideals and policies by which states accommodate diversity, including national and ethnic diversity. Within the philosophical literature, multiculturalism, *not ethnic diversity*, is often viewed as contributing to the decline of or weakness in redistributive policies. The concern in this literature is either that multiculturalism distracts political actors and social movements from pursuing policies that redistribute wealth more equally (see Fraser 1997, 11-40; Gitlin 1995) or that multiculturalism corrodes the bonds that unite members and that provide a source of group power to facilitate projects, such as the coordination of union activity or the implementation of large welfare state programs (Barry 2001). For example, the factions that emerge in labour unions, along lines of gender, ethnicity, or race, can distract organizations from pursuing collective action and corrode trusting relations among group members. This corrosion, even if not debilitating, at least increases the costs of cooperation (Creese 1999, 208-9).[1]

Multiculturalism also refers to a collection of different sorts of policies that range from acculturation programs to rules for group representation. Their differences are important to note here because some of them (usually those that are rarely implemented) are sometimes falsely represented as paradigms of multiculturalism. Broadly construed, multiculturalism includes policies whose goal is to ensure that ethnic membership or background is not a source of social, political, or economic disadvantage. The sort of policies that any state uses depends on the distinctive circumstances of the groups to which they are supposed to apply. To reflect this fact, Kymlicka (1995) divides multicultural policies into three categories: (1) those directed at immigrant groups or ethnic minorities; (2) those directed at national minorities[2]; and (3) those which address the circumstances of indigenous peoples.

Generally, the policies directed at immigrant minority groups are meant to facilitate their successful integration into mainstream society. Different strategies have been employed to ensure successful integration, some of which are more controversial than others. Most benign (yet still controversial in some societies) are acculturation programs, language training, affirmative action, employment equity, and policies that combat racism, such as, in Canada, human rights acts. These policies are the mainstays of Canadian multiculturalism, which means that most of the resources devoted to multiculturalism are devoted to these sorts of policies. Second, programs that recognize the contributions of distinctive ethnic groups, for instance, by relaying their history in high school textbooks, or highlighting their contributions through state-sponsored celebrations, provide the means of integration by ensuring that membership in an ethnic minority is consistent with being recognized as a full member of mainstream society.

Finally, the most controversial policies are those which provide legal exemptions or special treatment for ethnic minorities as a means by which to accommodate group practices or values. Examples of this sort of accommodation include exempting Sikh men from safety helmet laws and allowing (or directing) courts to consider cultural values as a mitigating factor in criminal sentencing.

Unlike ethnic minorities, national minorities and Aboriginal peoples often have historical claims to collective rights, constitutional protection for their language and culture, special rights to representation, and some measure of self-determination or self-government. In contrast, ethnic minorities, such as Sikh and Ukrainian Canadians, have no claim to self-government.[3] Within Canada, Aboriginal peoples and the Québécois strongly resist being categorized as ethnic minorities like all others in Canadian society and, therefore, policies specifically directed at addressing their concerns tend not to be viewed as part of Canada's "multicultural" framework. But, outside Canada, these policies are often viewed as fitting within what is generally thought to be multicultural politics and policies.[4]

If these distinctions seem reasonable, then in studies that seek to measure the consequences of ethnic diversity, the presence of ethnic diversity ought to be treated as independent of the presence of policies that promote multicultural ideals. Some ethnically diverse societies, such as Canada, are known to promote strong multicultural policies, while others, such as France, are thought to do less to accommodate or recognize their diversity. Moreover, in light of the different commitments that states might have to multicultural ideals, the question of how societies fare at enhancing equality in light of ethnic diversity would seem crucially to depend on whether they are willing to institute at least some types of multicultural policies. Therefore, the fact that societies in which the need for social assistance falls along ethnic lines are especially unsuccessful at sustaining strong redistributive programs (see Gould and Palmer 1988; Wilensky 1975) raises, rather than addresses, questions about whether multicultural programs that seek to integrate disadvantaged ethnic groups into mainstream society will help or hinder the conditions required for strong redistributive programs. The possibility, for instance, that the failure of some social welfare programs is caused by chauvinism or racism within mainstream society (Gilens 1996; also see discussion in Banting and Kymlicka 2003, 10-12 and 40-41), rather than by the mere presence of ethnic diversity, is neither ruled out nor even addressed by such studies. Similarly, the role that multicultural policies might play in addressing social problems (like racism) is left unexamined. In this context, it is no small irony that multiculturalism, which aims at enhancing equality, is sometimes viewed as undermining the conditions, such as the presence of trust, upon which the advancement of equality-enhancing policies depend. Studies that fail to distinguish between the presence of ethnic diversity and the presence of multicultural policies leave themselves open to the misleading conclusion that ethnic diversity weakens redistributive programs, when, in fact, the problem lies with the social conditions that multicultural policies aim to address, such as racism and cultural alienation.

Drawing this first distinction between ethnic diversity and multiculturalism is the most basic challenge for studies of social capital and ethnic diversity. The problem is not so much that studies have intentionally conflated these concepts. Rather, critics of multiculturalism sometimes substantiate their claims by citing studies of ethnic diversity and vice versa.[5] Yet, studies that show a correlation between diversity and weak redistributive programs provide little insight into the potential effects of multiculturalism because, on one hand, ethnic diversity and multiculturalism are independent variables and, on the other hand, multicultural policies are specifically directed at addressing social problems such as racism and cultural alienation, which are likely to affect the success of redistributive policies.

Insularity, Solidarity, Bridging, and Bonding

A large and growing literature in political theory and in studies of social capital links multicultural policies (not ethnic diversity) to a weak welfare state through the intermediate variables of social solidarity and trust. Studies that focus on social solidarity are often concerned more specifically with what they identify as the opposite of solidarity, namely ethnic fragmentation, "tribalism," and insularity. The social capital literature, for instance, discusses the problem of social solidarity/ethnic insularity partly in terms of a distinction between bridging and bonding relations. Bonding relations refer to connections among those who already feel connected because of shared identity-related characteristics such as ethnicity, religion, family, or language. Bridging refers to connections among people who are initially strangers and who do not share identity-related characteristics.

Although the social capital literature maintains that both bridging and bonding social capital can have "powerfully positive social effects," bridging social capital is viewed as more important to democratic community and as "creating more desirable outcomes" (Rothstein and Stolle 2002; Putnam 2000) because bridging the various cleavages within any society is important to forging a democratic community. In contrast, bonding social capital is often represented as hostile to democratic community (even though the democratic potential and contribution of bonding social capital, for example in relation to new immigrant communities, has not been the subject of much, if any, research [see Abraham, Chapter 8]). According to Robert Putnam, "bridging social capital can generate broader identities and reciprocity, whereas bonding social capital bolsters our narrower selves." Bridging relations are indicative of the presence of cooperation in society in general, while bonding relations create "strong in-group loyalty, [and] may also create strong out-group antagonism" (Putnam 2000, 23). Eric Uslaner makes a similar point, which he explains in terms of the distinction between moralistic and particularized trust. The particularized truster has strong bonds within her community, primarily has faith in her own kind, and may reject the idea of a common culture. She may get involved in civic associations, but only if these associations are within her own community. For instance, religious fundamentalists tend to do a significant amount of volunteering, but they almost exclusively volunteer within their own church communities. In doing so, according to Uslaner, they might exacerbate conflicts among different groups in society (Uslaner 2001b). Similarly, when ethnic politicians primarily serve their own communities, they may strengthen particularized trust but undermine the agenda in which moralistic trust is employed "to include rather than exclude folks who are different from themselves" (Uslaner 2002, 197). In contrast, moralistic trusters (those who build bridging relations), do not restrict themselves to membership in ethnic groups and especially religious organizations, where they would congregate only with people like themselves. In contrast to particularized trusters, moralistic trusters have faith in a wide range of strangers (Uslaner 2002, 28).

The message found in the social capital literature is that ethnic insularity is bad for democratic communities, and therefore policies that promote insularity or "bonding" forms of social capital are also bad. What makes this message so powerful is not only that empirical studies are said to provide evidence for it but also that it resonates with much of the social and political criticism of multicultural theory and policies. For example, Canadian multiculturalism, as pursued by the federal government, is commonly criticized for encouraging the leaders of ethnic groups to keep their members apart from the mainstream. In one critic's words, multiculturalism "amounts, at worst, to an apartheid form of citizenship" (Gwyn 1995, 234). According to another, by adopting multiculturalism, "too few who come to Canada end up accepting themselves – and one another – as simply 'Canadian,' thereby weakening the social fabric" (Bissoondath 1994, 219).

The suggestion that multiculturalism and ethnic insularity are causally linked can also be found in the philosophical criticisms of multiculturalism. For instance, David Miller has argued that national solidarity is crucial to the pursuit of social justice and that "radical" multicultural policies that celebrate ethnic identities at the expense of national identities threaten this solidarity (Miller 1995, 135). Miller's concern is that, under multiculturalism's ideals, minorities are encouraged to construct identities based on how they are "different" from rather than what they have in common with their co-nationals, and this makes them more vulnerable to social injustice because they are thereby alienating themselves from the group (namely the mainstream majority), which is in the best position to address these injustices. A far wiser strategy, according to Miller's analysis, would be to construct themselves as full members of the national community. Policies such as those that recognize special rights for minority groups or allocate to ethnic groups formal representation in legislatures undermine the common identification upon which community solidarity relies. In Miller's words, "If we believe in social justice and are concerned about winning democratic support for socially just policies, then we must pay attention to the conditions under which different groups will trust one another ... Trust requires solidarity not merely within groups but across them, and this in turn depends upon a common identification of the kind that nationality alone can provide" (Miller 1995, 140). Brian Barry makes a similar argument, though in less qualified terms. A "politics of difference," which Barry claims is exemplified by Canada's multiculturalism and theories of group-differentiated citizenship, "rests on a rejection of what we may call, in contrast, the politics of solidarity." Rather than citizens belonging to a single society and sharing a common fate, Barry argues, "the whole point of the 'politics of difference' is to assert that the right answer is for each cultural group to have public policies tailored to meet its specific demands" (Barry 2001, 300).

It is not unreasonable to suppose that some kinds of ethnic insularity undermine democratic community. Many multicultural theorists are well aware of potential threats posed by radically insular minorities such as Orthodox Jews, the Amish, and radical Mormon sects and have argued that insular minorities ought to be tolerated within democratic societies only insofar as they do not constitute a serious threat to civil society, which they don't mainly because they are so small. But these are not the groups that form the focus of discussions about the welfare state. For the most part, the focus of multicultural theory and policy and, one assumes, of debates about the welfare state and multiculturalism is relatively non-insular minorities, particularly those who participate in and enjoy the benefits of public institutions and social welfare programs.

Yet, if we set aside the radically insular minorities and focus instead on the non-insular minorities, the concerns about ethnic insularity seem to be greatly overstated, and the connections between these concerns and multiculturalism seem to be oversimplified. This is, first, because the main aim of multicultural policies in states that embrace multiculturalism is to combat insularity, not to reinforce it. It is *possible* that these policies fail to meet their goals. But the evidence suggests the opposite conclusion. With respect to Canada (a country with a relatively strong commitment to multiculturalism), indicators suggest that policies such as acculturation, language training, employment equity, and human rights education and protection are successful at breaking down barriers between the mainstream and minorities. Multicultural policy has eased the transition of immigrants, who then become devoted to Canada and are eager to identify with the political community and the government (Harles 1997, 734-35; Kymlicka 1998; also see Reitz and Breton 1994). Compared to other countries, Canada experiences relatively low levels of segregation in housing and education, only moderate ethnic inequality in income and earnings, and similar cultural participation rates across the labour market and in unions (Kurthen 1997, 261; Kymlicka 1998, 21-22). Kymlicka argues that, with respect to naturalization, political participation, and official language acquisition, immigrants are more integrated today than they were before multiculturalism was instituted (Kymlicka 1998, 18). Moreover, polling of the majority cultures has generally shown that cultural "acceptance, tolerance, and mutual understanding has ... increased over time" (Kurthen 1997, 260).

Of course, there is no telling whether these policies are responsible for Canada's successes or whether other factors such as the origins and timing of immigration or the wealth of immigrants have made significant contributions. A better test might be to measure the effects of more radical policies that actively accommodate some minorities through legal exemptions or, in the case of national minorities and indigenous peoples, through recognizing the collective rights of these groups to special representation or to self-determination. Policies that offer these sorts of accommodation seem to heighten the salience of ethnic identity in public life. Some critics argue that active accommodation policies of these sorts provide incentives for minorities to differentiate themselves from the mainstream so as to qualify for special consideration and exemptions. If this is true, then the concern about multiculturalism and insularity can be expressed as a concern that multiculturalism encourages individuals to form self-conceptions, interests, and organizations based on ethnic identity as a means by which to gain resources to advance particular interests.

Yet, three challenges have to be met before one can conclude that these more radical policies encourage ethnic insularity and, thereby, undermine democratic community. First, much depends on what counts as undermining rather than sustaining (or even supporting) the broader democratic community. As mentioned above, too few studies have been conducted on the social capital that immigrant communities bring with them and the distinctive ways in which they use their social capital to contribute to the democratic nature of their new state. According to Abraham (Chapter 8), the conventional indicators, which include voting and participating in political parties and other mainstream institutions, fail to account for grassroots efforts that have a profound effect not only on the public policies dear to a particular community, such as housing, daycare, and healthcare, but to the broader democratic vibrancy of the newly adopted domicile. In addition to the impact that immigrants have had on democratic politics in the United States, "first-generation Italians in Brazil and Argentina, Turks in Germany, Grenadians in Trinidad, Jews in Israel/Palestine, Indians in East Africa, Chinese in Malaya, and others have been important players in political, community, and labour struggles" (ibid., below, page 211). Canada has had similar experiences. A recent example is the case of Canadian Tamils, a community that has enhanced the democratic nature of both Canada and Sri Lanka. Tamil organizations in Canada closely monitor individual rights in relation to Canadian immigration, refugee, and deportation policies (as discussed in Chapter 8). At the same time, they provide a means by which Canada can exercise considerable influence on the peace process and democratic restructuring of Sri Lanka (Knox 2002, A1; Deverell 2003).

A second and related challenge is to clarify in social capital studies the place of programs that aim at restorative justice. One reason that the criticism that multiculturalism undermines social solidarity is misplaced is that it fails to comprehend the historical and social context in which such policies are sometimes developed. For instance, the objection that "radical" policies, such as those which recognize the self-determination of national minorities, promote ethnic insularity is misleading if it ignores the background conditions, of historical promises broken or incidents of injustice, against which policies that recognize self-government are formulated (Banting and Kymlicka 2003, 10). The conditions of social solidarity or societal trust could not be enhanced by ignoring constitutional promises made, for example, to protect the French language and culture in Canada, or by failing to address historical injustices upon which the claims of Aboriginal peoples are based. Indeed, the historical legacy of ignoring and breaking such promises has arguably done more to damage societal trust and solidarity in Canada than have policies of accommodation that attempt to mend relations between national minorities and majorities. No doubt these promises and injustices are costly and might even have a deleterious effect on welfare state policies. But the suggestion that multinational countries ignore these background conditions is a non-starter both in terms of the normative commitments to fostering democratic community and in terms of the sociological conditions that appear to build trust and solidarity.

A third challenge to be confronted relates to different degrees of institutional accessibility for different peoples. Bonding policies, which appear to accommodate the distinctive practices of a minority community, have to be assessed in light of the possibility that institutions within liberal democratic societies may not be equally accessible to members of ethnic and national minorities and majorities. Implicitly or explicitly, many political institutions complement and reinforce the particular ethnic and religious values of the mainstream, usually the majority group. Sometimes, favouring the majority's values is explicit, unavoidable, and unobjectionable, for instance, in the case of state recognition of an official language. English- and French-as-a-Second-Language (ESL/FSL) policies are a means of recognizing the unavoidable linguistic bias of public institutions and helping non-English or non-French speakers to overcome this bias. But other forms of bias are neither unavoidable nor as explicit, and many require precisely what some critics of multiculturalism deride, namely, a search for ways in which public policies can be amended so as to avoid unintentional bias in favour of one group and against others. In Canada, Sunday closing laws were reassessed in light of religious diversity (see *R. v. Big M Drug Mart Ltd.*, [1985] 1 S.C.R. 295). Laws and regulations that forbid children to bring weapons to school were reassessed because they conflicted with one of the practices of Sikhs, i.e., that each adult male carry a kirpan (see Banerjee 2002). Questions have also arisen about whether the cultural beliefs and practices of immigrants can be used as a mitigating feature in criminal sentencing. There is no doubt that some of these questions are difficult to resolve. But they are difficult not because rules, which are otherwise impartial, conflict with particular ethnic practices. Rather, the problem is that the rules in question may not be impartial; having an official language is not impartial, nor is choosing Sunday as a publicly recognized common day of rest, nor is allowing the traditional beliefs and norms of mainstream culture, but not minority cultures, to guide criminal sentencing. According to the ideals of multiculturalism, in some, though not all of these cases, cultural accommodation is justified. But, in all cases, cultural exemptions or special means of accommodation are favoured because the context is deemed culturally biased in the first place. Where bias is inevitable, as with language policy, or where it seems reasonable, as with regulations that ban carrying weapons, the policies that aim at multicultural accommodation compensate for the absence of impartiality.

Claims about the positive effects of bridging and the negative effects of bonding are especially dubious when considered from the perspective of how ethnic minorities experience impartiality. For example, in the social capital literature that focuses on ethnically diverse societies in which a strong majority ethnic group exists, there are good reasons to suppose that so-called "bridging" organizations are neither ethnically nor religiously neutral, even if they welcome all members of the public. It would be surprising and highly unlikely to find that longstanding civic associations, which form the focus of many social capital studies, are *not* biased in favour of particular cultural and religious values. The Girl Guides, Boy Scouts, and YMCA may welcome members from all walks of life, but this does not mean that, in any given community, they are organizations that reflect culturally diverse values. In Canada, outside a few urban centres, these organizations are overwhelmingly dominated by Christian and white-European values. The Boy Scouts may provide a civic starting point for all kids, but it is no less ethnically biased in favour of European, white, and Christian values than are many of the youth programs that count in research as ethnically based or church-run.

This is not to suggest that programs and organizations that attempt to bridge cultural and linguistic communities are not important within a multicultural framework. But two concerns follow from the third challenge. First, many policies are difficult to classify as either bonding or bridging because they do both. In some cases, policies that appear to clearly promote bonding rather than bridging are put in place to fulfill historical promises and, therefore, are one of the bases upon which intercommunity trust might develop. But even in the absence of promises, programs that seem clearly to bond members of a community together may, nonetheless, have a bridging function that is not at first obvious. One example of this sort is language instruction programs for immigrants in their own first language (e.g., not French or English). On one hand, these programs seem clearly to promote bonding, and even insularity, rather than bridging. On the other hand, evidence suggests that adult immigrants are unlikely to attain fluency in a second language (English or French) if they have not attained literacy in their first language (Kymlicka 1998, 49-53). More generally, fair and effective terms of acculturation may entail a process of incorporating cultural difference into the Canadian framework rather than imposing the dominant culture on soon-to-be assimilated minorities.

The third challenge amounts to a requirement that studies of social capital critically examine what counts as a bridging versus a bonding relation while keeping in mind that organizations dominated by the majority ethnic group are not necessarily culturally neutral. Citizens from the majority ethnic group who seem to succeed in forming strong "bridging" relations may be in the luxurious position of avoiding membership in ethnic-based associations

– where they would congregate with people like themselves – because so many of the *public* organizations that they join are ones in which they can expect to congregate with people like themselves. Similarly, the failure of some ethnic minorities to join bridging organizations is more accurately identified as a failure of public organizations effectively to bridge cultural groups.

The charge that multiculturalism heightens the salience of minority ethnicity may, in part, be correct. However, the connection between this sort of insularity and social solidarity is overly general and under-theorized in the social capital literature. It is possible, as some critics suggest, that multicultural theory raises questions about fairness in a way that encourages a troubling form of minority insularity to develop. Yet, this is neither the aim nor outcome of multicultural policies. Moreover, any measurement that claims to substantiate such a position needs to compare the ethnic insularity of minorities with the insularity of majorities within and outside of conditions of multiculturalism.

In addition, the question of whether ethnic insularity diminishes in the absence of questions about the fairness of public laws and practices toward ethnic minorities or of ethnic membership ratios in civic associations is not credibly an issue in societies that aim at treating people equally. In the absence of multiculturalism, the religious and cultural biases of the public sphere are likely to be no less salient overall, even though they may become less obviously salient to ethnic majorities. In contrast, where multiculturalism is actively promoted, mainstream culture may become less culturally insular and more sensitive to the ways in which seemingly impartial public policies and practices are not culturally, religiously, or linguistically impartial at all.

Multiculturalism, the Decline of Trust, and Equality

Like social solidarity, trust is viewed as crucial to social relations and potentially impaired by policies, such as multiculturalism, that emphasize how we differ from each other rather than how our fates are bound together. With respect to the ubiquity of trust in social and political relations, Annette Baier, in a seminal philosophical treatment of the subject, explains trust as that which entails giving to others discretion to affect our interests. With trust, we make ourselves vulnerable to another's goodwill in the sense that we leave ourselves open to the risk that others will abuse their power of discretion over us (Baier 1986, 235).[6] Exposing ourselves in this way might seem tolerable in contexts in which we are in a good position to assess and predict the risks involved in giving others such discretion, for example, within personal relations with intimate friends and family. But trust is crucial to all social relations, Baier emphasizes, including relations among strangers. We take the risk of trusting strangers whenever we ask for directions, eat food prepared in restaurants, or leave our children in the care of others. "We inhabit a climate of trust as we inhabit an atmosphere and notice it as we notice air, only when it becomes scarce and polluted" (ibid., 234).

In light of the concept's ubiquity, most studies of trust distinguish between different kinds of trust, and these different kinds now form a lengthy list: social trust, generalized trust, particular trust, moral trust, identity-group trust, institutional trust, personal trust, and so on. There is no consensus among social capital scholars about how many different kinds of trust are relevant to their analyses; nor is there agreement about how to define each kind. However, there is agreement about two broad characteristics of trust. First, the overriding message of studies of social capital and the welfare state suggest that a decline of trust leads to a decline in equality because, in the absence of trust, people are less willing to engage in cooperative relations of the sort required to sustain the welfare state. Second, most if not all scholars who work on trust and social capital note that social (or generalized) trust is distinct from personal trust (Banfield 1958; Putnam 1993a; Stolle 2002; Uslaner 2002; Yamagishi and Yamagishi 1994). This distinction is important to social capital analysis because it is only if trust is not personal that it can be helpful in explaining why strangers willingly cooperate in large-scale social programs like of those of the welfare state.

Both of these characteristics of trust, namely, the connection between trust and equality and the generalized or impersonal nature of social trust, are strongly implicated in a normative framework that influences how we might view social diversity and policy initiatives, such as multiculturalism, that aim at dealing with diversity. And, the message, overall, is negative. Despite the wide acknowledgement that trust is a morally ambiguous value because it can be used to sustain relations of "justice and fellowship" as well as "exploitation and conspiracy" (Baier 1986, 231-32), the overriding message of studies that focus on social capital, trust, and multiculturalism is that a decline of trust poses a problem for the welfare state. Research on social capital has suggested that social trust is in dangerous decline in Western democracies. A decline in trust has been linked to a decline in political participation and membership in civic associations (Putnam 1993a, 1995a, 2000), a decline in economic performance (Fukuyama 1995b), and shrinking support for social welfare programs (Miller 1995, 1998). Studies of the welfare state suggest that people in large, diverse communities trust less, participate less, and cooperate less than people in small homogeneous communities (see Aizlewood and Pendakur, Chapter 7). An array of factors have been cited as contributing to the general decline of social trust, including the family structure, shifting cultural norms, the dominance of television, and, of course, multiculturalism.

Two challenges follow from these agreed-upon characteristics of trust. The first challenge arises from the need to clarify whether equality is the foundation of trust or whether trust leads to equality. According to most studies of social capital, trust is the precursor to a healthy welfare state. However, the more conventional and pervasive observation in political analysis is that equality and egalitarian relations between those who trust each other are the precursor to valuable trust. When people are unequal to start with, valuable trust is unlikely to emerge between them.

The second challenge is to devise a way of distinguishing between self-regarding and other-regarding forms of trust and, thus, to clarify the difference between personal and social forms of trust. Despite the insistence by social capital scholars that personal and social trust are distinct dispositions, much of what counts as social trust seems to draw on personal and, especially, self-regarding values and to ignore other-regarding values that are more connected to fairness and fair play in the social sphere.

Trust and Equality

Although social capital theorists tend to focus on the ways in which trust sustains the welfare state and, by extension, conditions of equality, they are by no means unaware of the morally ambiguous nature of trust. In fact, part of the project within studies of social capital is to specify the circumstances in which a desirable form of trust can be developed. For instance, Putnam, in the context of presenting evidence that 9/11 caused a surge in trust, suggests that this form of trust could be turned into something useful and lasting if it were used to address social and economic equality in the United States. "Progressives," he suggests, "should work to translate that national mood into concrete policy initiatives that bridge the ethnic and class cleavages in our increasingly multicultural societies" (Putnam 2002). Trust could be rendered less morally ambiguous (or less morally undesirable) if government would institute policies that establish the conditions (in this case, bridging ethnic and class cleavages) under which a more meaningful and valuable trust can develop. Unsurprisingly, the conditions needed are ones that address social and economic inequality.

Although Putnam's work is usually cited to verify the claim that trust leads to equality and democracy (not vice versa), the converse view, namely, that equality is the foundation of a politically desirable form of trust, is the more conventional observation in political analyses of trust. For instance, Baier argues that social relations marked by profound inequality are often sustained by trust. Trust sustains exploitation whenever a privileged group trusts another less privileged group to pay more than their fair share toward sustaining a common project. The "trust" that others who have less will pay more is based on knowledge that, even though everyone benefits from the common project, the less privileged group is more vulnerable to the demise of the project than is the more privileged group. According to Baier, relations that are based on exploitation of this sort are more easily sustained when trust binds the exploited and exploiter together. Unlike the problem of free-riders, which sends common projects and trust into decline, trust and inequality, when combined, provide a powerful means by which exploitation can be sustained in the long term.

Because trust is widely recognized as morally ambiguous, its presence in political theory is usually framed by a prior discussion of the conditions in which a desirable form of trust might exist. For instance, theorists such as Locke and Tocqueville, both of whom wrote extensively about trust and identified it as an important social and political value, wrote only about trust between equal individuals and modelled trust-based relations on voluntary agreements among adults with relatively equal power (Baier 1986, 245). Their analyses also implied that not all trust-based relations were the right sort of relations upon which to model political society. For instance, the trust that exists between husbands and wives or slaves and masters was not the sort of trust that Locke or Tocqueville thought should shape liberal democratic societies *even though* these societies largely relied on such relations as a means of organizing social and economic life. In fact, these political theorists had difficulty reconciling the liberal values of political society with the exploitative relations upon which such societies were built (for discussion, see Pateman 1988, Chapters 2-5). Not all sorts of social relations, nor all forms of trust, could be justified from a liberal-democratic point of view. Only trust that exists between equals, only contracts that are signed between those with equal power, who are equally autonomous, count as valuable to the civil and political societies imagined by both of these theorists.

A similar context of equality operates in the case of the prisoner's dilemma, which is central to many analytic discussions of trust. Prisoner's dilemmas rely on a presumption that participants are equal, or at least equally vulnerable, and have equal access to enforcement mechanisms (Baier 1986, 252). The free-rider problem presumes roughly equal status among those engaged in trust-based relations in the sense that the free-rider has violated her obligations to others only because she is presumed to be an equal with others and is, therefore, equally capable of contributing to common projects. Children, for instance, are not viewed as free-riders because they do not have equal status in society and, therefore, are not in a position to assume the obligations upon which our cooperative relations are based. It is important to note, however, that this does not mean that children cannot engage in trusting relations. To the contrary, children are constantly in a position of having to trust others. Rather, the point is that the model of trust used in political and social analysis is poorly designed to understand how trust works among those with unequal power (Baier 1986, 249).

In some (though certainly not all) respects, the questions asked in surveys of social capital and trust aim at measuring politically valuable forms of trust – the sort of trust that Locke and Tocqueville were interested in – namely, trust between strangers who have to rely on each other to do the right thing. As I understand Putnam, this is the sort of trust that, he argues, is in dangerous decline. And, in some studies that draw on Putnam's research, this is the sort of trust whose decline is potentially debilitating to the welfare state. But these studies have been conducted in contexts in which individuals and groups are unequal in their access to economic resources as well as in their social and political power. Trust is understandably weak in such contexts. As Uslaner shows, a direct link between trust and economic inequality exists in the United States: "Changes in the Gini index alone account for almost two-thirds of the decline in trust" (Uslaner 2002, 186-87).[7] The reasons for this are not particularly difficult to fathom: "Those at the top can enforce their will against people who have less. And those at the bottom have little reason to believe that they will get a fair shake" (Uslaner 2002, 181; see also Seligman 1997, 36-37; Banfield 1958, 110). In other words, people willing to risk exposing themselves as vulnerable to strangers may be sufficiently well off that they can absorb an encounter or two with someone untrustworthy and still feel secure enough to believe that such encounters will be, at worst, occasional.

In addition to Uslaner, both Margaret Levi and Theda Skocpol point to the problems with studies that draw conclusions about social solidarity on the basis of surveys that measure trust within a context of inequality. Levi and Skocpol are particularly critical of the romanticism of Putnam's vision in "Bowling Alone" of a more trusting society, which they claim hearkens back to an era when the PTA, the Legion, and other grassroots associations were the life-blood of American democracy. Levi asks how changes brought about by women's equality and their entrance into the workforce figure into this analysis: Putnam "seems to decry the effects of this change rather than ... [to] search for institutional substitutes for the roles that women once performed" (Levi 1996, 52). Skocpol argues that civic disengagement may be largely the product of a growing class cleavage in America that has rendered participation and leadership in the American Legion or the PTA unimportant as "stepping stones" for professionals and business people and has thereby caused an unravelling of these civic associations for everyone else. "How ironic it would be," she argues, "if, after pulling out of locally rooted associations, the very business and professional elites who blazed the path toward local civic disengagement were now to turn around and successfully argue that the less privileged Americans they left behind are the ones who must repair the nation's social connectedness" (Skocpol 1996). Her implication is not only that trust is understandably weak where societies are divided by inequality but also that a decline in the sort of trust that helps to sustain unequal relations is appropriate and desirable from a democratic point of view.[8]

It is especially important for analyses that correlate social capital and multiculturalism that we understand whether trust is more a precondition or more a result of inequality because these analyses carry implications about whether states ought to adopt multicultural programs, which themselves aim at improving conditions of equality. In political and social theory, most accounts that discuss trust as politically valuable analyze the concept only in the context of relations among equals. The noted exception to this is survey research on trust and social capital studies (Uslaner's work being the important exception). Many of these studies focus on contexts in which racial, ethnic, and linguistic inequality characterizes the relations among people, while policies such as multiculturalism are in place for the purpose of improving conditions of inequality. In other words, at the same time as these studies measure trust outside of a context of equality, they are used to substantiate conclusions about, not only the correlation but also the causal relation between trust and equality, namely, that cooperative programs, such as social welfare, operate more efficiently where people trust each other. Of course, it is always possible that equality is both a precursor to and a result of trustful relations. Trust might well enhance cooperative relations of the sort that drive redistributive programs, while equality might also be a precursor to a politically valuable trust. If this turns out to be the case, then, perhaps, the correct conclusion to draw is that societies that already enjoy a high degree of equality are ones in which social welfare programs that sustain or enhance equality are most likely to succeed. Either way, the challenge for social capital studies is to sort out whether equality is a necessary precursor to valuable trust in addition to being the result of trusting relations.

Personal and Social Trust

The final challenge for social capital studies is to sharpen the distinction between personal and social (or generalized) trust and to offer a more detailed account of what makes personal trust personal and what makes social trust social and not personal. I don't mean to suggest that the social capital literature offers no guidance on the matter. To the contrary, it seems to offer lots of guidance, but, significantly, the distinctions drawn between social and personal trust are not as plain as analysts suppose.

Personal trust, according to these studies, is usually taken to exist among friends and family and is said to be based on intimate knowledge, familiarity, and direct connection to others (Yamagishi and Yamagishi 1994). Personal trust is crucial to the well-being of most individuals in the sense that having friends and family whom one trusts is important to leading a good life. But personal trust and the personal relations that are thereby sustained are clearly not appropriate bases on which to build legal and political relations in liberal-democratic societies. Personal trust is the wrong sort of trust on which to base public values and projects because it conflicts with the values of fair treatment, impartiality,[9] and individual equality to which liberal-democracies are committed. This is not to say that societies cannot be run on the basis of something like personal trust. Rather, the point is that societies run on the basis of personal trust, and thus, personal connections are generally viewed as corrupt from the vantage of liberal democracy. Personal and familial connections ought not to have public currency in liberal-democratic states, not only because of the corruption that might accompany such relations but also because of their inefficiency, as shown by Putnam's study of Italy (Putnam 1993a). Moreover, not only are actual family connections inappropriate in relation to liberal democratic values, but *imagined* or *quasi-personal* connections are also inappropriate. We would view the impartiality of our legal institutions as corrupted not only if a judge favoured defendants with whom she had a personal connection but also if the reasons for a judgment rested on an imagined or quasi-personal connection – for instance, if they were influenced by the fact that the defendant reminded the judge of her son or sister. Similarly, personal connections ought not to have political currency in liberal-democratic states because basic political values, such as equal treatment for individuals, preclude basing shared public political projects on affective ties forged in personal relations.

The suggestion repeatedly made about trust in the social capital literature is that personal trust would not get us very far in constructing a social welfare state and modern society. Nor will personal trust provide the appropriate basis upon which to facilitate large-scale projects meant to foster individual equality. For example, Eric Uslaner argues that trusting only those "who are our own kind" or "whom we know about" through reputation is not enough to sustain projects such as social assistance and public education across large populations. According to Uslaner, lots of good experiences with contractors or businesses do not add up to the "sunny disposition" that leads people to give to charity or to volunteer their time (2002). Trust among strangers, what Uslaner calls moralistic trust (ibid., 14-50), takes us beyond the people with whom we are familiar, beyond merely having faith in our own kind. Moralistic trust leads us to expose ourselves as vulnerable to others we have never met. Moralistic trusters see the world as a benign place, where people are generally well-motivated. They are the trusters who get involved in their communities, vote, pay taxes voluntarily, give to charities, volunteer their time, and maintain that "most people can be trusted" when asked by survey researchers.

Despite explicit and sometimes careful attempts to distinguish personal and social trust, such as those found in Uslaner's account, the pervasive practice in studies of social capital is to define and measure social trust in terms associated with personal dispositions and feelings of personal connection or familiarity, which have only limited relevance to whether people trust in a generalized way. Personal and social trust are said to be different sorts of things, yet social trust is often defined in terms that simply extend (or dilute) to strangers the same *kind*s of feelings and values that are at play in the intimate contexts of family and friends.

Consider in this regard the distinction between the trust we feel toward our intimates and friends and the trust we are willing to extend to strangers, in Putnam's understanding of the concept (1993a, 136) and in David Miller's influential explanation of the relation between trust and multiculturalism (Miller 1995, 90-99). Although there is a distinction between the sort of trust that we feel toward family and friends and the trust we extend to strangers, personal and social trust are the same kind of disposition in Putnam's and Miller's analyses. For Putnam, the relevant distinction is between *thick* and *thin* trust. He suggests that, as trust gets thinner or more diluted, it becomes less useful and powerful in anchoring norms of honesty and reciprocity (Putnam 1993a, 136). In Miller's account, the trust that arises among strangers sharing a strong national identity (which is crucial to solving collective action problems and, therefore, to facilitating large-scale cooperative projects, such as social welfare programs) also looks very much like an extended and diluted form of personal trust in that it is based on values of "imagined community." Miller is explicit that, in the modern era, national identity cannot be based on personal connection. Nonetheless, the bonds that he describes as national ones are striking in their similarity to the unconditional bonds of kinship: "In a national community the case can be made out for unconditional obligations to other members that arise simply by virtue of the fact that one is born and raised in that particular community" (Miller 1995, 42). As he states, "trust requires solidarity not merely within groups but across them, and this in turn depends upon a common identification of the kind that nationality alone can provide" (ibid., 140). Whereas national identity provides this sort of common identification, ethnic diversity may undercut it because, as Soroka, Johnston, and Banting point out, "it will be more difficult to foster identification with fellow citizens in societies that are ethnically or culturally divided" (Chapter 11, page 280). As they explain, "trusting individuals operates on degrees of personal acquaintance" (ibid., 282).

Whereas scholars of social capital maintain that social trust is an entirely different kind of disposition than the disposition at play in personal forms of trust, the difference between personal and social trust is characterized as one that is more of degree than of kind. The similarity between personal and social trust is especially clear when the standards used to measure personal and social trust are contrasted with the standards used to measure political trust. Whereas social trust is measured by extending personal values of familiarity to strangers and seeing how far it can be diluted (and with what consequences), political trust is measured according to principles and values of impartiality, fairness, and, according to one account, historical relations of justice "where, for decades, some groups have been political winners and other groups, losers" (ibid., 283).

Nowhere is this better illustrated than in the survey research. Personal dispositions and self-regarding values are used as standards by which social trust is measured, but values of impartiality and fairness – what might be called "other-regarding values" – are employed to measure political trust. In the ESC first wave survey and in the World Values Survey, the questions used to gauge personal trust and social trust are similar: in both cases, the respondent is asked a series of questions about whether s/he trusts familiars – i.e., neighbours (in the case of personal trust) and strangers including officials (in the case of social trust) to return his or her wallet (a personal possession) with or without the money in it. While this sort of question might accurately reflect a form of trust that is relevant to social capital, it tells us little about less self-regarding forms of trust, such as whether we trust strangers to have good judgment – even if what counts as good judgement does not directly serve our interests.

Political trust, in contrast, is measured by an entirely different set of questions. In contrast to social trust, political trust is measured by a series of questions about whether the respondent trusts the government to do "what is right." Political trust seems to be open to less partial and self-regarding values in the sense that it encompasses what respondents think public values ought to dictate rather than whether respondents view the system, or the officials within it, as reliably responsive to the respondents' personal interests.

Again, I don't mean to suggest that trusting strangers to return one's wallet is unimportant for good social relations among citizens. But it might be the wrong measurement of trust to use in studies about the support for redistributive policies. As social capital theorists are well aware, the sort of trust upon which the welfare state relies entails trusting people who exist largely in the abstract, as anonymous others in large populations of individuals who will never be personal acquaintances. But it might also require trusting people to value the principle of equality regardless of whether one expects to be on the receiving or giving side, to view the health of children as a communal responsibility regardless of whether or not one has children, and to view unemployment as a social rather than a personal problem. Measuring this sort of trust would seem to require indicators that measure trusting people to do the right thing regardless of the immediate impact on their personal self-interest. These indicators are more like the ones used to measure political trust than the ones that emphasize trust as an extension of personal and affective ties between intimates, i.e., the personal trust we have that people will consider and take care of their self-regarding interests.[10]

The sharp distinction drawn between, on the one hand, personal and political forms of trust and, on the other hand, the close connection between personal and social forms of trust influences the conclusions one can draw about trust and ethnic diversity. These conclusions indicate that ethnic diversity weakens the sort of trust required to facilitate large-scale cooperative ventures such as the welfare state. In short, ethnic diversity weakens social trust. Based on the way in which the survey questions measure the different types of trust, it may not be all that surprising to find that, while ethnic diversity is strongly linked to levels of social trust, its links with political trust are weak (see Chapter 11 below). This conclusion is unsurprising because, if one views social trust questions as tapping into the same values as personal trust, then the less familiar people are to us, the less willing we will be to give them the sort of discretion that we give to our family and friends (e.g., to look out for our interests). If social trust is diluted personal trust, then the more diluted, the less trust there is. In contrast, when questions tap into the values of political trust, which are values about others doing the right thing, the fact that people are unfamiliar does not affect our level of trust.

In sum, the analysis above suggests that the distinction between personal and social trust should be drawn more sharply for three reasons. First, on the face of it, it seems that social trust, when understood as the same kind of disposition as personal trust, is weakly related to liberal-democratic values such as impartiality and fair treatment. Second, as most studies of trust show, social trust does not seem to be the same sort of thing as personal trust, in the sense that it entails trust among people who are abstract others rather than among people who are acquaintances or intimates. Third, when social trust is employed in the context of studies of ethnic diversity and the welfare state, these personal connotations provide misleading conclusions about the relation between ethnic diversity and trust. Whereas it seems that ethnic diversity foments mistrust in society (though not toward government), a more accurate yet far less interesting interpretation of the survey research is that individuals are less likely to extend personal trust to those with whom they are unfamiliar. What weakens trust, then, are unfamiliar others.[11] While this might be true, it might be very weakly correlated (as the studies mentioned at the beginning of this essay suggest) to support for policies that aim at treating people fairly.

Conclusion

Multiculturalism has been implicated in eroding social solidarity and fragmenting community in a manner that jeopardizes the advancement of egalitarian policies, such as those which characterize the welfare state. Here I have argued that one of the obstacles to understanding the nature of this proposition is the uneven manner in which key concepts are employed in debates about multiculturalism and the welfare state. This analysis has focused on developing three sets of challenges that are aimed at clarifying the relation between multiculturalism and social capital.

The first set of challenges requires that the distinction between multiculturalism and ethnic diversity be clarified. Studies that conflate ethnic diversity and multiculturalism end up ignoring the ways in which most multicultural policies aim at integrating ethnic minorities into mainstream societies. They also tend to obscure the importance of policies that address historical injustices or those that improve trust and social solidarity among peoples by guaranteeing cultural, national and linguistic security, by means of constitutional guarantees for national minorities and indigenous peoples.

The second set of challenges is to examine the problem of ethnic insularity in a more even-handed manner. The assumption running through many studies is that insularity is characteristic of some minority communities and associations, not of majorities. The challenges for social capital studies are first to examine more critically what counts as evidence of insularity and to assess the contribution made by ethnic minorities, whether they are insular or not, to the democratic character of mainstream societies. A second challenge is to clarify within discussions of multiculturalism and social solidarity the place of programs that aim to rectify previous injustices. The third challenge is to balance the evidence of minority insularity with evidence of majority insularity both in the presence and absence of multicultural policies and in relation to the characterization of bridging versus bonding associations.

Finally, the third set of challenges focuses on trust. At a minimum, trust is a morally ambiguous concept that ought to be pursued in a manner that complements, but does not compete with, liberal egalitarian aims. But the relation between trust and equality is causally ambiguous and needs to be clarified. In addition, social trust ought to be measured in less personal and self-regarding terms so that studies that measure trust tap into the ways in which people think others ought to be treated and whether they believe that those around them share a sense of what is fair. This sort of measurement and this sort of trust would seem to be immediately important in the context of studies that aim to grapple with the difficult questions of how social, cultural, and economic equality ought to be pursued in diverse societies.

ACKNOWLEDGMENTS

This chapter was presented at the Equality, Security, and Community workshop held at the University of British Columbia in 2001. I am grateful to Fiona Kay and Richard Johnston for helpful comments on an earlier draft.

NOTES

1. Banting and Kymlicka (2003) divide the critical accounts of multiculturalism into those focused on (1) "crowding out" redistributive politics, (2) corroding the trust and solidarity within organizations and society, and (3) misdiagnosing the problem of racism.
2. Other than indigenous peoples, all members of a society are "immigrants." But national minorities are distinctive for a host of reasons including their role as founding peoples and the historical and constitutional promises that were made to protect them (their language and culture) as a community.
3. For an argument that fleshes out the reasons for this, see Kymlicka (1995, Chapter 2).
4. For instance, academic conferences held in the United States, at least in political science, commmonly convene panels that combine indigenous politics with multiculturalism.
5. Although this practice is pervasive, it is less a concern among critics of multiculturalism, such as Miller (1995) and Barry (2001), who focus explicitly on multicultural ideals and approaches, not on ethnic diversity. The confusion is more likely to arise in empirical studies of ethnic diversity, which refer to critical accounts of multiculturalism to underscore the challenges of ethnic diversity.
6. This aspect of trust is also emphasized by Hardin (1993, 507). The distinction between trusting others and relying on others depends according to Baier, on the presence (or absence) of goodwill.
7. See Uslaner's cross-national evidence (2002, Chapter 8). Also see Putnam (2001, 50-51, and Figure 7.9).
8. In Putnam's more recent contributions, such as the post-9/11 analysis of trust (2001), he endorses the need to bridge class and ethnic cleavages.
9. There are many thoughtful objections to the role that impartiality plays in liberal-democratic societies, some of which are extensively discussed in political theories that are committed to multiculturalism (e.g., see Young 1990, Chapter 4). Impartiality is also a central concept in social capital studies that focus on

trust in institutions (Rothstein 1998; Rothstein and Stolle 2002; Levi 1998) and a key concept whose use in these analyses also merits careful scrutiny.
10   One might argue that returning a wallet with the money intact *is* the right thing to do, so that the distinction I am suggesting amounts to no distinction at all, at least none relevant to the survey measures. But the distinction I suggest turns *not* on whether returning a wallet is the right thing to do but on how the question motivates respondents to think about their own interests or to think more broadly about public interests. The wallet example is self-regarding in the sense that it clearly asks the respondent to think about her own narrow interests in a particular situation – e.g., "Say *you* lost a wallet or purse with $100 in it." The trust-in-government question remains neutral about whose interests matter in asking "how much do you trust the government to do what is right?"
11   This also suggests that ethnic diversity will only be correlated to a decline in social trust if that diversity is unfamiliar or new. For those living in multicultural societies with stable levels of diversity and/or immigration, one might expect social trust to be high regardless of diversity.

Part 2
Studies of Social Capital and Determinants of Social Capital

5
Measuring and Modelling Interpersonal Trust

Stuart N. Soroka, John F. Helliwell, and Richard Johnston

The growing literature on trust, social capital, and well-being relies almost exclusively on a single survey measure of interpersonal trust: "Generally speaking, do you think that most people can be trusted, or that you can't be too careful in dealing with people?" Efforts at modelling responses to this balanced question are becoming increasingly sophisticated. Notable recent examples include Alesina and La Ferrara (2000) on the individual and contextual determinants of trust and Glaeser et al. (1999) on the link between responses to the question and actual behaviour in laboratory trust games. The measure underpins a cross-national growth industry, mainly through the World Values Survey (WVS). And international evidence from the WVS has been brought back home, as it were, to explain ethnic and regional differences in trust in the United States (Rice and Feldman 1997). Only rarely, however, is any attention paid to what a response to the question actually means. Most critically, does the question elicit a response – based perhaps on past experience – that indicates a person's real expectations of others' trustworthiness? Or does it register a moral predisposition, a statement about how one *should* react to others?

This chapter holds up a mirror to the standard question by comparing it with other renderings. Some of the alternatives are, like the original wording, about trust as a general proposition. Our most pointed demonstration, however, involves comparison with questions about a specific trust situation, a lost wallet. These questions mimic a widely publicized field experiment (Knack 2001). Part of the comparison involves simple response distributions, joined to observations on items' face validity. The most telling comparisons deploy multivariate techniques to plumb the sources of response. Where response to the traditional, highly general indicator is powerfully shaped by cultural norms, response to the specific, wallet question is sensitive to context and life experience. That said, the traditional indicator still gauges how much respondents believe others to be trustworthy.

In getting to this point, we also draw a lesson about Canada. Our sample and our questionnaire are rich in representation of Canada's ethno-religious diversity, of its high rate of immigration, and of its group life. In line with hypotheses that seemed plausible but were hitherto unsupported empirically, "bridging" groups appear to be more highly correlated than "bonding" groups with generalized trust. We also reproduce Rice and Feldman's (1997) finding that civic attitudes of immigrants are highly correlated with attitudes in their countries of origin. But the integrative power of Canadian society is also very much in evidence.

Concepts and Measures

Our opening generalization about lack of attention to the meaning and measurement of trust admits notable exceptions. Smith (1997) examines the trust question as part of a misanthropy scale, for instance, and finds that trusting responses decline when the question is preceded by questions on crime and victimization. "These items are especially prone to context effects," Smith suggests, "because they call for global assessments of people in general based presumably on one's entire life experience. Making judgements based on such massive, cognitive retrievals are difficult and open to variability" (ibid., 174). Controlling for these survey-based differences, however, Smith finds the misanthropy scale to be systematically and logically related to several other variables. Responses to the generalized trust question are valuable, but the placement of the question deserves attention.

Uslaner (2002) offers the most comprehensive consideration of responses to the generalized trust question to date, and the only one to explicitly link theories of trust with analyses of public opinion surveys. Uslaner distinguishes between *moralistic* and *strategic* trust, where the latter is based on individuals' experiences, and the former is something closer to a predisposition. When analysts in the rational choice tradition, economists especially, talk about trust, they tend to mean strategic trust, as in repeated games in which decisions to trust or not to trust are based on experiences in previous games. Moralistic trust, on the other hand, is rooted in our beliefs about others, which can be almost totally divorced from personal experience. Strategic trust is about how one thinks others will behave; moralistic trust is about whether one should trust others regardless of their behaviour (Uslaner 2002, 18-19).

Moralistic trust seems closer to Avigail Eisenberg's (see Chapter 4, this volume) emphasis on trust in strangers.

Uslaner's tests suggest that the generalized trust question is primarily about moralistic trust. Responses to the question are remarkably stable; they tend not to change based on experience; they are closely correlated with enduring feelings such as optimism, a feeling that one controls one's own fate, and with a willingness to participate in civic life. Although Uslaner makes a strong case that the question is primarily about moralistic trust, he does not go far in considering ways of measuring strategic trust or of measuring the role, however small, that strategic trust may play in responses to a moralistic trust question. Moreover, a lack of comparable alternative measures prevents Uslaner from performing a more detailed analysis of trust responses. He does a good job with what is available, but, as he notes, not much is available.

Measuring Trust

Wordings and frequencies for various trust questions in the Equality, Security, and Community (ESC) survey appear in Table 5.1.[1] The first four indicators gauge trust independently of context. Some of the aggregate differences among Questions 1 to 4 can be explained by the literature on survey question wording. In particular, Schuman and Presser's (1996) experiments on question wording suggest consideration of two related effects: (1) balance effects, where changing a question's wording to reflect a formal balance of alternatives (i.e., changing "do you favour" to "do you favour or oppose") has a significant effect on the distribution of responses, and (2) acquiescence effects, where respondents have a tendency to agree with attitude statements in survey items (see also Campbell et al., 1960; Peabody, 1961). Frequencies in Table 5.1 show evidence of both effects. While Q1 leads to a relatively even split between trusting and non-trusting respondents, unbalanced questions show evidence of considerable acquiescence effects. Q3 suggests that 74 percent of respondents are trusting; its opposite, Q4, suggests that 68 percent of respondents are not.

Differences in answers rest on more than acquiescence, however. Rather, dissimilar responses to different trust questions appear to be in large part a product of genuine differences in reasoning. Different trust questions, while addressing a similar subject, ask respondents to think about trust in different ways. The end result is a change in the distribution of responses representing a

TABLE 5.1

Trust questions in the ESC survey

Question	Not trusting %	Neutral/ DK %	Trusting %	Total (N)
TRUST QUESTIONS ...				
Q1 Generally speaking, would you say that most people can be trusted or that you can't be too careful in dealing with people?	42.8	4.4	52.7	(4,485)
Q2 People can be trusted until they prove otherwise. (Agree or Disagree)	14.2	2.9	82.8	(6,557)
Q3 Generally speaking, most people can be trusted. Do you agree or disagree?	22.7	3.5	73.8	(3,540)
Q4 Generally speaking, you can't be too careful in dealing with people. Do you agree or disagree?	68.0	4.4	27.6	(3,465)
WALLET QUESTIONS ...				
Q5 If you lost a wallet or purse that contained two hundred dollars, how likely is it to be returned with the money in it if it was found ... by someone who lives close by?	13.3	38.6	48.1	(6,408)
Q6 If you lost a wallet or purse that contained two hundred dollars, how likely is it to be returned with the money in it if it was found ... by a clerk at the grocery store where you do most of your shopping?	9.5	33.3	57.3	(6,413)
Q7 If you lost a wallet or purse that contained two hundred dollars, how likely is it to be returned with the money in it if it was found ... by a police officer?	5.5	23.1	71.3	(6,412)
Q8 If you lost a wallet or purse that contained two hundred dollars, how likely is it to be returned with the money in it if it was found ... by a complete stranger?	39.3	49.8	10.7	(6,380)

NOTE: Cells contain frequencies based on combined first wave, metro oversample, and resource community sample, unweighted.

more substantive difference, one that is particularly interesting for those studying interpersonal trust and the relationship between this and other variables.

For instance, the difference between responses to Q2 and Q3 is likely due to a subtle but important difference in wording. Agreeing with Q3 ("generally speaking, most people can be trusted") suggests that one has a positive, universal appraisal of whether people are trustworthy. Agreeing with Q2 ("people can be trusted until they prove otherwise") may suggest only that one approves of a particular trusting strategy. The strategy may be a relatively optimistic one, but it is also fairly safe. Agreeing with Q2 is easier than agreeing with Q3, then, and this is reflected in a 10-point increase in the percentage of trusting respondents. Another way of comparing Q2 and Q3 is to treat Q3 as having an implicit alternative category, since people who have not proven themselves trustworthy in the past are excluded from the group whose future trustworthiness is being assessed. This alone should guarantee that more people would agree with Q2 than Q3, as indeed they do. Differences between answers to Q3 (the blanket trust item) and Q4 ("you can't be too careful") are also likely to represent more than simply acquiescence effects. In particular, saying that you cannot be too careful in dealing with people is not the same as saying that people in general cannot be trusted. The former would reflect a cautious disposition, while the latter would simply be the reverse of Q1, the canonical measure.[2]

Questions 5 to 8 solicit a trusting response in alternative contexts, each time with a question about a lost wallet. These new questions are original to the ESC survey and are modelled after an experiment in which wallets containing fifty US dollars each were dropped in fourteen Western European and twelve US cities, and the number of returned wallets was used as a measure of how trustworthy residents are [as reported in *The Economist*, 22 June 1996]. Knack (2001, 184-85) has shown that more than one-third of the cross-regional and cross-national variation in answers to the balanced trust question can be explained by the frequency of return of experimentally dropped cash-bearing wallets. Our questions about the return of a wallet focus on a paradigmatic circumstance of trust. The situation provides no natural enforcement mechanisms, and nothing is said about a reward for trustworthy behaviour. Additionally, the questions specify alternative types of finder, making it possible for us to investigate in more detail the nature and radius of trust (Fukuyama 1995b). Police officers are considered the most likely to return lost wallets (Q7), followed by grocery clerks (Q6), neighbours (Q5), and finally strangers (Q8).

On the one hand, response to the wallet questions resembles that to the generalized questions, exactly as Knack (2001) implies. For example, a reliability analysis of all eight items in Table 5.1 yields a Cronbach's α of 0.68, and no subsetting of items yields a higher α.[3] Although the average inter-item correlation is about 0.4 among the generalized items, 0.3 among the wallet items, and only 0.1 to 0.15 between subdomains, factor analysis of the eight-item pool yields only one eigenvalue larger than one, and all items load similarly on this first factor.[4] The simplest representation of the overlap appears in Table 5.2, which cross-tabulates the canonical generalized question, Q1, with each wallet item. In general, someone who says that a wallet is "very likely" to be returned is 30 points more likely to say "people can be trusted" and 30 points less likely to say that "you can't be too careful." The wallet item with the least discriminatory power refers to a police officer, a reflection of how ubiquitous – and thus, how uninformative, relatively speaking – trust in the police is. The wallet item that evokes the least trusting response distribution, about strangers, produces the same discriminatory power as do the references to a neighbour and to a shop clerk.

On the other hand, Table 5.2 reveals plenty of slippage, more than we might expect from simple random measurement error. It is tempting to regard the general questions as relating to Uslaner's "moralistic trust," while the wallet questions refer to "strategic trust." Uslaner's language may be strained in relation to the general questions, as none asks about morality as the basis for motivation or behaviour. Still, the general question accepts ambiguity about the reference group the respondent might have in mind. This might invite responses that describe what persons think they *should* think rather than what they actually *do* think. The wallet questions are more precise, specifying both the nature of the event and the nature of the person whose trustworthiness is being evaluated. Intuitively, these questions seem to invite a probabilistic response. Indeed the response categories themselves are construed as probabilities.

Modelling Trust

To flesh out these intuitions, we need to model response at the source, so to speak. On one hand, we examine factors that index experience: immigrant status, indicators of social interaction, including aspects of neighbourhood context, marital history, spatial and non-spatial distributions of affiliation, and membership in formal organizations. On the other hand, we look at indicators of cultural orientation: respondents' own ethnicity (not to be confused

TABLE 5.2

Relationships between generalized trust and wallet questions

Wallet Questions		Generalized trust		
		Can't be too careful	Most people can be trusted	
Neighbour	Not at all likely	65.5% (359)	34.5% (189)	
	Likely	34.5% (688)	65.5% (1,307)	chi² = 170.8, $p < .001$
Clerk	Not at all likely	66.8% (268)	33.2% (133)	
	Likely	36.6% (879)	63.4% (1,522)	chi² = 129.8, $p < .001$
Police	Not at all likely	65.5% (146)	34.5% (77)	
	Likely	39.7% (1,192)	60.3% (1,811)	chi² = 56.8, $p < .001$
Stranger	Not at all likely	60.8% (996)	39.2% (643)	
	Likely	27.6% (124)	72.4% (325)	chi² = 155.8, $p < .001$

NOTE: Cells contain row percentages with counts in parentheses, based on combined first wave, metro oversample, and resource community sample, unweighted. Respondents in the middle category for either the generalized trust or wallet questions are omitted.

with immigration), aspects of their country or countries of ethnic origin, religion, and educational attainment. We also include controls to improve specification and to stabilize the estimation. When reporting differences, we generally emphasize differences (in boldface type) estimated to be significantly different from zero. To keep the number of observations as large as possible, we generally make use of the combined national, urban-oversample, and resource-community samples, although we also include variables designed to search for features of the results that may be specific to particular sample groups.

GENERALIZED TRUST

Table 5.3 presents logistic regressions for the traditional generalized trust question treated as a binary variable, where 1 is "most people can be trusted." Estimates are presented stagewise. In Model 1 appear demographic, ethnic, ethnic context, economic, and other contextual variables. Variables included

TABLE 5.3

Responses to general trust questions

		Dependent variables: generalized trust					
	Independent variables	Model 1		Model 2		Model 3	
Basic demographics	Female	-0.159**	(0.072) 0.853	-0.158**	(0.078) 0.854	-0.164**	(0.077) 0.849
	Age:						
	30-49	0.022	(0.087) 1.022	0.064	(0.097) 1.066	0.041	(0.100) 1.042
	50-65	0.548***	(0.117) 1.730	0.585***	(0.132) 1.796	0.597***	(0.131) 1.817
	66+	0.309**	(0.123) 1.362	0.321**	(0.133) 1.379	0.270**	(0.136) 1.310
	Education:						
	finished high school	0.326***	(0.103) 1.385	0.369***	(0.107) 1.446	0.339***	(0.110) 1.404
	started college/univ.	0.716***	(0.118) 2.047	0.694***	(0.126) 2.002	0.623***	(0.127) 1.865
	finished college/univ.	0.778***	(0.094) 2.178	0.835***	(0.105) 2.304	0.774***	(0.113) 2.167
	Religion:						
	Catholic	0.012	(0.087) 1.013	0.037	(0.095) 1.038	0.005	(0.097) 1.005
	Protestant	0.137	(0.097) 1.146	0.105	(0.108) 1.111	0.073	(0.111) 1.076
	French	-1.210***	(0.123) 0.298	-1.340***	(0.136) 0.262	-1.260***	(0.140) 0.284
	Immigrant	-0.227**	(0.098) 0.797	0.154	(0.178) 1.166	0.194	(0.188) 1.214
	Health	0.486***	(0.103) 1.626	0.470***	(0.121) 1.600	0.435***	(0.126) 1.545
	Resource oversample	0.055	(0.089) 1.057	0.050	(0.091) 1.051	0.061	(0.092) 1.063
Ethnicity	R is visible minority	-0.011	(0.283) 0.989	-0.030	(0.385) 0.970	-0.065	(0.397) 0.937
	Visible minority (%)	-0.181	(0.244) 0.834	-0.096	(0.273) 0.908	-0.036	(0.276) 0.965
	Interaction	-0.131	(0.490) 0.877	-0.031	(0.679) 0.970	0.010	(0.700) 1.010

		(1)	(2)	(3)
Economic situation	Economic outlook	0.206* (0.114) *1.228*	0.305** (0.127) *1.356*	0.297** (0.128) *1.346*
	Median income	−5.655 (4.393) *0.003*	−8.699* (5.223) *0.000*	−7.424 (5.326) *0.001*
	Income diversity	0.120 (0.680) *1.127*	0.198 (0.761) *1.219*	0.079 (0.779) *1.082*
Other contextual variables	Education (% > high school)	1.214*** (0.468) *3.367*	1.127** (0.530) *3.087*	1.030* (0.538) *2.802*
	Mobility (%, 5 yrs.)	−0.327 (0.234) *0.721*	−0.290 (0.239) *0.748*	−0.260 (0.243) *0.771*
	Population density	−0.027 (0.020) *0.974*	−0.020 (0.020) *0.980*	−0.020 (0.021) *0.980*
"National trust"	Imported trust		2.711** (1.057) *15.045*	2.909*** (1.073) *18.330*
	Parental trust		0.864 (0.705) *2.373*	0.658 (0.731) *1.932*
Networks	Divorced			−0.083 (0.091) *0.921*
	Sees family			−0.081 (0.100) *0.922*
	Sees friends			0.282* (0.155) *1.325*
	Sees neighbours			0.160 (0.094) *1.173*
	Religious memberships			0.252** (0.113) *1.287*
	Ethnic memberships			−0.203 (0.129) *0.816*
	Other memberships			0.090*** (0.030) *1.095*
Constant		−0.713*** (0.240)	−0.642** (0.261)	−1.021 (0.307)
N / PSUs		3,675/1,218	3,163/1,120	3,116/1,110
F (df)		14.33*** (22,1196)	12.08*** (24,1096)	10.62*** (31,1079)

NOTE: Cells contain coefficients, with standard errors (in parentheses) and odds ratios *in italics*, from a logit estimation using corrected standard errors. Results are based on combined first wave, metro oversample, and resource community sample, unweighted.

* $p < .10$; ** $p < .05$; *** $p < .01$.

All coefficients significant at $p < .10$ are in **bold**.

here give the basic structure of "domestic" factors in trust and are drawn, in large part, from the recent empirical literature on trust (e.g., Alesina and La Ferrara 2000; Glaeser et al. 2000; Helliwell and Putnam 1999; Uslaner 2002). Model 2 adds two representations of "national" trust, indicators of trust levels in immigrants' and immigrants' parents' countries of origin. This captures and extends the logic of Rice and Feldman's (1997) work exploring links between US immigrants' generalized trust scores and average scores in their countries of origin (discussed in more detail below). We look both at these variables themselves and at their impact on factors considered in Model 1. Does referring to national origin help interpret an earlier finding about ethnicity or immigrant status, for example? A similar logic applies to Model 3, where network variables are added.

Respondents with higher levels of education give more positive assessments to the general trust question, by an amount that increases with each level of educational attainment. This educational effect has been found in all previous analyses of answers to the balanced trust question and has been treated as support for the idea that education inculcates civic values (e.g., Helliwell and Putnam 1999). Some support for this interpretation comes from the fact that higher levels of education are positively correlated with survey answers whose relation to civic values is less ambiguous than in the case of the general trust question (e.g., Rice and Feldman, 1997). But if we are right to think of differences in response to the balanced trust question as being assessments of how well others can be trusted, then it is less clear why those with higher levels of education should give more positive assessments. Three hypotheses possibly explain the finding: (1) those with higher levels of education are more likely to encounter trustworthy behaviour; (2) ignorance breeds fear, which can then be dispelled by education; and (3) education raises other civic attitudes, increases awareness of the value of a trusting society, and incites respondents to put an optimistic twist to their assessments, thus making them embody some element of what should happen in a better world, reflecting the "moralistic" interpretation discussed earlier. If this more optimistic assessment is also reflected in personal behaviour – actions embodying trust – then higher levels of education should lead to higher levels of trust and trustworthiness within the community.

The "ignorance breeds fear" hypothesis is one way of explaining why those with higher levels of education provide more optimistic assessments of the trustworthiness of others. But the differential evaluations, to the extent that they refer to the same populations, might equally well represent excess optimism by those with more education. Are the less-educated excessively pessimistic, or are the more-educated too optimistic? If we had experimental dropped-wallet evidence, we might be able to address this puzzle by seeing whether the cross-community differences in answers to the dropped-wallet question were more accurately explained by the more-educated than by the less-educated respondents.

The third possibility, that the generally greater civic involvement of those with more education leads them to presume higher levels of trust, perhaps because this is more likely to support a high-trust society (the "moralistic" interpretation), is hard to distinguish from the "differential experience" hypothesis. The ambiguity may not matter overmuch, as there are likely to be positive spillovers from education in either event, although they might be presumed to be larger under the "civic culture" case than under the "differential experience" hypothesis. Research comparing the answers to the generalized trust assessment question with answers to more value-based questions might help to shed more light on the sources and consequences of the strong positive effect that education has on trust assessments.

Education effects persist when network connections are controlled. Education *does* lead to more participation in voluntary community organizations, which itself is often used as a measure of the strength of civic culture. This would tend to cause those with higher levels of education to spend more time with other civic-minded people and, hence, to give more positive answers to the general trust question. Be that as it may, Model 3 indicates that the education effect persists even when network ties are controlled.

Healthy people are more trusting. The coefficient on self-assessed health may reflect, in part, individual personality differences, with optimists assessing both their health and their communities in a more optimistic way. But epidemiological research also shows that those who are well-supported by family, friends, and community networks live longer and in better health than others – certain groups are more vulnerable to ill health due to their isolation or lack of social ties (Veenstra 2001; Curtis and Perks, Chapter 6, this volume; Berkman and Syme 1979). But our health effect captures more than this, since the coefficient shrinks only slightly when the same network variables are controlled. Then, too, the health effect may indicate network effects more subtle than those captured by our questions. It is also possible that the same events that produce some types of ill-health also place people in less supporting and less trustworthy environments than are those that are fully captured by our other individual and contextual variables.

Francophones are less trusting. Once again, we are unsure whether this reflects differences in optimism or differences in the trust environment that respondents are actually assessing. The finding puts us in mind of Knack (2001) who uses cross-country differences in responses to the general trust question to predict cross-country differences in the proportions of dropped wallets that are actually returned. His results show that France, which has very low trust assessments, is an outlier in his regression: the extent of trustworthy behaviour in France, as measured by the frequency with which dropped wallets are returned, is significantly higher than is forecast by answers to the generalized trust question. The frequency of wallet return is about at the European average, while the trust assessments are very low in France. If French origins are the key to the Canadian pattern, the footprint from earlier migration must be incredibly long.

Immigrants are less trusting than are the Canadian-born. This is a difference that glosses over ethnic differences among both immigrants and natives. If it is tempting to conclude that something in the experience of immigration makes new Canadians generally distrustful, the findings from the wallet questions should give us pause. And the explanation for generalized trust does not lie in the Canadian experience but in the country of origin. The home country leaves a "footprint," as just hinted for francophones. The idea of a footprint comes out of Rice and Feldman (1997), who find that trust assessments by immigrants reflect to a striking degree the (current) average trust assessments in the countries from which they or their ancestors immigrated. Strikingly, differences in the United States persist for a long time. The effect is as great for those with grandparents born in the United States as for those with parents born abroad. The two "national trust" terms test the "footprint" hypothesis in the Canadian context. "Imported trust" is an imputation to each respondent of the average trust score in his or her country of birth minus the average trust score in Canada, calculated from national samples in the most recent WVS. For those born in Canada, the value of the variable is naturally zero, while it is greater than zero for those who immigrated to Canada from higher-trust countries, and negative for those who came from lower-trust societies. As shown in Table 5A.1 (see appendix at end of chapter), the typical immigrant respondent came from a country with a slightly lower trust score than is Canada's, and the data show immigrants from countries with widely differing trust scores. This range of experience gives the data some variance to test the footprint hypothesis, while the negative average value offers the possibility that the footprint hypothesis explains the negative immigrant effect found in Model 1. The footprint of the origin county is indeed very deep. This is indicated by the coefficient on the "imported trust" term in Model 2. Furthermore, controlling imported trust turns the immigrant effect from negative to positive. The positive coefficient in this case is insignificant, but it suggests the possibility that, after allowing for the footprint effects of imported trust, the typical immigrant is more likely to give a *higher* than a lower trust answer than is a similarly situated Canadian-born respondent.

The footprint may be deep in the first generation, but it does not persist into later ones. Rice and Feldman (1997) were puzzled, and slightly troubled, that the footprint effect seemed as large two generations later as it was in the first generation, particularly in light of the "melting pot" image of the United States. To test the duration effect in our Canadian sample, we define a new variable ("parental trust") equal to the averaged trust score in the countries of birth of the respondents' parents minus the trust score in Canada, minus imported trust. This variable thus measures the trust-score difference between the countries of birth of the respondents and their parents. If our results were to mimic those of Rice and Feldman, we would find a positive coefficient on "parental trust" approximately equal to that on "imported trust." Instead we find that "parental trust" has only a small and insignificant effect. The Canada–United States contrast suggests, if taken literally, that "multicultural" Canada, in some important sense, absorbs immigrants into Canadian communities and values more quickly than does the United States "melting pot." This is consistent with the finding of Helliwell (2001) that the proportion of Canadians who self-describe their ethnicity as "Canadian" rather than one of a range of hyphenated alternatives is twice as high as the corresponding proportion in the United States. At the same time, it deepens the puzzle for francophones.

Network affiliations clearly matter, although some matter more than others, as indicated by Model 3. For Putnam (1993a, 1993b, 2000), trust is an asset that grows with use, and associational memberships build interpersonal trust because they encourage interaction. The success and effectiveness of regional governments in Italy is linked to the number of soccer clubs in each region; interpersonal trust has declined in America along with the popularity of bowling leagues. These are caricatures of Putnam's work, of course, although they do accurately illustrate his thesis. Individuals who participate in civic associations will tend to be more trusting, in part because these memberships provide opportunities for practising (and, perhaps, even learning) trusting behaviours. If the strong correlation between group memberships and interpersonal trust is well documented, the direction of the causal arrow is less clear. It may be that trusting individuals are the ones who join groups (see Stolle 1998), a hypothesis that complements a growing body of work suggesting that trust in government facilitates trust in individuals, rather than the opposite dynamic (Rothstein 1998). In any case, it is clear that trust and associational memberships are closely related.

That said, not all memberships have equivalent consequences, either for the members or for the community as a whole. Putnam distinguishes between *bonding* and *bridging* social capital, where the former reinforces connections between those who are similar in, for instance, class, ethnicity, or religion, and the latter builds links across these groups (see also Gittell and Vidal 1998; Tilly 1998). Groups are not easily divided into bridging and bonding, of course. Many groups will be both (Putnam 2000, 23), bonding in certain respects and bridging in others. Nevertheless, we should consider the possibility that some groups are more bridging than others, and that these groups are more effective at enhancing generalized trust.

We present network ties at successive removes from the individual, inside the household and outside to the extended family, to friends, to neighbours, and to formal associations. Among formal associations, we distinguish three types: religious, ethnic, and all others; for each type, the indicator is the number of memberships. We distinguish the types partly for empirical reasons and partly for conceptual ones. Table 5B.1 indicates that, in an exploratory factor analysis, religious and ethnic memberships load on a different factor from all other memberships, so these two should be distinguished from the others. And common sense dictates separating religious and ethnic associations from each other. Conceptually, ethnic and religious memberships tend strongly toward "bonding." Other groups, undoubtedly, have their exclusionary sides, even if not by design. But all things considered, the inventory of "other" groups almost certainly is more inclusive, more tilted toward "bridging," than is that of groups, such as ethnic and religious ones, that are exclusive by design.

In general, the wider the radius of action a network demands, the more positive impact on interpersonal trust is had by affiliation with it. The two family variables are insignificant, for instance, but those who regularly see friends or neighbours are relatively trusting. Among organized groups, ethnic group membership does not foster trust and may even inhibit it (the coefficient is negative but insignificant), strongly hinting that such groups indeed do not "bridge," however much they promote bonding. But "other" memberships do foster trust. So do religious groups. (Subsequent research using data from the Statistics Canada Ethnic Diversity survey suggests that social trust is favoured by participation in religious groups but is negatively related to the respondent's strength of religious belief, holding constant the level of participation. This suggests that it is the participation in these groups that provides the bridging influence.) Networks that appear to be more "bridging," then, are more positively related to various measures of interpersonal trust.

Most other variables have relatively weak effects. The age effect is curvilinear, with trust assessments most positive among those aged fifty to sixty-five and lowest among the youngest age group. In contrast to the initial finding for immigration, nothing in the realm of "visible minorities" matters for generalized trust (see Table 5.3). Individuals who belong to a visible minority do not differ from similarly situated members of the majority. Members of the majority are not affected by the visible minority percentage in their neighbourhoods, and the same is true of minority individuals themselves. No systematic effect appears from the respondent's own income, from the median income in the respondent's census district, or from income inequality in the district. The individual's assessment of whether his or her personal economic situation was likely to improve or worsen over the next twelve months does have an effect. This may reflect interpersonal differences in optimism, as discussed earlier for health effects, since the relationship also appears for each specific wallet question. Contextual effects were weak to null: average education levels and average mobility within the census area had no effect. Population density does seem to matter, but controls for "imported trust" suggest that the effect is spurious.

Some of these variables do matter for responses to the wallet question. The contrast between their lack of impact here and their importance below helps us interpret the meaning of each trust indicator. Also yielding a contrast is gender. In response to the general question, females appear to be less trusting than males. But this finding is not a universal. In a model of response to Q3, the one-sided trust question, the gender relationship is reversed. The reversal also appears in responses to the wallet question, reported below.

Specific Trust

Responses to the more specific wallet questions, as shown in Table 5.4, diverge interestingly from an individual's response to the general question.

TABLE 5.4

Responses to wallet questions

	Independent variables	Neighbour		Police		Dependent variables: wallet Clerk		Stranger	
Basic demographics	Female	0.067 (0.058)	1.069	0.281*** (0.061)	1.324	0.277*** (0.066)	1.319	0.205*** (0.055)	1.228
	Age: 0-49	0.361*** (0.071)	1.434	0.349*** (0.077)	1.417	0.284*** (0.091)	1.328	0.429*** (0.081)	1.536
	50-65	0.734*** (0.092)	2.084	0.630*** (0.093)	1.878	0.295*** (0.105)	1.343	0.630*** (0.093)	1.877
	66+	0.957*** (0.118)	2.603	0.825*** (0.134)	2.281	0.282** (0.133)	1.326	0.807*** (0.126)	2.241
Education:	finished high school	0.098 (0.089)	1.103	0.125 (0.092)	1.133	0.235** (0.107)	1.265	0.190* (0.097)	1.209
	started college/univ.	0.194** (0.099)	1.214	0.176 (0.108)	1.192	0.150 (0.135)	1.162	0.264** (0.112)	1.302
	finished college/univ.	0.284*** (0.083)	1.329	0.215** (0.091)	1.240	0.320*** (0.102)	1.378	0.495*** (0.100)	1.640
Religion:	Catholic	0.092 (0.083)	1.096	−0.072 (0.085)	0.930	0.144 (0.091)	1.154	−0.033 (0.077)	0.968
	Protestant	0.040 (0.080)	1.041	0.117 (0.084)	1.124	0.497*** (0.094)	1.644	0.037 (0.079)	1.038
	French	−0.851*** (0.101)	0.427	−0.972*** (0.093)	0.378	−1.348*** (0.106)	0.260	−1.096*** (0.100)	0.334
	Immigrant	0.178 (0.129)	1.195	−0.317** (0.144)	0.729	0.026 (0.144)	1.026	0.083 (0.140)	1.087
	Health	0.523*** (0.094)	1.688	0.307*** (0.092)	1.359	0.402*** (0.109)	1.494	0.402*** (0.094)	1.495
Resource oversample		−0.042 (0.078)	0.959	0.512*** (0.118)	1.668	0.426*** (0.082)	1.531	0.116 (0.078)	1.124

Ethnicity	R is visible minority	−0.273	(0.267)	0.761	−0.743***	(0.259)	0.476	−0.447	(0.303)	0.640	−0.500*	(0.264)	0.607
	Visible minority (%)	−0.474**	(0.228)	0.623	−0.814***	(0.245)	0.443	−0.403	(0.264)	0.669	−0.120	(0.239)	0.887
	Interaction	0.619	(0.540)	1.857	1.206**	(0.523)	3.342	0.801	(0.547)	2.227	0.724	(0.510)	2.062
Economic situation	Economic outlook	0.193**	(0.087)	1.213	0.259***	(0.099)	1.296	0.242**	(0.107)	1.273	0.206**	(0.090)	1.228
	Median income	0.025	(3.858)	1.026	−8.537**	(3.712)	0.000	−2.127	(4.274)	0.119	1.622	(3.723)	5.063
	Income diversity	−0.034	(0.574)	0.966	−0.524	(0.549)	0.592	−0.645	(0.612)	0.524	−0.787	(0.598)	0.455
Other contextual variables	Education (% > HS)	0.480	(0.440)	1.617	0.896**	(0.428)	2.451	0.907*	(0.483)	2.476	1.370***	(0.415)	3.934
	Mobility (%, 5 yrs)	−0.390**	(0.171)	0.677	−0.077	(0.192)	0.926	−0.350*	(0.208)	0.704	−0.249	(0.186)	0.779
"National trust"	Population density	−0.129***	(0.016)	0.879	−0.076***	(0.017)	0.927	−0.030	(0.019)	0.971	−0.040**	(0.016)	0.961
	Imported trust	1.315*	(0.734)	3.726	−1.321*	(0.791)	0.267	1.057	(0.972)	2.879	0.757	(0.891)	2.131
	Parental trust	1.023***	(0.608)	2.780	0.435	(0.602)	1.544	−0.062	(0.664)	0.940	0.499	(0.562)	1.647
Networks	Divorced	−0.226***	(0.078)	0.798	−0.016	(0.078)	0.984	−0.019	(0.088)	0.982	−0.166**	(0.072)	0.847
	Sees family	0.068	(0.073)	1.070	−0.116	(0.079)	0.891	0.025	(0.083)	1.026	0.037	(0.071)	1.037
	Sees friends	0.052	(0.117)	1.053	0.216*	(0.120)	1.241	0.333**	(0.141)	1.396	−0.059	(0.117)	0.943
	Sees neighbours	0.660***	(0.077)	1.935	0.100	(0.080)	1.105	0.043	(0.090)	1.044	0.152**	(0.077)	1.164
	Religious memberships	0.137	(0.088)	1.146	0.098	(0.093)	1.103	−0.010	(0.111)	0.990	−0.006	(0.084)	0.994
	Ethnic memberships	−0.090	(0.091)	0.914	−0.119	(0.103)	0.888	−0.097	(0.111)	0.907	−0.019	(0.103)	0.981
	Other memberships	0.072***	(0.021)	1.075	0.089***	(0.025)	1.093	0.018	(0.027)	1.018	0.113***	(0.022)	1.120
N / PSUs		4,757 / 1,654			4,778 / 1,659			4,763 / 1,655			4,736 / 1,649		
F (df)		23.14***	(31,1623)		18.73***	(31,1628)		18.35***	(31,1624)		15.25***	(31,1618)	

NOTE: See note to Table 5.3. Estimation is ordered logit.

TABLE 5.5

Summary of wallets measure

			Dependent variables: wallets measure					
	Independent variables	Model 1			Model 2			Model 3	
Basic demographics	Female	0.225***	(0.049)	1.253	0.233***	(0.052)	1.263	0.253*** (0.052)	1.287
	Age:								
	30-49	0.406***	(0.061)	1.500	0.443***	(0.066)	1.558	0.446*** (0.068)	1.562
	50-65	0.684***	(0.071)	1.982	0.736***	(0.078)	2.088	0.751*** (0.079)	2.118
	66+	0.918***	(0.110)	2.505	0.981***	(0.117)	2.668	0.964*** (0.119)	2.622
	Education:								
	finished high school	0.269***	(0.076)	1.309	0.261***	(0.080)	1.299	0.213*** (0.078)	1.237
	started college/univ.	0.297***	(0.087)	1.345	0.326***	(0.091)	1.386	0.240*** (0.093)	1.272
	finished college/univ.	0.529***	(0.074)	1.696	0.549***	(0.079)	1.732	0.439*** (0.081)	1.552
	Religion:								
	Catholic	0.021	(0.065)	1.021	0.085	(0.074)	1.089	0.061 (0.076)	1.063
	Protestant	0.211***	(0.061)	1.235	0.221***	(0.065)	1.247	0.188*** (0.068)	1.207
	French	−1.394***	(0.090)	0.248	−1.508***	(0.094)	0.221	−1.444*** (0.096)	0.236
	Immigrant	−0.065	(0.076)	0.937	−0.011	(0.122)	0.989	0.026 (0.121)	1.027
	Health	0.540***	(0.078)	1.716	0.584***	(0.085)	1.794	0.541*** (0.086)	1.717
	Resource oversample	0.210***	(0.068)	1.233	0.227***	(0.070)	1.255	0.256*** (0.070)	1.292
Ethnicity	R is visible minority	−0.525***	(0.186)	0.591	−0.596**	(0.239)	0.551	−0.560** (0.236)	0.571
	Visible minority (%)	−0.696***	(0.211)	0.499	−0.683***	(0.217)	0.505	−0.631*** (0.214)	0.532
	Interaction	0.763**	(0.363)	2.145	0.949**	(0.473)	2.583	0.918* (0.477)	2.505

Economic situation	Economic outlook	0.280***	(0.077)	1.323	0.243***	(0.083)	1.275	0.286***	(0.083)	1.331
	Median income	0.453	(3.118)	1.573	−0.627	(3.356)	0.534	−0.701	(3.469)	0.496
	Income diversity	−0.531	(0.516)	0.588	−0.713	(0.544)	0.490	−0.764	(0.553)	0.466
Other contextual variables	Education (% > high school)	1.085***	(0.375)	2.961	1.126***	(0.401)	3.084	1.085***	(0.411)	2.959
	Mobility (%, 5 yrs)	−0.497***	(0.146)	0.609	−0.427***	(0.145)	0.652	−0.346**	(0.147)	0.707
	Population density	−0.091***	(0.014)	0.913	−0.094***	(0.015)	0.911	−0.092***	(0.015)	0.912
"National trust"	Imported trust				0.938	(0.751)	2.555	1.023	(0.763)	2.782
	Parental trust				0.727	(0.464)	2.069	0.693	(0.474)	2.000
Networks	Divorced							−0.141**	(0.067)	0.869
	Sees family							0.001	(0.060)	1.001
	Sees friends							0.232**	(0.108)	1.261
	Sees neighbours							0.327***	(0.073)	1.387
	Religious memberships							0.098	(0.074)	1.103
	Ethnic memberships							−0.119	(0.093)	0.888
	Other memberships							0.094***	(0.020)	1.099
N / PSUs		5,230 / 1,735			4,614 / 1,638			4,560 / 1,619		
F (df)		44.47***	(22,1713)		39.62***	(24,1614)		32.74***	(31,1588)	

NOTE: See note to Table 5.3. Estimation is ordered logit.

Presentation of three stages for each of four questions would be tedious, so when we compare the tables, we focus on Model 3, the most fully specified variant. Table 5.5 presents the stagewise estimation for an index that combines the four wallet items (Cronbach's α = 0.66). That table tends to replicate evidence from Table 5.3, but averaged across the four specific questions, so readers may find the summary table more accessible. As quite a bit of the response is specific to each wallet situation, the text tends to refer to Table 5.4.

Tables 5.4 and 5.5 present quite a different picture from that of Table 5.3. On one hand, most individual differences in Tables 5.4 and 5.5, especially those with cultural implications, are much weaker. On the other hand, context – the reality that persons must deal with in making empirical judgments about trust and trustworthiness – comes through much more strongly.

Only two domains of individual difference are actually stronger for specific than for generalized trust: age and gender. The contrast between the oldest and the youngest is greater, and the pattern is essentially linear. Gender differences are both greater and of the opposite sign, though these results are largely in line with our observations regarding the different versions of the generalized trust measure. While women are less trusting than are men when the balanced trust question is used, they are more trusting than are men when the question without the "cannot be too careful" rider is used (Q3 in Table 5.1; see note 2). It may be cautiousness then, rather than different estimates of trustworthiness, that drive the gender difference in the balanced question. And, as the wallet questions do not include any kind of caution rider, women demonstrate more trust in three of the four wallet questions. Finally, for immigrants, there is an interesting divergence among specific wallet situations, even with "national trust" and networks controlled, where the distinctness is in the opposite direction between situations. Immigrants appear to trust neighbours more and the police less (although the first coefficient narrowly misses statistical significance).

The major finding, however, is for the power of context, much as social capital theory would suggest. Consider first the resource-community sample. Whereas for generalized trust these communities do not stand out, for specific trust, they are very distinct, especially for trust in the police but even for trust in strangers. These communities are generally small enough, and often isolated enough, that individuals are much more likely to know their neighbours, police, and those who work in local stores. Even strangers are more likely than elsewhere to have connections to the community. Thus, it is no surprise to find that resource-community residents think that their wallet will be returned regardless of who finds it. Moreover, the effect operates above and beyond that from population density. And density matters more for specific trust than for the general mode, as is also true for population mobility. Again, this seems as it should be, as density and mobility index experiential factors more than they do cultural ones. Residents of high-mobility and high-density communities are less likely to know their neighbours and, hence, are less likely to have forged the reciprocal trust that would assure a wallet's return. The owner would be more easily found, and his or her interests more likely to be valued by the finder, in neighbourhoods with less mobility.

Residents of communities with above-average levels of education think their wallets are more likely to be returned if found by neighbours, police, or strangers. This is in addition to the positive effect from the individual's own level of education. Thus, those with more education are regarded by their neighbours as more likely to return lost wallets. It is interesting that this contextual effect of education is stronger in the case of the more specific wallet question than it is in the generalized trust question. This suggests that the ambit of the general trust question is geographically broad. In contrast, expectations of honesty on the part of persons living and working nearby rest, almost by definition, on a smaller spatial range. A corollary is that local communities' average education levels carry more explanatory value for the wallet questions than for generalized trust.

Most striking, however, is ethnicity and ethnic context. Even with imported trust and networks controlled, coefficients on visible minority status are consistently negative, if not always significant by the conventional criterion. Particularly striking is the coefficient on trust in the police. Given all the controls, and given the weak-to-null relationships in the other situations, it is natural to wonder whether distrust in the police is specific to the Canadian experiences of members of visible minorities. Strictly speaking, the "visible minority" coefficient in each estimation captures the impact of minority status in neighbourhoods where no one else belongs to a visible minority. This is so because the setup also includes an interaction term combining the respondent's own majority/minority status with the neighbourhood's visible-minority percentage. The presence of an interaction term also means that the next coefficient, for the impact of the local percentage of visible minority residents, indexes the impact of ethnic context on members of the *majority*. And members of the majority are sensitive to context: the larger the local minority percentage the more distrustful are members of the "invisible" majority. The power of context is roughly the same for trust in neighbours, police officers, and grocery clerks. Interestingly, it is of no significance for the perceived trustworthiness of strangers. Finally, the interaction term estimates the difference between minority and majority persons in reaction to ethnic context; the actual effect for minority persons is the sum of the two coefficients. The interaction is always positive. It is statistically significant only once, but the patterns always converge: the positive value on the interaction is greater than is the negative value on the main effect. The indication is that visible minority respondents roughly mirror majority ones: as minority numbers grow, members of the minority feel more trusting. The strongest interaction is for trust in the police. So the strong negative sign on the individual-level term, whether or not the respondent belongs to a visible minority, indicates that minority persons are particularly distrustful of the police where their own numbers are small. As the minority group becomes the local majority, perceptions of the police become much more positive. Although there are strong indications of a similar gradient for other potential objects of trust, the police finding is the outstanding one.

Figure 5.1 translates "wallet" coefficients for ethnicity, ethnic context, and their interaction into real-world values. The figure draws upon the estimation for the summary "wallets" measure from Table 5.5 and presents results based on changes in these three variables, holding all other variables at their means. The vertical axis represents the probability that the respondent is, on balance, trusting. Where visible-minority respondents are relatively isolated in their neighbourhoods, they are much less trusting – much less likely to believe that the lost wallet would be returned – than are their majority neighbours. As the visible minority share in the neighbourhood grows, the trustfulness of majority respondents shrinks. In contrast, minority respondents become mildly more trusting. The majority/minority difference reverses when 60 percent of the neighbourhood's residents belong to a visible minority. As a practical matter, relatively few members of the majority live in any such place. In our sample, the median member of the majority lives in a neighbourhood with a visible-minority share of only 3 percent. In contrast, the median visible-minority person lives in a neighbourhood where the visible-minority share is 37 percent. In such a neighbourhood, majority/minority trust differences are small.

While ethnic and neighbourhood effects are stronger for the wallet measure, "national trust" effects are weaker. They are not entirely absent, to be sure, but they never do better than teeter on the brink of statistical significance.

FIGURE 5.1

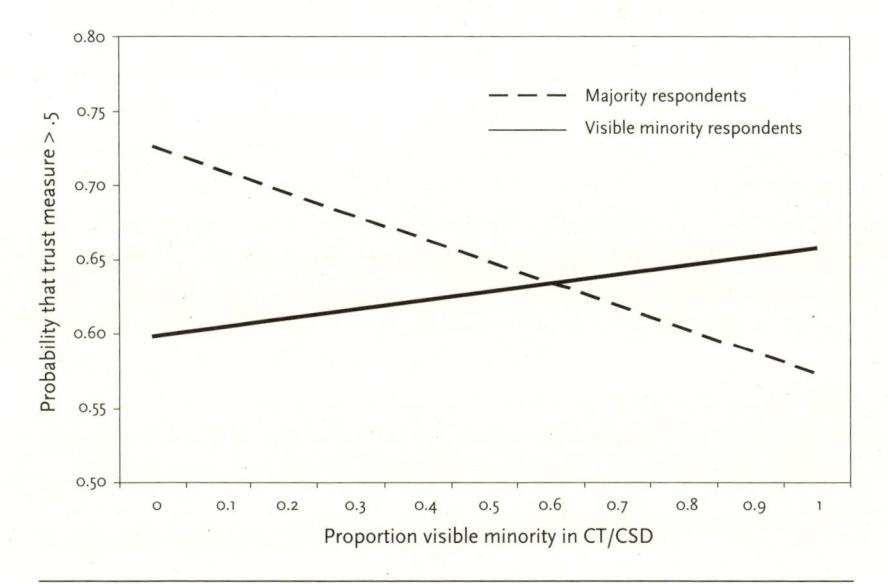

The effects of ethnicity on trust

[Line graph: x-axis "Proportion visible minority in CT/CSD" from 0 to 1; y-axis "Probability that trust measure > .5" from 0.50 to 0.80. Dashed line (Majority respondents) decreases from about 0.725 at 0 to about 0.575 at 1. Solid line (Visible minority respondents) increases from about 0.60 at 0 to about 0.66 at 1.]

And the values for "imported trust," in particular, are only about one-third the size of the generalized-trust coefficients. The difference between the "imported" and "parental" trust effects is smaller here than it is for generalized trust. So there is some suggestion that situational trust expectations persist. This seems to fly in the face of the very logic of the concept. But too much should not be made of the finding. For three of the four wallet items, the "parental trust" coefficient is smaller than it is in the generalized trust estimations.

Interpretation of the difference in "national trust" effects between the situational and the generalized estimation requires care. The easiest interpretation is that the difference is a measurement artifact. After all, the data from which "national trust" scores are derived are national means on precisely the measure that serves as the dependent variable in Table 5.3. And this measurement difference may indeed account for some of the difference in estimated effects. We doubt that this accounts for all of it, however. The divergence also accords with robust common sense. The rest of the pattern in Table 5.4 suggests that respondents employ information and experience from their Canadian milieu to derive situational expectations. This leaves less room for importing trust.

Finally, network effects matter less in the individual wallet estimations than in the generalized one. Individual coefficients stand out, of course. Seeing neighbours helps one trust neighbours – and strangers as well. Seeing friends helps one trust police officers and store clerks, although it is hard to think why it should help with these and not others. Membership in "other" groups has the most consistent effect and one whose power is roughly the same here as in Table 5.3. But the overall impact of network connections is not impressive. Partly, this reflects the absence in these estimations of one of the most powerful effects in the generalized one: from religious groups. The religious contrast goes right to the point, however. Its power in Table 5.3 and its weakness here indicates how the generalized question is linked to moral presuppositions.

Conclusion

Much remains to be done, obviously. We are conscious that key variables, such as optimism, are (necessarily) missing from our data and may account for some of the patterns we interpret substantively. However, the inclusion of the answers to the health question, which also are likely to be affected strongly by inherent optimism, helps to ensure that the other coefficients are less likely to be getting their power through a common correlation with the unmeasured optimism of the respondents. We essentially finesse questions of causal order, such as whether memberships induce trust or trust facilitates joining. Even so, the findings are rich and highly suggestive.

One clear indication is that where the generalized trust measure reflects cultural learning, the wallet questions call more upon experience and seem more plausible as indicators of the respondent's strategic expectations and the trustfulness he or she is likely actually to exhibit. Generalized trust is powerfully affected by education, by the cultural pattern of new Canadians' countries of origin, and by how involved the respondent is with religious organizations. Various aspects of community and neighbourhood context that seem plausible as factors in trust or distrust make little difference, in fact, for responses to the generalized measure. Generalized trust seems to be the sort of thing one learns in school or in church.

In contrast, neighbourhood context is very important – and in subtle ways – for the wallet measure. Residents of small, coherent resource communities stand out as peculiarly trusting, even of strangers. Neighbourhood density, mobility, and average education levels – all plausible factors in interpersonal trust – matter greatly to respondents' empirical beliefs about trustworthiness in specific trust situations. These factors matter hardly at all to generalized trust. Most striking, though, is the effect of diversity. If one belongs to a visible minority but is surrounded by members of the majority, one is less trusting than are neighbours in the "invisible" majority that a wallet will be returned, even by a neighbour. After all, in such a place, the neighbour may be ethnically very different from the visible-minority person in question. And a visible-minority person in such a place will be especially distrustful of the police. As the visible-minority percentage in the neighbourhood grows, so does the sense of trust that members of the visible minority repose in those around them. This is especially so for trust in the police. Conversely, members of the majority become *less* trustful.

These generalizations may be uncomfortable in themselves, but they are plausible and suggestive. We would never have reached them had we not unpacked the idea of trust. Different measures suit different purposes. Analyses of individual trust items suggest that generalized trust is a useful indicator. It still needs conceptual exploration, and this will require detailed empirical investigation. The centrality of church associations to generalized trust hints at the moralism that Uslaner (2002) believes to pervade the measure, for instance. But the continued power of "national trust," even if it indicates that generalized trust reflects experiences that are arguably no longer relevant, hardly seems like a story about moralizing. After all, field experiments with wallets, reported by Knack (2001), were the original inspiration for our battery of wallet questions. Response to the generalized question *is* related to response to the specific wallet questions. But the relationship is loose. Both kinds of question are necessary to triangulate the social space of trust.

Meanwhile, our analysis of trust has paid an unexpected dividend. The overall pattern may be read to vindicate the Canadian story of multiculturalism. It is true that the experiential world of the wallet questions unpacks a structure of implicit group antagonism. The story is mitigated, however, by the reality of residential distribution: most members of the "invisible" majority go about their business in neighbourhoods full of people like them.

The same is true, although not quite as one-sidedly so, for members of visible minorities. More important is what Canada seems to do in the realm of generalized interpersonal trust. Although new Canadians' trust levels reflect their countries of origin, such origin differences do not last past the first generation. It is tempting to infer that, by recognizing the multiplicity of Canadians' origins, we facilitate their acceptance of Canadian norms. Ironically, the Canadian mosaic seems to be a more powerful force for integration than is the US melting pot. And country-of-origin differences account for *all* differences between immigrants and natives. Indeed, when origins are accounted for, new Canadians are *more* trusting in the general sense than are their Canadian-born counterparts.

APPENDIX A: VARIABLE DESCRIPTIONS

The Equality, Security, and Community survey includes questions on demographics, economic situation, civic associations, political opinions, social policy preferences, and, of course, interpersonal trust. The sample has three basic components: a national probability sample, a metropolitan oversample weighted toward neighbourhoods with a high percentage of visible minority residents, and a BC resource community oversample. Merged with these data are a variety of contextual variables at the census tract or subdivision level from the 1996 Canadian Census, and aggregate results from the trust question asked in the World Values and European Values Surveys.

This appendix lists the details for each variable used in preceding analyses. Where necessary, question wording is included. The table that follows includes basic descriptives for these variables.

BASIC DEMOGRAPHICS

Female: dummy variable = 1 if respondent is female.
Age: dummy variables for 30 to 49, 50 to 65, 66 and over; residual category is
    < 30 yrs.
Education: dummy variables for "finished high school," "started college or university,"
    and "finished college or university"; residual category is "did not finish high
    school."
Religion: dummy variables for Catholic and Protestant; residual category is "other."
French: dummy variable = 1 if respondent speaks French at home.
Immigrant: dummy variable = 1 if respondent is an immigrant.
Health: self-reported health, based on the following question: "Compared to others
    your age, would you describe your health as excellent, very good, good, fair, or
    poor?" rescaled from 0 to 1 where 1 is excellent and 0 is poor.

Resource oversample: dummy variable = 1 if respondent is part of the resource oversample.

ETHNICITY

Visible minority: dummy variable = 1 if respondent is a visible minority, based on the Census definition (includes all individuals except aboriginals who are non-Caucasian in race or colour).

Visible minority percent: percentage of respondents' CT/CSD who are visible minorities, based on the Census definition (as above).

ECONOMIC SITUATION

Economic outlook: based on the following question: "What about the next twelve months? Do you feel your household's economic situation will improve, stay about the same, or get worse? = 1 if respondent feels that their household's economic situation will improve over the next twelve months, = .5 if they feel it will stay about the same, and = 0 if they feel it will get worse.

Median household income ($100,000s): median household income in respondents' CT/CSD, converted to $100,000s.

Income diversity: proportion of households in respondents' CT/CSD earning less than $10,000 and more than $90,000 (about the tenth and nineteenth percentiles for the majority of census subdivisions).

OTHER CONTEXTUAL VARIABLES

Education: proportion of individuals in respondent's CT/CSD with more than a high school diploma (started, but not necessarily finished, college or university).

Mobility: proportion of individuals in respondent's CT/CSD who moved in the five years previous to the 1996 Census.

Population density: number of individuals divided by the number of square kilometres for the individual's CT/CSD. This variable is heavily skewed to the right, so the log values are used.

NETWORKS

Divorced: dummy variable = 1 if respondent is divorced or separated.

Sees family: dummy variable = 1 if respondent sees family members (living elsewhere) once a month or more.

Sees friends: dummy variable = 1 if respondent sees close friends once a month or more.

Sees neighbours: dummy variable = 1 if respondent talks with neighbours once a month or more.

Religious memberships: dummy variable = 1 if respondent is a member of any groups related to their religion.

Ethnic memberships: dummy variable = 1 if respondent is a member of any groups related to their ethnicity.

Other memberships: dummy variable = 1 if respondent is a member of any other groups (service clubs, rec groups, political, youth, cultural, help).

"National Trust"

Imported trust: the national average of responses to the generalized trust question in respondents' country of origin, minus the Canadian national average. National averages were drawn first from the Third Wave of the World Values Survey; missing values were filled in using (in this order) the 2000 European Values Survey and the Second Wave of the World Values Survey.

Parental trust: the average of the two national averages of responses to the generalized trust question in respondents' parents' countries of origin, minus the Canadian national average, and minus Imported Trust. National averages are drawn from the same sources as above.

Trust and Memberships

See text.

TABLE 5A.1

Descriptives

Variable	N	Mean	Standard deviation	Minimum	Maximum
Female	6,579	0.543	0.498	0.000	1.000
Age	6,579	1.241	0.974	0.000	3.000
Education	6,448	2.781	1.158	1.000	4.000
Religion	6,014	1.006	0.793	0.000	2.000
French	6,579	0.138	0.345	0.000	1.000
Immigrant	6,520	0.214	0.410	0.000	1.000
Health	6,514	0.549	0.331	0.000	1.000
Resource	6,579	0.217	0.412	0.000	1.000
Visible minority	6,579	0.092	0.289	0.000	1.000
Prop. visible minority	6,569	0.121	0.149	0.000	0.519
Economic outlook	6,351	0.590	0.321	0.000	1.000
Median household income ($100,000s)	6,569	0.045	0.010	0.000	0.102
Income diversity	6,431	0.179	0.060	0.000	0.618
Education (prop > HS)	6,569	0.510	0.088	0.000	0.910
Mobility	6,569	0.444	0.121	0.000	0.831
Population density (log)	6,570	5.517	2.804	−5.186	9.642
Divorced	6,579	0.207	0.405	0.000	1.000
Sees family	6,543	0.765	0.424	0.000	1.000
Sees friends	6,541	0.915	0.279	0.000	1.000
Sees neighbours	6,512	0.804	0.397	0.000	1.000
Religious memberships	6,579	0.149	0.356	0.000	1.000
Ethnic memberships	6,579	0.122	0.327	0.000	1.000
Other memberships	6,579	1.473	1.401	0.000	6.000
Imported trust	5,996	−0.015	0.057	−0.381	0.176
Parental trust	5,658	−0.016	0.053	−0.347	0.333

NOTE: Results based on combined first wave, metro oversample, and resource community oversample, unweighted.

APPENDIX B: MEMBERSHIPS

The ESC survey asks about membership in eight distinct types of groups:

1   How many service clubs, such as Lions or Meals on Wheels, do you belong to?
2   How many recreational groups, such as sports leagues or clubs, music or hobby clubs, or exercise classes are you involved in?
3   How many organizations active on political issues, such as the environment or taxpayers' rights, do you belong to?
4   Sometimes people give time to various types of organizations. For instance, how many youth-oriented groups, such as Girl Guides or minor hockey, have you given time to in the last twelve months?
5   How about organizations providing cultural services to the public, such as a museum or music festival. How many of these have you given time to in the last twelve months?
6   How about organizations that help people, such as the Cancer Society or a food bank? How many of these have you volunteered time to in the last twelve months?
7   How many groups directly attached to your place of worship, such as a charitable group, are you a member of?
8   How many organizations connected with your own nationality or ethnic or racial group are you a member of?

The bridging-bonding dichotomy suggests that religious and ethnic groups might be distinguished from the other six types of groups. Religious and ethnic groups will certainly draw together people of the same religion or ethnicity, after all. Other groups might have a narrow social or economic focus (take, for instance, a country club), but not necessarily. By the same token, religious and ethnic groups may bring together people who share a religion or ethnic origin but have little else in common. Such groups may be bridging social and income gaps even as they are also bonding those in the same religious or ethnic group.

Unfortunately, we do not have detailed information about each of the groups in which respondents are members. We can nevertheless look at the relationships between group memberships, and predictors of group membership as indicators of the general membership of the eight different groups.

Table 5B.1 presents an unrotated principal components analysis of the eight different memberships variables. It is striking that the first six groups load on the first factor, while ethnic and religious groups load on the second. Results suggest a division between religious and ethnic (bonding?) groups, on one hand, and all other (bridging?) groups, on the other hand.

In Table 5B.2, we report equations estimating the number of organizations each person belongs to, with the types of organization divided different ways. The first column relates to ethnic organizations, the second to religious organizations, the third to all other organizations, and the fourth to total memberships, being the sum of ethnic, religious, and all other.

The first demographic variable considered is gender. Males are more likely than females to belong to ethnic groups, and females more likely to belong to religious groups. Among the types of other groups, Table 5B.3 shows females being less likely than males to be involved in service clubs, recreational groups, and political groups and more likely to be involved in cultural and help groups.

Memberships in ethnic and religious groups rise with age, while those in other groups follow more varied patterns. Memberships in service clubs and political groups rise with age, while memberships in recreational and youth groups fall with age. Help group memberships are highest among those aged fifty to sixty-five. Since we have survey results only from one year, we are unable to tell what patterns of cohort and life-cycle effects are being captured by these age variables, so we will not risk overinterpretation of the observed patterns.

Memberships in almost all types of organizations are more numerous among those with more education. For all eight types of organization, the positive effect of education on memberships is significant, and, in each case, it grows with the level of education. Going on to complete a higher level of education is associated with greater involvement across the whole spectrum of organization types.

TABLE 5B.1

Factor analysis of associational memberships

Membership type	Factor 1	Factor 2
Service	0.481	0.037
Recreation	0.585	−0.307
Political	0.448	−0.094
Youth	0.593	−0.301
Cultural	0.540	−0.081
Help	0.603	−0.113
Ethnic	0.327	0.696
Religious	0.422	0.633

NOTE: $N = 6,579$. Cells contain factor loading from a principal components analysis, unrotated, using membership dummy variables in the combined first wave, metro oversample, and resource community sample, unweighted.

TABLE 5B.2

Sources of associational memberships (ethnic, religious, and other)

		Dependent variables (number of memberships)							
	Independent variables	Ethnic		Religious		Other		All	
Basic demographics	Female	−0.036**	(0.016)	0.034*	(0.018)	−0.050	(0.072)	−0.053	(0.082)
	Age:								
	30-49	0.004	(0.021)	0.036*	(0.019)	−0.040	(0.097)	−0.000	(0.109)
	50-65	0.030	(0.025)	0.083***	(0.027)	−0.235**	(0.114)	−0.122	(0.129)
	66+	0.076***	(0.030)	0.241***	(0.036)	−0.226*	(0.123)	0.091	(0.144)
	Education:								
	finished high school	0.016	(0.024)	0.024	(0.029)	0.648***	(0.103)	0.688***	(0.119)
	started college/univ.	0.054*	(0.028)	0.057*	(0.030)	1.085***	(0.137)	1.196***	(0.147)
	finished college/univ.	0.069***	(0.025)	0.100***	(0.029)	1.361***	(0.101)	1.530***	(0.109)
	Religion:								
	Catholic	0.111***	(0.026)	0.168***	(0.019)	0.079	(0.106)	0.357***	(0.115)
	Protestant	0.013	(0.022)	0.220***	(0.025)	0.125	(0.103)	0.358***	(0.114)
	French	−0.088***	(0.025)	−0.108***	(0.024)	−0.846***	(0.117)	−1.041***	(0.131)
	Immigrant	0.108***	(0.032)	0.031	(0.025)	−0.602***	(0.120)	−0.463***	(0.140)
	Health	0.015	(0.029)	0.034	(0.027)	0.625***	(0.127)	0.674***	(0.149)
	Resource oversample	0.299***	(0.082)	0.111	(0.073)	−0.176	(0.265)	0.233	(0.334)
Ethnicity	R is visible minority	0.124**	(0.057)	0.027	(0.059)	−0.053	(0.258)	0.098	(0.294)
	Visible minority (%)	−0.103	(0.158)	−0.020	(0.152)	−0.202	(0.534)	−0.325	(0.656)
	Interaction	0.036	(0.030)	−0.047	(0.030)	0.033	(0.129)	0.022	(0.139)

Economic situation	Economic outlook	0.236	(0.989)	−0.816	(0.916)	−0.386	(4.829)	−0.966	(5.493)
	Median income	0.104	(0.163)	−0.190	(0.144)	−0.233	(0.738)	−0.319	(0.832)
	Income diversity	**−0.290****	**(0.117)**	−0.018	(0.105)	**1.349****	**(0.575)**	1.041	(0.652)
Other contextual variables	Education (% > high school)	0.016	(0.048)	**−0.093***	**(0.048)**	**−0.904****	**(0.222)**	**−0.981****	**(0.252)**
	Mobility (%, 5 yrs)	0.003	(0.004)	0.002	(0.004)	−0.004	(0.021)	0.001	(0.024)
	Population density	−0.039	(0.024)	**−0.050****	**(0.022)**	−0.027	(0.102)	−0.116	(0.119)
Constant		**0.135***	**(0.058)**	0.057	(0.053)	**1.173****	**(0.259)**	**1.365****	**(0.285)**
Observations		5,621		5,621		5,621		5,621	
R^2		0.05		0.05		0.07		0.06	

NOTE: Cells contain coefficients from an SLO estimation using corrected standard errors. Results are based on combined first wave, metro oversample, and resource community sample, unweighted.
* $p < .10$; ** $p < .05$; *** $p < .01$.
All coefficients significant at $p < .10$ are in **bold**.

TABLE 5B.3

Sources of associational memberships (service clubs and recreation, political, youth, cultural, and help groups)

	Independent variables	Service clubs	Rec. groups	Political	Youth	Cultural	Help
Basic demographics	Female	−0.033*** (0.015)	−0.112*** (0.030)	−0.028* (0.016)	−0.037 (0.025)	0.035* (0.021)	0.124*** (0.025)
Age:	30-49	0.050*** (0.016)	−0.136*** (0.042)	0.002 (0.018)	0.108*** (0.033)	−0.054** (0.026)	−0.010 (0.032)
	50-65	0.124*** (0.021)	−0.320*** (0.045)	0.053** (0.024)	−0.183*** (0.045)	−0.015 (0.034)	0.106** (0.043)
	66+	0.250*** (0.027)	−0.243*** (0.052)	0.086*** (0.032)	−0.328*** (0.043)	−0.041 (0.033)	0.050 (0.047)
Education;	finished high school	0.078*** (0.025)	0.255*** (0.041)	0.055*** (0.016)	0.110*** (0.036)	0.065*** (0.024)	0.084** (0.038)
	started college/univ.	0.110*** (0.031)	0.372*** (0.051)	0.108*** (0.022)	0.231*** (0.044)	0.159*** (0.030)	0.104** (0.048)
	finished college/univ.	0.101*** (0.020)	0.452*** (0.045)	0.177*** (0.019)	0.240*** (0.035)	0.189*** (0.023)	0.201*** (0.039)
Religion:	Catholic	0.013 (0.018)	0.051 (0.041)	−0.095*** (0.022)	0.098** (0.039)	−0.043 (0.027)	0.055* (0.032)
	Protestant	0.024 (0.020)	0.083* (0.042)	−0.091*** (0.022)	0.088** (0.037)	−0.062** (0.027)	0.083*** (0.031)
	French	−0.005 (0.025)	−0.287*** (0.044)	0.001 (0.024)	−0.284*** (0.039)	−0.030 (0.033)	−0.240*** (0.041)
	Immigrant	−0.027 (0.021)	−0.277*** (0.052)	−0.047** (0.022)	−0.162*** (0.034)	0.009 (0.033)	−0.098*** (0.034)
	Health	0.033 (0.024)	0.353*** (0.055)	0.039* (0.022)	0.150*** (0.042)	0.038 (0.035)	0.012 (0.042)
	Resource oversample	0.022 (0.050)	0.038 (0.111)	−0.116*** (0.032)	−0.004 (0.084)	0.018 (0.057)	−0.135 (0.089)

Ethnicity	R is visible minority	−0.030	(0.045)	0.050	(0.117)	0.004	(0.061)	−0.033	(0.089)	0.056	(0.077)	−0.100	(0.082)
	Visible minority (%)	0.015	(0.095)	−0.185	(0.206)	0.022	(0.072)	−0.087	(0.167)	−0.101	(0.128)	0.135	(0.171)
	Interaction	−0.013	(0.023)	0.007	(0.054)	0.055**	(0.027)	−0.057	(0.044)	0.005	(0.034)	0.037	(0.045)
Economic situation	Economic outlook	0.707	(0.805)	1.765	(2.098)	−0.907	(1.026)	2.198	(1.601)	−2.792**	(1.178)	−1.357	(1.610)
	Median income	0.015	(0.131)	−0.217	(0.326)	0.244	(0.192)	−0.085	(0.233)	−0.000	(0.159)	−0.190	(0.247)
	Income diversity	−0.021	(0.099)	0.567***	(0.206)	0.141	(0.111)	0.164	(0.198)	0.202	(0.146)	0.296	(0.185)
Other contextual variables	Education (% > high school)	−0.152***	(0.042)	−0.200**	(0.084)	−0.020	(0.048)	−0.213**	(0.085)	−0.122**	(0.051)	−0.198***	(0.076)
	Mobility (%, 5yrs)	−0.001	(0.004)	0.006	(0.009)	−0.005	(0.004)	−0.006	(0.008)	−0.004	(0.005)	0.007	(0.007)
	Population density	−0.004	(0.023)	0.114***	(0.043)	0.039	(0.024)	0.003	(0.044)	−0.024	(0.030)	−0.156***	(0.032)
Constant		0.044	(0.046)	0.283***	(0.099)	0.034	(0.052)	0.316***	(0.088)	0.234***	(0.068)	0.261***	(0.089)
Observations		5,621		5,621		5,621		5,621		5,621		5,621	
R^2		0.03		0.07		0.03		0.06		0.02		0.03	

NOTE: See note to Table 5B.2.

As for religion, respondents who describe themselves as either Protestant or Catholic are more likely to be involved in religious and youth groups (plus ethnic organizations in the case of Catholics) than are other respondents, while being less likely to be involved in political or cultural organizations. As for language, those whose first language is French are less likely to be involved in ethnic, religious, recreational, youth, and help groups. Immigrants are more likely to be involved in ethnic groups, and less likely to be involved in recreational, political, youth, and help groups. Visible minority respondents are more likely to be involved in ethnic and religious groups and less likely to be involved in political groups. All of these are, of course, partial effects holding constant all the other variables that enter the equations.

The variables with italicized titles refer to characteristics of the census tracts or subdivisions in which individuals live rather than to their own circumstances. Including both individual and community-level effects allows us to measure possible interaction effects. For example, we include whether the individual is visible minority and a contextual variable reporting the percentage of visible minority residents in the respondent's census division. We find that visible minority respondents are significantly more likely to be involved in ethnic and religious associations. Holding individual characteristics constant, those living in communities with high visible minority proportions are (insignificantly) more likely to be members of ethnic and religious organizations. When we add an interaction variable, it attracts a negative coefficient of about the same size as the individual effect. Thus, visible minority respondents are more likely to be members of ethnic and religious associations, especially if they live in census districts with low visible-minority proportions. One line of logic supporting these results is fairly straightforward: an ethnic organization is likely to have less to offer where ethnic diversity is higher, if this implies that the contacts and bonding opportunities are equally likely to be provided in offices, factories, and shops as in the association meetings. This logic would be stronger if there were more specificity in the ethnic mix data, since an increase in the simple measure of visible minority proportions does not imply greater proportions of those from the ethnic groups that are described in our membership questions.

Income is another variable through which we look for individual and contextual effects. We found little evidence of individual income effects, while our contextual effects include both the median income and the income diversity (as measured by the prevalence in the census district of those in either the first or the tenth decile of the overall population). In general, neither median income nor income diversity has any systematic relation with memberships. The only exception is that memberships in cultural organizations are lower, other things equal, in census districts with lower average incomes.

The final contextual variables include average education levels, population mobility, and population density. Education levels are included to provide a test of the Nie, Junn, and Stehlik-Barry (1996) hypothesis that membership activity rises with relative rather than absolute education levels. They argue that the oft-found positive linkage between individual-level education and participation is actually based on relative education, which implies that, if both individual-level and aggregate education levels are used in the same equation, they will have opposite signs and roughly equivalent magnitudes. This is, indeed, what they reported to find in their research. However, when Helliwell and Putnam (1999) repeated their analysis with more regionally specific and time-specific peer groups, the presumed negative effect of average education levels disappears for almost all types of organizations and becomes positive for some. That research was all based on US data. The ESC survey allows us to test the same hypothesis with Canadian data and to use a finer grid for comparative education than was possible with the US data. Our results show no significant effects of average education levels on membership levels (once each individual's own level of education has been taken into account), thus supporting the Helliwell and Putnam rather than the Nie et al. results for the United States. In the Canadian data, it would appear that the positive individual-level effects found to link education to social participation are not due to relative education and, hence, do flow through to the aggregate level (since they are neither offset nor augmented by significant community-level effects).

Population mobility, which we measure as the proportion of the population in the respondent's census district who have moved in the preceding five years, has a significant effect only in the case of religious organizations, where the effect is negative. The effects of mobility on memberships are less clear. Joining may help to build social structures for the newly arrived, and among those living temporarily in a community. On the other hand, more stable communities tend to foster increased interactions of many sorts, including, for example, the formation of new additional community-level organizations to meet individual and community needs. Our results reflect this ambiguity.

Population density may also have contrasting effects. In high density communities, typified by large urban areas, there are many more specialized organizations available to meet all interests, thus increasing the likely number of memberships. On the other hand, those living and working in large urban areas are less likely to know their neighbours and may live far from their places of work, thus spending more of their time commuting. In our Canadian sample, we find the partial effect of population density on membership activities to be generally insignificant. Memberships in political groups are less frequent in urban areas, but, in other cases, there are no significant effects.

ACKNOWLEDGMENTS
The authors are grateful to Keith Banting, Fiona Kay, Dietlind Stolle, and James Tansey for comments. The usual disclaimer applies.

NOTES

1 All analyses in this chapter use respondents from all three components of the ESC survey, described in detail in Appendix A. The variation across questions in number of cases was a result of CATI error. By the time this was discovered, it was too late to change the programming for the main sample. All respondents in the Vancouver, Toronto, and Montreal metropolitan oversamples and in the BC resource community sample, which went to field after the main sample, received all four questions.

2 Q3 and Q4 split Q1 into its components. In effecting this split, we hoped to shed light on an interesting feature of the split results that first appeared when Q1 and Q3 were asked of different halves of the 1983 US General Social Survey sample. As reported in Helliwell and Putnam (1999), men are significantly more trusting than women when asked Q1, while women are more trusting than men when asked Q3. Our supposition is that women were more inclined to be cautious, for a variety of possible reasons. We too find females to be less trusting when asked the balanced trust question (Q1), but more trusting than males when faced with the simpler question (Q3). Our survey also supports the US result that affirmative responses were much more likely to Q1 than to Q3 regardless of gender.

3 The indicators with the weakest link to an overall trust scale are Q2 and Q4, two of the unipolar agree-disagree items.

4 When the axes are rotated, the generalized and the wallet items load weakly on separate factors. The rotated solution does not obviously dominate the unrotated one, and it is natural to wonder how much of the separation is an artifact of response coding.

6
Gender, Early Experiences with "Social Capital," and Adult Community Participation

James Curtis and Thomas Perks

The purposes of this study are threefold. Using responses from a survey of a large national representative sample of adult Canadians, we ask: (1) whether females' and males' involvement levels in community voluntary activities differed during their school years; (2) whether women's and men's current levels of involvement in adult community activities differ; and (3) whether differential early experiences with community activities provide part of the explanation of current levels of participation in adult community activities for the genders.

Our measures of youth activities and current adult activities constitute alternative indicators of experiences, with "social capital" defined as "social connections among individuals" and their associated norms, knowledge and values of community participation (Putnam 2000, 19ff; cf. Portes 1998). The analyses explore gender differences, if any, in involvement with social capital at two points in the life cycle, the school years and current adulthood. Further, we ask whether the data suggest that access to social capital early in life "pays off" in access to higher levels of social involvement in the community later in adult life. Because we will employ data from a national sample of Canadian adults, "current adulthood" has different age reference points for the different age cohorts. Some younger adult respondents are only about five to ten years removed from their high school years; other adults are much more distant from the high school years. To check on the implications of this, we will conduct some of the analyses specific to age cohorts.

Relevant Literature

Over twenty years ago now, Hanks and Eckland (1978) reported the results of a study in which they assessed the relationship between activity in extracurricular activities in high school and involvement in voluntary associations somewhat later in life.[1] The results of this study, presented some time before the recent heightened interest in "social capital," gave interesting leads concerning important social sources of social capital among adults. Hanks and Eckland studied a national sample of about 2,000 US high school students who were interviewed in their sophomore year and then re-interviewed some fifteen years later at about thirty years of age. These researchers found that "participation in extracurricular school activities had a relatively strong direct effect on participation in adult secondary associations" (ibid, 481). Participation in extracurricular activity in high school was measured in terms of seven Likert-type items having to do with forms of voluntary activities closely associated with the school, such as creative writing, drama and music, and student government. (The questions on school activities were asked retrospectively in the second wave of the survey, not in the first survey while the students were in high school.) Participation in current voluntary association activities was measured by asking about a list of eight types of associations; for each type, respondents were asked about their membership, activity, and leadership roles.

Hanks and Eckland summarized their results in the following way: "Membership in adult voluntary associations is significantly related to its adolescent counterpart, participation in extracurricular school activities. Of particular interest is the fact that adolescent social participation has a stronger direct effect on adult social participation (beta = .234) than any other predictor in the model, including education, occupation, or income. Moreover, the beta is only slightly smaller than the zero-order coefficient (.282), indicating both that the relationship is largely direct and that it cannot be traced to any common antecedents that are controlled in this model: social class background, academic aptitude, or grade performance" (1978, 487-88).

Thus, participation in extracurricular activities in the school years was not simply a modest correlate of adult associational involvement; it was a stronger predictor of current adult associational involvement than were all other social background factors considered in the analyses, including three socioeconomic status factors that have been commonly described elsewhere in the literature as among the strongest social background predictors of voluntary association involvement. These social background factors are rivalled only by age in other research where the study population included a full range of adult age categories (for studies conducted in the United States and Canada, see, e.g., Almond and Verba 1963; Burns, Schlozman, and Verba, 2001; Chui, Curtis, and Grabb 1993; Curtis, Grabb, and Baer 1992; Curtis, Baer, and Grabb 2001; Cutler and Hendricks 2000; Knoke 1986; Milbrath and Goel 1977; Smith 1975; Verba, Schlozman, and Brady 1995; Wilson 2000; Wilson and Musick 1997).

Hanks and Eckland interpreted their results in terms of "social capital acquisition" without using these particular words. They argued as follows: "Our central thesis is that the extracurricular program can be viewed as a training ground for adolescents for participation in fundamentally similar organizations as adults, an arena in which the skills and habits conducive to membership in voluntary associations initially develop. Extracurricular activities expose students to a network of social relations, consisting in part of school staff and achievement oriented peers, which tends to bind their members to the school and to its normative structure just as adult voluntary associations ... are the cement which links the individual to the larger society" (1978, 481-82).

Hanks and Eckland indicated, further, that the "data ... provide strong evidence that participation in school activities provides role training that directly facilitates adult participation in voluntary associations" (ibid., 487-88).

There have been a limited number of follow-ups in other research on this topic. One interesting study, suggesting the same interpretations, is Janoski and Wilson's (1995) panel study extending across the high school years into early adulthood. These researchers drew on data from a national sample of about one thousand high school seniors interviewed eight years later and again seven years after that. They linked data on participation in high school extracurricular activities and parents' voluntary association activity on the one hand and adult activity in "self-oriented" versus "community-oriented" associations on the other hand. Their results showed that "when self-oriented (occupation and profession) and community-oriented (service, church, community, fraternal, and neighborhood) types of participation are distinguished ... family socialization explains community-oriented but not self-oriented participation" (ibid., 271). Their "family socialization" model, in multivariate analyses, was composed of four predictors: marital status, number of children, parents' voluntary association activity, and youth extracurricular activities. Socioeconomic status factors – income, occupational status, and education level – predicted well involvement in "self-oriented" associations but not community-oriented organizations.

In their explanation of the findings for community-oriented group participation, Janoski and Wilson emphasize the role of parents' socialization and not early youth experience in activities per se. They indicated that, for involvement in these associations, "parents ... socialize by example and even

... by direct contact and recruitment to the group in question. These kinds of associations are much more endogamous" (ibid., 289; cf. Knoke and Thompson 1977; Rotolo 2000).

Smith (1999) has recently used data from the National Education Longitudinal Study in the United States – a sample of Grade 8 students first interviewed in 1988 and later re-interviewed in Grades 10 and 12 and two years after graduation. The study showed that religious participation, participation in school extracurricular activities, close family relationships, and extensive connections to others, all measured in the school years, positively predicted political and civic involvement as a young adult. Smith does not report on the gender gradients for involvement in the youth activities, but she does indicate that gender was not a significant predictor of adult political participation when the effects of youth involvement and other controls were taken into account. Again, Smith interpreted her results in terms of the consequences or payoff of early social capital accumulation.

Burns, Schlozman and Verba (2001) have reported on extensive analyses of a US national sample survey of adults in which respondents were asked about their current political behaviours and, retrospectively, about the following aspects of the high school years: political activities of their parents, discussions about politics in their homes, and their levels of involvement in student councils, clubs, sports, and civic classes. The researchers found that women and men differed little on most of the measures of political involvement in the home and school, except that women had considerably more participation in high school clubs and men had more involvement in high school sports. The results also showed that the early political experiences in the home and in high school positively affected the political activity (a composite index) of adults, whether for females or males. These early factors did little, though, to account for gender differences in adult political activity. Females were somewhat less involved on the political activity index, which involved the sum of eight types of acts – voting, campaign work, contributing to a campaign, contacting an official, taking part in a protest/march/ demonstration, affiliation with an organization that takes political stands, and serving as a volunteer on a local board. Women did gain in political activity from the positive effects of involvement in high school clubs compared with men, because women were more involved in these activities in high school. Thus, early political involvement in the high school years did little to account for the adult gender gap, but it was a central part of the explanation of adult activity for each gender (ibid., Chapter 10).

Among the four studies we have just described, two of them used retrospective questions on youth activities, or asked adults to recall their activities from earlier periods (Hanks and Eckland 1978; Burns, Schlozman, and Verba 2001), and two of them were panel studies that "followed" and re-interviewed respondents over short periods of the life cycle after the high school years (Janoski and Wilson 1995; and Smith 1999).

The former studies rely on adults' reports of their youth activities, which may pose some recall problems. It is possible, for example, that adults who are more frequent community participants may better remember youth activities than do their currently inactive counterparts because the current activity reminds the former group of their past activities. The panel studies do not depend on recall for data on the youth years. However, these studies often have high levels of attrition (drop-outs) for the later wave or waves of the surveys. This becomes a problem if the continuing respondents are unrepresentative of the general population in some important ways. For example, it is a plausible hypothesis that people who are more active in the community might be more likely to continue to cooperate with the research organization and to participate in the further waves of the surveys. The panel studies are also much more expensive and time-consuming to execute. Time must be allowed to pass – the population must have time to age – and there are considerable expenses for repeatedly locating and interviewing respondents.

Thus, each of the two research approaches has its limitations, and results from each should be assessed against these characteristics. Data from both approaches are, however, useful in any attempts to better understand the effects of early involvement upon later involvement. We are best informed if we can compare across results of the two types of studies. For our present research problem, as shown by the four studies just reviewed, the two types of research yield the same patterns of results.

Not surprisingly, because of the much greater time requirement and financial costs of panel studies compared with retrospective studies, there have been few panel studies and more retrospective studies. (For literature reviews, see, e.g., Hooghe and Stolle 2003; Yates and Youniss 1998; Youniss, McLellan, and Yates 1997.) Further examples of panel studies relating early and later community activities can be found in the work of Jennings and Stoker (2002) and Plutzer (2002). Further examples of retrospective studies are provided by Beck and Jennings (1982), Hooghe (2003), Verba, Schlozman, and Brady (1995), among many others. Each of these is a non-Canadian study, most are for the United States, but not all. As yet, we have not had systematic

Canadian studies of the effects of early community involvement upon later involvement, whether using the panel or retrospective procedures. The US and international studies do show consistent positive relationships between early and later community activities (cf. Bibby 1994 for Canadian studies focused on religious activity, and Curtis, McTeer, and White 1999 for Canadian research on specifically sport and fitness involvement).[2]

There have been several US and Canadian studies of youths alone that show that they often report rather extensive experiences with a range of community voluntary activities, and that females often have higher involvement levels than males (e.g., Bianchi and Robinson 1997; Burt 1998; Flanagan et al. 1998; Sundeen and Raskoff 1994; van Roosmalen and Krahn 1996). Hanks and Eckland (1978) and Janoski and Wilson (1995) reported that there were no statistically significant gender differences in their data for either early involvement or later adult involvement. As we have said, the Burns et al. (2001) study showed a female disadvantage in political activity among adults, and some tendency, for some activities, for greater female involvement in the high school years. Smith's (1999) study showed no adult gender differences after controls and did not address differences among youths. The different patterns for the Hanks and Eckland and Janoski and Wilson studies may have occurred because the samples for those studies were quite small and each had suffered considerable attrition between surveys (the attrition was 50 percent and 35 percent, respectively). As we have said above, it may be that socially involved respondents, whether females or males, are most likely to continue to participate in panel studies. If so, results from panel studies with high attrition should provide an overestimate of involvement levels at Time 2 and later.

Still other research has shown that a large proportion of both female and male youths have part-time paid jobs, generally with males working more hours and receiving higher pay per hour (e.g., for Canada, see Desmarais and Curtis 1999; Loughlin and Barling 1999; van Roosmalen and Krahn 1996). Where there are gender differences in voluntary activities, with females having an advantage, the differential amounts of time given over to paid work may help account for this.

Also, much other North American research focused on adults has shown that, depending on the type of community involvement, females may either trail or exceed males in participation levels (e.g., Almond and Verba 1963; Burns, Schlozman, and Verba 2001; Booth 1972; Chui, Curtis, and Grabb 1993; Curtis 1971; Curtis, Grabb, and Baer, 1992; Curtis, Baer, and Grabb

2001; Curtis and Lambert 1976; Curtis, White, and McPherson 2000; Edwards, Edwards, and Watts 1984; Jennings and Niemi 1981; Knoke 1986; Lin 2000; Milbrath and Goel 1977; Smith 1975; Verba, Schlozman, and Brady 1995; Wilson 2000; Wilson and Musick 1997). One generalization suggested by this literature is that women are more likely to exceed men in the more time-consuming activities of informal volunteering and intensive volunteering with volunteer organizations; and they are sometimes surpassed by males in less time-consuming activities, such as nominal association memberships and voting. Also, women generally exceed men in the extent of visiting with family and neighbours and in church participation.

Research Questions

Because of the paucity of Canadian studies of early and later community activities, and the relationship between the two, we shall present available data on the topics for this county. We shall pursue the following five research questions suggested by the literature review:

1. whether the effects of extracurricular activities appear to extend to later periods in the life cycle, i.e., do effects of adolescent activities lessen or disappear with increased age of the adults (Hanks and Eckland's and Janoski and Wilson's respondents were only about fifteen years beyond the high school years; Smith's data covered a shorter period since high school; and Burns et al. did not assess the effects of time since high school)
2. whether there are effects from various forms of youth involvement in voluntary activities, extending to those undertaken outside the school system
3. whether the effects of early experiences with voluntary activities extend to adult involvement in a broad range of voluntary activities, ranging across formal and informal social involvement and across extra-family and family activities
4. whether the effects of early voluntary involvement are strong compared with effects of a broader range of social background factors
5. whether the patterns of predictors of voluntary activities involvement are similar for females and males; when judging from previous research, we might expect there to be some differences in levels of involvement in voluntary community activities both during the school years and later in adulthood.

Data Source and Method

Data Source

The data for our analyses came from the 1997 National Survey of Giving, Volunteering, and Participating (NSGVP). This survey was conducted by Statistics Canada through telephone interviews with a representative sample of Canadians aged fifteen and over. The content focus of the interviews was the three areas cited in the survey's title – giving to charities, volunteering time in the aid of organizations and individuals, and community participation. Each of these topics received several minutes of attention in the thirty-five-minute (average) interviews. The survey was especially suited to our present research purposes because it yielded a range of measures of community social participation. The survey also asked a few questions about community activities undertaken as a youth, the responses to which allow us to explore the predictive import of early participation in these activities for involvement in later adult activities. Because these questions were asked retrospectively of adults, without a panel design, we are able to avoid any possible problems of sample attrition that may be associated with social involvement levels.(For more details on the surveys, see Hall et al. 1998.)[3]

We chose as a working sub-sample from the NSGVP data file only respondents aged twenty-five and over (N = 15,912; the male component of this sub-sample was 6,823, and the females numbered 9,089). The Statistics Canada codes for the NSGVP data had placed all respondents under age twenty-four together in the same ten-year category (aged fifteen to twenty-four), at least for the coding in the public use data file. Therefore, respondents in their teens could not be separated from respondents in their early twenties. The age restriction of twenty-five and older for the working sample was chosen to assure that all respondents in our analyses had completed their schooling and were started on their work lives (whether in paid employment, household work, or both). Also, with this procedure, we could be certain that responses to the youth activities questions by each member of the working sample referred to activities from some time in the past and not to present activities. The latter, responding about current involvement as the referent for the youth activity questions, might be the case for any teenage respondent in the survey.

Measures

Our primary predictor variable was based on responses to a set of six questions asking: "As a youth during your school years did you/were you ... a participant in organized team sport?" ... "belong to a youth group?" ... "do some kind of volunteer work?" ... "go door to door to raise money?." ... "active in student government?" ... "active in religious organizations?" Two Youth Activity Indexes were constructed from the responses to these questions, where a score of one was given for each of the types of activities participated in during the school years and zero was assigned to non-participation; the scores were then summed, for each respondent. The first index, Youth Activity Index I, summed across the scores for all six types of activity, and the second, Index II, excluded sport team activity. This distinction between sport and other youth activity was made because, to anticipate our findings, it was only for sport activity that the participation rate of males was greater than that for females. Further details on the indexes and other measures used in the analyses are included in the appendix at the end of this chapter.

There were twelve alternative measures of current adult community participation as follows: volunteered informally in the community last year; volunteered for one or more organizations over the past year; total number of hours spent volunteering for organizations over the past twelve months; total number of organizations volunteered with over the past twelve months; total number of donations over the past twelve months; total amount of dollars donated to organizations over the past twelve months; total number of voluntary association memberships held last year; the number of recent elections voted in considering the last federal, provincial, and, municipal elections; an index of attention to current affairs; frequency of attendance at church services; frequency of socializing with parents and relatives; and frequency of socializing with friends outside the local neighbourhood (see appendix at end of chapter for more details). Thus, the measures cover a broad range of types of activity – across formal and informal activities, across volunteering of time and giving money, and for political, associational, and familial activities.

Social background characteristics, which we utilized as controls and predictors in portions of the analyses, were as follows: age group; marital status, presence of children in the home, language of interview, current employment status, personal income, and level of education completed. Unfortunately, no measures of ethnic background or visible minority status were available in the public use data (see appendix for more details).

Procedures

Our data analysis procedures involved comparisons of zero-order mean differences on the youth activity and adult activity measures across genders, correlations of the youth activity and adult activity measures by gender, and analyses of the relative predictive value of youth activities and other social background factors for adult activities within and across the gender subsamples. ANOVA with Multiple Classification Analysis (MCA) was used for the latter analyses.

ANOVA/MCA assesses the effects of a particular predictor variable on a dependent variable while simultaneously controlling for the effects of other factors. The procedure yields mean scores for the dependent variable for each category of the predictor variable, adjusted for the effects of the control factors and statistical interactions, and provides an F-test for statistical significance. The procedure also generates beta coefficients or partial correlation ratios for each predictor in the controlled analysis. These coefficients, when squared, roughly indicate the proportion of the total variance in the dependent variable accounted for by each predictor when partialling out the effects of the other predictors (see, e.g., Norusis 1993).

Results

Gender and Youth Community Activities

Table 6.1 shows the distribution by gender of responses to the questions on the six types of youth activities. We see that, for five of the six forms of activity, females were more likely than males to have participated some time during their school years. The exception was for organized sport, where a much larger proportion of males (about 73 percent) than females (about 56 percent) had been involved in these years. Three of the other five comparisons where females exceeded males – for involvement in youth groups, student government, and religious organizations – showed statistically significant differences (as did the differences for sport involvement). Not surprisingly, then, when responses on the activities were combined to create the two Youth Activity Indexes, one with sport activity included and the other not (see the bottom of Table 6.1), females showed significantly higher mean scores than males on each index. For females, the percentages involved in the six types of activities ranged from a high of 61 percent for youth groups, to 45-56 percent for sport, volunteer work, canvassing, and religious organizations, to a low of 19 percent for student government. The rank order of popularity of the youth activities for males was similar to that for females with the exception of the greater involvement in sport for males. The other five activities, while having lower levels of participation for males, had the same rank order of popularity.

Table 6.1

Participation in community voluntary activities as a youth, by gender, as reported by adult Canadians: national sample, 1997

Youth community activities, and youth activities index scores (N =)	Female subsample (9,089)	Male subsample (6,823)	Statistical significance of gender differences
Youth groups	61.2%	54.0%	***
Organized sports	55.5%	72.5%	***
Volunteer work	47.2%	45.8%	
Door-to-door canvassing	48.3%	47.1%	
Student government	19.3%	17.9%	*
Religious organizations	45.2%	32.6%	***
Youth Activities Index I	2.78	2.70	*
Youth Activities Index II	2.21	1.97	***

NOTE: (N =) means the smallest N for any of the analyses in the table. Index I is the mean number of youth community activities including organized sports (range = 0 to 6). Index II is the mean number of youth community activities excluding organized sports (range = 0 to 5).
$^*p \leq .05$; $^{**}p \leq .01$; $^{***}p \leq .001$.

Table 6.2

Participation in community voluntary activities as a youth, by gender, for age cohorts among adult respondents

Age cohorts	(N =)	Female subsample (9,089)	Male subsample (6,823)	Statistical significance of gender differences
SCORES ON YOUTH ACTIVITY INDEX I				
25-34 years old	(2,070/1,517)	3.08	2.94	*
35-44	(2,309/1,895)	3.00	2.78	***
45-54	(1,546/1,282)	2.91	2.85	
55-64	(1,161/917)	2.58	2.52	
65+	(1,843/1,066)	2.11	2.18	
SCORES ON YOUTH ACTIVITY INDEX II				
25-34 years old	(2,070/1,518)	2.42	2.13	***
35-44	(2,309/1,895)	2.37	2.02	***
45-54	(1,546/1,282)	2.36	2.12	***
55-64	(1,161/917)	2.09	1.84	***
65+	(1,843/1,067)	1.73	1.61	*

NOTE: See note to Table 6.1.

In Table 6.2 we look at gender differences across ten-year age cohorts ranging upward from age twenty-five to thirty-four to age sixty-five and older. We wondered whether there would be any suggestion from such analyses that the phenomenon of greater community involvement of females was a more recent occurrence, whether males who grew up in earlier decades had involvement levels more similar to those of females, or had an advantage over them then. The results in Table 6.2 do not suggest these patterns at all. To simplify the analyses, Table 6.2 includes only results for the two Youth Activity Indexes and not for the six individual components of the indexes. (Further analyses for the individual activities taken separately showed similar patterns to those in Table 6.2.) The table shows females to have been more active than males for all age categories except for age sixty-five and older for the index with sport team participation included (Index I). However, only the first two age cohorts showed statistically significant gender differences. For Index II, with sport activity excluded, all gender comparisons showed statistically significant greater female involvement.[4]

Turning to the comparisons across age categories for each gender, we find that the results are not consistent with the proposition that there may have been some decline recently in the amount of voluntary community participation. For both genders and both Youth Activity Indexes, we see that the older the respondent (representing progressively earlier periods for the growing up years) the less the youth activities. The relationships of youth activities with the age categories are inverse linear relationships in all instances (all $p \leq .001$).

Probably, we should view these latter temporal comparisons with some caution because, as we suggested earlier, to some extent, older respondents may not remember as well their youth activities and may under-report them. However, calling into question this interpretation is the fact that, for some of the specific school-years activities, in particular, for religious group involvement, there was a steady *increase* for increasingly older respondents, for both females and males. This is precisely the pattern that we would expect from evidence of declining religious group activity in studies comparing cross-sectional sample surveys from different points in time (e.g., Bibby 1994). These studies show that participation in religious services has steadily declined over the past several decades. Also, our NSGVP results showed no particular trend in involvement in youth groups over the age cohorts for either gender. (For more details on the patterns for individual types of youth activities over age cohorts in English Canada and Quebec, see Curtis, Baer, Grabb, and Perks 2003.)

To summarize, the set of results for youth activities suggest that: (1) girls have been either as active or more active than are boys, for five of the six types of activity, and this has been true over the decades; (2) boys have been more active in the one form of activity, sport involvement; and (3) involvement in most youth activities (religious and youth groups excepted) has increased for both genders over time.

Gender and Adult Community Involvement

Do similar patterns by gender – with greater activity by females – extend to community activity in adulthood? This is the question addressed in Tables 6.3 and 6.4.

Table 6.3 reports on levels of current participation in community activities for twelve measures. In only one instance, attending to current affairs, do males significantly exceed females in involvement. For six activities, females are significantly more involved – formal volunteering, informal volunteering, number of organizations given volunteer help, number of donations, level of church attendance, and socializing with parents and relatives. For the remaining five activities, women and men had similar levels of involvement.

TABLE 6.3

Levels of current participation in community activities, by gender, among adult respondents

Current community activities (N =)	Female subsample (9,089)	Male subsample (6,823)	Statistical significance of gender differences
Who did formal volunteering? (%)	63.5	58.2	***
Who did informal volunteering? (%)	82.3	79.1	***
Hours of volunteering (0-max.)	91.09	93.59	
No. of organizations volunteered with (0-20)	1.17	1.04	***
No. of donations (0-51)	4.68	4.02	***
Amount of donations ($0-max.)	$279.14	$287.64	
No. of current association memberships (0-7)	0.91	0.92	
Voting over three elections (0-3)	2.32	2.30	
Attention to current affairs (3-12)	10.56	10.87	***
Church attendance (1-5)	3.47	3.22	***
How often socialize with relatives? (1-4)	3.32	3.19	***
How often socialize with friends? (1-4)	3.00	2.99	

NOTE: (N =) means the smallest N for any of the analyses.
Parentheses in rows give ranges of scores for activity measures; see the text for further details.
*$p \leq .05$; **$p \leq .01$, ***$p \leq .001$.

Table 6.3 shows that, within each gender, a large majority had done some formal and informal volunteering one or more times during the past year; the volunteer hours averaged a little over ninety hours for the year; the volunteering was done for an average of a little over one volunteer organization; an average of four to five donations were given in the year, with the total amounts being nearly $300; about one voluntary association membership on average was reported; high levels of voting over three types of elections were reported; similar high rates of keeping track of current affairs were cited; and there were modest levels of church attendance and visiting with relatives and friends.

Table 6.4 shows that the same patterns by gender tended to hold across age cohorts, although only some of the gender differences were statistically significant because of the smaller subsample sizes for the age sub-categories. The one exception to the pattern among the significant differences is that males sixty-five and over reported more current voting than their female age peers. Females were more active in donations and gave their volunteer time to more organizations. Also, for all age categories, including the oldest, females were more active in church organizations and in visiting with parents and relatives. As in the overall gender comparisons, males in all age categories were more likely to report attention to current affairs.

Considering the patterns by age levels in Table 6.4, we see that there is no common relationship across types of activities, but the relationships for any particular activity are similar across genders. First, there are *curvilinear* relationships whereby activity increases from the younger age category to middle age and then declines in the older age categories. Such relationships occur for hours volunteered, number of volunteering organizations, and number of association memberships (all $p \leq .001$). These activities have in common that they require attendance outside the home in formal voluntary organizations. Second, *positive linear* relationships occur for amount of donations, voting, attending to current affairs, and church attendance. The first two activities require very little time commitment over the year, and attending to current affairs may be done at home through the media. Only frequent church attendance requires regular activity outside the home. The third pattern is a *negative linear* relationship whereby activity declines with age. Visiting with parents and relatives and visiting with friends show this pattern.

Effects of Youth Activities upon Adult Involvement

In Table 6.5, we turn to the question of the influence of early community activity during the school years upon later activity during adulthood. The

TABLE 6.4

Current participation in selected community activities, by gender, for age cohorts among adult Canadians

Dependent measures and age cohorts (N =)	Female subsample (9,089)	Male subsample (6,823)	Statistical significance of gender differences
HOURS OF VOLUNTEERING			
25-34 years old	71.62	77.95	
35-44	93.27	93.90	
45-54	104.84	102.65	
55-64	97.65	96.34	
65+	94.47	101.77	
NO. OF ORGANIZATIONS VOLUNTEERED WITH			
25-34 years old	1.05	.94	**
35-44	1.43	1.17	***
45-54	1.31	1.15	**
55-64	1.12	1.01	*
65+	.89	.84	
NO. OF DONATIONS			
25-34 years old	3.72	3.14	***
35-44	4.87	4.01	***
45-54	5.20	4.39	***
55-64	5.22	4.40	***
65+	4.71	4.48	
AMOUNT OF DONATIONS			
25-34 years old	153.90	172.20	
35-44	249.80	258.90	
45-54	334.14	312.24	
55-64	336.58	341.06	
65+	372.60	424.37	
NO. OF CURRENT ASSOCIATION MEMBERSHIPS			
25-34 years old	.72	.72	
35-44	.96	.93	
45-54	1.03	1.08	
55-64	1.00	1.01	
65+	.91	.92	
VOTING OVER THREE ELECTIONS			
25-34 years old	1.97	1.90	
35-44	2.30	2.24	
45-54	2.42	2.39	
55-64	2.53	2.59	
65+	2.51	2.61	**

▶

◀ TABLE 6.4

Dependent measures and age cohorts	(N =)	Female subsample (9,089)	Male subsample (6,823)	Statistical significance of gender differences
ATTENTION TO CURRENT AFFAIRS				
25-34 years old		9.68	10.23	***
35-44		10.41	10.74	***
45-54		10.82	11.02	**
55-64		11.16	11.40	**
65+		11.12	11.34	**
CHURCH ATTENDANCE				
25-34 years old		3.05	2.87	**
35-44		3.23	3.09	**
45-54		3.46	3.06	***
55-64		3.77	3.47	***
65+		3.97	3.78	**
SOCIALIZING WITH RELATIVES				
25-34 years old		3.44	3.35	***
35-44		3.31	3.16	***
45-54		3.24	3.09	***
55-64		3.35	3.16	***
65+		3.23	3.13	**
SOCIALIZING WITH FRIENDS				
25-34 years old		3.18	3.22	
35-44		3.01	3.01	
45-54		2.96	2.94	
55-64		2.99	2.89	*
65+		2.81	2.79	

NOTE: (N =) means the smallest N for any of the analyses.
*p ≤ .05; **p ≤ .01, ***p ≤ .001

table shows, for each gender, the correlations of the levels of involvement in the twelve measures of adult activities and scores on Youth Activity Index II. The results for the other Youth Activity Index were very much the same, so, to conserve space, they are not added to the tables. Table 6A.1 shows the same type of results separately for each age cohort.

Every correlation in Table 6.5 and in Table 6A.1 is positive and statistically significant except that for socializing with parents and relatives among males aged thirty-five to forty-four. Those involved in youth activities were more likely to be involved in the various adult activities, compared with those who were less active as youths. The pattern held throughout the separate social subgroups defined by gender and age (Table 6.A1). The correlations are quite modest in strength; they range, for example, in the overall subsample, from about .10 for socializing with relatives to about .30 for formal and informal volunteering, number of donations, number of volunteering organizations, and number of voluntary association memberships. Nonetheless, all the correlations are positive and statistically significant, except for the one just mentioned.

What is most remarkable about these correlations is that they do not appear to weaken over the life cycle. The apparent effect of early activity of youth upon current adult activity is not weaker for the older age cohorts than for the younger cohorts. The effect, for each form of adult activity, is as strong among adults fifty-five to sixty-four and sixty-five and over as it is for adults twenty-five to thirty-four, and for both genders. The results suggest the following proposition: the more involved one is in one's youth, the greater the likelihood of one's involvement as an adult, throughout the lifetime for both genders.

TABLE 6.5

Zero-order correlations of participation in community voluntary activities as a youth (Index II) and current participation in community activities, by gender

Measures of current participation as an adult	Female subsample ($N = 9{,}089$)	Male subsample ($N = 6{,}823$)
Formal volunteering	.26 ***	.30 ***
Informal volunteering	.25 ***	.27 ***
Hours of volunteering	.13 ***	.18 ***
No. of organizations volunteered with	.29 ***	.30 ***
No. of donations	.30 ***	.29 ***
Amount of donations	.12 ***	.15 ***
No. of current association memberships	.31 ***	.31 ***
Voting over three elections	.11 ***	.11 ***
Attention to current affairs	.10 ***	.13 ***
Church attendance	.10 ***	.14 ***
Socializing with relatives	.10 ***	.08 ***
Socializing with friends	.16 ***	.14 ***

*$p \leq .05$; **$p \leq .01$; ***$p \leq .001$.

Relative Effects of Youth Activities, Socioeconomic Status, and Other Social Background Factors

In Table 6.6, we consider further the issue of the effects of youth experiences upon adult activities. Here, we ask how strong is the effect of early youth activities upon later adult activities compared to the effects of other social background factors that are said in the literature to be important predictors of adult participation levels. With the present data source, we are able to explore in multivariate analyses the comparative effects of youth activity, age, marital status, children at home, language group, education level, employment status, and personal income level. The analyses in Table 6.6 also tell us whether the effects of youth involvement in community activities are statistically significant once we take into account the conjoint effects of the other social background factors. Table 6.6, once again, deals only with Youth Activity Index II, because both indexes showed the same patterns of results. The figures in the table are beta coefficients from ANOVA/MCA, which show the relative effect of each predictor of the dependent measure.

In Table 6.6, it is interesting that, for almost all measures of adult current activity, the predictive value of youth activities is greater than that for the other social background factors. Consider, for example, the first row of the table with results for the female subsample where Youth Activity Index II has a beta of .22 as a predictor of being a formal volunteer. While all the other social background factors are statistically significant predictors of formal volunteering, the betas are considerably smaller for these other factors than for the Youth Activity Index. The other betas range from .13 and .10 for education level and income down to .04 and .05 for marital status, language group, and employment status.

The same sort of pattern persists elsewhere in Table 6.6 for other forms of current community activity, for both female respondents and male respondents, and for all age cohorts. Youth activity is generally the best predictor of adult current social activities, however the latter is measured. The other social background factors, while statistically significant predictors, have weaker relationships with the adult activity measures throughout the analyses in the table. Thus, we find that early experience with voluntary community activity is a stronger predictor of current activity than current socioeconomic status (using the respondent's education level, income level, or employment status as indicators of socioeconomic status). Youth experience is also a stronger predictor than is the ascribed social characteristic of language group membership and age or the family status characteristics of marital status and children at home.

TABLE 6.6

Relative effects (betas from MCA/ANOVA) for participation in community activities as a youth (Index II) and seven other social background factors as predictors of current participation in community activities, for females and males

	Youth Activity Index II	Age	Marital status	Child in home	Language	Education	Employment status	Income	R^2
FOR THE FEMALE SUBSAMPLE									
Formal volunteering	.17***	.09***	.05***	.05***	.07***	.15***	.07***	.04**	.12
Informal volunteering	.20***	.11***	.04***	.04*	.03*	.04*	.03*	.03	.11
Hours of volunteering	.14***	.09***	.02	.02	.00	.09***	.07***	.01	.04
No. of organizations volunteered with	.21***	.13***	.03*	.10***	.09***	.17***	.06***	.03	.15
No. of donations	.23***	.29***	.16***	.06***	.08***	.12***	.03*	.17***	.21
Amount of donations	.08***	.21***	.05***	.05**	.08***	.12***	.05***	.15***	.08
No. of current association memberships	.25***	.25***	.04***	.07***	.02	.21***	.06***	.11***	.19
Voting over three elections	.13***	.33***	.11***	.04**	.15***	.08***	.05***	.07***	.11
Attention to current affairs	.11***	.27***	.06***	.04**	.06***	.10***	.03	.06***	.10
Church attendance	.15***	.32***	.05***	.09***	.05***	.05**	.03*	.04**	.09
Socializing with relatives	.06***	.10***	.08***	.02	.16***	.10***	.02	.04**	.07
Socializing with friends	.10***	.14***	.04**	.05***	.10***	.02	.02	.03	.06

▲

▼ TABLE 6.6

	Predictors							
	Youth Activity Index II	Age	Marital status	Child in home	Language	Education	Employment status	Income	R^2
FOR THE MALE SUBSAMPLE									
Formal volunteering	.22***	.07***	.05**	.08***	.05***	.13***	.04*	.10***	.15
Informal volunteering	.24***	.06***	.07***	.02	.04***	.01	.04**	.06**	.11
Hours of volunteering	.14***	.08***	.02	.04**	.01	.11***	.05**	.03	.05
No. of organizations volunteered with	.23***	.07***	.04*	.08***	.05***	.17***	.04*	.07***	.14
No. of donations	.22***	.24***	.13***	.04*	.07***	.09***	.03	.20***	.21
Amount of donations	.12***	.20***	.00	.03*	.09***	.08***	.05*	.18***	.10
No. of current association memberships	.23***	.18***	.06***	.01	.03*	.18***	.04**	.15***	.18
Voting over three elections	.10***	.31***	.10***	.01	.13***	.08***	.05*	.08***	.13
Attention to current affairs	.11***	.23***	.07***	.01	.07***	.08***	.02	.07***	.09
Church attendance	.16***	.27***	.11***	.08***	.07***	.07***	.03	.04	.11
Socializing with relatives	.06**	.11***	.12***	.02	.15***	.09***	.03	.05**	.07
Socializing with friends	.10***	.15***	.04*	.06***	.12***	.02	.01	.05*	.07

*$p \le .05$; **$p \le .01$, ***$p \le .001$

The detailed patterns of results for the various predictors of current activity could not be readily presented in the table without its becoming very large, but we can briefly summarize the patterns in the text here. As would be expected from previous studies, there was generally more current community activity if the respondent was: (1) middle-aged rather than elderly or younger (see also Table 6.4), (2) married rather than single or widowed/divorced, (3) living with children at home rather than not, (4) English-speaking rather than French-speaking, (5) higher in education, (6) full-time employed rather than part-time employed or not employed, and (7) higher in income.

The R^2 statistics, on the right-hand side of Table 6.6, show the extent to which the forms of adult activities are explained by youth activity and the other background factors. Of course, the higher the R^2, the more is total variance explained in adult activity by the set of predictors. Furthermore, the betas for youth activity suggest the amount of variance explained by youth activities alone (beta squared roughly equals the proportion of variance explained by the one predictor when others are controlled). As the table shows, some of the adult activities – formal volunteering, number of donations, number of organizations volunteered with, number of voluntary association memberships, and voting – are better predicted by the eight factors than are others of the adult activities. The total variance explained ranged from 21 percent for number of donations for both men and women, to 14 percent to 19 percent for number of volunteer organizations and number of voluntary association memberships, to 6 percent and 7 percent for socializing with relatives and friends.

It is appropriate to cautiously view the R^2 statistic as telling us how "socially structured" by the social background factors is a particular form of adult community activity. Seen in this way, the different forms of adult activity are differentially structured by social background factors. We see that the formal social activities in the wider community are more highly structured, compared with the more "informal" activities of interaction with relatives and interaction with friends. Yet, in all instances, the proportion of the structuring due to experience with youth activities is comparatively high.

The variance explained (beta squared) by youth activities, for females, ranges from about 6 percent for number of association memberships, to about 5 percent for number of donations, to 4 percent for number of organizations volunteered for and informal volunteering, to somewhat less for formal volunteering and church attendance, to less than 1 percent for the other dependent measures. The strengths of the relationships for males were as strong or stronger in all instances except for number of current association memberships and voting, where R^2 was slightly smaller than for females.

In analyses not presented in the tables, we looked at increases in levels of current activities across the detailed categories on the Youth Activity Index II after controls for the effects of the other social background factors. We found that, with each increase in the number of youth activities, ranging from no youth activities up to involvement in all five youth activities, there was a steady increase in current activity. For each adult activity, for both females and males, there was a linear relationship between the amount of community involvement as a youth and the amount of current adult community involvement. As suggested by Table 6.6, all the relationships for both genders were statistically significant ($p < .01$).

A similar pattern of comparatively strong effects of early activities upon later activities held in controlled analyses conducted separately for each of the age cohorts (data not presented in the tables). The relationships of early activities and later activities were always positive, nearly always linear, and generally statistically significant ($p < .05$ in all except three instances for those twenty-five to thirty-four, thirty-five to forty four, forty-five to fifty-four, and fifty-five to sixty-four). Thus, as with Table 6.4 before controls, the effects were consistent across young adults, for whom the youth activities were more recent, and older cohorts further removed from their youth activities.

Gender and Effects of Early Experience with Community Activities

We conclude the analyses with Table 6.7, where, using the merged subsamples of females and males, we ask how the gender differences in adult activities are affected by the differential early experiences by gender with community activities. The table shows how gender differences, where there were any, change under conditions of controls for: (1) early youth activities only, (2) the other seven social background factors only, and (3) all eight social background characteristics including youth activities.

The table shows that the differences between women and men in levels of involvement in some activities tend to become more marked once the effects of sociodemographic background factors are taken into account. This is true of the number of volunteer organizations joined or helped, the number of donations, the amount of donations, and, to some extent, voting. The other dependent measures show little change in the gender gradient after controls. What this indicates, for those activities with change, is that the distribution of background factors (particularly marital status, children at home,

TABLE 6.7

Levels of current participation in community activities (deviations from the grand mean), by gender, with statistical controls (MCA) for youth activities and seven social background factors

Dependent measures	Grand mean	None Female	None Male	Youth activities Female	Youth activities Male	Other factors Female	Other factors Male	All factors Female	All factors Male
Hours of volunteering	92.97	−1.06	1.42	−2.52	3.37	−3.00	4.00*	−4.92	6.58**
No. of organizations volunteered with	1.12	.06	−.08***	.05	−.06	.07	−.10***	.05	−.07***
No. of donations	4.42	.28	−.38***	.24	−.32***	.53	−.71***	.48	−.64***
Amount of donations	284.25	−4.00	5.36	−12.93	17.31*	23.41	−31.21***	15.53	−20.78**
No. of current voluntary organization memberships	.92	.00	.01	.03	−.02**	.05	−.06***	.02	−.03**
Voting over three elections	2.31	.01	−.01	.00	.00	.04	−.06***	.03	−.05***
Attention to current affairs	10.69	−.13	.17***	−.14	.19***	−.08	.11***	−.09	.12***
Church attendance	3.37	.10	−.15***	.07	−.10***	.09	−.13***	.06	−.09***
Socializing with relatives	3.26	.05	−.07***	.06	−.08***	.07	−.09***	.06	−.08***
Socializing with friends	3.00	.00	.00	.00	−.01	.01	−.01	.01	−.01

NOTE: "Other factors" are age, marital status, children at home or not, language group, education level, employment status, and income level. "All factors" are these other factors plus youth activities.
*$p \leq .05$; **$p \leq .01$; ***$p \leq .001$.

employment, and income) across the genders disadvantages women more than it does men for social participation. When these disadvantages are taken into account through controls, women are even more involved than men (see Burns, Schlozman, and Verba 2001, Chapter 10, for some similar results for political activity levels).

We might think that males would be handicapped in preparation for adult involvement, compared with females, because males have somewhat fewer youth experiences with involvement than females. However, the results (comparing across the uncontrolled and controlled analyses in Table 6.7) suggest that having fewer youth experiences does not tend to lessen adult involvement among men to the same extent that having differences from men on the other social background characteristics hinders women. We emphasize, though, that such patterns occur for only a few of the adult activities. For the other activities, the gender differences do not vary, particularly when the results are compared without and with controls.[5]

Discussion

The results of this study support the general proposition that early youth experience with community involvement predicts later adult community involvement. These results extend across women and men, but there are enough gender differences in other respects to warrant separate analyses by gender, or analyses of gender interactions, in future research on this topic.

To recapitulate, the results are as follows: Females exceed males in five of the six forms of youth community involvement, with sport activities being the only exception. Further, adult women are more involved in some current community activities than are men and are equal to adult men in all other forms of current activities except one – following current affairs – where men exceed women. The patterns by gender hold across comparisons for ten-year age cohorts, ranging from age twenty-five to thirty-four up to age fifty-five to sixty-four. Also, in multivariate analyses, experiences with youth activities is a stronger predictor of adult participation levels, compared with seven other social background factors, for each gender. Interestingly, early experience with voluntary activities predicts adult levels of community involvement over the various age cohorts, even into the older age cohorts. In other words, among women and men, early community involvement in the school years still predicts adult community activity decades later. Finally, social background predictors of adult participation are similar for females and males, and the different levels of experiences with youth activities across girls and boys appear to have small consequences for gender differences in current activities.

How should we interpret the evidence of effects of early community involvement? The effects certainly are consistent with the notion that social capital and/or cultural capital have been acquired in early involvement and that this has "paid off" later in adult activities. In other words, the results are consistent with the early interpretations of Hanks and Eckland (1978) for their similar, if less detailed, findings from years ago. Of course, the present results take us well beyond those of Hanks and Eckland, showing the generality of the results in various respects – the results appear to extend to comparisons over age cohorts and genders to a broader range of measures of youth activities and of adult activities, and to a contemporary national Canadian sample.

Our results are also consistent with views on the nature of social and cultural capital put forward by others since Hanks and Eckland's research. That is to say, as social and cultural capital theories suggest, the appropriate explanation may have to do with (a) skills or attitude orientations acquired in early involvement; (b) social contacts or social networks accessed through early involvement; or (c) orientations toward social rewards, or motivations, acquired from prior participation in community activity; (d) some combination of these (cf., e.g., Putnam 2000; Portes 1998). The patterns of our results are consistent with each of these avenues of interpretation.

Rewards and motivations acquired in early involvement may well be an especially important part of the explanation for the links between early and later community involvement. This theoretical interpretation may be found, too, in research on the community activity of elderly people. "Continuity theory," which emerged from such studies, argues that social activities, once started, are likely to be continued as long as: (1) they remain rewarding, (2) opportunities for participation are readily available, and (3) competing activities that are equally or more rewarding do not interfere with the activity in question. (This theory also pre-dates much of the development of social capital theory; for reviews, see, e.g., Atchley 1983, 1989; McPherson 1983.) As individuals age, it is argued, they strive to maintain some aspects of their leisure lifestyles because these activities continue to be rewarding and therefore are valued. The theory is normally applied to people as they move from middle to later ages, but there is little reason to suppose that the explanation would not be equally applicable to the transition from youth to adulthood. Still other psychological theorists have argued that key identities among adults are often acquired early in the life cycle through processes of imitation, social participation, and reinforcement through social interaction with others (e.g., see Bandura 1969; Bandura and Walters 1963; Csikszentmihalyi 1997). Identities acquired in this way are believed to be continually rewarded over the life cycle and to be rather persistent and resistant to change. For each of these reasons, too – continuance of rewarded activities and enduring identities – we might expect people involved in voluntary social activities early in their lives to be more involved in such activities later, compared with those without the early experiences. Presumably, these explanatory mechanisms reinforce links of early and later involvement, particularly where the above three conditions specified by continuity theory are met. Sometimes, current discussion of motivations and rewards by some "social capital" researchers echo these earlier arguments from continuity theory and psychological reinforcement theory.

We would be remiss if we did not point to yet another viable interpretation of the patterns of results for early and later involvement. Selectivity of personality characteristics may help account for the relationships. It may be that people who, as youths, are more attracted to engagement in social activities are more likely to get involved in early voluntary activities. Assuming there is considerable constancy in personality characteristics over the life course, this may be one of the reasons that it is many of the same people who are more likely to get involved early and later on in life. What types of personalities might get more involved at both stages in life? Perhaps it is those who are more gregarious and outgoing, more other-directed, more altruistic, or more prone to risk-taking (Hanks and Eckland suggested it was more achievement-oriented individuals, perhaps because they were studying activities and respondents based in the school system.) Certainly, we might expect extroverts to become more involved than introverts at both points in the life cycle. In other words, what appears to be the result of socialization to voluntary organizations or social capital accumulation through experiences in voluntary organizations may be, at least in part, selective recruitment of types of people to such organizations, both when they are young and at later stages in their lives (for parallel results and interpretations for the continuance of sport activity, see Curtis, McTeer, and White 1999). Of course, it is also possible that *both* selective recruitment of personalities and processes of social capital acquisition occur for voluntary activities.

If selectivity of personalities is involved as an explanation of the link between early and later activities, we would still need to ask what social circumstances lead to the development of types of personalities that seek to be more active, and how early socialization and early accumulation of social and cultural capital may be implicated in the development of the personalities. Moreover, if the key phenomenon is recruitment of personalities, it is intriguing to note that the results suggest that the relevant personality characteristics are at least as common among females as males and probably more so.

Assuming that females are somewhat more involved than are males, both in the school years and later as adults, why does this occur? Any of the explanatory mechanisms mentioned above may be patterned by gender in such a way that the attraction of voluntary community activities is greater for females than for males. For example, as we have just suggested, the relevant personality characteristics for community involvement may turn out to be somewhat more common among females. If so, this difference likely would be a result, in part, of differential socialization and experiences in the family, school systems, and wider community.

Another explanation warranting consideration is that alternative opportunities to engage in rewarding voluntary activity may be more readily available to females than to males. At least, this may have occurred for the types of activities making up the Youth Activity Index. Youth sport activity, however, is no doubt contrary to this pattern. For sport participation, opportunities have been much more readily available to boys than to girls. This likely accounts in large part for the greater involvement of boys than girls that we observed for this type of activity across the age cohorts (cf., e.g., Curtis, McTeer, and White 1999 for further analyses and a review of the literature on greater opportunities for males than for females).

The availability of competing rewarding activities may be at issue in a different way for some of the other gender differences in youth. If males are more attracted to sport activities and various other leisure activities not in the Youth Activity Index, and if these activities are readily available, they may successfully compete with activities in the Index for boys; the other activities may draw males away from the Index activities. Females, on the other hand, may have fewer attractive activities available to them beyond the types of activities in the Index. We should also remember that the previous non-Canadian literature shows inconsistent patterns of no gender differences in early voluntary activity involvement (e.g., Hanks and Eckland 1978; Janoski and Wilson 1995) and greater involvement by males or females depending on the activity considered (e.g., Burns, Schlozman, and Verba 2001; van

Roosmalen and Krahn 1996). One of the pressing needs in further data-gathering is clear and extensive mapping of the activity patterns among recent and current adolescents in Canada.

Turning to gender differences in adult activities, we find that the full range of explanations discussed above – social and cultural capital accumulation, differential opportunity structures, different socialization, and personality differences – are candidates for explanations for these differences too. As we said earlier in conjunction with Table 6.7, in the case of four particular adult activities – number of volunteer organizations pursued, number of donations, amount of donations, and voting – comparisons of the controlled and uncontrolled analyses suggest that, in their activity, females are more hindered by social background characteristics than are males. When women and men were "made similar" in terms of the social background factors, through controls, the females' levels of activity more greatly exceeded the male levels. In other words, married status and having children at home, because of the greater time commitments to home activities among females, probably means greater restraints on voluntary activity for women than for men. Also, when men have greater economic resources by virtue of their being more fully employed and with a higher income (and sometimes with higher educational status), this also increases advantages for voluntary involvement for men. The social background controls in Table 6.7 hold constant these advantages/disadvantages for involvement, and, in this circumstance, as we would expect, the activity levels of women increase relative to those of men.

Obviously, there remains much work to be done on our research questions before firm explanations can be nailed down. This is evident when we begin to contemplate the range of explanations, all possible or viable, as we have just done. Unfortunately, the design of the NSGVP survey, with its lack of details on behavioural and attitudinal correlates of early involvement and the lack of panel study data gathered over the respondent's life cycle, does not allow us to pinpoint the specific factors that account for the patterns of early and later involvement. To properly test the selectivity interpretation versus the socialization and social capital accumulation interpretations will require costly and time-consuming panel studies that follow cohorts of people, starting when they are children, over several decades of their lives, with detailed psychological, attitudinal, and activity measurements performed at several points in time during the life cycle. Unfortunately, we are many years away from having such data available for Canadian society because relevant studies are not yet under way and because a lengthy period is required for generating the requisite data. The common type of data source available for Canada is exemplified by the NSGVP, or the surveys recently mounted by the Equality, Security, and Community Project (ESC) and discussed elsewhere in this volume. These studies provide some detail on types of social involvements and some information on attitudes and beliefs at a particular point in the respondent's life. However, the respondents have not been, and probably will not be, followed over time as they age. Occasionally, the surveys have a few retrospective questions on earlier involvement, as with the NSGVP, but generally they do not (e.g., the ESC surveys have no such questions). This means that whatever measures there are for beliefs, motives, and behaviours are all made at about the same time in the respondent's life. Thus, whether current voluntary behaviours are caused by current beliefs and motivations, or the reverse, or whether they reciprocally influence each other, will remain unclear. We require ambitious panel studies, with low rates of attrition, to be able to better address the issue of causality and establish the causal order of variables. In the meantime, the present study of retrospective measures strongly suggests that important patterns of effects occur from early involvement. Therefore, it would be advisable to continue to monitor these patterns in this way while we await panel study data allowing better tests of alternative interpretations.

Before concluding, we should return to an interesting implication of the results on youth activities over the age cohorts. For both genders, the results suggested that voluntary activity as a youth has been on the increase over time. The younger the respondent (or the more recent their youth years), the more activity was reported. Persons twenty-five to thirty-four would have turned fifteen in the period 1980 to 1990; those thirty-five to forty-four would have turned fifteen during 1970 to 1980; those forty-five to fifty-four, during 1960 to 1970; and those fifty-five to sixty-four, during 1950 to 1960. As Table 6.2 showed, an increase in activity for each more recent cohort was true of both Youth Activity Indexes for both genders. In further analyses not reported in the tables, this pattern held for each separate type of youth activity in the indexes except for religious activity (where we see the expected steady decline with each newer age cohort) and youth groups (there was little change over the cohorts).

These findings directly contradict Putnam's conclusion that voluntary association activity has declined over recent years in the United States, at least among adults eighteen and older (2000, Chapters 3 and 7). It is true that Putnam's conclusion has been disputed by Rotolo (1999) and Paxton (1999), who re-analyzed Putnam's original data source and found no clear decline after appropriate controls. Yet, Putnam's theory of decline – his thesis that people are increasingly "bowling alone" – has captured the attention of researchers and policy makers. Many have lamented the possibility that Americans (and perhaps Canadians) are becoming less involved in society. Our present results suggest just the opposite, at least for Canadian youth. We have also shown elsewhere (Curtis, Baer, and Grabb 2001; Curtis, Baer, Grabb, and Perks 2003) that comparisons of cross-sectional survey data for Canadian adults for 1981 and 1991 show either small increases or constancy in levels of voluntary association activity. The results of that study and of the present analysis give little reason for alarm about declining associational activity. Instead, the evidence that youth activity seems to be a good predictor of adult activity, and the fact that the former appears to be on the rise, give us reason for optimism about levels of adult involvement in the future.

APPENDIX: MEASURES USED IN THE ANALYSIS

Youth Activities
Respondents were asked whether they did any of the following activities when they were in grade school or high school:

1. Youth groups: "Did you belong to a youth group (such as Guides, Scouts, a 4H Club, a choir)?"
2. Organized sports: "Did you participate in an organized team sport (such as a baseball league, hockey league, etc.)?"
3. Volunteer work: "Did you do some kind of volunteer work?"
4. Door-to-door canvassing: "Did you go door to door to raise money for a cause or organization?"
5. Student government: "Were you active in student government?"
6. Religious organizations: "Were you active in a religious organization?"

Youth Activity Index I
A score of one was given for each "yes" answer to the above six questions, and zero was assigned to each "no" answer. The scores were then summed for each respondent. The index ranged from 0 to 6.

Youth Activity Index II

The sum of the "yes" answers for each of the above types of youth activity, excluding sport team activity. The index ranged from 0 to 5.

Adult Community Involvement

Volunteered Informally

Respondents who answered "yes" to having helped others outside the home, independent of an organization with any one or more of the following activities in the past twelve months: "housework; yard or maintenance work; shopping or driving others; providing care or support to the sick or elderly; visiting the sick or elderly; babysitting without pay; write letters, solve problems, find information or fill out forms for others; unpaid teaching or coaching; helping someone in operating a business or farm work; help in any other way."

Volunteered for Organizations

Respondents who answered "yes" to having volunteered in any one or more of the following ways *through an organization* in the past twelve months: "canvassing, campaigning, or fundraising; as a member of a board or committee; helping educate, influence public opinion, or lobby others; consulting, executive, office or administrative work; teach or coach; provide care or support; provide health care; as a member of a self-help group; collect, serve, or deliver food or other goods; maintain, repair, or build facilities; help with first-aid, fire fighting, or search and rescue; activities aimed at protecting the environment or wildlife; in any other way not mentioned yet."

Hours of Volunteering

The sum of all hours reported for volunteering in organizations in the past twelve months.

Number of Volunteer Organizations

"For how many organizations did you volunteer in the past twelve months?"

Number of Donations

Based on responses to a set of questions that determined the number of donations given over the past year in each of the following ways: "responding to a request through the mail; to attend a charity event; using payroll deductions; sponsoring someone in an event; made 'in memoriam'; when asked by someone at work; someone doing door-to-door canvassing; someone canvassing for a charitable donation at a shopping centre or street corner; responding to a telephone request; through collection at a place of worship; responding to a television or radio request;

approaching a non-profit or charitable organization on your own; made in any other ways." The measure recorded the sum across all these forms of donation, for a range of 0 to 51.

Amount of Donations
This was the sum of the amounts of money given in the past twelve months in response to various questions on donations.

Number of Current Association Memberships
The number of voluntary association memberships currently held was reported in response to a set of questions asking about current membership in: "a service club or fraternal association; a political organization; a cultural, education, or hobby organization; a religious affiliated group; a neighbourhood, civic, or community association or school group; any other organization." The measure ranged from 0 (for no membership) to 7.

Voting over Three Elections
The measure was based on responses to three questions that asked: "Did you vote in the last federal election?" "Did you vote in the last provincial election?" and "Did you vote in the last municipal election?" Each affirmative answer was given a score of one, and the scores were summed, for a range of 0 to 3.

Attention to Current Affairs
Attention to current affairs was based on three questions that asked: "How frequently do you follow news and current affairs that are local and regional?" "How frequently do you follow news and current affairs that are national?" and "How frequently do you follow news and current affairs that are international?" Responses to each were coded as: rarely or never = 1; several times each month = 2; several times each week = 3; and daily = 4. Then the responses to the three questions were summed, for a range of 3 to 12.

Church Attendance
"Other than on special occasions (such as weddings, funerals, or baptisms), how often have you attended religious services or meetings in the past 12 months?" The responses were coded: not at all = 1; only once or twice = 2; at least 3 or 4 times = 3; at least once a month = 4; at least once a week = 5.

Socialize with Relatives
"Please tell me whether you do the following activities every week, a few times a month, a few times a year, or not at all. How frequently do you socialize with parents

or other relatives?" The responses were coded: not at all = 1; a few times a year = 2; a few times a month = 3; every week = 4.

Socialize with Friends

"Please tell me whether you do the following activities every week, a few times a month, a few times a year, or not at all. How frequently do you socialize with friends who live outside the neighbourhood?" The responses and codes were the same as for "socialize with relatives" above.

SOCIAL BACKGROUND CONTROLS

Age

Respondents = ages were coded as: twenty-five to thirty-four = 1; thirty-five to forty-four = 2; forty-five to fifty-four = 3; fifty-five to sixty-four = 4; sixty-five and over = 5, after responses to "What is your date of birth?"

Marital Status

"What is your marital status?" was asked, and marital status was coded as: married = 1; single/never married = 2; widow/widower = 3; separated/divorced = 4.

Children at Home

Presence of children less than age eighteen in the household was coded as none = 0 and yes = 1.

Language of Interview

Respondents were asked whether they would prefer to be interviewed in English or in French.

Employment Status

Employed = 1; unemployed = 0.

Personal Income

The question was "What is your best estimate of your own total personal income before taxes and deductions from all sources in the past twelve months?" Statistics Canada coded personal income as: none = 1; less than $20,000 = 2; $20,000 to $39,999 = 3; $40,000 to $59,999 = 4; $60,000 and over = 5.

Educational Status

Respondents were asked "What is the highest level of education you have completed?" Statistics Canada coded educational status as: less than high school = 1; graduated from high school = 2; some post-secondary = 3; post-secondary diploma = 4; university degree = 5.

TABLE 6A.1

Zero-order correlations of participation in community voluntary activities as a youth (Index II) and current participation in community activities, by gender and age cohorts

Measures of current participation as an adult	Female subsample	Male subsample
AGED 25-34 (2,096/1,540)		
Formal volunteering	.24***	.26***
Informal volunteering	.24***	.29***
Hours of volunteering	.15***	.13***
No. of organizations volunteered with	.27***	.26***
No. of donations	.33***	.27***
Amount of donations	.17***	.13***
No. of current association memberships	.32***	.30***
Voting over three elections	.14***	.12***
Attention to current affairs	.14***	.21***
Church attendance	.17***	.23***
Socializing with relatives	.08***	.07**
Socializing with friends	.12***	.13***
AGED 35-44 (2,347/1,933)		
Formal volunteering	.27***	.28***
Informal volunteering	.24***	.23***
Hours of volunteering	.14***	.19***
No. of organizations volunteered with	.31***	.29***
No. of donations	.34***	.26***
Amount of donations	.08***	.15***
No. of current association memberships	.35***	.29***
Voting over three elections	.14***	.10***
Attention to current affairs	.16***	.14***
Church attendance	.19***	.18***
Socializing with relatives	.10***	.04
Socializing with friends	.16***	.10***
AGED 45-54 (1,572/1,311)		
Formal volunteering	.25***	.32***
Informal volunteering	.20***	.25***
Hours of volunteering	.14***	.19***
No. of organizations volunteered with	.28***	.32***
No. of donations	.33***	.35***
Amount of donations	.14***	.16***
No. of current association memberships	.29***	.33***
Voting over three elections	.15***	.15***
Attention to current affairs	.13***	.12***

▶

◀ TABLE 6A.1

Measures of current participation as an adult	Female subsample	Male subsample
Church attendance	.12***	.13***
Socializing with relatives	.10***	.06*
Socializing with friends	.13***	.14***
AGED 55-64 (1,176/933)		
Formal volunteering	.24***	.32***
Informal volunteering	.22***	.31***
Hours of volunteering	.13***	.23***
No. of organizations volunteered with	.28***	.33***
No. of donations	.33***	.35***
Amount of donations	.16***	.19***
No. of current association memberships	.30***	.32***
Voting over three elections	.10**	.18***
Attention to current affairs	.19***	.12***
Church attendance	.10**	.15***
Socializing with relatives	.14***	.09**
Socializing with friends	.19***	.14***
AGED 65+ (1,898/1,106)		
Formal volunteering	.24***	.31***
Informal volunteering	.24***	.28***
Hours of volunteering	.14***	.19***
No. of organizations volunteered with	.25***	.29***
No. of donations	.29***	.32***
Amount of donations	.18***	.20***
No. of current association memberships	.32***	.34***
Voting over three elections	.16***	.20***
Attention to current affairs	.10***	.19***
Church attendance	.13***	.15***
Socializing with relatives	.08***	.12***
Socializing with friends	.16***	.13***

NOTE: The figures in parentheses are the N for females in the age cohort and the N for males in the age cohort.
*$p \leq .05$; **$p \leq .01$, ***$p \leq .001$

ACKNOWLEDGMENTS

We acknowledge with thanks that our data source was made available by Statistics Canada as a public use file, and that the Social Sciences and Humanities Research Council provided funding for our work through a research grant to Dr. Jon Kesselman and others. Also, we owe thanks to Terry Stewart for his very helpful assistance with the analysis. Direct correspondence to Thomas Perks, Department of Sociology, University of Lethbridge, Alberta, Canada T1K 3M4 (thomas.perks@uleth.ca).

NOTES

1. Before Hanks and Eckland's study, Snyder (1970) had, in a local school study in the United States, followed up on members of a graduating high school class five years later. He found, as did Hanks and Eckland, that those with higher levels of involvement in high school groups (two involvement levels were compared) were more likely to belong to voluntary organizations five years later. Smith and Baldwin (1974) looked at parental influences in local survey data.
2. There has been some panel research on voluntary association activity over short time periods in adulthood (e.g., Babchuk and Booth 1969; Curtis, White, and McPherson 2000; McPherson and Lockwood 1980 cover periods up to eight years). In these studies, prior involvement does predict later involvement, but the results also show large increases and decreases in association affiliations and activity levels for some respondents.
3. Statistics Canada has presented the zero-order relationships of youth activity involvement and selected adult community activities in Hall et al. (1998) and Jones (2000).
4. In further analyses (not reported in the table), we confirmed that there were no statistical interactions between gender and age for either of the two indexes or for any of the six separate activities.
5. We inspected possible interactions for gender and youth activities. There was only one that was statistically significant: hours given to volunteering ($p \leq .001$). Here experience with youth activities has stronger yield for males than for females, perhaps because, with the double day (i.e., the extra burden of domestic responsibilities), women had more difficulty finding as much time for volunteering as men.

7
Ethnicity and Social Capital in Canada

Amanda Aizlewood and Ravi Pendakur

Social capital is, in theory at least, about working together to pursue common objectives. It manifests itself as specific forms of social conduct – including networks, norms, and trust – that allow people to interact in ways that encourage the production of social goods. The past decade has spawned a good deal of work that has sought to define social capital and to identify the appropriate personal and community characteristics that lead to higher levels of community cooperation, trust, and participation (see in particular Brehm and Rahn 1997; Fukuyama 1995b; Putnam 1993a, 1995a; Putnam et al. 1993). To date, social capital has been shown to be positively associated with high levels of education, confidence in public institutions, and participation in social, cultural, and political activities. These positive associations are appealing to policy makers, given the hypothesis that trust, reciprocity, and cooperation will correlate with higher outcomes on quality of life indicators such as public safety, health, and life satisfaction and will create value not only for individuals, but for communities and societies in general.

Not all studies have yielded encouraging results. Though a great deal of attention has been focused on the identification of "good" conditions for the creation of social capital, a small body of work carried out in the United States suggests that other things – ethnic diversity in particular – may work to reduce it. These findings are not limited to qualitative conjecture; a modest body of survey-based empirical research consistently shows that negative relationships exist between social capital and indicators of ethnic diversity at the individual and community levels (see Alesina and LaFerrara 1999, 2000; Glaeser et al. 2000; Johnston and Soroka 2001; Marschall and Stolle 2004; Saguaro Seminar 2000). Some hypothesize that it is the differing levels of "civic-ness" exhibited by ethnic groups themselves that account for lower overall stocks of social capital (see Banfield 1958; Black 1982, 1987; Fukuyama 1995b; Inglehart 1988, 1990; Putnam 1993a; Rice and Feldman

1997; Verba, Schlozman, and Brady 1995). Others maintain that the answers lie in the social-psychological aspects of majority-minority societal interaction and that the presence of diverse elements in communities inhibits trust and reduces civic and cooperative behaviour among dominant groups (see Coleman 1990a; Forbes 1997; Miller 1995; Uslaner 2002).

From a Canadian perspective, these arguments suggest that there is reason to worry. Canada has high immigration associated with settlement in large cities that serve as homes to ethnically diverse populations. A domestic line of inquiry seems prudent: do indicators of social capital vary based on ethnic origin and degree of ethnic diversity in Canada as they do in the United States? Using data from the 2000 Equality, Security, and Community survey, we test these hypotheses in the Canadian context. We look at the broad relationships between ethnic diversity and social capital in order to further our understanding of the impact of ethnicity and ethnic diversity on civic attitudes and behaviours in Canada. This study moves beyond the scope of previous efforts by examining not only visible ethnic differences but also the specific attitudes and behaviours of twenty-two distinct ethnocultural groups. We compare the relative and absolute strengths of individual and community level characteristics in predicting outcomes on social capital measures. Individual-level characteristics refer to personal markers, such as ethnocultural ancestry, immigrant status, and visible minority status. Community-level characteristics refer to the features of the environment in which an individual lives, such as the local proportion of visible minorities, the area's cultural diversity, and the size of the community. We seek to further our understanding of (1) the impact of community-level characteristics on civic attitudes and behaviours; (2) the impact of individual-level characteristics on civic attitudes and behaviours; and (3) which, if any, holds greater explanatory power in the Canadian context.

Our results suggest that, in Canada, individual ethnocultural characteristics do not appreciably affect scores on social capital measures but that broad designations of ethnicity, such as visible-minority and immigrant status, do so, though weakly. Community-level factors play a more ambiguous role: we find that larger community size, in particular, is a consistent predictor of lower interpersonal trust, lower propensity to join organizations, and less time spent with friends. We also find that scores on social capital indicators tend to increase as community-level diversity increases but that such differences do not withstand the addition of more individual-level ethnocultural attributes. Individual sociodemographic characteristics such as age, education, and income hold greater explanatory power that remains consistent despite the presence of other statistical controls. We speculate that, in Canada, where community size, diversity, wealth, and education are so closely and positively correlated, an urban lifestyle, or "city effect," may be a more accurate predictor of civic attitudes and behaviours.

The Literature

Why would diversity interfere with or reduce trust and cooperative behaviour among citizens? Social capital writ large represents the potential willingness of individuals to work together and to engage in cooperative civic endeavours collectively. The concept of social capital has, thus, come to mean the willingness and ability of individuals to create and sustain relationships through voluntary associations (Portes and Landolt 1996b). This role is an important one in societies that require senses of community, solidarity, and mutual obligation in order to support collective undertakings such as a welfare state (see Soroka, Johnston, and Banting, Chapter 11, this volume) There is a fundamental weakness with such characterizations, however, since social capital does not necessarily have to be inclusive in nature. High levels of trust and association within a group do not necessarily translate to high levels of trust and networking when dealing with people from outside the group. It is well documented, for example, that ethnic enclave economies draw from in-group members and rarely from those outside the group (see, e.g., Li 1998; Portes and Stepick 1993). In ethnically diverse settings such as urban areas, broader community cohesion may be threatened if individuals from both majority and minority populations bond exclusively on ethnic terms, thereby creating socially isolated communities that do not trust or cooperate with each other. Despite the fact that social networks based on ethnic criteria present outward signs of high social capital and are useful to members in social and economic terms, they are based on exclusive rather than inclusive criteria and, thus, do not necessarily result in high levels of cohesion across groups (see Etzioni 2001; Portes and Landolt 1996b; Varshney 2002).

This dilemma is noted in a broad cross-section of social capital literature, from which two hypotheses can be identified. The first hypothesis suggests that broad social capital is relatively easy to build in ethnically homogeneous communities and is more difficult to sustain in ethnically diverse settings. Individuals are more disposed to trust others like themselves and less likely to trust those they perceive to be different (Uslaner 2002). According to this view, ethnocultural homogeneity produces a smoothly functioning society in which the insertion of diverse elements creates friction and stress. Homogeneity facilitates trust and cooperation because "like" individuals share cultural values and expectations, or what Granovetter calls "strong ties" (1973; see also Coleman 1990). Conversely, diversity creates real or perceived barriers to communication and understanding among people and leads to apprehension among so-called unlike individuals (see, in particular, Miller 1995; see also Eisenberg, Chapter 4 of this volume). Majority groups, in particular, are believed to be negatively affected by diversity because the presence of "difference" threatens individual or collective identities (Forbes 1997; Wilton 1998) and leads to a reduced sense of trust and lower levels of cooperative activity. If group identity is threatened, formerly dominant groups may reduce their participation participation in the community, which in turn, reduces social capital. In this context-based line of reasoning, it is the diversity that surrounds an individual or group on a micro- or macro-scale that influences attitudes and behaviours.

A second hypothesis proposes that it is an individual's group-based ethnocultural characteristics that drive his or her attitudes and behaviours, or what Johnston and Soroka (2001) term "compositional" arguments. In this view, social capital is a cultural attribute that is inherited or learned and not easily shed. As a result, some ethnocultural groups have more or fewer "civic" qualities than others, and these qualities present themselves in personal attitudes and behaviours that remain constant across generations and even oceans (see Banfield 1958; Black 1982, 1987; Fukuyama 1995b; Inglehart 1988, 1990; Putnam 1993a; Rice and Feldman 1997; and Verba, Schlozman, and Brady 1995). The social capital of a community is the sum of an individual's and, in turn, a group's, contribution. In the aggregate, if a community has high social capital, it is because it is composed of civic-minded groups. The overall stock of social capital can be reduced if groups with low social capital enter the community, a situation that seems particularly salient for societies with large-scale, ongoing immigration. In this composition-based line of reasoning, it is the personal ethnocultural identification of individuals or the aggregate ethnocultural identification of a homogeneous group that determines the social capital of a community.

Both hypotheses can be and have been supported empirically and, therefore, most survey-based studies incorporate both individual and contextual indicators in their attempts to identify the key predictors of social capital measures. The vast majority of research in this domain is conducted in the United States, and results for the Canadian context are few. Results from the

Social Capital Community Benchmark project in the United States show that scores on trust and participation are substantially lower in ethnically diverse communities (Saguaro Seminar 2001). Individuals in such communities are less likely to trust others, are more likely to be personally isolated, have fewer friends, spend less time socializing with friends and family, and express a lower sense of community than do individuals in ethnically homogeneous communities. These results, suggest the authors, hint at a pervasive, generalized mistrust in diverse settings; despite the expectation that individuals may be less trusting of members of other ethnocultural groups, researchers have found that in areas of high ethnic diversity, lack of trust is indiscriminate and extends to members of the respondent's own ethnic group. Johnston and Soroka's study of the Canadian component of the World Values Survey examines these issues directly, but poor available indicators of ethnicity and community-level diversity hamper the usefulness of the findings (2001). They do find that, broadly speaking, both individual and community-level ethnic diversity affect scores on social capital measures, but their results fail to definitively uphold the hypotheses of either the contextual or compositional arguments. They find that ethnic differences in social capital do exist and, while somewhat blunted, remain important even in the face of statistical controls such as age and education. In Canada, provinces with high ethnic diversity do not demonstrate lower scores on civic measures, but, rather, diverse regions present high scores on social capital measures.

In the United States, results do not appear to vary according to which element of social capital – trust, participation, or interaction – is being studied. Alesina and La Ferrara (2000) find that ethnic origin and religious affiliation are not significant predictors of trust, but having low income and little education and living in an ethnically diverse area all negatively influence the degree to which trust is extended to others. In a separate study, the same researchers find that, after controlling for individual characteristics, scores on participation measures are significantly lower in ethnically fragmented communities. They conclude that, on the whole, individuals "prefer to interact with others who are similar to themselves in terms of income, race or ethnicity [and] prefer to join groups composed of individuals with preferences similar to their own" (Alesina and La Ferrara 1999, 2). Overall, the authors' "aversion to heterogeneity" hypothesis is supported: for participation and the development of trust, individuals require similarity rather than difference.

This seemingly broad negative relationship also extends to more intimate settings. The acquisition of close, personal networks reflects position in the social structure, which, in turn, intersects with "dimensions of opportunity and constraint," argues Fischer in his study of urban networks (1982, 11). Educational resources, employment status, and ethnic membership all combine to expose individuals to specific groups of contacts from whom opportunities and advantages are gained. These findings are reinforced by the results of Glaeser et al. (2000), who observe that, in personal encounters, differences in race and nationality reduce the level of perceived trustworthiness. The notion that likeness and familiarity breed trust is also reinforced by social-psychological literature, in which individuals are shown to be most strongly influenced by members of their own "primary" groups, namely those with whom they engage in regular, daily interaction (Frank and Yasumoto 1998). A 1994 study of self-help support groups found that interaction in small, diverse settings leads to lower trust among participants (Wuthnow 1994). Using a survey of one thousand American support group members, Wuthnow found that individuals in heterogeneous groups are generally less likely to report high levels of trust than those in homogeneous groups. In a related argument, Wilton (1998, 178) suggests that negative reactions occur in small, yet diverse settings because individuals who are in places they think of as their own encounter "people who don't appear to belong."

Other studies find that an accounting of both context and contact is needed to explain the relationship between diversity and civic attitudes and behaviours. With respect to context, beneficial social interactions can be achieved through participation in formal activities but also in informal activities such as social encounters (Edwards, Foley, and Diani 2001). The frequency of such contact is important, but encounters are made especially meaningful if interaction takes place in ethnically diverse settings. Stein et al. (2000) do suggest that, for majority groups at least, living in diverse settings results in lower trust scores. But they offer an interesting corollary: that an increase in the frequency of contact between groups significantly offsets the negative effects of a diverse context. Simply living near minority groups but not interacting with them increases feelings of threat among the majority group, and this finding reinforces the results of Jackman and Crane's earlier study of black and white communities in the United States in which similar effects were observed (1986). Marschall and Stolle (2004) also find that context plays an important positive role in shaping civic attitudes and behaviours. Despite their initial observation that individuals in heterogeneous areas are much less likely to trust others than individuals in more homogeneous areas, they find that interactions among individuals in ethnically diverse settings play an important role in the development of generalized trust. When individuals living in heterogeneous neighbourhoods have positive, direct interactions with members of other ethnic groups, they are also more likely to extend trust to other strangers. Positive social interactions among "unlike" individuals contribute more to the development of generalized trust and civic orientations than do similar experiences among individuals who share common characteristics, attitudes, and behaviours.

The relationship between an ethnically diverse context and civic attitudes and behaviours seems particularly relevant to Canada. Canada is one of the most urbanized countries in the world, with close to 80 percent of citizens living in cities or metropolitan areas (Statistics Canada 2005). Urban living occupies a central role in studies of social contact because of the implication of city life in the decline of traditional forms of community-based interaction (see Guest and Wierzbicki 1999). Traditionally, "community" has referred to something resembling a neighbourhood, an entity that implies physical ties based on geographical proximity or spatial location. People interact and are familiar because they encounter one another regularly in the street. The term has, over time, been reconceptualized in terms of social networks, especially non-geographic, non-local ones (see, e.g., Wellman 1999b). These are non-local because they arise from something other than geographic proximity and focus on interests, social relations, and social networks as a basis for relationships. These networks may be seen to threaten the production or maintenance of social capital if urbanization is the producer of "a social order in which the traditional ties of community-shared space, close kinship links, shared religious and moral values were being replaced by anonymity, individualism and competition" (Forrest and Kearns 2001). There is some evidence to support this fear. Guest and Wierzbicki find in their 1999 study in the United States that there is "a relatively continuous, albeit slow, decline in the importance of social ties on the basis of neighbourhood and, in turn, an even smaller upward growth in the importance of non-neighbourhood social ties ... neighbourhood and non-neighbourhood ties are becoming disassociated over time" (109).

Coupled with the effects associated with urbanization is the reality that immigration and ethnic diversity in Canada are essentially urban phenomena. In Canada, diverse communities are synonymous with large communities. In 2001, 48 percent of immigrants and refugees settled in Toronto, 15 percent in Vancouver, 12 percent in Montreal. However, there is less ethnocultural segregation in Canadian than in American urban spaces, which alters the impact of ethnocultural diversity, and Canadian cities cannot be characterized as cities are in American social capital studies. Germain's 2000 study that finds that in Montreal neighbourhoods, recent immigrants tend to share residential space with others of different origins, and with people of French or British origins, "creating a much more cosmopolitan landscape where diversity rather than ethnic or racial concentration is the rule" (13). In Canada, poverty is neither as spatially nor as ethnically determined, and there is greater diversity of ethnocultural groups in poorer Canadian neighbourhoods than there is in comparable neighbourhoods of American cities.

Data, Measures, and Methods

The Data

What is the impact of ethnicity and ethnic diversity on social capital in Canada? In order to study this question directly, we use the Equality, Security, and Community (ESC) survey, a large, national, and stratified random sample of the Canadian population who speak an official language (English or French) and are over eighteen years of age. In order to include the contextual factors of local diversity and city size as controls in the analysis, we augment the ESC by linking it to municipal data from the 1996 Census.

The ESC survey is particularly suited to the investigation of issues of ethnicity and social capital for a number of reasons. First, the survey was administered to 5,152 respondents, 1,051 of whom live in census tracts in Montreal, Toronto, and Vancouver that include four times the average number of visible minorities for that Census Metropolitan Area (CMA). This urban oversample means that the total number of visible minorities available for meaningful analysis is substantial for a survey of this size. Second, the ESC features proportional weight, cluster, and strata information, all of which we use to allow results to be generalized to the population.[1] Third, the survey has a large and varied set of questions on ethnic identity, ancestry, and affiliation that far exceed the depth publicly available in other surveys, including the Canadian census. Fourth, the survey poses detailed questions related to interpersonal and political trust, forms of participation, and formal and informal kinds of social interaction, all of which are widely used to operationalize the concept of social capital.

We examine the relationship between personal trust, political trust, participation, and social interaction as dependent variables, on one hand, and an array of personal and community-level characteristics as independent variables on the other. Ours is a general study; we intend only to reveal the strength of relationships between dependent and independent variables in each of five separate models and do not attempt to uncover causal relationships across the dependent variables themselves.[2]

Dependent Variables: Measures of Social Capital

We operationalize social capital according to four thematic indicators: interpersonal trust, political trust, formal participation, and informal social interaction. The indicator of *interpersonal trust* is constructed using the aggregate of four related questions concerning the fate of a lost wallet. This instrument of inquiry in the area of trust is unique to the ESC survey. The respondent is asked whether a wallet containing $200 would be returned intact if it were found by a neighbour, a police officer, a grocery clerk at a local shop, or a complete stranger. The resulting variable is measured on a nine-point scale, on which a low figure represents low trust and a high figure represents high trust. Our measure for *political trust* is the sum of two questions that ask whether the respondent trusts the federal or provincial government "to do what is right." The new variable is measured on a seven-point scale, ascending numerically from low trust to high trust. We enlist two variables to measure *informal social interaction*: frequency of seeing friends and frequency of talking to neighbours. Both are measured on seven-point scales, ascending numerically from low to high frequency. *Formal participation* is measured using a binary variable that taps respondents' propensity to join organizations. It is drawn from seven questions that probe membership in service, community, and recreational clubs, political groups, youth-oriented service organizations, volunteer organizations, or any other type of formalized organization. As long as the respondent is a member of any club or organization, he or she is considered to have joined.

Independent Variables: Contextual Level

Our independent variables come in two varieties: individual-level variables and contextual/community-level variables. Community-level variables are so called because they refer to the general characteristics of the area in which a respondent resides, rather than to the personal attributes of each respondent.

Each variable is linked on a case basis to census subdivision (CSD) population and ethnicity data from the 1996 census. In this way, three variables are derived for the analysis. The first is the natural log of the total population of the CSD in which a respondent lives *(size of the community)*. Community size is important for two reasons: first, larger communities in Canada are more likely to be home to a diverse population and a larger proportion of immigrants and, second, larger communities are expected to exhibit different attitudes and behaviours than do smaller communities. The two other contextual variables measure the diversity of a respondent's community. The *index of diversity* variable measures the chance that two randomly selected cases within the CSD will differ. As the index value increases, contextual diversity increases. The final contextual variable is the *percentage of visible minorities* in the respondent's CSD.[3]

Independent Variables: Individual Level

Individual-level variables are divided into two types. The first type includes the basic demographic markers that exist independently of ethnocultural ancestry but are implicated in discussions of social capital.[4] This group includes *age, sex, educational attainment, marital status, employment status, subjective income,* and whether the respondent has *children living in the household*. The second group includes variables that are ethnocultural in nature. This group includes *ethnic ancestry, household language, religious affiliation, visible minority affiliation, immigration status,* and, for immigrants only, the *length of time a respondent has lived in Canada*.[5]

The derivation of the ethnic-ancestry variable merits a more detailed explanation. Categorizing ethnic identity is a complex and amorphous task because there are myriad ways in which people may define membership in a particular group. Identity in ethnocultural terms weaves together a broad spectrum of concepts, including ancestry, religion, language, and socialization to name just a few. In general terms, however, ethnicity refers to a group's distinctiveness and is, therefore, also a measure of culture. This ethnocultural grouping comprises a bundle of membership criteria, including: self-categorization and identification as means of identifying group members and non-members; a shared descent that suggests commonality and includes a notion of history; specific cultural traits such as customs or language; and a social organization for interaction both within the group and with people outside the group. These are, by and large, ascribed criteria; individuals have these characteristics through cultural reproduction and knowledge acquisition. It is not necessary for members to fulfill all criteria, but a few of the criteria must be fulfilled for the essence of the ethnicity to be maintained.

The ESC project is a rich source of information on ethnic affiliation, by virtue of its unique collection instrument. A set of four questions asks specifically about ethnic affiliation. The first asks "To what ethnic or cultural group(s) do you belong?" and allows the respondent up to four mentions, prompted by the question "Are there any others?" With these data, it is possible to construct a clear picture of ethnocultural origins, including, in particular, individuals with multiple origins. If the respondent answers "Canadian" as a first response, a probe question seeks additional information: "In addition to being a Canadian, to what ethnic or cultural group did you or your ancestors belong upon first coming to this continent?" For our purposes, we use responses from the first two questions (first and second mention) and the Canadian probe question to categorize respondents into a set of ethnic groups that includes both people who report only one ethnic origin and those who report more than one origin. Sixteen categories of single responses can be drawn from the first mention. If the first response is Canadian, the answer to the probe question is used instead, if any is provided. If a second response is provided, it is then combined into a series of multiple response categories.

Our review of other studies in this area prompts us to consider that ethnocultural origin alone is not sufficient for examining the impact of diversity on social capital. Ethnic identity can also – rightly or wrongly – be ascribed by others. Indeed, "the man in the street can see that men differ in physical appearance and he is certain that the differences are more than skin deep" (Simpson and Yinger 1965). To account for the relative visibility of some ethnocultural groups, we aggregate separately Europeans, *visible minority* groups and *Aboriginals* in ways analogous to the constructing of employment equity categories. In order to maintain the cultural element of the compositional social capital debate, we further divide the European group to differentiate between *majority whites* (i.e., British, French, and Canadian) and *non-majority whites* (i.e., German, Italian, Ukrainian, etc).

Analysis

The data are explored in two stages. In the first stage, we present simple means comparisons of the five social capital measures alone, and according to selected indicators. From these results, we can identify basic patterns in the data and prepare for the second, more advanced, analytical stage. In the advanced stage, our hypotheses are tested according to the criteria discussed in the previous section. To test our hypotheses, we use a three-phase multiple regression model.[6] In the base-line phase, standard demographic control variables and community-level population and diversity characteristics are examined. Added at the second phase are broad ethnocultural indicators: employment equity (e.g., visible minority) categories, immigrant status, recentness of arrival in Canada, household language, and religion. In the third and final phase, we augment the model with the inclusion of specific ethnocultural ancestry markers. At each phase, we explore the impact of each independent variable on the respective dependent variables. We also identify changes to the relative explanatory power of each independent predictor due to the inclusion of increasingly precise control variables.

If contextual-level arguments apply to Canadian communities, we should expect indicators of community diversity to bear significant negative weight on our dependent social capital variables. If individual-level arguments are valid, we expect personal ethnocultural attributes to assume positions of explanatory strength in our models. Finally, if neither contextual nor compositional indicators hold exclusive weight, we should expect standard controls such as age, education and income to play important roles in explaining variance in the five dependent variables. Although we do take the liberty of drawing conclusions as to the usefulness of independent variables both within and among the models, each regression is a separate analysis and, thus, must be considered independently.

Findings

Comparisons of Means

Table 7.1 presents the basic characteristics of the five social capital variables in the analysis, including the number of observations, proportions, weighted means, and standard deviations. Formal participation is measured dichotomously (i.e., a respondent is a member of an organization or is not). In this sample, 73 percent have joined at least one organization. The variables for informal interaction are measured on seven-point scales. Overall, respondents see friends fairly often (5.23) and talk to their neighbours slightly less often (4.95). Respondents have mid-level trust in others (5.95 on a scale of 9) and low overall trust in government (3.28 on a scale of 7).

What patterns emerge with respect to markers of diversity? Table 7.2 presents a comparison of means for each measure of social capital according

TABLE 7.1

Characteristics of social capital measures

	N	Proportion who join
Formal participation	4,999	73%

	N	Mean	Standard deviation	Scale
Interpersonal trust	4,738	5.95	1.85	1 to 9
Political trust	4,908	3.28	1.47	1 to 7
Seeing friends	5,117	5.23	1.33	1 to 7
Talking to neighbours	5,096	4.95	1.69	1 to 7

to employment equity categories and immigrant status. Group-based differences can be observed for each component of social capital, with the exception of "seeing friends," for which differences are marginal. In general, majority whites and non-majority whites exhibit higher scores, while visible minorities and Aboriginal peoples exhibit lower scores. Visible minorities exhibit the lowest scores for "talking to neighbours" and have a lower propensity to join organizations. There are some clear exceptions. Visible minorities and immigrant visible minorities are the most trusting of government, and Canadian-born visible minorities socialize with friends most often.

Immigrant status plays a role, though a clear pattern is not easy to identify. Immigrant status reduces most scores as compared to Canadian-born respondents. The story changes, however, when the category is broken down into white and visible minority groups. The most striking group-based differences appear within the interpersonal trust variable. Here, visible minorities exhibit the lowest scores, regardless of immigrant status. Interestingly, the immigrant factor also plays a role for whites, though in the opposite direction: this group exhibits the highest score for interpersonal trust. For visible minority groups, it is likely that recentness of arrival may partly explain differences.

These initial results suggest that differences do exist among individual-level indicators of ethnicity and with community-level diversity. We now turn to multiple regression modelling to uncover the impact of individual and community-level factors on these differences. If distinctions remain after repeated plausible controls are introduced, we can conclude that these variations are indeed the product of diversity-related factors.

TABLE 7.2

Comparisons of means for social capital measures according to employment equity categories and immigrant status

	Formal participation	Interpersonal trust	Political trust	Informal social interaction — Seeing friends	Informal social interaction — Talking to neighbours
All	0.73	5.95	3.28	5.23	4.95
Majority white	0.73	6.02	3.25	5.25	5.03
Non-majority white	0.75	6.01	3.20	5.26	4.97
Visible minority	0.67	5.48	3.66	5.21	4.42
Aboriginal	0.73	5.72	3.11	5.34	4.85
Immigrant	0.69	5.88	3.54	5.11	4.49
Immigrant white	0.68	6.16	3.43	5.13	5.00
Immigrant visible minority	0.69	5.50	3.76	5.13	4.55
Canadian-born	0.73	5.97	3.22	5.26	4.98
Canadian-born white	0.74	6.01	3.23	5.27	5.03
Canadian-born visible minority	0.62	5.46	3.38	5.46	3.97

BASIC MODEL

The basic model includes a group of individual-level demographic predictors and the respondents' community-level population and diversity characteristics. Results for five independent regressions are presented in Table 7.3. The leftmost column lists the independent variables included in the analysis. Two types of regression are used: for the formal participation model, a weighted survey logistic regression model is used to measure the propensity to join organizations. The other four models use weighted survey linear regression analyses. Each cell of the table shows the coefficient of the independent variable and its significance.

The five models vary in strength. Political trust is the weakest model, with only 2 percent of the variance of the dependent variable explained. Interpersonal trust is the strongest model, with 13 percent of the variance explained.

In these models, contextual-level variables fare well, with community size and index of diversity displaying the most consistent results. With the exception of political trust, as community size increases, scores on social capital measures decrease. This effect is most powerful for the interpersonal

TABLE 7.3

Basic model

		Formal participation	Political trust	Interpersonal trust	Informal social interaction – Seeing friends	Informal social interaction – Talking to neighbours
	N	4,837	4,651	4,562	4,804	4,780
	F	15.05 ***	11.94 ***	70.35 ***	52.41 ***	17.03 ***
	r^2	—	2%	13%	8%	6%
CONTEXTUAL VARIABLES	Community size (ln)	-0.09 ***	0.02	-0.25 ***	-0.07 ***	-0.04 *
	Index of diversity	1.12 ***	-0.27	2.46 ***	0.65 ***	0.27
	% visible minorities	-0.73 *	0.02	-0.81 **	-0.42 *	-0.26
INDIVIDUAL-LEVEL VARIABLES						
Sex (female)	Age	0.00	-0.01 **	0.02 ***	-0.01 **	0.02 ***
	Male	-0.08	-0.12	-0.27 ***	0.17 **	0.08
	Subjective income	0.17 ***	0.08 *	0.11 **	0.04	-0.04
	Children at home	-0.06	0.07	0.12	0.03	0.16
Education (less than high school)	High school	0.60 ***	0.06	0.23	-0.04	0.12
	Some technical	0.44 ***	-0.14	0.27 *	0.05	-0.11
	Technical certificate	0.59 ***	0.22	0.29 *	-0.09	0.18
	Some university	0.71 ***	-0.02	0.31 *	0.02	0.27 *
	BA	0.98 ***	0.21	0.52 ***	-0.13	0.00
	MA/PhD	1.27 ***	0.22	0.55 **	-0.09	0.03
Employment status (employed)	Unemployed	-0.11	-0.06	-0.08	-0.05	-0.06
	Student	0.56 *	0.17	0.23	0.16	0.08
	Retired	-0.19	0.09	-0.08	0.00	0.12
	Homemaker	-0.06	0.24 *	0.00	0.20	0.28 *
Marital status (married)	Single	-0.04	0.10	-0.18	0.59 ***	-0.34 ***
	Divorced/separated	-0.05	-0.01	-0.29 *	0.15	-0.23
	Widowed	-0.04	0.28	-0.43 **	0.17	-0.04

NOTE: Table entries are regression coefficients based on the ESC survey, first wave with metropolitan oversample, weighted. Significance t and F tests: *p < .05, **p < .01, ***p < .001.

trust model and weakest for "talking to neighbours." The effect appears to be counteracted by the index of diversity variable. In all cases, the negative impact of community size is balanced by the positive impact of the diversity of the municipality. The percentage of visible minorities in a respondent's CSD displays a consistently negative relationship among its coefficients, though this result is significant for formal participation rates, interpersonal trust, and seeing friends. Overall, the picture is mixed: community size and the presence of visible minorities reduce social capital scores, and ethnocultural heterogeneity increases scores.

Do the demographic controls shed any light on these results? The answer is yes, but only within models and not across them. Our basic model for explaining political trust provides few answers. Growing older appears to reduce trust in government, and having a higher perceived income appears to increase it. Educational attainment has a strong positive impact on formal participation and interpersonal trust. These effects are particularly strong among those who have earned post-secondary credentials. This may in part explain why students also appear as strong factors in the participation model, as well as do those who believe that they earn higher incomes relative to others. Demographic variables such as age, sex, marital status, and the presence of children in the home have no significant impact on an individual's propensity to join. Men are as likely to join as women, and people who are married are as likely to join as those who are divorced, separated, single, or widowed. Interpersonal trust is seen to increase with age but to diminish among men. Our two models for informal social interaction show dissimilar trends. Age has a positive effect on talking to neighbours, but the frequency of seeing friends decreases with age. Being single has the opposite effect: single individuals talk with neighbours less but socialize with friends more. Men are more likely to see friends than women, but are no more likely to talk with neighbours on a regular basis. Education, employment status, and income do not play major roles, suggesting that sociability is not a product of socioeconomic circumstance.

Broad Model: Adding General Ethnocultural Attributes

The basic models suggest that social capital measures are driven by a combination of community-level diversity characteristics and basic demographic attributes. What impact do individual-level cultural attributes have on the model? The second phase explores the impact of broad ethnocultural characteristics on measures of social capital. The results can be found in Table 7.4.

Perhaps the most striking change is the reduction in predictive power of the contextual level variables, save community size. What could account for this effect? In phased regression modelling, if the addition of control variables reduces the predictive power of existing variables, we can conclude that one of the new variables now explains that variance more effectively. If a coefficient does not shrink, it can be said that the added control variable has failed to rule out the original coefficient as an explanatory factor.

The strength of each model is increased, with the most significant gain made for the model for interpersonal trust. Political trust remains the weakest model. In almost all cases, we observe a reduction in the size of the contextual-level coefficients with a concomitant loss of statistical significance. The key exception is the continued power of community size to predict interpersonal trust, formal participation, and seeing friends. The magnitude of the coefficients is reduced, but not sufficiently to affect their significant role in the model. In this case, the addition of ethnocultural markers does not impinge on the statistical impact of city living on interpersonal trust. The same cannot be said for markers of contextual diversity, all of which are statistically insignificant. The new broad ethnocultural controls must explain the change, since age, education, marital status, and income all remain statistically significant, and their relative impacts do not change.

With the exception of speaking French at home, the ethnocultural coefficients do not form a clear pattern across the models. Religious identification does not appear to play a strong role in interpersonal trust, but French speakers, Aboriginals, visible minorities, and long-time visible-minority immigrants all exhibit lower scores for this variable. The broad political trust model reveals the continued positive influence of ethnocultural attributes. In this model, community-level indicators are weakened by the positive effect of immigrant controls, in particular, recent immigrants. Religion does play a role in propensity to join and talking to neighbours. Being a Protestant exerts a positive influence on participation. Among the broad ethnocultural variables, being a visible minority, being a recent white immigrant, and speaking French as one's household language all exert strong negative influences. Interestingly, however, long-time visible-minority immigrants exhibit a strong positive propensity to join, and non-majority whites are not as likely to join.

The models for informal social interaction have some similarities. Sociodemographic predictors significant in the basic model continue to be so in the new model. Religion plays an important role in neighbourly

TABLE 7.4

Broad model

		Formal participation	Political trust	Interpersonal trust	Informal social interaction Seeing friends	Talking to neighbours
	N	4,837	4,651	4,562	4,804	4,780
	F	11.42 ***	21.41 ***	65.58 ***	42.29 ***	30.74 ***
	r²	—	4%	19%	10%	8%
CONTEXTUAL VARIABLES	Community size (ln)	−0.04 *	0.00	−0.15 ***	−0.04 **	−0.01
	Index of diversity	0.39	−0.01	0.20	−0.26	−0.32
	% visible minorities	−0.33	−0.17	−0.34	−0.24	−0.01
INDIVIDUAL-LEVEL VARIABLES	Age	0.00	−0.01 **	0.02 ***	−0.01 **	0.02 ***
Sex (female)	Male	−0.05	−0.12	−0.26 **	0.18 **	0.12
	Subjective income	0.15 **	0.09 **	0.10 *	0.03	−0.05
	Children at home	−0.08	0.06	0.11	0.02	0.13
Education (less than high school)	High school	0.64 ***	0.04	0.22 *	−0.03	0.13
	Some technical	0.49 *	−0.14	0.24 *	0.06	−0.08
	Technical certificate	0.61 ***	0.17	0.29 *	−0.09	0.19
	Some university	0.74 ***	−0.05	0.30 *	0.02	0.28 *
	BA	1.10 ***	0.16	0.57 ***	−0.10	0.06
	MA/PhD	1.45 ***	0.16	0.65 ***	−0.05	0.13
Employment status (employed)	Unemployed	−0.10	−0.10	−0.15	−0.07	−0.05
	Student	0.72 **	0.09	0.24	0.17	0.10
	Retired	−0.18	0.06	−0.11	0.01	0.12
	Homemaker	−0.07	0.24 *	−0.07	0.19	0.26 *

Marital status (married)	Single	−0.04	0.12	−0.17	0.61 ***	−0.33 ***
	Divorced/separated	−0.10	0.01	−0.31 **	0.14	−0.24 *
	Widowed	−0.05	0.28 *	−0.47 **	0.17	−0.05
Religion (no religion)	Protestant	0.27 *	0.16	0.20 *	0.09	0.16
	Catholic	0.10	0.25 **	0.06	−0.04	0.34 ***
	Evangelical Protestant	0.41 *	0.11	0.19	0.08	0.24 *
	Other religion	0.49	0.02	0.11	−0.01	0.35 *
Household language	Language – French	−0.45 *	0.10	−1.46 ***	−0.52 ***	−0.59 ***
	Language – Other	0.07	−0.19	−0.27	0.00	0.16
EE category (majority white)	Visible minority	0.06	−0.08	−0.19 **	−0.04	−0.10
	Non-majority white	−1.01 **	0.26	−0.27	−0.12	−0.71 **
	Aboriginal	0.03	−0.07	−0.39 *	0.03	−0.23
Immigrants (Canadian-born)	VM immigrant (<5)	−0.31	0.76 *	0.07	−0.19	0.07
	VM immigrant (5-9)	0.44	0.47	0.08	0.25	0.11
	VM immigrant (10-20)	0.25	0.38	−0.26	−0.15	0.01
	VM immigrant (20+)	0.66 *	0.20	−0.75 *	0.14	0.34
	White immigrant (<5)	−1.29 *	1.10 *	0.10	0.43 **	−0.27
	White immigrant (5-9)	−1.22 *	0.60	0.09	−0.26	−0.18
	White immigrant (10-20)	−0.25	0.74 **	0.05	−0.12	−0.34
	White immigrant (20+)	−0.28	0.18	−0.15	−0.01	−0.14

NOTE: See note to Table 7.3. Reference category for household language is English.

interaction. Aside from Protestants, respondents reporting a religious affiliation also report higher contact with neighbours. No similar effect is seen for the "seeing friends" model. As with interpersonal trust, speaking French as one's household language is a negative influence on both measures of informal social interaction.

Full Model: Adding Specific Ethnocultural Attributes

Results from the broad models allow us to conclude that community-level measures of diversity do little to explain variance in the five social capital variables in the face of broad ethnocultural controls. These results favour individual-level hypotheses over community-level ones by suggesting that broad group characteristics assume greater predictive strength in our five social capital models. Community size remains an important determinant in three models. What of individual-level ethnocultural attributes? The final phase of regression analysis allows us to examine the compositional argument with greater precision. In Table 7.5, the broad ethnocultural groups have been broken out into twenty-two distinct categories – sixteen single ethnicities and six groups in which respondents claim more than one ethnic origin. Also added are immigrant status variables by recentness of arrival.[7] If compositional hypotheses are valid, we should see significant differences between ethnic groups.

It is apparent from the results that the addition of specific ethnocultural characteristics has little impact on the variables in the previous model. No patterns appear across the models with respect to the detailed ethnic groups. At the same time, contextual-level indicators of diversity remain insignificant, with the exception of the impact of community size on interpersonal trust, formal participation, and seeing friends, which remain strong. No ethnic groupings have significant impacts within the "seeing friends" model. In general, groups do not appear to differ significantly from the British reference category. There are some exceptions: Chinese talk to their neighbours less and exhibit lower interpersonal trust. Latin Americans talk to their neighbours less, but trust government more. Blacks and South Asians also trust government more. Eastern Europeans and Filipinos are less likely than the British to join organizations. Ukrainians and "other Asians," a group composed of, among others, those of Vietnamese, Korean, and Japanese ancestry, also extend less trust to others.

Standard individual-level demographic attributes appear to withstand with ease the addition of the new controls. The contribution of the demographic

TABLE 7.5

Full model

		Formal participation	Political trust	Interpersonal trust	Informal social interaction — Seeing friends	Informal social interaction — Talking to neighbours
	N	4,837	4,561	4,652	4,804	4,780
	F	14.95 ***	17.45 ***	63.37 ***	50.18 ***	30.93 ***
	r²	—	5%	20%	10%	9%
CONTEXTUAL VARIABLES	Community size (ln)	−0.05 *	0.00	−0.14 ***	−0.03 *	−0.01
	Index of diversity	0.40	−0.03	0.16	−0.25	−0.32
	% visible minorities	−0.40	−0.15	−0.28	−0.20	0.01
INDIVIDUAL-LEVEL VARIABLES	Age	0.00	−0.01 *	0.02 ***	−0.01 **	0.02 ***
	Male	−0.04	−0.12	−0.25 ***	0.18 **	0.12
Sex (female)	Subjective income	0.15 **	0.09 *	0.09 *	0.03	−0.04
	Children at home	−0.07	0.07	0.10	0.02	0.14
Education (less than high school)	High school	0.64 ***	0.04	0.24 *	−0.03	0.13
	Some technical	0.49 *	−0.13	0.26 *	0.04	−0.09
	Technical certificate	0.63 ***	0.18	0.30 **	−0.08	0.20 *
	Some university	0.74 ***	−0.06	0.31 *	0.02	0.29 *
	BA	1.10 ***	0.16	0.59 ***	−0.11	0.06
	MA/PhD	1.43 ***	0.15	0.69 ***	−0.06	0.13
Employment status (employed)	Unemployed	−0.12	−0.11	−0.14	−0.08	−0.06
	Student	0.66 **	0.11	0.27	0.16	0.09
	Retired	−0.21	0.06	−0.10	0.00	0.10
	Homemaker	−0.12	0.23 *	−0.06	0.19	0.27 *

▼ TABLE 7.5

		Formal participation	Political trust	Interpersonal trust	Informal social interaction — Seeing friends	Informal social interaction — Talking to neighbours
Marital status (married)	Single	−0.05	0.12	−0.15	0.60 ***	−0.34 ***
	Divorced/separated	−0.05	0.00	−0.32 **	0.15	−0.21
	Widowed	−0.03	0.28 *	−0.47 **	0.15	−0.05
Religion (no religion)	Protestant	0.28 *	0.16	0.20 *	0.10	0.17
	Catholic	0.13	0.23 *	0.08	−0.03	0.34 ***
	Evangelical Protestant	0.37 *	0.11	0.14	0.10	0.26 *
	Other religion	0.63	−0.07	0.04	−0.04	0.16
Household language	Language – French	−0.46 *	0.12	−1.39 ***	−0.53 ***	−0.57 ***
	Language – Other	0.10	−0.27	−0.22	−0.03	0.28
Immigrant status (Canadian-born)	< 5 years	−0.24	0.62 **	0.25	0.10	−0.21
	5-9 years	−0.75 *	0.97 ***	0.27	0.01	−0.20
	10-20 years	−0.21	0.48 *	−0.01	−0.20	−0.34
	20+ years	−0.15	0.14	−0.28 *	−0.02	−0.10
Group status (British)	Majority (multiple)	−0.02	−0.07	−0.09	−0.02	−0.12
	French	0.01	−0.03	−0.15	0.02	−0.01
	Canadian	0.00	−0.11	−0.19	0.17	0.06
	Northern European	−0.20	−0.10	−0.07	0.06	0.05
	Maj. with Northern European	0.03	−0.13	−0.27	−0.02	0.04
	German	0.56	−0.10	0.25	−0.04	−0.36
	Ukrainian	0.21	−0.09	−0.76 **	−0.19	0.06

Southern European	0.19	−0.35	−0.18	−0.23
Eastern European	−0.85 **	−0.21	0.06	−0.36
Other European	−0.10	−0.25	−0.17	−0.07
Maj. with other European	0.32	−0.23	0.25	0.30
European – Multiple	0.58	0.01	0.10	0.11
Black/Caribbean	−0.31	−0.32	−0.15	−0.42
Latin American	−0.15	−0.28	0.16	−0.74 *
Chinese	−0.16	−0.80 **	−0.09	−0.72 ***
South Asian	−0.57	−0.28	0.01	−0.07
Filipino	−1.06 *	−0.40	−0.16	−0.22
Other Asian	−0.94 *	−0.95 **	0.29	−0.40
Visible minority and other	−0.96 **	−0.03	−0.33	−0.65 *
Aboriginal	−0.29	−0.57	0.23	−0.44
Aboriginal with other	0.36	−0.25	−0.10	0.01

NOTE: See note to Table 7.3. Reference category for household language is English.

variables in Table 7.5 closely mirrors that seen in Table 7.4: higher education and income positively affect participation and interpersonal trust, younger individuals trust government more and socialize more with friends but less with neighbours, and older individuals trust others more. Men and single individuals are more likely than women or married people to see their friends and talk to their neighbours, but are also less trusting of others.

Broad, structural identifiers of diversity such as immigrant status, religion and language remain important contributors to several models. These effects remain strong despite the presence of more precise markers of ethnicity. There is a clear immigration effect within the political trust model, with immigrants exhibiting a clear positive pattern. Not surprisingly, immigrants who have arrived in Canada within the last five years are significantly less likely to join an organization. Speaking French continues to exert strong downward pressure across four of the models, while speaking a non-official language makes no impact whatsoever on any model.

Discussion

Our goal was to explore the relationship between diversity and social capital across a broad range of indicators. The research was motivated by findings that suggested that diversity exerts a negative influence on civic attitudes and behaviours. Our findings differ markedly from those of previous research, particularly in regard to studies carried out in the United States. We find that, in Canada, while differences based on ethnocultural identifiers do exist, they are the exception rather than the rule. If diversity were detrimental to social capital, we would expect to see negative effects across either immigrant or visible-minority groups. By and large, we do not. There is no consistency across groups in any of our measures. An examination of bivariate means suggested slight differences across broad ethnic categories in such attributes as political and interpersonal trust and informal social interaction. However, controlling for individual and contextual characteristics using survey regression methods caused most of these differences to disappear. Indeed, in the case of trust in government, visible minorities and immigrant groups exhibit higher scores than the comparison groups. We also find that scores on social capital indicators tend to increase as community-level diversity increases, but such differences do not withstand the addition of individual-level ethnocultural attributes.

We suggest that, in Canada, where community size, diversity, wealth, and education are so closely and positively correlated, an urban lifestyle may be a more useful explanation for variance in civic attitudes and behaviours. Cities are places in which myriad world-views, languages, and cultures meet. Perhaps the dominant finding is the effect of community size on measures of social capital. In three of the five models – participation, interpersonal trust and seeing friends – the larger the city of residence, the less likely people are to participate, trust, and socialize. This may be accounted for by the effect of living in a city – the constant presence of strangers and social networks based on individual interest more than local attachments (non-local networks). Generalized trust is reduced in cities because familiarity is a more selective, network-based phenomenon.

Mitigating the effect of city size are the individual characteristics of education and income. Having higher levels of schooling and having a higher perceived income result in increased scores on measures of participation and interpersonal trust. From a political perspective, these findings are encouraging. Indicators of social capital are politically important only if we know what levers can be used to make a situation better. How do we increase levels of trust and membership? Based on our research, controlling diversity is neither justifiable nor realistic; but more importantly, it does not appear to be the answer. Education and income appear to be far more effective levers for affecting social capital.

APPENDIX

This appendix describes the variables used in the analyses and their basic descriptives (see also Table 7A.1). Variables are obtained from the 2000 Equality Security Community survey or from the 1996 Canadian Census linked through forward sortation postal codes and Census subdivisions. Most variables have been recoded, combined, or reconstructed for the purposes of the analyses.

Social Capital Variables

Frequency of seeing friends: A seven-point scale variable derived from the question: "How often do you see close friends – not your husband or wife or partner or family member, but people you feel fairly close to?" Ranges from 1 – "never" to 7 – "every day."

Frequency of talking to neighbours: a seven-point scale variable derived from the question: "And how often do you talk with your neighbours?" Ranges from 1 – "never" to 7 – "every day."

Formal participation: Dummy variable, membership = 1, derived from the following questions: "How many service clubs, such as Lions or Meals on Wheels, do you belong to?" "How many recreational groups, such as sports leagues or clubs, music or hobby clubs, or exercise classes are you involved in?" "How many organizations active on political issues, such as the environment or taxpayers' rights, do you belong to?" "Sometimes people give time to various types of organizations. For instance, how many youth-oriented groups, such as Girl Guides or Minor Hockey, have you given time to in the last twelve months?" "How about organizations providing cultural services to the public, such as a museum or music festival. How many of these have you given time to in the last twelve months?" "How about organizations that help people, such as the Cancer Society or a food bank? How many of these have you volunteered time to in the last twelve months?" and "Do you belong to or volunteer for any other groups or organizations that we have not asked about?" The reference category is 0 – "no reported memberships."

Interpersonal trust: A nine-point scale constructed from four questions: "If you lost a wallet or a purse that contained two hundred dollars, how likely is it to be returned with the money in it if it was found by (someone who lives close by / a clerk at the nearest grocery store / a police officer/a complete stranger); would you say very likely, somewhat likely or not at all likely?" Ranges from 1 – "lowest trust" to 9 – "highest trust."

Political trust: A seven-point scale constructed from two questions: "How much do you trust the government in Ottawa to do what is right? Do you trust it almost always, most of the time, only some of the time, or almost never?" and "How much do you trust the government in [province] to do what is right? Do you trust it almost always, most of the time, only some of the time, or almost never?" Ranges from 1 – "lowest trust" to 7 – "highest trust."

COMMUNITY-LEVEL VARIABLES

Community size: The natural log of the population of the respondent's municipality of residence, as derived from the 1996 Census of Canada.

Index of diversity: The index of diversity = 1 – sum of squares of the proportions of all the groups in the CSD (1996 Census of Canada). The minimum value (for a CSD in which everyone shares the same ethnicity) is zero – ID = (1-12) = 0. The maximum value varies, depending on the number of groups represented. All majority ethnic groups were combined (British, French, and Canadian) in order to avoid problems of interpretation in cases of CSDs reporting only British and Canadian ethnicity. Counts for twenty-five minority ethnic groups were included in order to calculate the index in each CMA. It should be noted that not all CMAs have people from each ethnic group.

Percentage of visible minorities: The percentage of visible minorities in a respondent's municipality of residence, as derived from the 1996 Census of Canada.

INDIVIDUAL-LEVEL VARIABLES

Education: Dummy variables for "high school," "some technical school," "technical certificate," "some university," "bachelor's degree," and "MA/PhD." Reference category is "less than high school."

Religion: Dummy variables for "Catholic," "Protestant," "Evangelical Protestant," and "other religion." Reference category is "no religion."

Household language: Dummy variables for "household language – French," "household language – other." Reference category is "household language – English."

Subjective income: Five-point scale derived from the following questions: "If you had to guess, would you say your household income is above average, average, or below average?" "Would you say it is a little bit above average or a lot above average?" and "Would you say it is a little bit below average or a lot below average?" The resulting categories are 1 – "a lot below," 2 – "a little below," 3 – "average," 4 – "a little above," and 5 – "a lot above." This variable was used because over one-quarter of respondents did not answer the reported income variable.

Sex: Dummy variable = 1 if the respondent is male. The reference category is female.

Immigrant status and recentness of arrival in Canada: For immigrant respondents only, dummy variables for "immigrant who has arrived in the last five years," "immigrant who arrived between five and nine years ago," "immigrant who arrived between ten and twenty years ago," and "immigrant who arrived more than twenty years ago." The reference category is "Canadian-born."

Employment equity markers: Dummy variables for "visible minority," "Aboriginal," and "non-majority white." Reference category is "majority white."

Visible minority/immigrant status/recentness of arrival: Dummy variables for "white immigrant who has arrived in the last five years," "white immigrant who arrived between five and nine years ago," "white immigrant who arrived between ten and twenty years ago," "white immigrant who arrived more than twenty years ago," "visible minority immigrant who arrived less than five years ago," "visible minority immigrant who arrived between five and nine years ago," "visible minority immigrant who arrived between ten and twenty years ago," and "visible minority immigrant who arrived more than twenty years ago."

Marital status: Dummy variables for "single," "divorced or separated," and "widowed." The reference category is "married or living common law."

Employment status: Dummy variables for "unemployed," "student," "homemaker," and "retired." The reference category is "employed."

Children living at home: Dummy variable = 1 if respondent has at least one child living at home. The reference category is "no children living at home."

Table 7A.1

Descriptives

Variable	N	Mean	Standard deviation	Minimum	Maximum
Community size (ln)	5,142	10.90	2.31	4.17	13.81
Index of diversity	5,142	0.60	0.23	0.00	0.89
Subjective income	4,933	2.96	0.94	1.00	5.00
High school	5,152	0.24	0.43	0.00	1.00
Some technical school	5,152	0.07	0.25	0.00	1.00
Technical certificate	5,152	0.17	0.38	0.00	1.00
Some university	5,152	0.08	0.27	0.00	1.00
Bachelor's degree	5,152	0.18	0.39	0.00	1.00
MA/PhD	5,152	0.07	0.25	0.00	1.00
Age	5,016	44.30	16.34	18.00	95.00
Male	5,152	0.46	0.50	0.00	1.00
R has children at home	5,152	0.74	0.44	0.00	1.00
Divorced/separated	5,152	0.12	0.32	0.0	1.00
Single	5,152	0.26	0.44	0.00	1.00
Widowed	5,152	0.06	0.24	0.00	1.00
Household language – other	5,152	0.11	0.31	0.00	1.00
Household language – French	5,152	0.18	0.38	0.00	1.00
Retired	5,152	0.16	0.37	0.00	1.00
Unemployed	5,152	0.08	0.27	0.00	1.00
Student	5,152	0.07	0.26	0.00	1.00
Homemaker	5,152	0.05	0.22	0.00	1.00
Protestant	5,152	0.25	0.43	0.00	1.00
Evangelical Protestant	5,152	0.08	0.27	0.00	1.00
Catholic	5,152	0.39	0.49	0.00	1.00
Other religion	5,152	0.06	0.23	0.00	1.00
Recent immigrant (<5 yrs)	5,152	0.03	0.17	0.00	1.00
Recent immigrant (5-9 yrs)	5,152	0.03	0.17	0.00	1.00
Immigrant (10-20 yrs)	5,152	0.04	0.21	0.00	1.00
Immigrant (20+ yrs)	5,152	0.10	0.30	0.00	1.00
Canadian	5,152	0.08	0.27	0.00	1.00
French	5,152	0.15	0.35	0.00	1.00
Northern European	5,152	0.02	0.13	0.00	1.00
German	5,152	0.04	0.19	0.00	1.00
Southern European	5,152	0.02	0.15	0.00	1.00
Eastern European	5,152	0.02	0.14	0.00	1.00

▶

◀ TABLE 7A.1

Variable	N	Mean	Standard deviation	Minimum	Maximum
Ukrainian	5,152	0.02	0.12	0.00	1.00
Other European	5,152	0.02	0.13	0.00	1.00
Chinese	5,152	0.04	0.19	0.00	1.00
Filipino	5,152	0.01	0.11	0.00	1.00
Other Asian	5,152	0.02	0.13	0.00	1.00
Black/Caribbean	5,152	0.02	0.13	0.00	1.00
South Asian	5,152	0.03	0.17	0.00	1.00
Latin	5,152	0.01	0.09	0.00	1.00
Native	5,152	0.01	0.11	0.00	1.00
British/French/Canadian	5,152	0.04	0.20	0.00	1.00
British with Other	5,152	0.04	0.19	0.00	1.00
British with other European	5,152	0.01	0.12	0.00	1.00
Multiple European origin	5,152	0.02	0.14	0.00	1.00
VM with other origin	5,152	0.01	0.12	0.00	1.00
Aboriginal with other origin	5,152	0.01	0.10	0.00	1.00

NOTES

The opinions expressed in this report are those of the authors and do not necessarily reflect the views of the Department of Canadian Heritage.

1. There are thirteen strata and 153 clusters in this dataset.
2. For discussions of causal relationships between indicators of social capital, see Brehm and Rahn (1997) and Muller and Seligson (1994).
3. Further detail as to the construction of these variables can be found in the appendix above.
4. For a study of the impact of age on social capital, see Robinson and Jackson (2001); for education, see Helliwell and Putnam (1999) and Nie, Junn, and Stehlik-Barry (1996).
5. The method of preparation of these variables for analysis is described in the appendix of this chapter.
6. Data are analyzed using STATA's survey regression procedures. Using this program allows us to specify the characteristics of the sampling design (e.g., strata, clusters, and weights) and obtain unbiased point estimates and efficient standard errors. See StataCorp (1999).
7. The former ethnic comparison group has been broken out into three single origins – British, Canadian, and French and one multiple-origin group made up of

individuals claiming combinations of British, French, and Canadian. In this table, the comparison ethnic group is people claiming only British origin. The European group has been split into six single-origin groups (German, Ukrainian, Northern European, Eastern European, Southern European, and other European) and one group for people claiming combinations of European origins (European multiple). The visible minority category has also been split into six single-origin groups (Black/Caribbean, Latin American, Chinese, Filipino, South Asian, and other Asian) and one group for those claiming a visible-minority origin in combination with another origin. The Aboriginal group has been split into those claiming only Aboriginal origins and those claiming Aboriginal origins in combination with another origin. As well, there are two categories for people claiming a combination of European origins with majority origins (Majority with Northern European, and Majority with other European).

8
Social Capital and Political Struggles of Immigrants: Sri Lankan Tamils and Black Caribbean Peoples in Toronto

Sara Abraham

Debates on social capital have bolstered the assumption that activated networks in civil society can expand or deepen democratic practice. In this chapter, I extend this analysis to look at how transnational networks of immigrant populations in metropolitan countries can do the same. I focus on the first generation of two visible-minority communities concentrated in the Greater Toronto Area – the Sri Lankan Tamil and the Black Caribbean. I offer the hypothesis that these immigrant groups, drawing upon transnational discourses and networks, have demonstrably brought with them strong notions of reciprocity, community,[1] and justice, and have consequently struggled to transform dominant structures of exclusion upon arrival, thereby expanding and deepening Canadian structures of democracy. In this way, I question the terms on which the loaded notions of "integration" and "social cohesion" are usually posited, i.e., the immigrant acceptance of Canadian political and social norms, and the latter as the desirable standard (see Li 2003). The concept of social capital is useful for this task for two reasons: its normative neutrality, i.e., it is a "type of social relation," and its capacity for "working" at the level of network and association-building, contributing to an explanation of immigrant political activity. Yet, other concomitant social relations also ensure the limits of social capital in monopolizing the explanation for immigrant political activity. I explore some of these limits in the conclusion of this chapter.

Type of Social Relation: Ideology and Social Capital

In this chapter, I argue that persons of these two particular immigrant communities have "understood" each other by means of a non-assimilable idiom learnt "from" (if not "in") their "past" and that this has allowed them to agitate together to gain "access and resources" (Foley and Edwards 2001, 277). Specifically, I suggest that these immigrants have understood each other through shared experiences at a generalized level. This permits them to bond around new goals and spurs them to action in an environment in which they are not yet out-networked and in which they have no political experience. Loizos (2000) has made a similar argument about the settlement of refugees: "New relationships were formed in which a modicum of trust was extended simply because a person was linked to a *known* community, and the knowledge of that community was both shared ... and a basis for future association" (130).

I suggest that "understanding" of this kind creates a pool of people who are neither strangers nor social acquaintances. Understanding permits social interaction and the creation of shared projects. While Eisenberg (Chapter 4, this volume) suggests the centrality of trust to preferred political relations (between equals), my argument on this score is less normative. I simply argue that "understanding" in the Sri Lankan Tamil and anglophone Caribbean communities has been rooted in the ideologies of nationalism that hold them together, and political trust (within the pool) has been strictly contingent on this understanding. Whereas social capital usually refers to a "real" set of linkages, the social capital produced from shared nationalist understanding gives rise to "weak ties" and is premised on "the imagined community." Nonetheless, the effects are real and significant.

Black Caribbean and Tamil organizations in Toronto, of two relatively "poor" communities in the city, collectively have provided community members with a venue and a space, a source of network, cultural production, skills development, informal counselling, rights education, occasional employment, elder housing, and sports and recreation, all of which have been crucial for their settlement and quality of life. The documented public contributions have been in the form of strong intervention into numerous political debates and of opposition to systemic discrimination – through challenging policing practices, using human rights codes against discrimination, monitoring and broadening immigration criteria, participating in fair housing and fair employment struggles, feminist theorizing and movement building, promoting refugee rights, and defending civil liberties. Tangibly, a number of programs – including the Transitional Year Programs that enable underprivileged students to gain entrance into the University of Toronto and York University, the Heritage Classes in Toronto schools, Caribana (the largest national festival), and Black and Tamil track and sports events producing outstanding athletes – have been significant outcomes of the efforts of the communities.

The influence of Black musicians and musical traditions has also been highly significant in the development of popular Canadian culture.

Both these political and social histories, I argue, have been driven by an ideology of "nationalism," which itself has transnational linkages. These ideologies (and the belief-systems attached to them) have spurred collective action, and it could be said that ideologies are a part of what Edwards and Foley refer to as "the cultural reserves" from which identities are constructed and social capital "appropriated" (1997). Further, these extensions of ethnic communities into a wider Canadian life should not be viewed as arbitrary or exceptional but as transformative. They have sought to de-racialize the wider polity, sometimes independently and sometimes in tandem with other social justice organizations in the city. However, these forms of collective action can be perceived to run against the grain of "the social collective," and it is worth considering that the very debate on the possible "disintegrating" effect of "diversity" works from this premise. For instance, Minkoff (1997) has suggested that the rise of social movement organizations (such as civil rights groups and gay and lesbian advocacy groups) in the United States is evidence of the weakness of the claim of a "decline in civil society," and yet, since these organizations are perceived to generate "social conflict," they are not considered positively. I take her critique a step further. I argue that the wide de-racializing effects of Tamil and Caribbean mobilization have been good, not just for immigrants but also for Canada, and that they reflect the continuing production of positive forms of social capital.

Finally, my discussion shares with Eisenberg (see Chapter 4) a heavy qualification of the importance of the idea of "trust" to political-social capital, though for different reasons. Competing networks of social capital are endemic to community formation, and we see it in the two cases discussed in this chapter. For instance, nationalism as a patriarchal ideology frequently counteracts other resources of social capital, such as women's networking. As it turns out, women were very active in Caribbean-based nationalist institutions in Toronto, but then "broke away" to collectively institutionalize a distinct social capital. Yet, I argue that the nationalist organizations were a source of an important oppositional and resistant consciousness.

This argument is based on secondary and primary literature and interviews with key activists within both communities, and is part of an ongoing research project on the political participation of these two communities (Abraham 2002).[2] I have chosen to undertake a comparative study so as to more sharply demonstrate the point – in two cases – that transnational linkages of nationalist ideology, specifically Pan-Africanism and Tamil Nationalism, have been a critical element in creating local social capital and are central to explaining immigrant political activity.

Arrival and Institution-Building

Caribbean and Sri Lankan Tamil peoples migrated in large numbers to Canada in the post-1962 era, settling for the most part in the Greater Toronto Area. The Caribbean population arrived, on average, fifteen years before the Sri Lankans. According to their own estimates, each community numbers well above 200,000 in the Greater Toronto Area, composing what might be argued to be "political interest groups" (Jabbra 1997, 101). Both communities have shown vigorous political organizing in the first generation of their arrival. These are populations that are also similar on other important indices – they have been slotted into the formal and informal working class, they face particular hardships as visible minorities, and they come from deep original political cultures – but the details of the differences matter to the forms of politics they have demonstrated.

Caribbean middle-class and working-class immigrants, during the 1960s, faced a white settler society that was adjusting to a "flood" of non-white immigrants. Consequently, they were jointly at the forefront of a struggle for acceptance, serving as a wave of pioneers to de-racialize Canada in the major sectors of education, employment, housing, and the state – struggles that continue to this day. The majority of early migrants in the new stream of Caribbean migration were women working in racialized service sector occupations, followed by family members and men. With daily and systemic acts of exclusion confronting immigrants, "race" was the ground for much of the agitational politics developed by the community, which was conceptualized in studies of the community as anti-racism (Calliste 1996, 2000; Henry 1994; Stasiulis 1982), though the term was not used by the movement till the mid-1980s.[3] Black-based organizing around community, labour, cultural, and political issues has since produced a minor stream of alternative discourse, politics, and culture.

Sri Lankan Tamil migrants (with a pattern of men first followed by women and children) came into a more racially accustomed environment in the 1980s and 1990s. Yet, being predominantly a refugee population, they have had to endure particular forms of government surveillance as well as Western culture, a flexible low-wage labour market, and language barriers to employment, education, and political participation. As many of the migrants are petty bourgeois or professional in origin and have aspirations, the Canadian experience for this first generation has been very discouraging, and their experiences of exclusion, quite distinctive. In other words, distinct structures of exclusion inhibited their "integration." Their political identities, however, have been largely shaped by the conflict in Sri Lanka, and this is the touchstone of their organizing efforts in Canada.

Over a thirty-year period, seventy significant organizations have grown out of the Black Caribbean population, including secular, politically-oriented community organizations, women's groups, media organizations, and those connected to annual events. The high period of Caribbean organizational activity (first decade of arrival) was the 1970s, with a subsequent decline in activist organizations through the 1990s. Similarly, the Sri Lankan Tamil population has seen the formation of over thirty such organizations over a twenty-year period (see a full list of the organizations at the end of this chapter).

The key institutions that both communities organized in their first few years have had wide recognition and visibility within their respective communities. Most of these institutions have been interventionist and have contributed to the conditions for "self-determination" within the Canadian nation-state. Many of these organizations were founded with a view to making the community more self-reliant (e.g., they provide education for the community by the community) and self-defining (i.e., they stress the meaning of being "Black" or "Tamil"). Youth have had a prominent place in the more activist organizations of both communities. They have been some of the sharpest advocates of "nationalism." In the following section, I sketch what these ideologies have offered to activists upon their arrival and settlement in Toronto and demonstrate how they have shaped identity formation as well as institution-building.

Pan-Africanism

Transnational links between Canada and the Caribbean are many centuries old, based primarily on the fish trade, mining, and banking interests in the island region. For at least a century, Canada has been a destination for Caribbean migrants who have been drawn through links created by these trades and industries. Within this colonial relationship, the transnational ideology[4] of Pan-Africanism came to crystallize the thought of many Caribbean radicals in Canada. The most powerful expressions of this body of thought and action have included Garveyism in the 1930s and 1940s and Black Power in the

1960s and 1970s. When Caribbean immigrants started arriving in large numbers in the 1960s, a few activists found two key Black community organizations, the Home Services Association and the UNIA (United Negro Improvement Association), already in existence in Toronto.

The UNIA, formed as a Garveyite institution, was located downtown on College Street and soon became a point of reference for Caribbean immigrant activist youth. Its members had already been involved with Sleeping Car Porters, the most significant of the Black (male) labour struggles of the previous generation. It now came to share its building with the most successful of the new collective projects, the Black Education Project, from the early 1970s. The Home Services Association, formed by Nova Scotian Black Canadians who had settled in Toronto, had even closer and more immediate links with many of the activists who arrived in the late 1960s. It also had a building in the heart of the activist base in the city – the Bathurst-Bloor region – and was already engaged in educational work with school age children and youth, a key form of community involvement that the new activists picked up. Some of the leading youth activists at the time were, in fact, not US or Caribbean transplants but were Black Canadians who had grown up around the Home Services Association. In other words, two generations of Pan-Africanists came together in this period. Meetings were held often in the Home Services building where members discussed not only the issues of immigration but also of African and Black history.

A major collective project to establish a Black community centre was devised but did not come to fruition. However, the more immediate imperative, to address severe inequities in schooling and youth education, drew plenty of community interest and involvement. The Black Education Project schooled hundreds of Caribbean children in an effort to redress what parents were observing as hostility, as well as a lack of preparedness, in the Toronto education system for large numbers of Caribbean immigrant children. The children were not succeeding in school and were facing overt hostility not only from peers but also from teachers, causing extreme concern to parents who had migrated in many cases for "a good education" for their children. The confrontation with institutional exclusion and a lack of state support created the need for "a coming together," and intra-community bonds were forged. It was not until the mid- to late 1970s that "bridging capital" in the form of links with sympathetic trustees on the School Board began to encourage public discussion of more ambitious changes in the school curriculum.

The activists that started and ran many of the community organizations were high school, university, and former students. As Caribbean migrants, they did not necessarily arrive with a strong "Black" consciousness, yet they could quickly come to identify with the broader political currents and larger changes sweeping North America at the time. In Canada, they were able to experience firsthand these changes, which helped crystallize their political orientation. They met with Black conscientious objectors who came to Canada in the 1960s (among an estimated 60,000 Americans). Stokely Carmichael, leader of the Black Panther Party, a US Black nationalist organization, spoke to a large crowd in Toronto in 1966. An African Liberation Support Committee (there were branches all over the United States) was formed in Toronto in 1968. There already were regular protests at the South African embassy in the city. One interviewee states that, within a week of arriving in Canada in 1974 as a high school student, she attended a demonstration protesting the killing of sixteen-year-old Michael Habib by a white man "who was out to get one of them that day." She was immediately drawn from then on to Pan-Africanist ideas. The names of most of the organizations formed in that decade (see the list at the end of this chapter) carried the word "Black" – not "Caribbean" and rarely "Canadian," generating divisions among sections of the community,[5] but also indicative of the larger context for the local mobilization.

Organized events attracting a few thousand people included the Black Writers Congress in Montreal in 1968, a huge Black Conference in Toronto in 1970, and African Liberation Day celebrations in Toronto in 1972. These events brought together new Caribbean migrants to Canada with African Americans involved in civil rights struggles, Caribbean-based radicals facing exile from the region, and other Black activists already living in Canada. They made real the transnational connections between the activists and consolidated the ideology of Black Power in Canada. Discussions on Black identity filled the early issues of the Toronto-based community newspaper *Contrast*, as did accounts of African struggles and US civil rights folk heroes. The repercussions of the Sir George Williams University (now Concordia University) showdown in 1969 in Montreal led to a tour of the Caribbean by activists who spoke of their experiences using a Pan-Africanist analysis. Such analyses grounded the activists' sense of the larger mission of what was still a burgeoning movement in Canada.

Meanwhile, young people in the Caribbean faced increasing repression as new national governments sought to curb the incursion of Black Power ideology into the region. Those who moved to Canada could draw on their own national histories to understand the resistance they faced in Canada, and this allowed them to enter the networks. In an interview, a leading Jamaican-born activist recalls that the anti-Vietnam struggle was the major issue that he participated in at York University in 1967-68. Only subsequently did he encounter organizations and individuals linked with Pan-Africanism, but, when he did so, they became the base of his networks. Thus, as he put it, he moved from the political philosophy of self-reliance as propounded by Ho Chi Minh toward that of Marcus Garvey, C.L.R. James, and Walter Rodney, finding no essential difference. Utilizing his links with supportive faculty and administrators, he went on to spearhead the establishment of the Transitional Year Programs in the Toronto universities. Selective socialist groups in Montreal and Toronto also came to be seen as supportive of the same "anti-colonial" mindset, and working links were established with groups such as Latin American Working Group. The aftermath of the Sir George Williams events also impacted community politics by allowing a political relationship to form between the Montreal Caribbean community and the Toronto Caribbean community, along with other socialist organizations that offered support and publicity to the detained students. Social clubs and Black musical artists of reggae, soul, and funk from the US also linked the members of the diaspora. Music and dance provided key spaces in which social links, between men and women as well as within the genders, could be made.

Most of the organizations (see list at end of chapter) included women and men, and almost none were dominantly male. The mass conferences tended to showcase articulate men, but the organizations themselves were run with women and youth power. A next generation of activism, from the mid-1970s onward, saw the development of women-led and women's-issue activities, such as those related to the struggles of domestic workers and nurses. However, all the major Black and Caribbean women activists who came into their own through the 1980s and 1990s still credit the Black consciousness and social movement as a venue for learning their own politics, creating new networks, and deepening their thinking. Without homogenizing the experiences, Black women's organizing and ideology, as it subsequently developed, was part of an internationalist movement in which, according to poet-activist June Jordan, "black women's visions are not limited to a narrow and essentialist identity politics" (Sudbury 1998, 2).

A number of the Caribbean activists – Rosie Douglas (later prime minister of Dominica), Jacqueline Creft (later minister of education of Grenada),

Horace Campbell (leading Pan-Africanist intellectual), among others – left Canada and became significant political actors in their home countries or within an international Pan-Africanist movement, which demonstrates the seriousness of the political work undertaken in Canada and belies the suggestion that agitation was a mere youthful phase for these individuals. Black organizations and issues have continued to run parallel to the mainstream in Toronto, even as many of the base communities have parted ways and developed "national" cultural identities, compounded by the complexities of engaging with the post-1980s immigrants from Africa.

In summary, I have argued that a vigorous social movement that was rooted and routed through organizations and networks of Caribbean immigrants, along with Canadian Black community members, spun out from the consciousness of Pan-Africanism as it was being articulated and developed in the 1960s and early 1970s. It lasted for about a decade and laid the groundwork for intra-community unity and bond-building.

Tamil Nationalism

Tamil nationalism traces its roots to the Dravida movement of South India in the 1930s and 1940s. This was an anti-colonial, anti-caste, and nationalist struggle. The ideas of women's liberation, cross-caste marriage, rationalism, and anti-Brahmanism propelled a mass sub-nationalist movement of progressive anti-colonial resistance. This early movement paved the way for the contemporary Tamil aspirations for political and cultural liberation that have developed with particular intensity in Sri Lanka.

In Sri Lanka, Tamil Nationalism is rooted in the minority Tamil community's resistance to a Sinhala-ethnic chauvinist state and its army, its militant and armed struggle for a particular territory, and its defence of a particular culture. It is classically nationalist – self-serving, myth-making, and hegemonic in its definition of peoples' history and culture. It has been tremendously strengthened by the brutal war waged against the people by the Sri Lankan Sinhala army, with little international effort to resolve the conflict, and has fed into the strong resistance offered by the Liberation Tigers of Tamil Eelam (LTTE) in fighting for the "liberation" of the Tamil homeland.

The official international leadership of Tamil Nationalism lies in the World Tamil Movement (WTM), now situated in numerous countries. The material resources of the World Tamil Movement far surpass those of the Pan-Africanist movement. They support offices, staff, and an infrastructure of communication and trade, creating a political leadership for Tamils in

Toronto. In Canada, activists working out of the WTM, the Canadian Council of Tamils, and the Tamil Eelam Society (TESOC) closely monitor immigration, refugee, and deportation policies. With many families still divided between continents and many people still arriving and claiming refugee status, it is crucial to the Tamil community in Canada that the doorway to Canada remains open. A number of Tamils have been denied asylum, many families have not been reconnected, and a few individuals have been deported, thus educating the community to a less benign view of Canada as a "refugee haven."

The activists are varied in origin and experience. A significant proportion of the membership and leadership of organizations such as TESOC, the Canadian Tamil Congress (CTC), and Canadian Tamil Youth Development (CanTYD), the largest locally oriented groups today in Toronto, were not politically active in Sri Lanka, for they were too young, were not from Jaffna (the epicentre of the movement), or had emigrated to Africa, Canada, or the UK in the 1970s or earlier. The class and cultural differences, as well as the differences in direct experience of war, are glossed over to create a "unified voice." On this point, it is worth considering that only one of the cases of deportation generated public mobilization. In 1997, over 850 Tamils gathered outside the Parliament Buildings in Ottawa to protest the planned deportation of the WTM coordinator,[6] which is an indication of the controlled and strategic orientation of Tamil Nationalist ideology. The one independent Tamil women's group that formed, Villipu, eventually folded under a series of intra-community rumours and accusations about the personal lives of its feminist leaders as well as about ideological views that challenged some premises of Tamil Nationalism.[7]

Central to Tamil Nationalist ideology has been the continuous production of nationalist feeling, necessarily visceral (in the context of war), romantic (to promote heroism), and propagandistic (to achieve "consensus"). A second task of the ideology, particularly in Canada, has been the publicizing of Tamil arrival and settlement with a view to advertising its successes and supporting the settlement and advancement of "our people" through promoting a model minority ideology and appealing to Canadian power brokers on that promise. A third task has been to provide social support – employment-related, legal, and social recognition – for Tamil migrants and their families, as a reinforcement of "our people." Finally, the ideology is strongly gendered and familial, upholding values of stable intra-community marriages with traditional roles for men and women, respect for elders and tradition, passing on language and culture to the children, and personal and material sacrifice for "nation."

The ideology of Tamil Nationalism has thus intervened in the consolidation of Tamil community in Toronto at a number of levels. It has attempted to keep alive the community's loyalty to the struggle and the language through multiple newspapers, constant news updates, editorials eliciting support, radio stations, TV stations (with similarity to Latinidad, another language-based culture), phone lists updating "members" about political developments and obligations, and a number of relief organizations that maintain community support, materially and ideologically, for the struggle and for the rehabilitation of victims and refugees in Sri Lanka. The relative success of the transnational ideology also arises from the fact that some of the key, younger community activists, now graduated from Canadian universities, remember scenes of war or of the poverty of life under war, but have no memory of life before the war. The seeking of international recognition of the legitimacy of LTTE, an ongoing struggle in itself, informs the goals of the local activists and makes their work viable. At the same time, the cultural spaces offered by local multicultural policy have offered the possibility for youth to be Canadian and Tamil, combining, albeit uneasily, their own desires with those of their parents and the Movement.

In developing a framework for local political intervention, some youth have begun to critique mainstream media as perpetuating stereotypes regarding the struggle at home and the lives of Tamils in Toronto. The media is accused of distorting key facts in their descriptions of the community, for instance, remittances become "coerced extraction," victims of state violence become "terrorists," and so on. Following a spate of such *National Post* articles in 2000, a press release from the Canada-wide Tamil students' organization CUTSU stated that over thirty-five recent articles have "consistently depicted the Tamil community as terrorists, drug smugglers, people smugglers, frauds, and criminals. These false accusations have created a negative environment for the Tamil-Canadian community to work, study, socialize, and be fully contributing members of Canadian society." The same press release pointed out that Tamils in Canada "are making great strides in education as a vast majority of our youth are going on to post-secondary education ... We have established scholarships and bursaries at universities, raised money for hospitals, the Cancer Society, the Red Cross, the Food Bank."[8] The Canadian federal election of 2000 followed the above-mentioned events and saw, according to my survey, a very high voter turnout from the community, ten points above the Canadian average. This helps establish the hope that there can be a Tamil voting bloc and also indicates a highly internally networked community.

In my own survey within the community (Abraham 2002), I found that major local concerns included the negative media portrayal of the community, the cost of housing, the lack of remunerative employment, and cultural problems faced by parents. In tackling the media rather than the "living condition" issues of which they are aware, Tamil youth appear to betray a preoccupation with "image"; however, image is, indeed, important in restoring the credibility of a community associated with violent politics here and at home. Where they can, they make their own interventions, as in youth counselling for which they have set up networks through the CanTYD. This youth organization as a matter of course stresses the cultural value of being Tamil, maintaining Tamil gender norms, and keeping the language in use.

The primary work of Tamil Nationalism in Canada has thus been to achieve in-group consolidation in order to produce support for the liberation struggle at home. The activist youth (with some school board support) have struck relationships with more high-risk Tamil youth. There are also strategic, quiet networks extending into the Canadian state, political parties, and media. The combination of supporting the struggle at home with developing mechanisms of support for Tamils in Toronto produced the agenda of the First Convention of the Canadian Tamil Congress (CTC) on 1-2 June 2002. The CTC, a body that calls itself the "united voice" of Tamils in Canada, is modelled after the Canadian Jewish Congress. Its leadership overlaps with the leadership of CanTYD, as well as with long-time activists in various other social service Tamil organizations such as TESOC, and claims hegemony over community organizational space. Strong resolutions at the Convention around the peace process (in Sri Lanka), business development (in Canada), media coverage (of Sri Lanka and immigrants), and Human Rights (in Sri Lanka) suggest that the interests of the Tamil community are linked to these issues. International concerns dominate the framework for local involvement, but the organizations also offer some resources for a struggling first generation, as well as producing spokespeople to represent their Tamil issues to the Canadian state. "Politics" rather than "protest" has been the preferred strategy toward the local environment.

Conclusion
I have argued that Black Caribbean and Sri Lankan Tamil immigrant groups

in Toronto have drawn on, albeit differently, transnational discourses and networks to enact strong notions of reciprocity, community, and justice through internal community development in order to transform dominant structures of exclusion and to meet their own interests. The stigma of racialization, itself reflecting the negative value of social capital (one is denied or harassed based on putative links with a community), has been challenged through mobilization around the complex nationalist politics of "being Black" and "being Tamil." (Whether nationalist politics is sufficient to tackle the ongoing state racialization of the youth and the "gangs" of both communities is obviously doubtful.) In making this argument, I have used the concept of social capital, primarily, as linked to the cultural-political resources of ideology, in order to trace some of the processes of community formation. I have argued that transnational ideologies have shaped new immigrants into a collective of shared perspectives and thus have provided the impetus toward in-group bonding, with key activists bridging across subcommunities. Bridging between the community and the state has been recognized by the communities for its value, yet, on the whole, has been made difficult by complex and profound, sometimes oppositional, community interests, producing an inherent instability that needs further study as to its implications for the utility of the notion of social capital.

Further, neither ideology nor organization-building can by themselves explain the two political movements described here. It is, rather, in the interrelationship between the two kinds of "capital" that we see the formation of the new social capital of interlinked and synergized community organizations. Such "movements" are hardly unique. International political ideological currents (such as Bolshevism or Garveyism), as well as support for politics "at home" (such as nationalist feeling), have often influenced migrant workers' politics and their creation of new political organizations (Gonzales and Strikwerda 1998). First-generation Italians in Brazil and Argentina, Turks in Germany, Grenadians in Trinidad, Jews in Israel/Palestine, Indians in East Africa, Chinese in Malaya, and others have been important players in political, community, and labour struggles – even leaders on occasion – with variants of "nationalism" frequently fuelling the agitation. Immigrant encounters rooted in emancipatory ideas or transnational streams have also been heavily documented from the nineteenth century onward for the United States (James 1998; Roediger 1991; Voss 1993). More contemporaneously, language-based political cultures such as Latinidad have radicalized migrant workers who have then turned their attention to local injustices (Davis 2000). It seems quite clear that the notion of social capital does not alone capture the processes and dynamics of these social movement-like developments.

A third qualification of the utility of the notion of social capital lies in the processes of integration. While I have suggested the efficacy of the initial creation of social capital, the subsequent decline in movement organizing coincides with an increasing hegemony of Canadian cultural norms, the effects of multicultural structuring of community social action (see Stasiulis 1982), and the rise of the Canadian-born generation. Whether the fate of these communities is in-group stratification with "advanced marginalization" for some, linked to social control by their own more privileged community members (a heavily gendered process), as theorized in Cohen's insightful study of African Americans in the United States (1999, 33-77), remains to be seen. On this cautionary note, we might also ask about the dampening effect of integration on intra-community bonds, which leads to an individualization of struggle and a defeat for community interests. Yet, more optimistically, perhaps, the new organizational forms, new ideas, and new linkages have stuck. We could also ask whether there has been an infusion of transnationally circulating ideas into Canadian social structures and institutions, as pushed by immigrants and activists for a betterment of the lives of themselves and others. I hope to have shown that the concept of social capital, as it links idea to understanding to institution to network, within and across communities, allows us to closely follow these processes.

APPENDIX

Major Secular Community Organizations, Media, and Annual Events in the Sri Lankan Tamil and Black Caribbean Communities

ANGLO-CARIBBEAN

1960s	CO	UNIA (defunct)
	CO	Home Services Association (defunct)
	CO	Canadian Negro Women's Association (defunct)
Late 1960s	CO	African Liberation Support Committee (defunct)
	CO	Jamaican Canadian Association
	CO	National Black Canadian Conference (defunct)
	CO	Congress of Black Women of Canada (BWC)
	M	Contrast (defunct)
	M	Black Liberation News (defunct)
	M	Islander (defunct)

▶

◂ Appendix

	M	Share
	CO	Tenants Hotline of Don Vale Community Centre
	CO	Black Education Project (BEP) (defunct)
	CO	Black Resources Information Centre (defunct)
	CO	Black Youth Organization (BYO) (defunct)
	CO	Black Student Unions
	CO	Black Theatre Canada (defunct)
	CO	African Liberation Support Committee (defunct)
	CO	Brotherhood Community Centre Project (BCCP) (defunct)
	CO	Black Liaison Committee (defunct)
	CO	Harriet Tubman Youth Centre
	CO	Black People's Library (defunct)
	CO	Ryerson Afro-Caribbean Association
	CO	Coalition of Black Trade Unionists
	CO	IMMICAN (defunct)
	CO	Afro-Caribbean Theatre Workshop
	CO	Black Women's Support Program
	CO	Black Sisterhood
	CO	Grenada Support Group (defunct)
	CO	Association of Concerned Guyanese (defunct)
	AE	African Liberation Day
	AE	Caribana
1980s	CO	Caribbean and Black Action Group (defunct)
	CO	Canadian Alliance of Black Educators
	CO	International Committee on Racism
	CO	Sistervision Press
	CO	Black Women's Collective
	CO	Coalition in Support of Black Nurses
	CO	Committee for Racial Equality (against the KKK) (defunct)
	CO	CIRPA
	M	Our Lives
	M	Caribbean Camera
	M	Pride
	M	Indo-Caribbean News
	AE	International Rastafarian Conference
	AE	Rodney Memorial Events
1990s	CO	Peel Sisters in Action
	CO	Black Action Defense Committee
	CO	Coalition for Black Nurses
	CO	Garvey-Rodney-Committee (defunct)
	CO	Cheddi Jagan Centre
	CO	Tropicana
	M	Flo 89.5 (2001)
	CO	African Canadian Legal Clinic

▶

Appendix

	CO	Masani Productions
	CO	African Canadian Coalition against Racism (2000)
	CO	Black Youth United (2001)
	CO	Black Youth International (2001)
	AE	International Dub Conference

Sri Lankan Tamil

1970	CO	Tamil Eelam Society (TESOC)
	CO	Canada Sri Lanka Association
1980s	CO	Senior Tamils Centre
	CO	World Tamil Movement (WTM), with affiliate organizations
	CO	SECAM
	CO	CAFTARR (defunct)
	CO	Tamil Resource Centre (Thedagam) (TRC)
1990s	CO	Villipu (Women's Organization) (defunct)
	CO	Vasantham Wellness Centre
	CO	Tamil Service Providers' Network
	CO	Canadian Tamil Youth Development (CanTYD)
	CO	FACT (apex organization)
	CO	Tamil Academy of Fine Arts and Technology
	CO	TEEDOR (Technical Help for Reconstruction of Eelam)
	CO	TEEMS (Medical Services)
	CO	Various University Tamil Student Organizations and CUTSU
	CO	Canadian Tamil Congress (2000) (CTC)
	M	24 hour Digital TV Channel
	M	24 hour Radio Stations (4)
	M	Defunct Newspapers (3)
	M	Eelanadu
	M	Eelamurasu
	M	Nammaadhu
	M	Ulagar Thamilar
	M	Mukhamukham
	M	Udayan
	M	Senthirai
	AE	Great Warrior Day
	AE	Black Tigers Day
	AE	Women's Day of Tamil Eelam
	AE	Rajani-De Sousa Memorial (defunct)

NOTE: This is a list in construction.
CO = community organization (these were mostly all initially community-financed and run)
M = media (not including the Internet since local readership and popularity is hard to ascertain)
AE = annual event
SOURCE: Interviews by the author and fieldwork notes; Stasiulis (1982); Cheran (2001); *Share Magazine* (Caribbean weekly), 1981-84.

ACKNOWLEDGMENTS

I would like to acknowledge the generosity of my friends in both communities who set up interviews for me. I would like to thank all the interviewees for their trust and time. I would also like to thank the reviewers of this volume for pushing me to better understand my use of the notion of social capital.

NOTES

1. The idea of community as a good needs to be heavily qualified by feminist analysis of the relations of patriarchy, property, hierarchy, caste, and other violent relations within communities of origin (see Banerji 1999) and of the attempts by male elites to recreate such communities after settlement. My point thus solely applies to other relations also found within communities – of shared culture and language, affinity, familiarity, supportive relations of kinship, solidarity against discrimination, the pooling of resources, and so on.
2. I have published some of the empirical findings that follow in Abraham (2004). In this chapter, I explore the details in relation to the notion of social capital.
3. Agnes Calliste, conversation, 28 May 2002.
4. Flows of transnationalism can be traced at many levels other than ideology – material (remittances), kin (immediate, extended, and fictive), culture (Caribana is the most obvious, but musical genres, musicians, and sub-cultures), technology and science, to name the most common, though I cannot explore these dimensions within this chapter.
5. The *Caribbean Chronicle* in March 1968 had this to say – "It is extremely difficult to understand what good it will do West Indians to stir up a civil war in Canada in the name of Black Power. Canada has opened its doors to thousands of West Indians in search of betterment for themselves and their families. With the growing rumblings of Black Power it is quite easy for Canada to decide to shut the door, or at least make it much more difficult for would-be immigrants from the Caribbean."
6. TamilNet, 28 September 1997.
7. Other autonomous groups, reflecting the diversity of opinion and the history of competing Tamil groups in Sri Lanka itself, have also not always found space in which to organize.
8. One respondent told me that the media gives no indication of the enormous contribution that diaspora Tamils were making to infrastructural and humanitarian development in Eelam/Sri Lanka through professional expertise, developing a plan for a postwar reconstruction of Tamil society, and charity contributions.

Part 3
Consequences of Social Capital: Policy and Government Programs

9
Social Capital and Intergenerational Coresidence: How Ethnic Communities and Families Shape Transitions to Adulthood

Barbara A. Mitchell

Over the past several decades, there has been a profound transformation in the home-leaving behaviour of young adults in many areas of the industrialized world. Young people are increasingly likely to remain in their parents' homes until later ages, leading some researchers to characterize this generation as "on hold" due to their prolonged dependency on parental household resources (Côté and Allahar 1994). Notably, Canadian census data show that 41 percent of the 3.8 million young adults aged twenty to twenty-nine lived with their parents in 2001, a rise from 27 percent two decades earlier. Moreover, almost one-third of all young adults have "boomeranged" home – 33 percent of young men and 28 percent of young women (Statistics Canada 2003), thereby contributing to a growing phenomenon of "crowded" and "refilled" nests. At a macro-level, tougher economic conditions for young people, increased post-secondary enrolment, later ages of marriage, and continuing high rates of immigration are the chief reasons underlying these trends (Mitchell, Wister, and Gee 2004).

Indeed, research finds that ethnocultural factors play a significant role in the formation of intergenerational living arrangements (e.g., Boyd 2000; Goldscheider and Goldscheider 1993, 1999). Looking at Canadian census data, Boyd (2000) documents that ethnic origin, controlling for other co-variates, is one of the strongest factors related to coresidence at this phase of the family life cycle. The highest rates of coresidence are exhibited by Greek, Italian, Balkan, Portuguese, South Asian Chinese, Jewish, and other Southeastern Asian groups.

The probability of young adults living at home is also affected by other family background factors, such as family structure and intergenerational relationship quality. For instance, Mitchell's (1994) research finds that young adults growing up in certain types of family structures (e.g., step-families) are more likely to leave home at an early age. Young people with more positive parent-child relations are more likely to remain at, or return, home than those with weak or conflictual family ties (e.g., Mitchell, Wister, and Gee 2000). Several materially based factors, such as family socioeconomic status, as well as characteristics of the young adults themselves (e.g., gender, age, marital status, personal income, and employment status), are also found to predict the likelihood of coresidence (Boyd and Norris 2000; Gee, Mitchell and Wister 1995; Goldscheider and Goldscheider 1999; Mitchell, Wister, and Gee 2004). For example, females generally leave home earlier than males, and young persons with jobs are more likely to establish a separate residence than those who are chronically unemployed.

Although this body of research highlights the importance of considering cultural, social, economic, and sociodemographic factors, a detailed examination of how these mechanisms operate with respect to specific Canadian ethnic groups is lacking. In particular, there is a paucity of research focusing on how social resources, embedded within structured networks of association, affect living arrangements and the transition to adulthood. Young adults from traditional ethnic groups, for example, may be exposed to normative structures that affect their choices as to when, and under what circumstances, they should leave the parental home. Clearly, this information is crucial to an understanding of contemporary family life in a highly multicultural society that is undergoing rapid social and economic change.

Moreover, this research can uncover patterns that show how disparities in resources can translate to unequal opportunities during the transition to adulthood, which may have profound lifelong consequences. Substantial research, for instance, documents that many early home-leavers – particularly those that leave home before the completion of high school – may face a lifetime of disadvantage. This is often due to a lack of social capital in the form of a supportive and stable family environment (e.g., see Simons and Whitbeck 1991).

To gain an understanding of how cultural and social factors influence coresidence and transitions to adulthood, we need to develop conceptual frameworks that can connect macro and micro processes across individuals, families, communities, and society. A synthesis of the concept of "social capital" and tenets of the life-course perspective offers a theoretical approach that has the potential to meet these goals. Consistent with other authors in this volume (e.g., Kay and Bernard, Chapter 2; Curtis and Perks, Chapter 6; Aizlewood and Pendakur, Chapter 7; and Abraham, Chapter 8), I define social capital as "social connections among individuals" such that it "inheres in the structure of relations" (Bourdieu 1986; Coleman 1988, 1990b; Putnam 2000). Unlike economic capital, which is more "tangible," access to social capital can generate valuable resources (i.e., social support) that exist in networks of relations. It can be found in cultural groups that emphasize "familistic" norms and values, or it can be found within mutually supporting, close-knit families. Linking social and other types of capital (e.g., economic) to the notion of life-course transitions and transition reversals represents a dynamic perspective that is well suited to framing family diversity in social capital during the transition to adulthood.

Given the existing conceptual and research gaps, the primary objective of this chapter is to explore the relative importance of ethnic and family background factors (as forms of social capital) in the timing of leaving home and the propensity to return home after an initial "launch." Coresidence may be indicative of social capital (e.g., stronger networks of relationships) within the parental household, which can generate a number of social and economic benefits for young adults as they navigate their way to "full adulthood." In this sense, the ethnic and family nexus is inextricably linked to home-leaving timing and to pathways into and out of the parental home through various types of social resources. The four ethnocultural groups under study here include Canadian young adults of British, Chinese, Indian (Indo/East Indian), and Southern European origin, between the ages of nineteen and thirty-five. These groups were chosen on the basis of their diversity and their constituting some of the major ethnic groups in Canada. The results of this analysis will have implications for contemporary transitions to adulthood, social inequality, social policy, and community programs.

Life-Course Theory and Social Capital

The life-course theoretical perspective has its roots in a wide range of disciplines, including sociology, demography, economics, and developmental psychology (see also Mitchell 2003 for a discussion of the origins of this perspective). This framework is useful for studying family-related transitions and behaviours within structural contexts as well as amid social and economic change (Elder 1978, 1985; Hagestad 1990). As a concept, the life course reflects the intersection of social, cultural, economic, and historical factors with personal biography. The life course consists of interlocking trajectories or pathways across the life span, which are marked by sequences of transitions that are marked by behaviours such as young adults' home-leaving. However, transitions do not necessarily proceed in a given order or sequence, and transition "reversals," such as a "boomerang" home, may occur.

This perspective is useful for studying how household living arrangements, embedded within a sociohistorical time period and geographical location, are formed over the life course and how they affect the transition to adulthood. Living arrangements are shaped (and reshaped) by family background and cultural factors (e.g., relationship quality, norms, values) and traditions embedded within family and social histories (Hareven 1996). Therefore, it is assumed that one's cultural and family environment and the opportunity to draw upon parental resources are pivotal in the timing and pathways of home-leaving, which influences the transition to adulthood in profound ways, both in the short and long terms.

Two major tenets of the life-course perspective have particular relevance for this study. The first theme is the recognition of heterogeneity in levels of and access to resources that affect the timing and pathways of life course events. The second theme is "the ripple effect," that is, the conditions under which events or transitions experienced earlier in life affect subsequent life-course patterns (George 1993). The concept of "social capital" will be used to embellish both of these themes.

Heterogeneity and Social Capital

Researchers commonly challenge the assumption that there is an "institutionalized life course" (George 1993; Meyer 1986). Instead, diversity in transitional behaviours is emphasized, and researchers are paying close attention to how heterogeneity in social structures and processes shape family development over the life course. Of relevance to the present study is the idea that life-course patterns can vary according to the "stock" of social capital that is present or available during transitional points or events. As such, this concept alludes to some measure of inequality since it includes certain people in networks with access to resources, thereby excluding others (as noted by Kay and Bernard in Chapter 3).

The concept of social capital has been defined in numerous ways (e.g., Bourdieu 1986; Coleman 1988, 1990b; Lin 2001a) and has its limitations. Yet, there is a growing consensus that social capital represents the ability of actors to secure benefits by virtue of membership in social networks or other social structures (Portes 1998). Pioneering this term in the 1970s, Bourdieu used this concept to characterize the advantages and opportunities accrued to people through membership in particular communities. He states that social capital is "the aggregate of the actual and potential resources which are linked to possession of a durable network of more or less institutionalized relationships of mutual acquaintance and recognition – or in other words, to membership in a group which provides each of its members with the backing of the collectively owned capital" (Bourdieu 1986, 248-49).

Unlike economic capital, which is more concrete (e.g., income, savings), social capital "exists in the relations among persons" (Coleman 1988, S100). Beginning with a theory of rational action, Coleman argues that people have both control over and interest in maintaining certain resources. Ethnic groups, for example, often have a strong desire to maintain and perpetuate their cultural heritage. Social capital is a particularly valuable resource in that it is productive – it makes possible the achievement of certain ends that would be unattainable in its absence. For example, as discussed by Abraham (Chapter 8), social capital can contribute to identity and interest formation among recent immigrant groups. More generally, involvement in social networks can also build social structure and enhance community integration (Putnam 2000).

Since social capital resides in social relationships, it can be found when young adults are embedded within certain ethnic communities and within certain families. It manifests itself as social connectedness or support, and it is influenced by ethnic or cultural factors. In particular, cultural groups can transmit important norms, values, and expectations. As previously noted by Kay and Bernard (Chapter 3), these normative structures not only reproduce social capital and become enacted in micro-social relationships but also establish expectations for future interactions. Young adults raised in tight-knit or traditional ethnic communities, therefore, are often exposed to operating principles that reproduce existing stocks of social capital. These communities are characterized by a high degree of institutional closure, which promotes community cohesion and integration.

Within these ethnic communities, social capital maintains its strength and value through regular activation of networks via the normative structures of key socializing institutions. As discussed by Abraham in Chapter 8, groups can share "ideologies and traditional behaviours that can be sustained through shared understandings." They can also participate in activities that reinforce adherence to traditional ethnic customs and mores. Ideologies and traditional behaviours, therefore, can be sustained through shared understanding and participation in activities that reinforce adherence to traditional ethnic customs and mores. Furthermore, regular participation in religious activities and association with peers from the same ethnic peer group promote structures of exclusion and inclusion. In this way, and as previously articulated by Kay and Bernard (Chapter 3), "norms are crucial to determining who is 'in' and who is 'out.'" Individuals who conform to group norms maintain membership within the group, while failure to comply with dominant norms can result in negative sanctions and exclusion from the group.

The present study assumes that cultural membership on both a macro- and a micro-level can mould norms and expectations and choices regarding home-leaving. In particular, cultural groups create and reproduce their own "social capital," which generates distinctive "social timetables." These refer to the normatively scheduled occurrence of key life course events that provide individuals and their families with social and cognitive "road-maps" to guide life-course decisions (Hagestad and Neugarten 1985). Individuals adhere to cultural group expectations pertaining to when and under what circumstances they should make transitions in order to avoid the negative social sanctions associated with being "out of sync" or "off time." As a result, ethno-cultural environments perpetuate unique social timetables that govern expectations about the appropriate timing and pathways under which young adults leave the parental home.

Young adults from more familistic or "traditional" cultural backgrounds (e.g., Asians and Southern Europeans) are, therefore, expected to display different patterns of home-leaving than do young adults from British backgrounds. Asian and Southern European young adults are expected to leave home for marriage, school, or for employment rather than to achieve independence, because of the high value their communities place on familistic behaviours and educational achievement. Indo young adults, in particular, are expected to be likely to stay home until the time of marriage. In this cultural group, parents continue to play a major role in helping their children choose a marital partner, and they often encourage children (especially daughters) to leave home at the time of marriage rather than to pursue individualistic goals (Mitchell, Wister, and Gee 2004). These pathways may translate into later ages of leaving home and fewer returns after an initial departure, especially among those who leave to marry and start building a family.

Conversely, young adults from more individualistic cultural backgrounds (e.g., British) may be encouraged to leave home to achieve "independence," often coupled with work or school, rather than for family-related reasons (e.g., to marry). British cultural groups often place a high value on individual goals and autonomy, and remaining at home until marriage is no longer a dominant cultural norm. This would likely result in younger ages of home-leaving and a higher proclivity for a subsequent return home because of an "incomplete" launch.

Another interrelated source of social capital found within families can stem from the quality of parent-child relationships, which can be considered apart from ethnocultural membership. Indeed, Coleman (1988, S111) states that, "even if adults are physically present, there is a lack of social capital in the family if there are not strong relations between parents and children." This is crucial for enabling the child to profit from access to other kinds of resources. Coleman points out: "The social capital of the family is the relations between children and parents ... That is, if the human capital possessed by parents is not complemented by social capital embodied in family relations, it is irrelevant to the child's educational growth that the parent has a great deal, or a small amount of human capital" (S110).

In this way, social capital can represent a filter through which the financial and human capital of parents is transmitted to and employed by children (Teachman, Paasch, and Carver 1997). As such, social capital can either enhance or dilute the presence of other parental resources (Coleman 1990b). Thus, if parent-child relationships are not strong, children may not be able to "profit" from other types of capital (e.g., parental material resources), and this could affect their transition to adulthood. Strong supportive family relations, therefore, benefit children because they constitute an important source of social support that can be drawn upon when needed. For example, young adults with positive parent-child relationships tend to remain in the home longer than do those with weaker ties (e.g., Mitchell 2000b, 1994). Conversely, young adults with weak or conflictual family ties (often found in step-families, as observed by Coleman) have been found to leave the parental home earlier than do those with stronger ties. Access to this type of social capital, therefore, is hypothesized to influence the kinds of adaptations or strategies that can take place within a particular situation (e.g., returning home if unemployed), as well as the long-term consequences of transitional behaviours.

How the Past Shapes the Future

Another hallmark of the life-course perspective is that earlier life-course decisions, opportunities, and conditions can affect later outcomes (Mitchell 2003). In fact, Coleman (1988) argues that a lack of social capital can lead to negative outcomes, such as dropping out of school at an early age. The past, therefore, has the potential to shape the present and future through a process conceptualized as a "ripple" effect. The timing and conditions under which earlier life events and behaviours occur set up a chain reaction or "domino effect" of experiences for individuals and their families.

An example of this phenomenon applied to the present research is leaving home "prematurely" (e.g., because of intergenerational conflict). This may also increase the probability of a return home in the short term, due to an "incomplete launch." And, although the issue is beyond the scope of the present analysis, it is well established that, in the long term, a young adult unable to complete high school may face disadvantages in the labour market and in other realms. The past, therefore, can significantly affect later life outcomes such as socioeconomic status, career, and family-building trajectories, as well as mental and physical health outcomes. This long-term view, with its recognition of cumulative advantage or disadvantage, is particularly valuable for understanding social inequality and for creating effective social policies and programs (O'Rand 1996).

Data and Methods

Sampling

The data presented in this chapter are drawn from a three-year study entitled, "The Culture and Coresidence Study" (1999-2002), involving a survey of 1,907 young adults aged nineteen to thirty-five residing in the Greater Vancouver metropolitan area. The sample includes only young adults who self-identify with one of four ethnocultural groups – those of British, Chinese, Indo, or Southern European origin. The British group consists of persons who self-identify as English, Scottish, Irish, or Welsh (or any combination thereof); the Chinese group consists of persons with origins in Hong Kong, Taiwan, and Mainland China; the Indo group contains individuals of Indian, Pakistani, or Sri Lankan backgrounds, and the Southern European group consists of persons of Greek, Italian, Spanish, and Portuguese origins, the latter two subgroupings including persons of Latin American heritages. These groupings are not homogeneous, but they do form distinctive groups on the basis of historical, familial, and kinship patterns.

Two random sampling techniques were used to recruit respondents. The vast majority of respondents (90 percent) were obtained through randomly sampling a purchased list of Greater Vancouver household telephone numbers (with subfiles of Chinese and Indo-Canadian surnames), in combination with Greek, Italian, and Chinese ethnic directories. Another 10 percent of respondents were drawn using a random digit dialling process. A CATI system was employed for contact, callback, screening, and telephone-based interviews. A number of the interviewers were bilingual or multilingual in English and Cantonese and/or Mandarin, or in English and the languages of South Asia. In total, about 8 percent (or 76) of the Chinese and Indo-Canadian interviews were conducted in the interviewee's home language. The response rate is calculated at 51 percent, after disqualifying persons who did not meet age and ethnocultural identification criteria.

Overall, the sample consists of 790 (41.4 percent) men and 1,170 (58.6 percent) women aged nineteen to thirty-five. Our target of at least 450 persons in each ethnocultural group was met – 502 respondents of British origin, 462 of Chinese origin, 487 of South Asian origin, and 456 of Southern European origin – thus ensuring approximately equal percentages of each group in the overall sample. The mean age of the total sample is 26.5 years. Despite the random sampling techniques used, the Chinese origin sample is statistically significantly younger (mean age of 25.2 years) than are the other three groups, a fact that must be kept in mind in across-group comparisons.

INTERVIEWS

Several versions of structured interviews were administered to the various home-leaving groups: home-stayer, home-leaver, or home-returner/"boomerang kid." Home-stayers are defined as persons who have never left home for more than one four-month period. Home-leavers are those who have left home for at least one four-month period and have never returned for a period of four or more months. Home-returners are young adults who have left (for at least four months) and have returned for at least one four-month period. Each respondent was asked several questions related to their home-leaving category, their relationship with parents and exchanges of support, their ethnocultural identity and membership, attitudes about family life and gender roles, and so on. While many questions were identical, unique questions were also asked of the different home-leaving groups; for example, reasons for returning home were only asked of the home-returners.

All interviews were conducted by telephone, in the preferred language of the respondent, and ranged from thirty-five to fifty-five minutes in duration. Finally, all interviewees were assured of confidentiality and anonymity, and were informed that they could discontinue the interview at any time and not answer any question that made them feel uncomfortable.

Measurement

The two dependent variables of interest for this chapter are (1) age at first home-leaving and (2) number of years between home-leaving and the most recent return (see the appendix at the end of this chapter for a complete listing of all variables). For the home-leaving analysis, young adults who had not left home by the date of the survey were censored. This means that they are included as non-leavers for each age of home-leaving until their age at the time of the survey date, at which point they are removed from further analysis (censored). This allows for maximum use of available information on the dependent variable. For the home-returner analysis, we included only persons who had left home, since those who had not left home are not exposed to the risk of returning home. Again, we censored those who had not returned by the date of the survey, thereby using the number of years in a home-leaving state up until the survey, since we do not know when they might return in the future. Last return was used in lieu of first return home because of the availability of variables (such as main activity and marital status) that were only measured at the time of last return.

Measurement of the independent variables is straightforward, and they are presented in the same order in which they are included in the event history analyses. Most of the variables are identical for the two analyses, except in the cases of the sociodemographic block of factors, in which differences are highlighted between the two analyses.

Ethnocultural Identity

Ethnocultural identity is measured as: "British," "Chinese," "Indo," or "Southern European," capturing the ethnic group to which the respondent most closely identifies.

Family Environment

Eight variables are included as measures of family environment. *Family structure* is constructed using two questions about the relationship of the woman and man who mostly raised the respondent. It is, therefore, a measure of family structure while growing up. The four categories include: (1) intact, two-parent biological families; (2) step-families; (3) single-parent families; and (4) other (e.g., other family relative). *Father's education* was recoded into four categories: (1) less than high school, (2) high school graduate, (3) some college/university, and (4) university degree or higher.

Mother's and father's birth country was used to measure foreign-born status and was collapsed into two categories: (1) born in Canada, United States, or Britain; and (2) born outside of these countries. The United States and Britain are included with Canada because of similarities in family value systems. *Mother's religiosity* is measured by means of a question that asks respondents about the frequency of their mothers' religious attendance: "How often does your mother attend religious services [not counting special ceremonies like weddings or funerals]" and were recoded into three groups: (1) rarely/not at all, (2) monthly or yearly, and (3) at least once a week. Father's attendance was not included because of similarity with mother's. *Number of siblings* is measured as the number of brothers and sisters that the respondent has resided with during their last coresidence in the parental household (current situation for non-home-leavers). Finally, *relationship with mother and father* was also measured when the respondent was last living in the parents' home. The ordinal categories include: poor, somewhat poor, good, very good, and excellent.

SOCIODEMOGRAPHIC FACTORS

Three sociodemographic variables were used in the home-leaving analysis. *Sex* of the young adult was simply measured as male or female. *Birth cohort* represents three age groups based upon the respondent's year of birth: (1) 1964-69, (2) 1970-74, and (3) 1975-80. *Main activity* is measured as the main activity of the young adult at the time of the survey for home-stayers and at the time of home-leaving for those deemed to have left home, with the following responses: (1) employed, (2) looking for work, (3) school, (4) homemaker, and (5) other.

For the home-returning analysis, three additional variables were added to further capture dimensions of home-leaving transitions that may influence subsequent returns home. *Reason for first home-leaving* is based on a question asking respondents to identify the primary reason for their leaving home the first time for four or more months. The categories include (1) employment, (2) school, (3) conflict at home, (4) marriage/cohabitation, and (5) other. *Age left home* is measured as an interval scale. *Marital status* of the young adult is also measured at the time of the survey or at last return, depending on the transition status of the young adult. The categories are (1) single, never married; (2) divorced, separated, or widowed; and (3) married/

common law. Since the vast majority of young adults are single at the time of home-leaving, this variable was only included in the returner analysis.

Ethnocultural Factors

Five additional ethnocultural variables are included in the analysis. *Familism* is an additive scale constructed from a series of Likert scale items that focus on the importance of extended family to the individual respondent (strongly agree, agree, disagree, or strongly disagree). The following statements were used: "The emotional and financial welfare of the extended family (such as grandparents, aunts, and uncles) is of utmost importance," "The needs of the extended family are more important than your own," and "A main function of the extended family is to provide emotional and financial help to other family members in time of need." The scale has a range of 3-12 and a Cronbach's alpha of .60.

The variable, *gender-role traditionalism*, is measured using Greenstein's (1995) scale capturing attitudes toward gender-roles in the family. A four-point Likert scale (strongly agree, agree, disagree, or strongly disagree) was applied to the following items, "A woman's place is in the home, not in the office or shop," "A wife who carries out her full family responsibility doesn't have time for full employment," "The employment of mothers leads to more youth crime," "Women are much happier if they stay at home and take care of their children," "It is much better for everyone concerned if the man is the achiever outside of the home and the woman takes care of the home and family," and "Men, rather than women, should be the head of the family and household." This scale has a range of 6-23 and a Cronbach's alpha of .80. *Young adult's religiosity* is measured in the same manner as parental religiosity. Finally, *language at home* and *language with peers* are measured by responses to the questions: "What language do you currently speak most often at your parent's home?" and "outside of the parental home, with friends?" Answers were placed into either English or non-English. Since very few cases were missing (less than .5 percent), missing values were assigned to the mean for interval measures and the modal category for ordinal and categorical variables in order to maximize the sample size.

Statistical Analyses

Two statistical techniques were used to analyze the data – initial bivariate analyses followed by multivariate analyses of age of home-leaving and age of last return. Event history analysis was used to model the risk of an event's occurring, or survival in a particular state, using cross-sectional data (Yamaguchi 1991). In order to retain a focus on coresidence, this method is used to analyze the survivor rate of home-staying and the risk of returning home after an earlier "launch" (Teachman and Hayward 1993).

Bivariate Results

Figure 9.1 provides a cross-tabulation of living arrangement by ethnic group. With regard to home-leaving, the British young adults are more likely to have left home at the time of the survey (61.9 percent) than are members of the other groups. They are also more likely to have "boomeranged" home than are members of the other groups (23.5 percent, compared to 17.3 percent Chinese, 8.7 percent Indo, and 15.8 percent Southern European). However, the rate of returning relative to those who left home (i.e., those at risk of a return) is slightly higher in the Chinese sample (42 percent) than in the British sample (38 percent). This is also observed in the subsequent survival analysis (Model 1). In addition, young adults who identify with Chinese, Indo, or Southern European cultural backgrounds exhibit a similar pattern of home-staying (41.6 percent, 36 percent, and 36 percent, respectively),

Figure 9.1

Living arrangement by ethnic group

Ethnic group	Stayer	Leaver	Boomerang
British	14.5	61.9	23.5
Chinese	41.6	41.1	17.3
Indo	36.0	55.3	8.7
Southern European	36.0	48.2	15.8

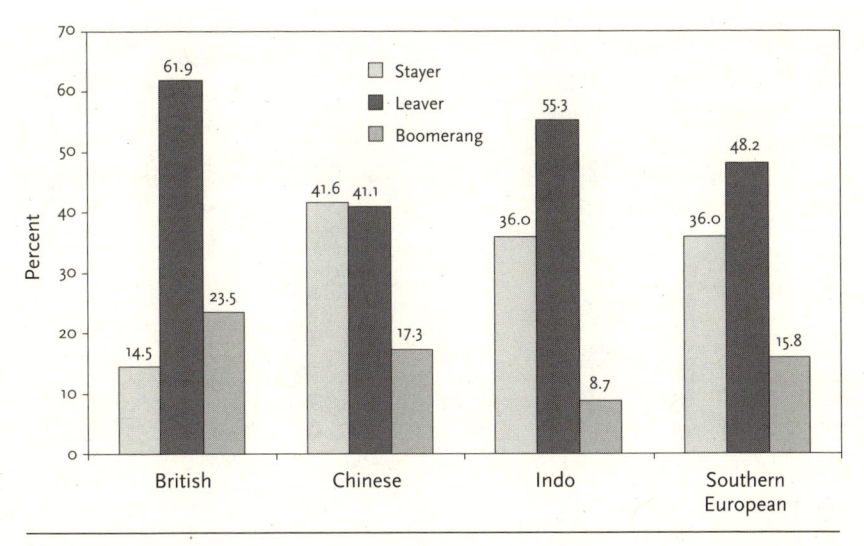

N = 1,907
SOURCE: Culture and Coresidence Study, 1999-2000.

although Chinese young adults have the highest rate of intergenerational coresidence.

Figure 9.2 shows the main reason for (first) home-leaving by ethnic group. One striking trend is that British and Southern European young adults are more likely to state that they left home in order to seek "independence" (34.3 percent and 34.9 percent respectively) than the Chinese and Indo young adults (9.3 percent and 6.4 percent respectively). Another dramatic finding is that Indo young adults tend to leave home to marry/cohabit – in fact 70.1 percent of Indo Canadian home-leavers report that they left home at the time of marriage, compared to only 13.5 percent of British young adults. It should also be noted that almost half of these young adults told the interviewers that their marriages involved some kind of arrangement in which parents played a pivotal role. Finally, home-leaving for school-related reasons is most common for Chinese young adults (53.7 percent), and leaving due to "conflict" at home is more commonly cited among British (8.9 percent) and Southern European young adults (7.9 percent) but is extremely rare among Chinese (1.5 percent) and Indo (1.3 percent) young people.

FIGURE 9.2

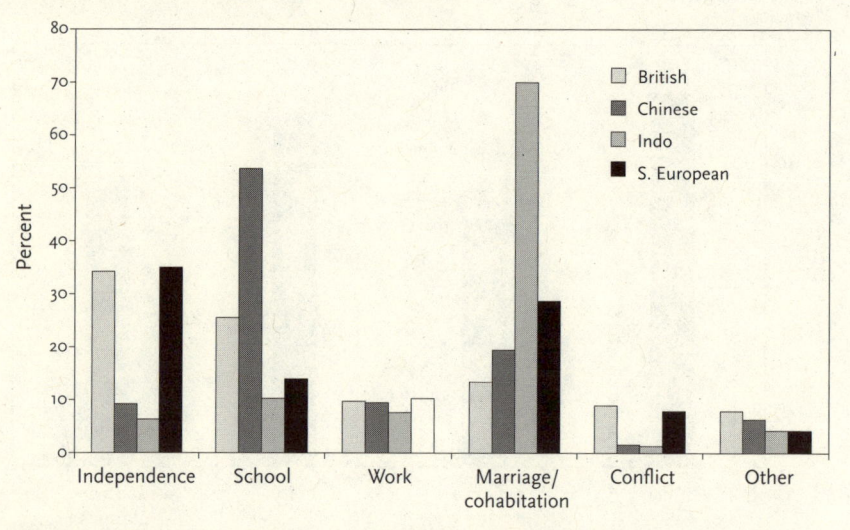

Reason for (first) home-leaving by ethnic group

N = 1,302
SOURCE: Culture and Coresidence Study, 1999-2000.

Survival Analysis

A series of parametric regression models was estimated using the LIFEREG procedure in SAS for censored survival data of age of home-leaving, and duration in years between home-leaving and last return home, using the Weibull model. Since the shape of the survival distribution is known, and we do not use time-dependent covariates, this method is preferred (Allison 1995). Based on previous research (Mitchell 1994; Mitchell, Wister, and Gee 2004), we assume a Weibull distribution, which models the natural logarithm of the survival times $[\log T]$. The log-survival time model is expressed as:

$$[\log T] = B_0 + B_1 x_1 + B_2 x_2 + B_k x_k + \sigma \varepsilon,$$

where B is the parameter estimate, x is the independent variables in the model, σ is the scale parameter, and ε is a vector of errors assumed from the Weibull distribution (Allison 1995). The parameter estimates are logged estimates of duration of surviving without experiencing the event. The logged estimates are converted into percentage increases (positive coefficients) or decreases (negative coefficients) in expected survival times by applying the formula: $100 [\exp (B) - 1]$. As observed in Tables 9.1 and 9.2, a positive survival time can be interpreted as the percentage increase in the expected survival time before the event for each one-unit increase in the variable, or compared to a reference category for categorical variables, controlling for all other covariates (Allison 1995; Teachman and Hayward 1993).

The Weibull model is also a proportional hazards model, so that its coefficients can be interpreted as relative hazard rates. The log survival coefficients can be converted to log-hazard format by simply reversing the sign and dividing by the scale parameter shown at the bottom of each table. As stated by Allison (1995, 67): "The change in signs makes intuitive sense ... If the hazard is high, the events occur quickly and the survival times are short ... When the hazard is low, events are unlikely to occur and survival times are long." In keeping with our hypothesis that young adults who identify with more traditional ethnocultural groups will have longer durations in the home, we report survival rates rather than hazards rates.

We employ a hierarchical analytical strategy with four blocks of variables in order to ascertain how each cluster affects the original association of ethnicity with home-leaving and returning-home behaviour. These blocks include family background factors, characteristics of the youth, and a set of additional ethnocultural factors. Significant changes in the original association between ethnic identity and the two youth transitions with the inclusion of the variable blocks will be presented in this chapter. The results from the final block will follow. Only the final estimates will be shown in Table 9.1 (home-leaving analysis) and Table 9.2 (returning-home analysis). The correlation matrix of the independent variables (available upon request) does not reveal problems of multicollinearity. Also, several interaction effects were examined (e.g., among social capital measures, such as between ethnicity and family relationships), yet these did not produce any statistically significant results and are not included, though they are available upon request.

HOME-LEAVING ANALYSIS

All four models are statistically significant and all of the ethnic identity contrasts reveal a clear association with home-staying. Since the scale parameter (.17) is between 0 and .5, the Weibull regressions indicate that the survival rate of leaving home is increasing (Allison 1995). In the initial block (not shown in Table 9.1), the association between ethnic identity and home-leaving results in all three contrasts being statistically significant, at which point no other independent variables are included. The expected survival rate at home of the non-British groups exceeds that of the British by 28 percent for Indos, 22 percent for Chinese, and 20 percent for Southern European origin young adults. This means that all three non-British ethnic groups stay home longer before a first home-leaving experience.

The inclusion of the family background factors (family structure, father's education, parental birth country, number of siblings, and relationship with mother and father) in the second block reduces these associations by more than half, to the levels observed in the final block. However, they all remain statistically significant. Table 9.1 displays the final model results for home-staying, which is again found to be statistically significant (chi square = 4,211, $p < .001$). It is observed that the expected survival rate of staying at home is 12 percent among Indos, 11 percent for Chinese, and 6 percent for Southern European origin young adults, compared to those of British background, all of which are statistically significant.

With regard to family background factors, seven of the eight variables are statistically significant. The strongest associations are observed for relationship with mother. Compared to that of those who report poor relationships with their mothers, the expected survival rate of remaining in the home is increased by 15 percent among young adults who report an excellent

TABLE 9.1

Final survival analyses model for staying at home

	Beta		Standard error	Survival rate (%)
ETHNIC IDENTITY (ref = British)				
Chinese	.11	***	.11	11
Indo	.12	***	.11	12
Southern European	.06	**	.02	6
FAMILY BACKGROUND				
Family structure (ref = two biological)				
Step	−.09	**	.03	−9
Single	−.01		.02	—
Other	−.08	***	.02	−8
Father's education (ref = less than high school)				
High school	−.02		.01	—
Some post-secondary	−.01		.02	—
University degree	.01		.02	—
Mother's birth country (ref = Can/US/Britain)				
Outside Can/US/Britain	.05	**	.01	5
Father's birth country (ref = Can/US/Britain)				
Outside Can/US/Brit	.06	**	.02	6
Mother's religiosity (ref = very rarely/not at all)				
Once a year/once a month	.03	*	.01	3
At least once per week	−.02		.01	—
Number of siblings	−.02	***	.01	−2
Relationship with mother (ref = poor)				
Excellent	.14	***	.03	15
Very good	.15	***	.03	17
Good	.12	***	.03	12
Somewhat poor	.08	**	.03	8
Relationship with father (ref = poor)				
Excellent	.05	*	.02	5
Very good	.04		.02	—
Good	.06	*	.02	6
Somewhat poor	−.02		.02	—
YOUNG ADULT SOCIODEMOGRAPHIC FACTORS				
Sex (ref = male)				
Female	−.05	***	.01	−5
Age group (ref = 1964-69)				
1975-80	.01		.01	—
1970-74	−.02	*	.01	3

▶

◀ TABLE 9.1

	Beta	Standard error	Survival rate (%)
Main activity (ref = employed)			
Looking for work	.07 **	.03	7
School	−.07 ***	.01	−7
Homemaker	.08 *	.03	8
Other	−.06 *	.03	−6
YOUNG-ADULT ETHNOCULTURAL FACTORS			
Familism	.01	.01	—
Traditionalism	.01	.01	—
Religiosity (ref = very rarely/not at all)			
Once a year/once a month	−.03	.01	—
At least once per week	.03	.01	—
Language at home (ref = English)			
Non-English	−.02	.01	—
Language with peers (ref = English)			
Non-English	−.02	.01	—

NOTE: $*p < .05$, $**p < .01$, $***p < .001$.
Final model chi square = 4211.18, $p < .001$.
Log-likelihood of Weibull = −263, scale = .17.

relationship, 17 percent among those with a very good relationship, 12 percent among those with a good relationship, and 8 percent among those with a somewhat poor relationship. Only two contrasts of relationship with father result in statistically significant associations, whereby having a good or excellent relationship (compared to a poor relationship) increases the survival rate of home staying by 6 percent and 5 percent, respectively, for each contrast.

In addition, two contrasts for family structure are found to be statistically significant. The survival rate of staying at home decreases by 9 percent for youths exposed to step-families and decreases by 8 percent for the "other" category, as compared to youths growing up with both biological parents. This can be interpreted as meaning that youths raised in a step-family or "other" environment stay at home for shorter durations than those raised in two-parent families. Having a mother or father born outside Canada, the United States, or Britain slightly increases the survival rate of staying (5 percent and 6 percent, respectively), and having a mother who attends religious services once a month to once a year, compared to very rarely or not at all, increases the expected survival rate by 3 percent. Also, having more siblings decreases the rate of staying by a factor of 2 percent for each sibling. No statistically significant relationships are found for the contrasts representing father's education.

The three sociodemographic variables related to young adults also result in statistically significant associations. The survival rate at home is decreased by 5 percent among females compared to males. Also, young adults born during 1975-80 have slightly higher (3 percent) rates of staying at home than those born during 1964-69. In addition, three of the four contrasts for main activity show statistically significant associations. Survival rates of staying are decreased for young adults attending school (survival rate = –7 percent), compared to being employed, as well as those who left home for "other" reasons (survival rate = –6 percent). However, the survival rates are increased by 8 percent for homemakers and 7 percent for those looking for work compared to employed young adults. None of the five additional ethnocultural variables related to young adults are found to be statistically significant (familism, traditionalism, religiosity, language at home/with peers).

Returning-Home Analysis

Table 9.2 provides the parameter estimates for duration until last return home. The Weibull scale parameter (.71) for this analysis indicates that the rate of returning home is increasing at a decreasing rate, which is also consistent with earlier research. A positive survival rate indicates an increase in survival time and a negative one shows a decrease in survival time for a given covariate. Again, all four blocks are found to be statistically significant. In the initial block with only ethnic identity as an independent variable (not shown in Table 9.2), only the Chinese/British contrast of the ethnic identity variable results in a statistically significant association with the likelihood of returning – the Chinese youths have a 7 percent decrease in survival time compared to the British. However, the inclusion of the family background variables in the second block (not shown in Table 9.2) results in this association becoming not statistically significant.

As shown in Table 9.2, after all of the blocks are entered, ethnic identity does not result in a statistically significant association with returning home. However, four family background factors surface as important predictors – father's education, father's birth country, and relationship with mother/father. Indeed, the strongest relationships are uncovered for relationship with mother. Those youths with excellent relationships (compared to poor ones) have a significant decrease in survival time between home-leaving and a final return (survival rate = –23 percent). Also, those with very good, good, and somewhat poor relationships also have shorter survival durations than those with poor relationships (survival rates are –23 percent, –19 percent, and –19 percent, respectively). Thus, youths with better relationships with their mothers return home faster. Similarly, the survival rate is decreased significantly among those reporting an excellent relationship with father, as well as those with very good and good relationships, compared to those with a poor relationship (survival rates are –12 percent, –13 percent, and –9 percent, respectively). Moreover, the expected survival rate is increased 6 percent among young adults whose fathers graduated from high school compared to those whose fathers did not. Survival times are also decreased by 14 percent among those whose fathers were born outside Canada, the United States, and Britain compared to those born inside these countries.

Turning to sociodemographic factors related to young adults, five of the six variables emerge as statistically significant. The survival time between home-leaving and returning is increased by 46 percent among young adult "homemakers" compared to employed young adults. Those "looking for work" have a 7 percent lower survival rate than those who are employed. Marital status also shows a clear association to returning – those who are married/cohabiting have a 27 percent longer survival time than those who are single, never-married. Birth cohort also affects the probability of home-returning – it is decreased by 24 percent among those born during 1970-74 compared to those born during 1964-69, and 12 percent among those born during 1975-80 compared to the oldest age group. The reason for first leaving home also surfaces as important; those who left home due to conflict have a 23 percent lower survival time than those who left for independence. Similarly, leaving for employment or school compared to independence also decreases the survival rate by 14 percent and 8 percent, respectively. Furthermore, the survival time away from home is lengthened by 2 percent for each successive year at which a young adult originally left home. Thus, leaving home at younger ages results in a faster return.

Finally, only one supplementary variable related to young adult ethnocultural factors (identical to those in the home-leaving analysis) results in a statistically significant association. Specifically, the survival rate is inflated by 12 percent among youths who used non-English at home compared to those who use English at home.

TABLE 9.2

Final survival analysis model for returning home

	Beta	Standard error	Survival rate (%)
ETHNIC IDENTITY (ref = British)			
Chinese	−.03	.05	—
Indo	−.02	.05	—
Southern European	.01	.04	—
FAMILY BACKGROUND			
Family structure (ref = two biological)			
Step	−.03	.06	—
Single	−.04	.04	—
Other	.11	.06	—
Father's education (ref = less than high school)			
High school	.06 *	.03	6
Some post-secondary	−.01	.04	—
University degree	−.04	.03	—
Mother's birth country (ref = Can/US/Britain)			
Outside Can/US/Brit	.04	.04	—
Father's birth country (ref = Can/US/Britain)			
Outside Can/US/Brit	−.15 ***	.04	−14
Mother's religiosity (ref = very rarely/not at all)			
Once a year/once a month	.02	.03	—
At least once per week	.01	.03	—
Number of siblings	.02	.01	—
Relationship with mother (ref = poor)			
Excellent	−.27 ***	.07	−23
Very good	−.27 ***	.07	−23
Good	−.21 **	.07	−19
Somewhat poor	−.22 **	.07	−19
Relationship with father (ref = poor)			
Excellent	−.13 **	.05	−12
Very good	−.14 **	.05	−13
Good	−.10 *	.05	−9
Somewhat poor	−.06	.05	—
YOUNG-ADULT SOCIODEMOGRAPHIC FACTORS			
Sex (ref = male)			
Female	−.02	.02	—
Age group (ref = 1964-69)			
1975-80	−.27 ***	.03	−24
1970-74	−.12 ***	.03	−12

▶

◀ TABLE 9.2

	Beta	Standard error	Survival rate (%)
Reason for first leave (ref = independence)			
Employment	−.15 ***	.04	−14
School	−.08 *	.03	−8
Conflict at home	−.26 ***	.05	−23
Marry/cohabit	.01	.05	—
Other	−.15	.04	−.14
Age left home	.02 ***	.01	2
Main activity (ref = employed)			
Looking for work	−.08 *	.04	−7
School	−.05 *	.03	—
Homemaker	.38 **	.13	46
Other	−.09	.05	—
YOUNG-ADULT ETHNOCULTURAL FACTORS			
Marital status (ref = single, never married)			
Divorced/separated/widowed	.11	.07	—
Married/common-law	.24 ***	.03	27
Familism	.01	.01	—
Traditionalism	.01	.01	—
Religiosity (ref = very rarely/not at all)			
Once a year/once a month	.01	.03	—
At least once per week	.02	.04	—
Language at home (ref = English)			
Non-English	.11 **	.04	12
Language with peers (ref = English)			
Non-English	−.01	.03	—

NOTE: *$p < .05$, **$p < .01$, ***$p < .001$.
Final model chi square = 668, $p < .001$.
Log-likelihood of Weibull = −325.9, scale = .71.

Discussion

Results of this study reveal considerable diversity in home-leaving trajectories among Canadian young adults and support key tenets of the life-course theoretical perspective synthesized with the concept of social capital. While it is recognized that contemporary youth transitions are affected by broad macro-economic conditions (i.e., need for post-secondary education, employment opportunities, and so on) and societal-level sociodemographic change (i.e., later ages of marriage), life course events are heterogeneous and socially structured. A principal theme connecting the findings in this study is that ethnocultural communities and family bonds can generate different types and levels of social capital, which, in turn, differently influence living arrangement patterns and the transition to adulthood.

Specifically, home-leaving trajectories are found to be strongly influenced by two sets of social capital resources related to ethnocultural membership and intergenerational relationship quality. Consistent with previous research, this study finds that ethnocultural membership affects patterns of coresidence (e.g., Boyd 2000; Goldscheider and Goldscheider 1993, 1999). In this study, young adults identifying with Asian backgrounds (Indo or Chinese) tend to remain at home longer than British or Southern European young adults. They are also less likely to leave home to seek "independence" than British or Southern European young adults. Indo young adults tend to leave home predominantly to marry, while Chinese young adults tend to depart for school-related reasons. However, with regard to home-returning at the multivariate level, ethnic identity does not appear to affect the probability of a return, after controlling for other factors.

Other influential ethnocultural factors affecting home-leaving transitions include the foreign-born status of parents (slightly longer durations of staying at home among those with foreign-born parents) and mother's religious attendance (slightly longer durations of staying at home if mother attends monthly/yearly compared to rarely/not at all). In addition, the rate of returning is lower among youths who speak non-English at home compared to those who speak mainly English at home. Taken together, these findings suggest that ethnocultural communities transmit and reproduce social capital via norms, values, and expectations, and this can influence the timing and pathways of transitional behaviours into adulthood. In particular, more traditional ethnocultural groups appear to support longer durations in the home before an initial launch.

The second major generator of social capital – intergenerational relationship quality – is found when young adults are enmeshed in positive family relations. Indeed, young adults who report having better or higher-quality relationships with their mothers are more likely to remain at home, and return at faster rates, than those with poor relationships. Associations are also found for relationship with father, although they are considerably weaker and less consistent. In fact, the quality of intergenerational relationships shows the strongest associations with age at home-leaving, controlling for all other factors. Furthermore, young adults exposed to step-families are also found to leave home earlier than those who live with both biological parents, which supports previous literature indicating that family structure can be an important generator of social capital (e.g., Coleman 1988; Mitchell 1994).

Finally, several important sociodemographic factors related to young adults are also found to affect the home-leaving process, consistent with previous research. These include: gender, number of siblings, age cohort, main activity, and reason for leaving. Females tend to stay at home at lower rates than males and, thus, leave home earlier. The 1970-74 birth cohort shows a slightly longer rate of staying than the 1964-69 cohort. Main activity of the young adult also affects the probability of remaining at home and the likelihood of home-returning. Compared to young adults who are working, young adults attending school stay at home slightly shorter times, whereas the opposite pattern is observed for young adults who are looking for work or are homemakers.

Furthermore, compared to the employed group, young adults who are homemakers are considerably less likely to return home, whereas those looking for work are more likely to experience a transition reversal. Age cohort and marital status also affect the probability of a home return; more recent birth cohorts are more likely to return than the 1965-69 birth cohort. And young adults who are married/cohabiting have a reduced rate of home return as compared to that of the non-married, as expected.

Finally, the age and reason for first leaving home surfaces as important in determining whether or not a young adult returns home. What is noteworthy is the observation that leaving home at an early age increases the probability of a home return. Those leaving for employment, school, or conflict, compared to those leaving for independence, have decreased durations away from home. These findings support the notion that the conditions under which the initial home-leaving occurred can set up a "chain reaction" of events that affects the probability and pace of later transitional behaviours. This draws our attention to the issue of inequity in the transition to adulthood, which has profound implications for current social, economic, and political issues in Canadian society.

Implications for Social Inequality and Social Policy

Several important implications for social inequality, social policy, and community programs can be identified from this research. One important outcome of heterogeneity in social capital, as manifested by differences in patterns of home-leaving behaviour, is that some subgroups of Canadian young adults may have less access than others to social capital during the transition to adulthood. This is a worrisome situation, given that we live in an era of widening social inequality, a retreat from the welfare state, and economic restructuring. Continued government cutbacks and reductions in social services will invariably create an increasing period of reliance on parental households.

As a result, some youths will be more vulnerable than others to lifelong adverse effects if they lack supportive cultural or family household environments (social capital) as they mature into adults. Two of the strongest sets of predictors of home-leaving timing relate to the strength and quality of parent-child relationships and, to a lesser extent, ethnocultural factors. This finding indicates that leaving home "prematurely" due to a lack of social capital (e.g., because of intergenerational conflict) or, in some cases, a search for "independence" could potentially have far-reaching long-term consequences for many realms of a person's life. These domains might include family formation patterns and kin relations, as well trajectories related to schooling, work, health, and socio-emotional well-being (e.g., see Booth, Crouter and Shanahan 1999). This implication is also supported by the general finding by Curtis and Perks (Chapter 6) that access to social capital earlier in life can provide important "payoffs" later in adult life.

In particular, young adults can experience personal or professional barriers in the transition to adulthood if they cannot draw upon household resources when needed. Additional research using this data set shows that a major benefit of living at home until later ages is that it can offer young people additional emotional support from their parents. Thus, coresidence can strengthen intergenerational ties and enlarge one's stock of social capital. It also provides young people with an opportunity to save money, enjoy the "comforts of home," and accumulate other material resources (e.g., a car, furniture) in order to facilitate successful independent living (e.g., see Mitchell 2000b). Therefore, some young adults living apart from parents because strained or unsupportive relations prevent them from living at home may find it difficult to cope on their own, attend post-secondary school, or survive financially. Furthermore, based on additional qualitative data, some young adults in this study experienced negative consequences later in life because they felt they were being "pushed" out of the family nest at a relatively young age (e.g., aged eighteen to nineteen). In these cases, although they tended to complete high school, there was the sense that they did not feel quite "ready" to make it on their own. Yet, they felt obliged to try to establish a separate residence in order to conform to parental expectations of independence and autonomy. Some of these young people also reported that they did feel that they would be welcomed back in the parental home in the event of personal problems, such as unemployment or divorce.

However, as discussed by other contributors to this volume (e.g., Kay and Bernard Chapter 3; Aizlewood and Pendakur, Chapter 7), it is also important to recognize how "social capital" can encompass both positive and negative elements, since social structures can be both enabling and constraining. Generally, there is a tendency to equate social capital with a multitude of benefits. In this study, observed benefits focus on how young adults with higher social capital tend to remain at home longer than those with lower levels, resulting in distinct social and economic advantages (e.g., parental emotional and financial support). From this perspective, a supportive family environment can serve as a safety net or buffer against personal or economic hardship and daily challenges. Yet, it is important to recognize that there can also be "too much of a good thing" since some young adults with high stocks of social capital can experience disadvantages during the transition to adulthood. This finding alerts us to the notion that social capital can represent an important element of informal social control with respect to institutionalized social relations.

Specifically, while many young adults in this study felt that the decision to leave home was to some extent their own "choice," a significant number perceived a lack of options with regard to when and under what circumstances they could leave home. Also, some young people in our study who were from very traditional backgrounds reported that they felt "forced" to remain at home until later ages due to strong cultural traditions (also see Mitchell 2004). This normative pressure created a number of perceived negative consequences because these young people felt that they were unable to pursue their own individual goals. In particular, some young women (especially those from patriarchal ethnic backgrounds) felt that their daily lives were too closely regulated and monitored. They also reported that their individual mobility was hampered by cultural or family values that gave primacy to marital and family-related home-leaving trajectories rather than to the achievement of occupational goals.

In light of the multidimensional nature of social capital, several recommendations can be made in the areas of social policy and community programs. Young adults employed in the labour force require "living wages," since current minimum wage standards are inadequate to meet the needs of many young people, particularly if they are living apart from their parents. They also need access to affordable housing and adequate social assistance if living apart from parents is a desired goal. Monthly income assistance rates for a single person in British Columbia, for example, are only about $510 per month, and recent changes to the welfare system will drastically cut the number of people who can apply for this support (McInnes 2002). Also, given the strong need for post-secondary education, young adults need sufficient government-sponsored student loans and grants. Many Canadian young adults are currently faced with rising tuition fees and very expensive housing markets in major urban areas.

Moreover, based on the finding that social capital influences home-leaving timing and pathways, preventive strategies are necessary in order to identify youths most at risk of dire consequences, such as those who leave home before the completion of high school. This could be done by high-school teachers, counsellors, and social workers. With regard to intervention, crisis services, safe housing, and life skills training could be very beneficial to young adults who lack ethnic community or family support and are having problems living at home. Furthermore, many families could benefit from family life education, conflict resolution training, and support groups, particularly if intergenerational conflict is the result of other family problems. Generally, community-based organizations would be helpful in providing information, resources, and culturally sensitive sociocultural activities to young adults, and their families, who would like to strengthen their social networks and their reservoir of social capital.

Limitations and Future Research

This exploratory research has several limitations and highlights many fruitful areas for future research. One limitation is that only four cultural groups residing in the Greater Vancouver Regional District of British Columbia are the focus of this research, which also does not fully explore diversity within each cultural group. Inclusion of a wider variety of ethnic groups across Canada, as well as additional cultural measures (e.g., immigration history, participation in ethnic-group-related activities) and geographical mobility patterns could, therefore, help to elucidate the mechanisms underlying the observed cultural effects. It is also important to incorporate the reality that increasing numbers of young adults identify with multiple ethnic origins. Inclusion of more direct questions on values and preferences would also be helpful for understanding how cultural groups sustain, reinforce, and reproduce existing levels of social capital and how these affect home-leaving processes. There is also a need for research that includes a richer set of socioeconomic measures (e.g., parental income, intergenerational financial transfers) to disentangle these elements from macro processes and sociocultural factors.

Future research should also uncover how parents and children negotiate home-leaving decisions, as well as adjacent issues related to power and control dynamics that produce intergenerational solidarity or conflict. In a similar vein, attention should also be paid to empirical investigations of the negative consequences of social capital. For example, Portes (1998) discusses how social capital can literally produce "family ties that bind." This can occur when there is intense pressure to conform to group norms and expectations. One might expect constraints on behaviour to be more restrictive for females than for males, but future research is needed on this topic. Moreover, future studies on home-leaving need to consider "semi-autonomous" stages of leaving home, such as living in college/university dorms or residences (Goldscheider and Goldscheider 1999), and how this phase interrelates with social and other types of capital. Perhaps a refinement of the very concept of home-leaving is also required, since there may be different dimensions that go beyond physical separation and entail social-psychological and financial degrees of separation.

Finally, while the statistical analysis lends support to the synthesizing of a life-course approach with the concept of social capital, the multivariate analyses were limited by a cross-sectional research design. Results suggest that certain families and ethnic groups may be uniquely advantaged with regard to a variety of social, economic, educational, and health-related outcomes, yet, data limitations prevent a full investigation of these linkages. The ideal research design would be a longitudinal study of young adults, beginning with a baseline study of the circumstances preceding the decision to leave home. These youths could be re-interviewed in follow-up studies in order to directly assess "returns" on social capital, including both short-term and long-term implications of these transitional events. In the face of changing family structures, economic and political change, and high levels of immigration in an increasingly multicultural society, it is evident that future research is required if we are to gain a clearer understanding of how social capital shapes the passage to adulthood.

Table 9A.1

Frequency distribution for home-leaving and home-returning analysis

Variables	Category/Range	Home-leaving analysis (N = 1,907) n	%	Home-returning analysis (N = 1,302) n	%
DEPENDENT					
Age of first home-leaving	interval range = 10-32	$\bar{X}=$ 21.2 s.d. = 3.6		—	—
Duration between home-leaving and last return	interval range = 0-18	—	—	$\bar{X}=$ 6.7 s.d.= 4.5	
INDEPENDENT					
Ethnocultural identity	British	502	26.3	429	33.0
	Chinese	462	24.2	270	20.7
	Indo-Canadian	487	25.6	311	23.9
	Southern European	456	23.9	292	22.4
Family structure	two biological	1,611	84.5	1,068	82.0
	step-family	34	1.8	32	2.5
	single parent	177	9.3	132	10.1
	other	85	4.4	70	5.4
Father's education	less than high school	581	30.5	395	30.3
	high school grad	768	40.3	530	40.7
	some college/university	260	13.6	177	13.6
	university degree	298	15.6	200	15.4
Mother's birth country	Can/US/Britain	590	30.9	490	37.6
	outside Can/US/Britain	1,317	69.1	812	62.4
Father's birth country	Can/US/Britain	534	28.0	453	34.8
	outside Can/US/Britain	1,373	72.0	849	65.2
Mother's religiosity (attendance)	very rarely/never	728	38.2	520	39.9
	once/year–once/month	473	24.8	303	23.3
	at least once/week	706	37.0	479	36.8
Number of sibs	interval range = 1-10	$\bar{X}=$ 1.0 s.d.= 1.1		$\bar{X}=$ 1.0 s.d.= 1.1	
Relationship with mother	excellent	859	45.0	578	44.4
	very	478	25.1	302	23.2
	good	353	18.5	242	18.6
	somewhat poor	145	7.6	113	8.7
	poor	72	3.8	67	5.1

▶

◀ TABLE 9A.1

Variables	Category/Range	Home-leaving analysis ($N = 1{,}907$) n	%	Home-returning analysis ($N = 1{,}302$) n	%
Relationship with father	excellent	825	43.3	564	43.3
	very good	401	21.0	259	19.9
	good	381	20.0	241	18.5
	somewhat poor	185	9.7	140	10.8
	poor	115	6.0	98	7.5
Sex	females	1,117	58.6	813	62.4
	males	790	41.4	489	37.6
Birth cohort	1964-69	618	32.4	571	43.9
	1970-74	580	30.4	443	34.0
	1975-81	709	37.2	288	22.1
Main activity	employed	970	50.9	810	62.2
	looking for work	74	3.9	71	5.5
	school	779	40.9	226	17.4
	homemaker	34	1.8	157	12.0
	other	50	2.6	38	2.9
Reason first leave	to work	—	—	122	9.4
	for school	—	—	328	25.2
	home conflict	—	—	69	5.3
	left to marry/cohabit	—	—	413	31.7
	independence	—	—	294	22.6
	other	—	—	76	5.8
Age left home	interval			$\bar{X}=$	20.3
	range = 10-32			s.d.=	3.6
Marital status (last return)	married	—	—	641	49.2
	common-law	—	—	97	7.4
	single never married	—	—	528	40.6
	divorced/sep/wid	—	—	36	2.8
Familism	interval	=	8.6	=	8.6
	range = 1-10	s.d.=	1.5	s.d.=	1.5
Traditionalism	interval	=	11.9	=	11.8
	range = 1-10	s.d.=	3.1	s.d.=	3.2
Religiosity (attendance)	very rarely/never	796	41.8	564	43.3
	once/year–once/month	628	32.9	427	32.8
	at least once/week	483	25.3	311	23.9
Language at home	English	865	45.4	644	49.5
	non-English	1,042	54.6	658	50.5
Language with peers	English	1,262	66.2	880	67.6
	non-English	645	33.8	422	32.4

NOTE: Range, mean, and standard deviation shown for interval variables, except number of returns (frequency shown).
$\bar{X}$ = mean
s.d. = standard deviation

ACKNOWLEDGMENTS

An earlier version of this chapter was presented at the Equality, Security, and Community project annual meeting at the University of British Columbia in Vancouver, British Columbia, November 2001. The research reported here was supported by a Social Sciences and Humanities Research Council of Canada grant (#401-1999-102). The author acknowledges the assistance of Doug Talling with computer runs as well as the contributions made to this project by the late Dr. Ellen Gee and Dr. Andrew Wister.

10

Social Capital and Health in Canada: (Compositional) Effects of Trust, Participation in Networks, and Civic Activity on Self-Rated Health

Gerry Veenstra

Social relationships have powerful effects on health. Early research into these effects, mostly conducted during the 1980s, explored the significance of social ties and participation in networks by utilizing simple quantitative measures such as number of close friends and relatives and membership in religious groups and other voluntary associations (Berkman et al. 2000). They found that involvement in such networks and associations was often positively associated with health and well-being. Since then, a plethora of research has focused on qualitative aspects of social relationships, such as the provision of social support, in attempts to explain *how* social relationships promote or detract from well-being (ibid.).

Social support is not the only pathway by which social relationships influence health, however, and more attention is needed in regard to the broader social context and structural factors that influence the various types of networks and support available to people. Indeed, Lisa Berkman and her colleagues argue that we should return to a Durkheimian orientation to network structure and social context by exploring the social and cultural contexts that shape the nature of networks themselves and also shape the development of social and economic inequalities, given that the latter are often embedded within and reinforced by the former and have profound effects on health and well-being. Specific aspects of social structure that may shape the character of social networks and the distribution of resources and rewards (and then health) include but are not limited to the nature of the labour market, global and national economic pressures and trends, industrialization and organizational relations, social class dynamics, rapid cultural and social change, and such demographic phenomena as changing age and ethnic compositions and the movement of populations to cities.

The "social capital" literature has the potential to contribute to this sweeping imperative by virtue of its focus on wedding aspects of macro social and economic structure to social networks at the meso (intermediate) level. For example, social resources of the kind described by this literature, such as dense webs of social networks and high levels of interpersonal trust, are thought by some researchers to influence aspects of the economy (e.g., Helliwell and Putnam 1995; Woolcock 1998) and the polity (e.g., Putnam 1993a; Rice and Sumberg 1997), with subsequent consequences for the health of individuals and populations (e.g., Kawachi et al. 1997; Veenstra 2001; Veenstra and Lomas 1999). The social capital discourse thus takes the Berkman et al. imperative even further by noting that the macro context influences the nature of social relationships (and then health) *and* that the nature of social relationships influences the shape and character of the larger sociopolitical and economic context – it pays close attention to the interconnectedness of the individual, the networks that (s)he participates in, the shape and character of networks within communities, and the macro context within which the networks operate. Since the early 1990s the social capital and health discourse has grown quickly in scope and sophistication, and the means by which social capital is thought to (potentially) influence health are many and varied. This chapter will clarify some of these means, informed by a review of some empirical findings from various international contexts, and will then provide additional empirical support for the Canadian context. The empirical investigation is accomplished via a cross-sectional analysis of survey responses from a representative sample of Canadian adults in order to determine the health effects of specified aspects of social capital.

Social Capital: What Is It?

Social capital has been defined as features of social structure that facilitate resolution of collective action problems (Coleman 1988; Putnam et al. 1993), features that may serve to further the ends of specified individuals but may also act as resources for entire groups (Lin 2001b). There is no single social capital as such; rather, each instance of a social resource of this kind directs attention to the specific attributes of specific structures, and the relationships embedded within these structures, that facilitate certain kinds of actions and outcomes for certain people or social groups (Veenstra 2001). Researchers may implicitly argue that specific attributes of social structure, broadly conceived, work to achieve a multitude of ends, but this should never be assumed to be the case – social capital is always specific to the particularities of contexts, actions, and outcomes.

Social capital can be considered "social" because it is embedded within social relationships and social structure. It can be considered a "capital" because, like other forms of capital, it serves as a valuable resource for the accomplishment of goals. In comparing social capital with economic capital, for example, Hawe and Shiell (2000) describe these requisite characteristics: (1) it must be durable (i.e., it should be a stock of value that continues to provide a flow of productive services over time); (2) it must require one to invest resources now in order to generate benefits over the productive life of the asset; (3) it must be difficult to value (since the benefits of social capital may not always be reducible to an overt economic form); (4) it must reside in networks (such that property and ownership rights are not applicable); (5) it must not be portable, and ownership cannot be transferable between individuals; (6) it must not depreciate with use (but instead should have a multiplier effect, such that the more it is used the larger the stock of social capital, at least to a point); and (7) it should have a public good quality (i.e., it should be difficult to exclude persons from reaping its benefits – non-rivalrous). According to these criteria, only certain aspects of social structure that serve as resources and facilitate collective actions should be included within the rubric of social capital. Thus, trust, norms of reciprocity, and social networks, in common parlance thought to be primary ingredients of social capital, are only a social resource – a social capital – when they provide a durable, contextually specific, and accessible resource, and so on.

While it seems sensible to limit the analytical focus to resources in relationships and networks that are durable and non-rivalrous, it also seems reasonable to prioritize social relationships that are housed in civil society; otherwise, most aspects of social structure could be deemed a health-producing or health-damaging social capital. We could argue, for example, that intensely competitive social class relations serve to strengthen the cohesion of the dominant class, leading to better health for that class and poorer health for the subordinate class (Veenstra 2001). This class cohesion might be called "social capital," an aspect of social structure that facilitates certain actions and achieves certain ends (population health) for a certain group (the dominant class). The concept loses analytical meaning when it can encompass nearly all of social relations, however, and in this instance disobeys the public good dimension. (Eisenberg, in Chapter 4, argues for recognition of the public goods quality of social capital by paying careful attention to the ways in which trust, in particular, can sustain exploitation rather than militate against it.) The nature of social relations in the *civil space* only and the *non-zero-sum* ends they facilitate for groups and individuals delimit a more manageable conception of social capital.

In summary, according to the literature, social capital resides in the structure of the civil space rather than in individuals themselves, although individual acts contribute to its character. It serves as a resource that enables groups or individuals to accomplish their goals, but its nature is always defined by the particularities of a given context. Its generation and maintenance is unique among the capitals, and it serves a public rather than exclusively private good. It can be located at various levels of structure, from the micro (e.g., individuals in networks) to the macro (e.g., state-society relations). So, how might this broad and sweeping conceptualization of social capital serve as an orienting scheme for understanding social, economic, and political determinants of health? Health researchers have only recently begun to create theoretical models for determinants of population health that incorporate meaningful consideration of relationships in, and the structure of, the civil space.

Social Capital and Health: Theoretical Possibilities and Empirical Findings

Health research generally focuses on individual-level outcomes – physical and mental health. In an attempt to address the multiple levels of analysis that permeate the social capital discourse, health researchers have analytically distinguished *compositional* from *contextual* effects of social capital on health (Kawachi and Berkman 2000). Compositional effects are the direct influences of civic participation, participation in networks, or a sense of trust, for example, on the health of the participants simply by virtue of their participating or trusting. That is, certain actions and attitudes that are thought to contribute to the store or maintenance of social capital may be intrinsically health-inducing. Empirical testing for such compositional effects is generally conducted at the level of the individual (e.g., Lavis and Stoddart 1999; Rose 2000; Veenstra 2000). Contextual effects, on the other hand, refer to those aspects of social structure that influence the health of groups or populations via direct or indirect means. That is, social capital as a resource for achieving certain collective goals that are then health-inducing is the analytical focus that is relevant to pursuing contextual effects, regardless of how and whether the individual contributes to the store of a given social capital. Empirical testing for such contextual effects of social capital for health is generally ecological or multi-level in character, often relating measures of social capital in communities to ecological measures of health such as mortality rates or life expectancy (e.g., Kawachi et al. 1997; Lynch et al. 2001; Putnam 2000; Veenstra 2002b) or to individual measures such as self-rated physical and mental health via the utilization of hierarchical multi-level modelling (e.g., Kawachi, Kennedy, and Glass 1999; Weitzman and Kawachi 2000; Ellaway and Macintyre 2000).

COMPOSITIONAL EFFECTS

The actions that individuals engage in or the values and ideals that they express, all of which contribute to the store of a given social capital, might be intrinsically health-inducing. Thus, Wilkinson (1996) suggests that friendship patterns can reflect social ease and confidence or anxiety and inner angst that may influence health directly. Knowledge of the resources inherent in one's networks may promote a sense of mastery or personal locus of control and reduce stress, a well-known determinant of health. There is a broad literature on the general effects of various kinds of social support and social relationships on individuals' health status (House, Landis, and Umberson 1988; Berkman et al. 2000) and patterns of mutual acquaintance in a social capital context may serve to sustain health along these lines. In short, engaging in those actions or expressing those sentiments that contribute to a so-called social capital may directly influence the health of the contributors themselves.

Table 10.1 highlights empirical evidence for individual-level relationships that reflect compositional effects of social capital on health. With respect to social trust, Lavis and Stoddart (1999), utilizing the World Values Survey, showed the relationship of the expression of trust to self-rated health status in five of seven nations studied, including Canada, while Rose (2000) demonstrated the relevance of trust for the self-reported health of Russians. On the other hand, multiple measures of social and political trust were found to be mostly unrelated to self-rated health status in a study based in the province of Saskatchewan, Canada (Veenstra 2000). With respect to participation in networks in the civil space, both Lavis and Stoddart (1999) and Veenstra (2000) found little reason to believe that membership in associations is related to self-rated health status in the Canadian context, and Ellaway and Macintyre (2000) did not find individual-level relationships between participation in a local association and self-rated health status in Scotland. Conversely, however, Baum et al. (2000) reported that participation in the

TABLE 10.1

Social capital and health: individual-level findings

Author	Context	Measure of health	Social capital indicator	Relationship
Lavis and Stoddart (1999)	World Values Survey in Canada, US, UK, France, Germany, Italy, and Japan (n = 1,333 in Canada)	Self-rated health status	Social trust; membership in voluntary associations	Trust was significantly associated with health in Canada, US, Germany, Italy, and Japan, even after controlling for sociodemographic factors (in the Canadian case, odds ratio of 1.54 while controlling for age, income, education, and employment grade). Number of memberships was not significantly related to health.
Veenstra (2000)	Survey in eight health districts in Saskatchewan, Canada (n = 534)	Self-rated health status	Social and political trust; commitment; social engagement; civic participation	Trust and commitment unrelated to health. Frequency of socialization with workmates (eta = .145) and attendance at religious services (eta = .136) significantly related to health. Number of associations only relevant for the health of elderly (eta = .278). Nature of participation in associations, the character of associations, and civic participation irrelevant for health.

▼ TABLE 10.1

Author	Context	Measure of health	Social capital indicator	Relationship
Baum et al. (2000)	Survey in Western suburbs of Adelaide, Australia ($n = 2,542$)	Health status measured by the SF-12 (physical and mental health status)	Six categories of participation (informal social contact, activities in public spaces, group sports or hobbies, civic activity singly and in a group, participation in community groups)	Many aspects of participation bivariately related to both physical and mental health, more strongly so to the latter.
Ellaway and Macintyre (2000)	Survey in western Scotland ($n = 605$)	Self-rated health status; report of symptoms	Belonging to a local association	Membership not related to health after controlling for age, sex, and social class.
Rose (2000)	Survey in Russia ($n = 1,904$)	Self-reported health	Involvement in or exclusion from formal and informal networks; trust	Markers of social capital significantly related to health before and after controlling for human capital (age, income, sex, subjective social status, and education).

civic space was related to mental health status (and physical health status too, but less strongly) in one Australian city, while Rose (2000) showcased significant relationships between membership in groups and health in Russia. In summary, some evidence exists for compositional effects of social capital on health, the former measured by trust and associational membership, in some international settings, but the evidence is still meagre (and even contradictory). This chapter adds to the literature by providing evidence for compositional effects of trust and participation in the civil space on the self-rated health of adult Canadians.

CONTEXTUAL EFFECTS

At the macro-level, social capital may influence the performance (i.e., the effectiveness and/or efficiency) of political institutions (Putnam et al. 1993; Rice and Sumberg 1997), with indirect implications for the health of the governed populations. Thus Veenstra and Lomas (1999) speculate about the means by which social capitals may affect the governing performance of Canadian regional health authorities, in particular, with implications for the provision of health care. More generally, other characteristics of political institutions that might be influenced by social relations in the civil space, such as degree of adherence to welfare state principles, may be especially pertinent for the health of populations. Kawachi and Berkman (2000) argue, for instance, that societies or communities with low levels of trust are less likely to invest in human security or provide generous safety nets. They contend that interpersonal trust coincides with more egalitarian patterns of political participation, where the passage of policies pertaining to education, transportation, pollution, child welfare, and zoning laws beneficial to the well-being of all citizens is more likely. (In Chapter 11, Soroka, Johnston, and Banting describe how the nature of the redistributive state is rooted in a sense of community and collective responsibility.) A state that seeks to redress social inequality in general may serve to reduce income inequality through welfare measures, potentially improving the population's health by those materialistic or psycho-social means that link income inequality to health (see Kaplan et al. 1996; Kawachi et al. 1997; Kennedy, Kawachi, and Prothrow-Stith 1996; Lynch and Kaplan 1997; Wilkinson 1992). Social capital may also influence access to valuable services and amenities, as socially cohesive communities may be more successful at uniting to ensure that budget cuts do not affect health and social services.

Social relations and interpersonal trust in the civil space may influence economic development and growth (Helliwell and Putnam 1995; Woolcock 1998, 2001), a possibility again described in depth by Soroka, Johnston, and Banting (Chapter 11). To the degree that wealth aggregated to the level of the community contributes to average levels of health (see Veenstra 2002b), the influence of social relations in the civil space upon economic productivity will have implications for population health. Also, to the degree that social relations within the civil sphere affect deep social structure, social capitals may mitigate class, racial, ethnic, gendered, religious, and other power imbalances, that is, networks of mutual acquaintance spanning these potential chasms may introduce people to perspectives different from their own and produce a spirit of tolerance, thereby lessening the magnitude of influence that embedded relations have upon social relations in general and upon health inequalities along racial lines in particular (Veenstra 2001). At the micro- and meso- levels, some forms of social capital may influence health-related behaviours by promoting diffusion of health-related information, thus increasing the likelihood that healthy norms of behaviour are adopted, or by exerting social control over deviant health-related behaviour, thereby mitigating the incidence of crime, juvenile delinquency, and access to firearms within communities.

Social capital has been found empirically relevant for some of these potentially health-inducing ecological characteristics of communities or societies, but mostly without consideration of aggregate health as a primary dependent variable. For example, the prevalence of voluntaristic activities such as participation in soccer clubs and church choirs and civic activities such as voting or reading a local newspaper was found to be empirically related to the performance of political institutions among Italian regions (Putnam et al. 1993). A similar result, utilizing a more comprehensive measure of social capital and referring to state governments, was reported for the United States (Rice and Sumberg 1997). Knack and Keefer (1997) used the World Values Survey to find, at the national level, that, although group memberships appeared unrelated to trust and civic norms, both trust and civic norms appeared to have significant impacts upon economic activity. Kennedy et al. (1998) reported that social capital was related to the incidence of violent crime among US states, as was income inequality, concluding that social capital mediated the relationship between income inequality and crime (both of which may influence overall levels of health).

TABLE 10.2

Social capital and health: ecological findings

Author	Context	Measure of health	Measure of social capital	Relationship
Ellison (1999)	Nations ($n = 23$)	Aggregated self-reported health status	Aggregated social trust	Aggregated social trust and health related bivariately (r-squared = 25.0%) but not after controlling for GNP and income inequality (0.0%).
Lynch et al. (2001)	Nations of Luxembourg Income Study ($n = 16$)	Life expectancy; age- and sex-specific mortality rates; age-standardized all-cause mortality rates; cause-specific mortality rates (in 12 categories); low birth-weight rates; self-rated health status	Aggregated distrust and membership in organizations (from World Values Survey)	Social capital measures not significantly related to age-specific mortality, life expectancy, and self-rated health. Distrust related to CHD mortality ($r = -.61$) and unintentional deaths <1 ($r = .63$). Associational membership related to cirrhosis deaths ($r = -.58$). (All relationships controlled for GDP/capita.)
Kawachi et al. (1997)	American states ($n = 39$)	Age-standardized mortality rates; cause-specific mortality rates (coronary heart disease, malignant neoplasms, cerebrovascular disease, unintentional injuries)	Aggregated participation in civic associations, three social trust questions	Social trust ($r = .77, .79, .71$) and group membership ($r = -.49$) significantly related to all-cause mortality in bivariate relationships. Social trust significantly related to total mortality, malignant neoplasms, infant mortality, and stroke after controlling for state-level poverty. Group membership significantly related to total mortality, coronary heart disease, malignant neoplasms, and infant mortality after controlling for state-level poverty.

▼ Table 10.2

Author	Context	Measure of health	Measure of social capital	Relationship
Putnam (2000)	American states ($n = 50$)	Healthy state index of 23 items, 1993-98; mortality rate, 1990	Social capital index of fourteen items (including serving in local organizations, number of club memberships and meetings attended, turnout in elections, attending public meetings, etc.)	Social capital was strongly related to the healthy state index ($r = .78$) and the mortality rate ($r = -.81$).
Veenstra (2002a)	Health districts in Saskatchewan, Canada ($n = 29$)	Age-standardized mortality rates	Social capital index including: density of secondary associations, aggregate of associational memberships, and proportion of eligible voters who voted in three elections	Social capital index and mortality not significantly related ($r = -.327, p = .083$). Density of associations almost significantly related to mortality ($r = -.356, p = .058$).

Much more work is needed, however, to determine whether and how these community-level or society-level relationships between social capital, governance, and economy translate into better or worse health for some or all of the members of communities.

Table 10.2 highlights some empirical ecological relationships between measures of social capital and population health in a number of international contexts. Among twenty-three Western nations, Ellison (1999) found that the prevalence of trust was relevant for health before but not after controlling for societal wealth and income inequality. In a smaller sample of Western nations, Lynch et al. (2001) did not find many relationships between social capital and health after controlling for societal wealth: the only significant relationships reported pertained to very specific causes of mortality – CHD mortality, unintentional deaths and cirrhosis deaths. Kawachi et al. (1997) argue that social capital mediates the relationship between income inequality and health status among US states, and found that higher levels of trust and greater associational participation in the aggregate were associated with lower levels of mortality from most of the major causes of death among US states. Also among the US states, Putnam (2000) showed that another measure of state-level social capital was related to a health status index, even after controlling for multiple sociodemographic characteristics of states. Among health districts in Saskatchewan, Canada, Veenstra (2002b) found that social capital was negatively related to mortality rates, albeit not quite significantly so. In summary, social capital research has found some empirical relationships between simple measures of social capital and aggregate measures of health in several international and North American contexts, but not in all studied contexts. In addition, not all relationships persisted after controlling for economic attributes of societies or communities, suggesting that civil society and the economy are linked to one another and that, to the degree that they serve as determinants of the overall health of populations, they do so jointly.

It is important to note that, if trust and participation in voluntary associations are related to health at the level of the individual, then we might expect to find relationships between aggregate measures of trust, participation, and health at most levels of aggregation, relationships that could then be considered statistical artefacts. Table 10.3 highlights results from multilevel studies linking social capital to health, the only statistical way of being confident that an ecological attribute of social structure is not an artefact. (Soroka, Johnston, and Banting in Chapter 11 provide an example of an approach to incorporating multiple levels of analysis into one model that, with respect to individually professed trust rather than health, incorporates both individual and contextual effects.) Thus Kawachi et al. (1999) found that individuals living in US states with low social capital were at increased risk for poor self-rated health after controlling for individual risk factors such as low income, low education, smoking, obesity, and access to health care. Among US colleges, social capital was related to binge drinking, a predictor of well-being, after controlling for various characteristics of students (Weitzman and Kawachi 2000). Finally, Ellaway, and Macintyre (2000) report a significant effect for associational membership aggregated to the postcode level in Scotland after controlling for some individual-level measures. In summary, there is some evidence for contextual effects of social capital on the health of populations operating above and beyond compositional effects, but more work of this kind is needed, especially in Canada.

This chapter explores individual-level relationships between trust, social engagement, civic participation, and self-rated health status using cross-sectional data from a survey of randomly selected adults in Canada. Are trusting Canadians healthier than those who suspect others? Does participation in associations positively influence health? Do Canadians who contribute to the political-civic life of society experience a higher sense of well-being? If relationships are found between these indicators of social capital and self-rated health status, then we have evidence of compositional effects of social capital upon health for Canadians, especially if the relationships hold after controlling for sociodemographic and socioeconomic characteristics of survey respondents. If there are few relationships of this kind, then the challenge is renewed to find other, more intricate (and contextual) pathways through which interpersonal trust, for example, may influence health. Identifying compositional effects is an important first step toward identifying the role, if any, of social capital in promoting or sustaining the health of Canadians.

Data: Survey Sample of Canadian Adults

In summer 2000, a telephone survey of randomly selected Canadian adults was conducted by the Institute for Social Research at York University for the Equality, Security, and Community project at the University of British Columbia. The survey sample used in this chapter was composed of 4101 respondents, representing a 50 percent response rate, and analysis was weighted by household size and province of residence for purposes of representativeness. Because of its national representativeness and its incorporation of

TABLE 10.3

Social capital and health: multi-level findings

Author	Context	Measure of health	Measure of social capital	Relationship
Kawachi et al. (1999)	American states ($n = 39$)	Self-rated health status	Aggregated participation in civic associations, three social trust questions	Living in a social capital "high" vs. "low" state was significantly related to health before and after controlling for age, sex, and race at the individual level (e.g., odds ratio of 1.41 for living in a high vs. low trust state).
Weitzman and Kawachi (2000)	Four-year American colleges ($n = 140$)	Binge drinking	Aggregated average time volunteering in past month	Contextual social capital was significantly related to binge drinking before and after controlling for individual volunteering, age, sex, race, and parents' educational attainment.
Ellaway and Macintyre (2000)	Survey in localities in western Scotland ($n = 605$)	Self-rated health status; report of symptoms	Belonging to a local association, aggregated to postcode sector	Aggregate membership significantly related to health after controlling for individual age, sex, and social class.

multiple measures of social capital, this survey data set provides an excellent means of assessing compositional health effects in Canada. However, because of the small number of provinces in the country and the small number of survey respondents in many Census Tracts, the data set does not facilitate the exploration of contextual effects by means of multi-level modelling at these two levels of analysis.

Health was assessed by a single self-rated health question, a simple survey measure known to be a predictor of other, more objective, measures of health (Idler and Benyamini 1997). The survey data set also contained measures of social and political trust, social engagement, and civic participation, three supposed aspects of social capital utilized frequently in the health literature. Social trust was captured by one straightforward measure of generalized trust (people can be trusted until proven otherwise) and four trust questions with specific referents (neighbours, police officers, grocery store clerks, and strangers). Political trust was addressed by two survey questions, one pertaining to trust in the federal government and a second to trust in the provincial government. Social engagement was assessed by participation in informal and formal networks, that is, with respect to family, friends, and neighbours and with respect to formal voluntary associations and organizations. Finally, several aspects of civic activity were measured, namely, voting in elections and attention to local and international news.

The survey items, variables, and their coding are described in more detail in the appendix.

Methods: Analytical Steps and Modelling Techniques

The analysis begins by highlighting multivariate relationships between self-rated health and basic demographic (age, gender, number of siblings) and sociodemographic attributes (marital status, number of children, education and income, employment status, language at home, and immigrant status). Basic demographic variables can only be antecedent to relationships between the human aspects of social capital – trust, participation in networks and civic activity – and self-rated health. To the degree that they make such relationships spurious by simultaneously causing perceptions of health and these indicators of social capital, it is sensible to control for them in a multivariate analysis of relationships between social capital and health. Sociodemographic characteristics of respondents are more problematic. One could argue that some or all sociodemographic variables are antecedent to social capital and health relationships and should be controlled for in multivariate analysis. It is also plausible to posit, however, that past connections, that is, past access to social capital resources, may have helped people obtain their jobs, influenced educational experiences, and even influenced immigration choices and ethnic affiliation, and, if current networks of association reflect the character of former networks, then such variables are properly interpreted as intervening variables. (Supporting this possibility, Curtis and Perks in chapter 6 above demonstrate a strong relationship between activity in extracurricular activities during school years and civic activity as an adult, indicating a degree of continuity over time with respect to extracurricular involvement.) In the interest of removing as much spuriousness as possible from social capital and health relationships, the first approach is adopted here. Backward step-wise logistic regression is used to create a parsimonious model of sociodemographic variables representing all of the demographic and sociodemographic variables, which are then controlled for when exploring relationships between social capital and health.

The analysis then describes relationships between the individual-level aspects or indicators of social capital (social and political trust, participation in informal networks, associational membership, and civic activity) and self-rated health before and after controlling for sociodemographic variables, and in some instances after controlling for one another as well. Throughout the analysis, precise details for the statistically significant results are reported in the text of the chapter, and several of the multivariate models are presented in tables.

With respect to multivariate modelling, the dependent variable was dichotomized (fair/poor health was compared to excellent/very good/good health) and binary logistic regression models were created. For a given logistic regression model, the model chi-square provided a test of significance for the entire model, Nagelkerke's pseudo-R-squared provided an estimate of the explanatory power of the model as a whole, and the B, Exp(B), and p-value statistics indicated the nature of the contribution of each variable to the model.

Results: Compositional Effects in Canada

Table 10.4 shows results from a multiple logistic regression incorporating only the demographic variables. Age and number of siblings were statistically significant, although only a little variability in self-rated health status was explained by the model as a whole (perhaps to be expected, given that respondents were asked to describe their state of health in comparison with others their own age and gender). Table 10.5 displays results from a logistic

Table 10.4

Multivariate logistic regression: basic demographic predictors of fair or poor self-rated health status

	Logistic regression		
	Beta	Exp(B)	Significance
Year of birth	−.016	.984	<.001
Number of siblings	.081	1.084	<.001
Gender (dummy variable, 1 = female)	.092	1.096	>.05

NOTE: $N = 3,964$, model chi-square = 73.533, $p < .001$, Nagelkerke R-squared = 3.4%.

Table 10.5

Multivariate logistic regression: sociodemographic predictors of fair or poor self-rated health status

	Logistic regression		
	Beta	Exp(B)	Significance
Year of birth	.003	1.003	>.05
Number of siblings	.067	1.069	<.001
Gender (dummy variable, 1 = female)	.101	1.107	>.05
Marital status (versus "never been married")			>.05
Married			
Living with a partner			
Separated			
Divorced			
Widowed			
Number of children	.016	1.106	>.05
Education	−.137	.872	<.001
Employment status (versus "homemaker")			<.001
Self-employed	−.215	.807	>.05
Working for pay	−.264	.768	>.05
Retired	.638	1.893	<.05
Unemployed/looking for work	.663	1.941	<.05
Student	−.344	.709	>.05
Language spoken at home (versus "other")			>.05
English			
French			
Country of birth (dummy variable, 1 = "Canada")	.064	1.066	>.05

NOTE: $N = 3,693$, model chi-square = 148.161, $p < .001$, Nagelkerke R-squared = 7.3%.

TABLE 10.6

Multivariate logistic regression: sociodemographic predictors of fair or poor self-rated health status, parsimonious version

	Logistic regression		
	Beta	Exp(B)	Significance
Number of siblings	.069	1.071	<.001
Education	−.137	.872	<.001
Employment status (versus "homemaker")			<.001
Self-employed	−.292	.747	>.05
Working for pay	−.284	.753	>.05
Retired	.514	1.671	<.05
Unemployed/looking for work	.669	1.952	<.05
Student	−.294	.745	>.05
Language spoken at home (versus "other")			>.05
English			
French			

NOTE: $N = 3{,}798$, model chi-square = 148.429, $p < .001$, Nagelkerke R-squared = 7.2%.

regression additionally including the sociodemographic variables, in which number of siblings, education and employment status were the statistically significant contributors to the model.[1] Table 10.6 shows the parsimonious logistic regression model representing the sociodemographic determinants of self-rated health status used in subsequent exploration of relationships between indicators of social capital and health, obtained by implementing backwards step-wise regression (Likelihood Ratio) on the model displayed in Table 10.5.

Next, multivariate relationships between various individual-level indicators of social capital – social and political trust, social engagement, and civic participation – and self-rated health status are presented.

TRUST AND HEALTH

Of the five measures of social trust, two were significantly related to self-rated health, such that more trust in neighbours and in police officers corresponded with lower odds of reporting fair/poor health scores (with the sociodemographic controls, $p < .001$ for the entire variable, Exp(B) = −.630 for the "very likely" response, in particular, $N = 3{,}717$; and $p < .001$ for the entire variable, Exp(B) = −.707 for "very likely," in particular, $N = 3{,}713$, respectively). The two measures of political trust were also significantly related to health before and after adding the controls (for federal trust, $p < .01$, Exp(B) = 0.903, $N = 3{,}676$ with controls; for provincial trust, $p < .001$, Exp(B) = 0.864, $N = 3{,}686$ with controls). These findings indicate that more-trusting Canadians tend to report better self-rated health scores, an insight consistent with the international results described by Lavis and Stoddart (1999) and Rose (2000) in Russia but at odds with that reported by Veenstra (2000) in Saskatchewan.

Thus, it seems that people who are open to interacting with others, who believe in the inherent good will of others, and so on may benefit from this attitude. (See Veenstra 2002a and Soroka, Helliwell, and Johnston in Chapter 5 of this volume, for in-depth explorations of the multifaceted nature of trust.) Why? Kawachi and Berkman (2000) speculate that interpersonal trust facilitates knowledge transfer of new health innovations and influences voluntarism and participation in collective action, both of which may subsequently influence well-being. It is also possible that trusting people are less likely to feel lonely and isolated or are more likely to have well-developed skills for dealing with stress. Of course, causality may run in the other direction, so that trust stems from healthfulness rather than influencing it. Although a cross-sectional study such as this one cannot ascertain causal directionality, there is some support in the literature from longitudinal designs for the causal priority of trust over health (Barefoot et al., 1998). Still, the nature of the relationship between trust and health, especially between political trust and health, remains mostly unknown.

SOCIAL ENGAGEMENT AND HEALTH

With respect to social engagement, informal networking with family members, close friends, and neighbours were all positively and significantly related to health, but only the latter was significant after introducing the sociodemographic controls ($p < .05$, Exp(B) = 0.935, $N = 3763$). Participation in more associations was also related to better health; participation in recreational groups, youth groups, groups that help people, political groups, and cultural service organizations appeared to be the main contributors to this relationship. Still, after controlling for sociodemographic characteristics, only participation in recreational groups remained significantly related to self-rated health ($p < .05$, Exp(B) = .886, $N = 3{,}789$). (The total amount of money contributed to associations [$p < .01$, Exp(B) = .924, $N = 3{,}432$] was also pertinent, but likely reflects economic circumstance more than anything else.) Upon noting that the recreational category includes exercise classes and sports groups, suggesting a reversed direction of causality (given that a certain level of health is undoubtedly required to participate in some exercise classes and sports teams), it seems that associational membership in general did *not* represent a compelling compositional effect in this sample.

Civic Activity and Health

Finally, of the four indicators of civic activity, only civic interest in the form of attention to the television news was significantly related to self-rated health status before and after adding controls ($p < .01$, $Exp(B) = .944$, $N = 3,774$ with controls). Even though television watching, in general, is known to be associated with poorer health outcomes, especially obesity, in this sample, watching television news, in particular, was associated with *better* overall self-rated health.

Table 10.7 shows results from a multivariate logistic regression containing several of the most relevant individual-level social capital items. It is notable that each of the social trust, political trust, membership in recreational groups, and television news indicators included in the model remained statistically significant predictors of self-rated health after controlling for various sociodemographic characteristics and for one another. Achieved with a nationally representative sample of adults, this result provides preliminary but compelling evidence for a compositional effect of social trust, political trust, and civic attention on the health of Canadians.

Discussion: Does Social Capital Really Matter for the Health of Canadians?

This exploration for compositional effects of social capital on health in Canada was quite fruitful. As discussed in the introduction, social trust, participation in various kinds of networks, and political participation of a civic nature may influence health status in and of themselves, perhaps by virtue of the social support inherent to close relationships that affect self-esteem, for example, or perhaps as indicators of the degree of meaningful participation in shared social life, an elemental state of being in which physical well-being accompanies an elemental state of social and political well-being. Individual-level relationships between such phenomena and health support this view, in general, and statistically significant relationships of this kind were found in this data set that is representative of Canadian adults. Even after controlling for demographic and human capital measures such as age, gender, education, and income, it was found that trust in other people

TABLE 10.7

Multivariate logistic regression: sociodemographic and social capital predictors of fair or poor self-rated health status

	Logistic regression		
	Beta	Exp(B)	Significance
Number of siblings	.074	1.076	<.001
Education	−.116	.890	<.001
Employment status (versus "homemaker")			<.001
Self-employed	−.406	.667	>.05
Working for pay	−.443	.642	<.05
Retired	.455	1.577	<.05
Unemployed/looking for work	.550	1.733	<.05
Student	−.361	.697	>.05
Language spoken at home (versus "other")			<.05
English	−.536	.585	<.05
French	−.188	.829	>.05
Social trust II (versus "not at all likely")			<.01
Very likely	−.496	.609	>.05
Somewhat likely	−.229	.795	<.05
Political trust I	−.078	.925	<.05
Talks with neighbours	−.038	.963	>.05
Recreational groups	−.114	.892	<.05
Watches TV news	−.046	.955	<.05

NOTE: $N = 3{,}553$, model chi-square = 164.327, $p < .001$, Nagelkerke R-squared = 8.5%.

(social trust), trust in governments (political trust), participation in recreational groups, and civic attention to the news were significantly related to self-rated health status. In this sample, Canadians who professed trust and claimed to participate in the social and political "space" in these ways tended to report good overall health.

Are these individual-level relationships truly reflective of causality at the individual level? Unfortunately, it is impossible to say, given the limitations inherent in a cross-sectional data set of individual survey responses. Some of these relationships obviously refer to individual-level phenomena, while others are more suggestive of the social structural aspect of social capital (reflections of structural phenomena). Informal networks with neighbours, family, and friends, in particular, and also formal membership in associations, suggest the importance of social support, a well-known determinant of health at the individual level. Close relationships with others may provide people with reassurance and resources to deal with daily problems, possibly enhancing self-esteem and militating against depression. But how does *trust* influence health? Why would civic attention to the news matter for well-being? These latter individual-level relationships are not obviously and necessarily compositional effects, but they may, instead, be rough indicators of the social and political milieu that respondents live in, a milieu that may be replete with (or devoid of) political activism and broadly based networks of association and, thus, may be a milieu that promotes (or dissuades) the health of its citizens via other means. If so, these individual-level relationships may be statistical artefacts, with true causality operating at a higher level of analysis. A fundamental question for further exploration, then, is this: at which higher level of analysis, at which type of "community," are trust and associational and political participation on one hand, and the health of community residents on the other, truly fostered? Is this community geopolitical in nature or is it, instead, one of the other communities, infinite in number, within which human beings as social beings align themselves? These questions remain mostly unaddressed in Canada.

A second fundamental issue pertains to the very nature of social capital itself. If social capital is of an abstract nature and comes in a number of different forms and manifestations, to what degree does a generalized social trust, for example, form a common ingredient? If a particular social capital, such as loosely knit networks with colleagues and acquaintances in many countries, which enable someone to obtain information about potential job opportunities elsewhere, is based on a specific form of trust – on trust in one's colleagues but not necessarily on trust in people in general – does a relationship between social trust broadly conceived and health reflect the influence of this social capital? Probably not. Thus, the compositional results regarding trust displayed in this chapter pertain only to those manifestations of social capital that are built upon a generic trust. Studies such as this one that ask general questions of large populations are inherently limited in scope, and more work on the varied manifestations of social capital, and their relationships with health, is needed.

A third fundamental unaddressed and unresolved issue pertains to the inherently consensual nature of social capital discourse, and the paucity of "power" and structured inequality as orienting schemes in this discourse. The discourse in the field of health research tends to focus on shared norms, trust among people, participation in networks, dense networks in communities or societies and collective or collaborative action. Where is social class? Is there room to accommodate deep schisms that exist in some societies, such as those between and among races or genders? People have different opportunities to exercise power and influence, an array of life chances given them by structural characteristics of the social world, which may be related to their ability to access the resources embedded in social relations. Analyses that ignore aspects of social structure that may play a big role in the determination of life chances might be considered somewhat sociologically naïve.

These fundamental unresolved issues notwithstanding, this chapter demonstrates the possible relevance of social capital for the health of Canadians. The social capital and health discourse represents an exciting entry into the world of social theory for health researchers. It serves to expand focus from a narrow consideration of the determinants of health – focused on the health care system and actions and behaviours of individuals, such as dietary choices and exercise – to the complex and largely unseen world of interpersonal relationships and social structure. The field of social capital research suggests that social structure matters, at multiple levels of analysis, and, although locating determinants of health in the world of social relationships is an intimidating and complicated task, with few signposts to guide analytical exploration, the potential reward for understanding variability in the health of Canadians seems to be high.

APPENDIX

This appendix describes the variables used in the preceding analysis.

Health

Self-reported health status: "Compared to others your age, would you describe your health as excellent, very good, good, fair, or poor?" All response categories were utilized in bivariate analyses. The variable was dichotomized for use in multivariate modelling by distinguishing excellent (25 percent of responses), very good (33.5 percent), and good (27.8 percent) responses from fair (10.3 percent) and poor (3.1 percent) responses.

Demographic Characteristics

Gender: "What is your gender?" Dummy variable = 1 if respondent is female. 53.7 percent of survey respondents were female.

Year of birth: "In what year were you born?" The average age in the sample was 42.7 years.

Number of siblings: "When you were fourteen years of age, how many brothers and sisters did you have?" The average number of siblings was 3.3.

Sociodemographic Characteristics

Marital status: "Are you presently married, living with a partner, separated, divorced, widowed, or have you never been married?" 63.8 percent of respondents were married or living with a partner, whereas 23.3 percent had never been married.

Number of children: "How many children do you have, including any no longer living with you?" 32.8 percent of respondents had no children, 12.7 percent had one child, and 30.0 percent had two children.

Education: "What is the highest level of education that you have completed?" Coded as 1 = no schooling, 2 = some elementary school, 3 = completed elementary school, 4 = some secondary/high school, 5 = completed secondary/high school, 6 = some technical/community college, 7 = completed technical/community college, 8 = some university, 9 = bachelor's degree, 10 = master's degree, and 11 = professional degree or doctorate. In the survey sample, 41.9 percent of respondents had completed only high school and 24.7 percent had completed a university degree.

Employment status: "Are you currently self-employed, working for pay, retired, unemployed or looking for work, a student, a homemaker, or something else?" 12.6 percent of respondents were self-employed, 55.0 percent worked for pay, and 15.2 percent were retired.

Household income: "What is the best estimate of the total income of all family who live with you at this household, including yourself, from all sources for the year ending Dec 31, 1999?" Coded in dollars.

Language spoken at home: "What language do you usually speak at home?" 24.5 percent spoke French and 67.8 percent spoke English at home.

Country of birth: "In what country were you born?" Dummy variable = 1 if respondent was born in Canada. 83.0 percent of respondents were born in Canada.

Social Trust

Social trust I: "People can be trusted until they prove otherwise." Dummy variable, coded = 0 if disagree, = 1 if agree. 85.9 percent of respondents agreed with this statement.

Social trust II, III, IV, and V: "Say you lost a wallet or purse with $100 in it. How likely is it that the wallet or purse will be returned with the money in it if it was found by a [neighbour]? Would you say it is very likely, likely, or not at all likely?" The question is repeated four times, for a neighbour (someone who lives close by), a police officer, a clerk at the local grocery store, and a stranger. Coded = 1 for not at all likely, = 2 for somewhat likely, and = 0 for very likely. In the survey sample, 45.7 percent of respondents thought it was very likely that the money would be returned by someone who lives close by, 50.9 if found by a clerk at a grocery store, and 66.6 percent if found by a police officer. Only 9.4 percent thought it was very likely to be returned by a stranger.

POLITICAL TRUST

Political trust I: "How much do you trust the government in Ottawa to do what is right?" Coded 1 = almost never (includes never), 2 = some of the time, 3 = most of the time, and 4 = almost always (includes always). 21.9 percent of respondents chose "almost never," whereas only 5.6 percent chose "almost always."

Political trust II: "How much do you trust the government in [province] to do what is right?" Coded 1 = almost never (includes never), 2 = some of the time, 3 = most of the time, and 4 = almost always (includes always). 25.2 percent chose "almost never," whereas 5.7 percent chose "almost always."

INFORMAL NETWORKS

Sees family members: "How often do you see family members who do not live with you? Would you say every day, several times a week, at least once a week, at least once a month, several times a year, or less often?" Coded 1 = less often, 2 = several times a year, 3 = at least once a month, 4 = several times a week, and 5 = every day. 12.5 percent of respondents see family members every day, and 8.1 percent see them less often than several times a year.

Sees close friends: "How often do you see close friends – not your husband or wife or partner or family member, but people you feel fairly close to?" Coded 1 = less often, 2 = several times a year, 3 = at least once a month, 4 = several times a week, and 5 = every day. 18.8 percent see a close friend every day, whereas only 8.5 percent see a close friend several times a year or less.

Talks with neighbours: "And how often do you talk with your neighbours?" Coded 1 = less often (includes never), 2 = several times a year, 3 = at least once a month, 4 = at least once a week, 5 = several times a week, and 6 = every day. 22.6 percent of respondents talk with neighbours every day, whereas 12.8 percent speak with neighbours less often than several times a year.

FORMAL NETWORKS

Service clubs: "How many service clubs, such as Lions or Meals on Wheels, do you belong to?" Only 11.7 percent of respondents belonged to one or more service clubs.

Recreational groups: "How many recreational groups, such as sports leagues or clubs, music or hobby clubs, or exercise classes are you involved in?" 45.8 percent of survey respondents belonged to at least one recreational group.

Political organizations: "How many organizations active on political issues, such as the environment or taxpayers' rights, do you belong to?" 12.0 percent belonged to one or more political organizations.

Youth-oriented groups: "Sometimes people give time to various types of organizations. For instance, how many youth-oriented groups, such as Girl Guides or Minor Hockey, have you given time to in the last twelve months?" 30.7 percent belonged to one or more youth-oriented groups.

Cultural services organizations: "How about organizations providing cultural services to the public, such as a museum or music festival. How many of these have you given time to in the last twelve months?" 15.1 percent belonged to a cultural services organization.

Volunteer organizations: "How about organizations that help people, such as the Cancer Society or a food bank? How many of these have you volunteered time to in the last twelve months?" 30.7 percent belonged to a volunteer organization.

Ethnic organizations: "How many organizations connected with your own nationality or ethnic or racial group are you a member of?" 14.3 percent belonged to such an organization.

Religious groups: "How many groups directly attached to your place of worship, such as a charitable group, are you a member of?" 19.7 percent belonged to one or more religious groups, although the question was not asked of all respondents.

Other organizations: "Do you belong to or volunteer for any other groups or organizations that we have not asked about? How many of these other groups do you volunteer for or belong to?"

Number of hours volunteered: "Thinking about the last twelve months, about how many hours in a typical month did you volunteer for all of the various organizations and charitable and social service activities we've mentioned?"

Amount of money contributed: "Thinking about the past twelve months, including membership dues, about how much money, in total, did you contribute to any charity, or any social service organization?"

Attends religious services: "How often do you attend religious services, not including weddings and funerals?" Coded 1 = never, 2 = less than once a year, 3 = once or twice a year, 4 = several times a year, 5 = about once a month, 6 = two to three times a month, 7 = nearly every week, 8 = every week, and 9 = more than once a week. 16.6 percent never attend religious services, whereas 32.7 percent attend services at least once a month.

CIVIC PARTICIPATION

Voted I: "Did you vote in the last federal election in 1997?" Dummy variable, 1 = yes. 73.0 percent of respondents voted in this election.

Voted II: "Did you vote in the last provincial election in [date]?" Dummy variable, 1 = yes. 69.6 percent voted in the last provincial election.

Reads newspaper: "In a typical week, how many days do you read a daily newspaper?" Only 16.7 percent of respondents do not read a newspaper at all, and 30.5 percent read one every day of the week.

Watches TV news: "In a typical week, on how many days do you watch the news on television?" Only 8.7 percent of respondents claimed that they do not watch the TV news, and a full 43.9 percent watch the news seven days a week.

NOTE

1   Income reduced the *N* substantially and so was not included in this model. Still, upon its addition to the model it was non-significant (results not shown).

11
Ethnicity, Trust, and the Welfare State

Stuart N. Soroka, Richard Johnston, and Keith Banting

Contemporary democratic politics is multicultural politics. During the second half of the twentieth century, new patterns of international migration altered the demographic landscape of liberal-democratic countries, increasing the ethnic, racial, religious, and linguistic diversity of their societies. These new forms of social difference have generated new political pressures and new policy issues. Governments must manage tensions between cultural majorities and minorities, and find their way through potentially explosive issues embedded in immigration and refuge policies, anti-discrimination programs, and the integration of newcomers into the social fabric. But multiculturalism may bring an even broader transformation of political life and policy regimes. In particular, it may call the welfare state into question. New forms of social diversity spark debates about traditional conceptions of identity and community and about the rights and mutual obligations embedded in citizenship. Shifts in such broad orientations toward government and society have the potential to reshape the frame of reference within which basic economic and social programs are debated, and to reconfigure the political constituencies that sustain them.

The social role of the state would seem particularly sensitive to such shifts (Banting 2000). Many commentators have wondered whether relatively diverse societies are less likely than relatively homogeneous ones to invest in redistributive and social insurance programs. A growing body of evidence from a variety of settings points in this direction. For example, analysts have pointed to different levels of social diversity in explaining differences between US and European social welfare programs (e.g., Alesina, Glaeser, and Sacerdote 2001; Gould and Palmer 1988). Studies comparing social expenditures across American cities and states find that ethnically heterogeneous states tend to spend less on redistributive programs (Alesina, Baqir, and Easterly 1997; Hero and Tolbert 1996; Plotnick and Winters 1985). And development economists have found similar patterns across a wide range of countries, including the richest and poorest nations in the world: spending on private education tends to be higher in countries with considerable religious and ethnic diversity, and income transfer payments tend to be lower in such countries (Easterly and Levine 1997; James 1987, 1993). It is difficult, these studies suggest, to sustain strong social welfare programs in the face of comparatively high ethnic diversity.

Why would this be the case? One theory starts from notions of community and mutual obligation. In this view, the expansion of the welfare state in the twentieth century was underpinned by a sense of community and collective responsibility of citizens for each other (Marshall 1950). These bonds of community seem more difficult to sustain as the population becomes more diverse. Logically, defection from a commitment to strong social programs might come from two directions. On the one hand, minorities might argue that universal public services tend to reflect the norms of the dominant culture and are insensitive to distinctive minority needs and belief systems. In such circumstances, some minority groups might prefer private schools and social services rooted in their own religious and cultural community. On the other hand, cultural majorities may come to resent social programs that they see as transferring resources to "outsider" minorities. For most analysts, this represents the largest threat to the social solidarity underpinning the welfare state, an hypothesis that is supported to a certain extent by research on the tension between immigration and support for social welfare in Western Europe, the United States, and other countries (Banting 1999, 2000; Carens 1988; Fullinwider 1988; Kitschelt 1995). Thus, the essential premise of this approach is that the redistributive state is rooted in a sense of community and collective responsibility, and that this solidarity becomes more difficult to sustain as a population becomes increasingly diverse.

The social capital literature provides a subtly different perspective, with an emphasis on trust as the solution to collective action games. The argument is best described by Miller (1995, 90-99): Mutual trust facilitates solutions to collective action problems that are inherent in social welfare programs, where citizens must trust each other to both take part as contributors and not take advantage as beneficiaries. Trust is aided by identification with fellow citizens. Identification with fellow citizens is easiest in ethnically and culturally homogenous societies, however, so it will be more difficult to foster identification with fellow citizens in societies that are ethnically or culturally divided. More diverse societies are consequently more likely to lack support for social welfare programs.

Miller's narrative is similar to the preceding "community"-focused explanation, but its particular appeal to social capital theorists is that it highlights *trust* as an important intermediary variable between diversity and support for social welfare. "Interpersonal" or "social" trust has been a central component in the study of social capital. For example, a growing body of economic research, closely allied with social capital themes, explores the link between increased ethnic diversity and decreased trust. Ethnic / linguistic / cultural diversity appears to be negatively correlated with growth rates (Easterly and Levine 1997; McCarty 1993; Zak and Knack 1998; Zucker 1986); there also appears to be a greater need for governmental mechanisms enforcing contracts and property rights in countries that are more ethnically diverse (Knack and Keefer 1995, 1997; Zak and Knack 1998). These studies feature trust as the explanatory variable and suggest that Miller's work is particularly valuable in pointing to the potential importance of trust in explaining support for social welfare programs.

Although several literatures propose that ethnic diversity affects support for social welfare, empirical discussions of this link must still rely on triangulation. In short, to date, no empirical study has explored the connection between individuals' opinions and perceptions as affected by the experience of diversity, on one hand, and support for the welfare state, on the other. This chapter seeks to fill this gap by examining these relations as they play out in the case of Canada.

Canada represents a good case for these purposes. First, although the Canadian welfare state has always been more limited than those established in northern Europe (Esping-Anderson 1990), its social commitments have been much more ambitious than those prevailing in the United States. As measured both by program structures and social expenditures as a proportion of GDP, the Canadian welfare state has historically fallen midway between the US and European patterns. Second, Canada has high levels of multiculturalism. It has long been an immigrant society; it has one of the highest proportions of citizens born outside of the country among all OECD countries, and its official policies embrace multiculturalism as a defining feature of Canadian life. Moreover, its minority populations are quite concentrated in certain regions and especially urban areas, making it relatively easy to compare the views of people living in diverse as opposed to homogenous communities. Third, Canadian diversity may have competing dimensions, so to speak. At the same time as Canada has maintained a relatively open door to immigration, it has all along been communally segmented on traditional European lines, between French and English linguistic communities.[1] So the Canadian case poses the issues well. Although past research suggests no clear link between diversity and Canadians' trust in individuals, trust in government, or national pride (Johnston and Soroka 2001), these analyses were weakly specified in the key variables.

The empirical base of the chapter is the Equality, Security, and Community survey supplemented by census data for neighbourhoods. In most respects, variables and data are as described in Chapter 5 (Soroka, Helliwell, and Johnston). This chapter extends the analysis to include indicators of welfare state opinion and political and demographic factors that may be relevant to formation of that opinion.

Modelling Trust

As a first step in examining the link between ethnicity and support for social welfare, we consider the impact of individual and contextual variables on trust in individuals and trust in government. The importance of interpersonal trust has been outlined above – it is a critical intermediary variable between ethnic diversity and support for social welfare. Trust in government warrants further explanation.

Political trust ought to be a factor in support for the welfare state. The success of new regimes seems contingent on political support (e.g., Mishler and Rose 1997), and the logic ought to extend to consolidated systems. In this vein, Scholz and Lubell (1998, 399) suggest that "'vertical trust' between citizen and state can expand the range of collective problems that legal authorities are able to tackle." Their evidence indicates that trust in government (as well as trust in individuals) affects US respondents' compliance with tax laws. The implication is that individuals are more willing to pay taxes when they believe that the money will be spent appropriately. If taxes are the precondition for spending, then a similar dynamic should hold in support for the welfare state.

The two kinds of trust are quite different, especially, perhaps, in Canada. Trusting individuals operates on degrees of personal acquaintance, and, correspondingly, on expectations of reciprocity. Trusting a government entails a much greater leap of faith, since we rarely know government officials personally, and we cannot expect the government to reciprocate (Hardin 2000). Trust in government may embody history, where, for decades, some groups have been political winners and other groups, losers. Accordingly, there is considerable slippage between the two (Johnston and Soroka 2001; Newton 1999; Newton and Norris 2000; Orren 1997). In particular, the structural foundations of each can be quite distinct.

Although they are distinct mental states, the two types of trust should still have some positive empirical link, and, ideally, we should allow for it rather than risk an omitted-variables problem. But there is serious confusion about the causal direction of the link. Intuition suggests that political trust is a generalized form of interpersonal trust. This is an implicit assumption in Putnam's (1993a) work linking high civic engagement with the success of new regional governments in Italy, for example. However, a growing body of evidence suggests that influence runs in the opposite direction. Muller and Seligson (1994) find that a country's years of experience with democracy is a powerful predictor of its average score on the interpersonal trust measure; Brehm and Rahn's (1997) structural model of United States GSS data also suggests that the direction of influence leads from trust in government to trust in individuals (see also Sztompka 1996). The implication may be that personal relations flourish under the shadow of Leviathan: mutual trust becomes possible when we already trust institutions to catch and penalize defectors. Of course, influence could be reciprocal.

The problem is that estimating the true interdependence of interpersonal and political trust is next to impossible. OLS setups that include one as an "exogenous" predictor of the other are under-identified. To unpack the simultaneity in the system, we might employ two-stage least squares (2SLS) estimation, where exogenous variables are used to create "instrumented" versions of the endogenous variables, the instrumented variables are then used in place of the original variables, and the system is thereby purged, supposedly, of simultaneity bias (Kennedy 2003, 188-89). As is commonly the case, our attempt to find suitable instruments failed. We just present each in the estimation model for the other and accept the strong likelihood of simultaneity bias. Omission of the trust terms has very small effects on the remaining parameters, and structural differences between the trust forms will come out in divergence of parameters between estimations.

With this in mind, we examine trust in individuals and government with the following regression model:

$$Trust^1 = \alpha_1 + \omega Trust^2 + (\beta_1 REth + \beta_2 CEth + \beta_3 REth*CEth)$$
$$+ (\rho_1 RFre + \rho_2 Que + \rho_3 RFre*Que)$$
$$+ \Sigma\delta Ind + \Sigma\gamma Con + \pi Vote + \varepsilon_1, \qquad (1)$$

where $Trust^1$ is trust in individuals, $Trust^2$ is trust in government, Ind is a set of individual-level variables, Con is a set of contextual-level variables, $Vote$ is respondents' vote in the most recent federal and provincial elections, α is a constant, and ε is an error term that subsumes all unmeasured variation.[2]

The two terms in parentheses represent our test of the effects of ethnicity on trust. Ethnicity is represented here on two dimensions: French/English and "visible minority"/majority. The former is Canada's longstanding linguistic division – a division that may have mutated into a geographic one, between Quebec and the rest of Canada. We prefer to focus on the primordial contrast and to let Quebec enter the analysis as the marker for linguistic context; we return to this below. The latter dimension refers to visible markers as opposed to audible ones. Historically, Canada thought of itself as composed of two founding peoples, one British and the other French. As a result, while immigrants from Britain and France were not seen as different, people coming from other parts of the world, including western and central Europe, were seen as "other" and classified as "ethnic." In contemporary debates over multiculturalism, the focus has narrowed to people who are racial minorities, or what are often referred to as "visible minorities." This study follows contemporary usage – "visible minority" is meant to connote all individuals who are non-Caucasian in race. The largest groups who fall into this general category are Chinese, South Asians, and Blacks.[3]

As for the variables themselves, $REth$ corresponds to dummy variables that represent whether or not the respondent belongs to a "visible" minority. $CEth$ is the contextual equivalent: the proportion of visible minorities in each respondent's census tract (CT in metropolitan areas) or census subdivision (CSD in all other areas), as of the 1996 Census.[4] The $REth*CEth$ interaction captures the possibility that ethnic context has a different effect on minority respondents than on majority ones. The second term in parentheses is the equivalent for francophone respondents: $RFre$ is dummy variable referring to francophone status;[5] the contextual variable is residence in or out of Quebec (Que).[6]

$Vote$ variables are included in both estimations, although we conjecture that the $Vote$ group pertains only to political trust. Trust in government should at least partly reflect whether respondents support the party in power. Two dummy variables are included, one for the federal and one for the provincial government; the variable is equal to 1 if the respondent voted for the party currently in power.

Additional individual-level variables (*Ind*) include most basic demographics: *gender, age, education, religion* (Catholic/Protestant/other), and *immigration status*. Inclusion of these variables reflects analyses in Chapter 5 as well as the literature on social capital and the welfare state.[7] Here we add *household income*, as it is critical to welfare state opinion.

Our indicator of interpersonal trust is the four-item "wallet" measure described in detail in Chapter 5. Each item asks about the likelihood that a lost wallet would be returned, respectively, by a neighbour, a police officer, a clerk at the local grocery store, and a stranger. As indicated earlier, this measure taps the radius of trust based on experience. In contrast, the standard "generalized trust" indicator captures a more moralistic propensity. As a factor in welfare-state opinion, the standard indicator is, unsurprisingly, more powerful. But, as Chapter 5 shows, the standard indicator is *not* a mediator of forces embedded either in ethnicity or in ethnic context. The wallet measure, in contrast, powerfully captures the zone of impact from diversity.

The trust in government measure combines (1) "How much do you trust the government in Ottawa to do what is right?" (2) "How much do you trust the government in [province] to do what is right?" (3) a feeling thermometer for federal government, and (4) a feeling thermometer for provincial government. Results are rescaled from 0 to 1, where 1 is most trusting. Trust in one governmental level is highly correlated with trust in the other level, so combining the two does not present a problem and helps avoid difficulties with collinearity.

Results are presented in Table 11.1.[8] Unsurprisingly, the two forms of trust *are* linked, although not all that strongly. There is a hint that political trust explains more of interpersonal trust than the reverse. More strikingly, the pattern for ethnicity and ethnic context differs sharply between the political and the interpersonal. For interpersonal trust, both racial and linguistic factors are implicated and context is key. For political trust, language matters a bit and context not at all. For interpersonal trust, the consistently striking relationship links the minority's local preponderance with the majority's reaction. For visible minorities, the pattern is roughly as described in Chapter 5: members of the "majority" are generally more trusting than visible-minority persons. But the larger the minority share in the neighbourhood, the less trusting the "majority" is; and, beyond some point, visible-minority persons are more trusting than persons of European origin (at this point, the minority is, in fact, the local majority). The French/non-French contrast has some affinities with the European/non-European one. Non-francophones respond to the local preponderance of francophones roughly as Europeans do to non-Europeans. Living in Quebec reduces a non-francophone's interpersonal trust about one-eighth the maximum possible distance. Francophones outside Quebec, adrift on an English sea, are less trusting than members of the linguistic majority. But francophones in Quebec are even less trusting than those outside the province. So anglophones are always more trusting than francophones, regardless of context, and Quebeckers are always less trusting than non-Quebeckers, regardless of language.[9]

But none of these differences and none of these sensitivities is that impressive. First, consider the absolute scale of impact. The initial difference between majority and minority individuals on each dimension is about 0.06 on a 0,1 range. The maximum effect of contextual shift for the majority on each dimension is about 0.12. That is, moving from a place in which there are essentially no members of the minority to a place where there are essentially no members of the majority would reduce a "majority" respondent's trust by about one-eighth the total possible movement. Put another way, it would reduce trust about half a standard deviation.[10] In the real world of visible minorities and "invisible" majorities, variance like this would be outlandish. The median majority respondent lives in a census subdivision with a tiny visible-minority percentage and very few live in tracts or districts where the minority constitutes so much as one-sixth of the local population. Visible minorities tend, unsurprisingly, to live where other minority persons concentrate, so that few find themselves in the situation implicit in the dummy-variable coefficient, that is, where there are *no* other members of the minority. So their trust level will almost never actually be as far below that for the majority as implied by the main-effect coefficient. For language contrasts, contextual coefficients do capture something ubiquitous. Francophones dominate Quebec locales as thoroughly as anglophones dominate non-Quebec ones (notwithstanding the fact that the number of anglophones dwelling in Quebec exceeds the population of several other provinces). Still, on both dimensions, the significance of the contextual and even of the individual ethno-linguistic structure is more theoretical than actual.[11] Coefficients describe what *would* follow if certain other things were true. But those other things are true for only a modest fraction of Canadians.

TABLE 11.1

Modelling trust

Independent variables	Dependent variable			
	Trust in individuals		Trust in government	
TRUST				
Trust in individuals	—		0.164 ***	(0.015)
Trust in government	0.180 ***	(0.017)	—	
ETHNICITY				
R is visible minority	−0.057 **	(0.027)	0.021	(0.026)
Visible minority (prop)	−0.130 ***	(0.028)	0.016	(0.023)
Interaction	0.105 **	(0.052)	0.031	(0.045)
LANGUAGE				
R is French	−0.053 **	(0.025)	0.060 ***	(0.021)
Quebec (dummy)	−0.114 ***	(0.019)	−0.002	(0.016)
Interaction	−0.039	(0.032)	−0.026	(0.026)
VOTE VARIABLES				
Voted for govt party (fed)	0.004	(0.007)	0.037 ***	(0.007)
Voted for govt party (prov)	0.002	(0.007)	0.039 ***	(0.008)
ECONOMIC SITUATION				
Economic outlook	0.015	(0.011)	0.046 ***	(0.011)
Household income	0.018 ***	(0.007)	−0.014 *	(0.007)
Median income	−0.706	(0.436)	0.016	(0.385)
Income diversity	0.002	(0.066)	−0.017	(0.063)
OTHER CONTEXTUAL VARIABLES				
Education (prop > HS)	0.117 **	(0.051)	0.053	(0.048)
Mobility (prop, 5 yrs)	−0.045 **	(0.020)	−0.023	(0.022)
Population density	−0.008 ***	(0.002)	0.002	(0.002)
BASIC DEMOGRAPHICS				
Female	0.025 ***	(0.007)	0.004	(0.006)
Age (30-49)	0.063 ***	(0.008)	−0.040 ***	(0.008)
(50-65)	0.083 ***	(0.010)	−0.061 ***	(0.010)
(66+)	0.113 ***	(0.015)	−0.063 ***	(0.014)
Education (finished high school)	0.024 ***	(0.010)	0.013 ***	(0.011)
(started college/univ.)	0.016	(0.012)	0.031 ***	(0.012)
(finished college/univ.)	0.047 **	(0.010)	0.037 ***	(0.010)
Religion (Catholic)	−0.003	(0.009)	0.031 ***	(0.009)
(Protestant)	0.011	(0.008)	0.018 **	(0.008)
Immigrant	−0.014	(0.010)	0.031 ***	(0.009)
Health	0.041 ***	(0.010)	0.032 ***	(0.010)
Resource sample	0.029 ***	(0.010)	−0.056 ***	(0.009)
Constant	0.505 ***	(0.024)	0.232 ***	(0.025)
N (CT/CSDs)	1,449		1,449	
N (individuals)	3,799		3,799	
R^2	0.233		0.111	

NOTE: Cells contain coefficients from OLS regressions with standard errors (corrected, based on the number of CT/CSDs) in parentheses. Contextual variables are in italics.

$p < .10$, * $p < .05$, ** $p < .01$, *** $p < .001$. Coefficients significant at $p < .10$ are in **bold**. Results are based on combined first wave, metro oversample, and resource community sample.

And there is hardly any ethnic story – even a theoretical one – for trust in government. Only French language affects trust in government, and this effect is the mirror image of that for interpersonal trust: francophones are *more* trusting than others. Strikingly, for all the angry talk around jurisdiction, Quebec residence makes no further contribution. Francophones in Quebec are no less trusting of Ottawa than francophones elsewhere in the country, a pattern that places interesting question marks around the significance of ongoing intergovernmental battles for the attitudes of the public.

Other divergences between the forms of trust will be noted only in passing. Both forms of trust increase with education and educational context. Both decrease with the mobility of the local population.[12] Population density and gender matter only for interpersonal trust. Vote for election winners, the respondent's economic outlook, religion, and immigrant status matter only for political trust. Age and income have contrasting effects: each increases personal trust and decreases political trust.

Modelling Support for the Welfare State

The degree to which ethnicity and ethnic diversity affect support for social programs is tested with the following model:

$$Support = \alpha_2 + \omega_1 Trust^1 + \omega_2 Trust^2 + (\beta_1 REth + \beta_2 CEth + \beta_3 REth*CEth) \\ + (\rho_1 RFre + \rho_2 Que + \rho_3 RFre*Que) \\ + \Sigma\delta Ind + \Sigma\gamma Con + \pi Vote + \varepsilon_2, \qquad (2)$$

where *Support* is respondents' support for various social welfare programs. We examine three domains of the welfare state separately. The domains differ subtly in rationale and in the degree to which they are vulnerable to arguments about moral hazard. Empirically, response is correlated much more weakly across than within domains. The final form for each index was reached by a combination of factor analysis and reliability tests.[13] In our measurement scheme, all dependent variables are scaled from 0 to 1, whether they are based on one item or several.

The first domain is *Employment Insurance and Welfare*, which employs the following questions:
- Many unemployed persons could find work if they really wanted to. [Agree or disagree]
- How many do you think could find work: about one quarter, about one half, about three quarters, or almost all of them could find work?

- In Canada today, do you think it is too easy or too hard to get unemployment insurance?
- Is the unemployment benefit, that is, the amount of money people receive when they are unemployed, too high or too low?
- Which is closer to your own view:
  - *One*, refusing welfare to single parents is unfair to their children / *Two*, giving welfare to single parents rewards irresponsible behaviour.
  - *One*, people on welfare are usually there for only a short time and are unlikely to be on it again / *Two*, once people get on welfare they usually stay on it.
  - *One*, the government should see to it that everyone has a decent standard of living / *Two*, the government should leave it to people to get ahead on their own.
- The government must do more to reduce the income gap between rich and poor Canadians. [Agree or disagree]

What these questions all have in common is some notion of "decommodification" of labour, in the sense intended by Esping-Andersen (1990). An affirmative response, as we code it, indicates a concern that withdrawal from the labour force should not unduly penalize a person. Generous access and benefits in the unemployment insurance system, for instance, should raise the reservation wage. Although classical welfare (whose targets are commonly single parents and unemployables) and Employment Insurance (EI) have somewhat different rhetorical props, both address the matter of the price of not working. Both policy domains are similarly vulnerable to arguments from moral hazard. For EI, the issue is centrally about voluntary withdrawal as opposed to involuntary imposition of joblessness. For welfare, the imagery of "welfare queens" taps the same logic as do claims about voluntary unemployment, and the system also evokes rhetoric about bad personal behaviour. This domain seems absolutely central to the moral economy of capitalism. Yet it is also a magnet for arguments from trust in human nature.[14]

The second domain is *Health Care*, which we explore with a single item: "Which is closer to your own view: *One*, everyone should have equal access to health care, even if that means waiting for treatment, OR [*Two*, if you can afford it you should be able to buy faster access to health care.] / OR [*Two*, if you are willing to pay for it you should be able to buy faster access to health care.]"[15]

This item strikes us as getting to the core of current disputes over the Canadian system: equality of access versus length of queues. As a domain, health care strikes us as less susceptible to moralizing about fellow citizens than employment insurance and welfare. The moral hazard lies in frivolous visits to doctors and hospitals, and some of the anti-system rhetoric raises this spectre; it forms part of the argument for deterrence fees. If we had such a question, we would have tried it out as a possible companion for this question, but we did not. And all citizens worry about their own potential access to health care, even as they tend to see sickness and accident as essentially actuarial phenomena.[16]

Finally, we consider support for publicly provided *Pensions*. Here we deploy two items: "When it comes to saving for retirement would CANADA/CANADIANS/YOU be better off if the Canada Pension Plan was shut down and individual Canadians/you were able to invest their money for themselves/yourself?"[17] and [agree or disagree] "Government pensions are the only way to ensure that all Canadians have at least some income in their old age."

The first focuses specifically on the CPP, a contributory scheme, which, as such, is amenable to arguments that the savings are better off in private hands. The second question covers the CPP, but also addresses by implication a general argument for public pensions, including ones funded out of general revenue. Our expectation is that this will be the least moralized area in the whole domain. There is a sense in which general-revenue pensions reward those who fail to save, and so could be described as a transfer not just between income classes but from the prudent to the imprudent. But this is not true for the CPP, and, to the extent that everyone pays taxes, is not true for the general scheme either.

Estimation proceeds in stages. In the first step, we estimate welfare-state support without any trust indicator in the model. This allows us to see whether there is any basic relationship between ethnicity or ethnic context and welfare-state opinion. We occasionally refer to this setup as the "reduced form." Then we enter both kinds of trust into the estimation. Obviously, the effect of trust is interesting in its own right, and we do expect it to differ across domains. But it is also interesting as an intervening variable, as an account of the mental state whose variation helps explain the original ethnic/ethnic context relationship. This argument applies to interpersonal trust, in particular, as Table 11.1 indicates that political trust is not really implicated in ethnicity. A mediating role for trust will be indicated by *shrinkage* in ethnicity or ethnic context coefficients as estimation moves from stage 1 to stage 2. Results appear in Tables 11.2-4.

TABLE 11.2

Modelling support for social programs: EI/Welfare

Independent variables	Dependent variable: Employment Insurance/ Welfare			
	Without trust		With trust	
TRUST				
Trust in individuals	—		0.042 **	(0.018)
Trust in government	—		−0.002	(0.018)
ETHNICITY				
R is visible minority	−0.031	(0.023)	−0.038	(0.025)
Visible minority (prop)	0.015	(0.026)	0.027	(0.027)
Interaction	−0.020	(0.040)	−0.015	(0.044)
LANGUAGE				
R is French	0.057 ***	(0.021)	0.059 **	(0.025)
Quebec (dummy)	−0.023	(0.017)	−0.009	(0.019)
Interaction	−0.006	(0.028)	−0.016	(0.031)
ECONOMIC SITUATION				
Economic outlook	−0.006	(0.010)	0.003	(0.010)
Household income	−0.062 ***	(0.008)	−0.065 ***	(0.009)
Median income	−1.493 ***	(0.466)	−1.533 ***	(0.487)
Income diversity	−0.003	(0.060)	−0.006	(0.065)
OTHER CONTEXTUAL VARIABLES				
Education (prop > high school)	0.038	(0.048)	0.041	(0.051)
Mobility (prop, 5yrs)	−0.041 *	(0.022)	−0.040 *	(0.023)
Population density	0.004 **	(0.002)	0.003 **	(0.002)
BASIC DEMOGRAPHICS				
Female	0.046 ***	(0.006)	0.046 ***	(0.007)
Age (30-49)	0.034 ***	(0.008)	0.033 ***	(0.008)
(50-65)	0.040 ***	(0.009)	0.035 ***	(0.010)
(66+)	−0.034 ***	(0.011)	−0.027 *	(0.014)
Education (finished HS)	−0.007	(0.010)	−0.008	(0.011)
(started college/univ.)	−0.008	(0.010)	−0.007	(0.012)
(finished college/univ.)	0.017 *	(0.010)	0.014	(0.011)
Religion (Catholic)	−0.016 *	(0.009)	−0.016 *	(0.009)
(Protestant)	−0.018 *	(0.010)	−0.018 *	(0.010)
Immigrant	−0.005	(0.010)	−0.006	(0.011)
Health	−0.040 ***	(0.010)	−0.046 ***	(0.010)
Resource sample	0.024 **	(0.010)	0.022 **	(0.011)
Constant	0.647 ***	(0.022)	0.624 ***	(0.025)
N (CT/CSDs)	1,488		1,401	
N (individuals)	4,082		3,614	
R^2	0.070		0.070	

NOTE: See note to Table 11.1.

TABLE 11.3

Modelling support for social programs: health care

	Dependent variable: health care	
Independent variables	Without trust	With trust
TRUST		
Trust in individuals	—	0.057 * (0.034)
Trust in government	—	0.082 ** (0.034)
ETHNICITY		
R is visible minority	−0.095 * (0.054)	−0.091 (0.058)
Visible minority (prop)	−0.052 (0.047)	−0.041 (0.051)
Interaction	0.003 (0.105)	−0.051 (0.109)
LANGUAGE		
R is French	−0.035 (0.041)	−0.032 (0.045)
Quebec (dummy)	−0.122 *** (0.043)	−0.101 ** (0.045)
Interaction	0.031 (0.060)	0.024 (0.064)
ECONOMIC SITUATION		
Economic outlook	−0.021 (0.020)	−0.029 (0.021)
Household income	−0.055 *** (0.019)	−0.063 *** (0.019)
Median income	0.368 (0.932)	0.381 (0.966)
Income diversity	−0.090 (0.121)	−0.108 (0.127)
OTHER CONTEXTUAL VARIABLES		
Education (prop > HS)	−0.171 * (0.094)	−0.214 ** (0.099)
Mobility (prop, 5yrs)	−0.044 (0.042)	−0.027 (0.045)
Population density	0.001 (0.003)	0.002 (0.004)
BASIC DEMOGRAPHICS		
Female	0.065 *** (0.013)	0.067 *** (0.013)
Age (30-49)	−0.002 (0.017)	0.003 (0.018)
(50-65)	−0.015 (0.020)	−0.019 (0.022)
(66+)	−0.078 *** (0.027)	−0.066 ** (0.030)
Education (finished HS)	−0.037 * (0.020)	−0.043 * (0.022)
(started college/univ.)	−0.031 (0.021)	−0.040 (0.024)
(finished college/univ.)	−0.025 (0.018)	−0.019 (0.021)
Religion (Catholic)	0.006 (0.018)	−0.002 (0.019)
(Protestant)	−0.001 (0.016)	−0.005 (0.017)
Immigrant	−0.017 (0.020)	−0.022 (0.021)
Health	−0.041 (0.019)	−0.054 *** (0.020)
Resource sample	−0.053 *** (0.019)	−0.051 ** (0.021)
Constant	0.941 *** (0.044)	0.895 *** (0.052)
N (CT/CSDs)	1,543	1,449
N (individuals)	4,302	3,796
R²	0.040	0.040

NOTE: See note to Table 11.1.

TABLE 11.4

Modelling support for social programs: pensions

	Dependent variable: pensions			
Independent variables	Without trust		With trust	
TRUST				
Trust in individuals	—		0.031	(0.024)
Trust in government	—		0.092 ***	(0.027)
ETHNICITY				
R is visible minority	−0.005	(0.041)	0.016	(0.046)
Visible minority (prop)	0.051	(0.037)	0.049	(0.039)
Interaction	−0.104	(0.079)	−0.143	(0.090)
LANGUAGE				
R is French	0.013	(0.035)	0.017	(0.035)
Quebec (dummy)	0.008	(0.027)	0.022	(0.030)
Interaction	−0.012	(0.046)	−0.023	(0.048)
ECONOMIC SITUATION				
Economic outlook	−0.050 ***	(0.015)	−0.054 ***	(0.016)
Household income	−0.050 ***	(0.011)	−0.049 ***	(0.012)
Median income	−0.268	(0.649)	−0.430	(0.673)
Income diversity	−0.124	(0.088)	−0.115	(0.092)
OTHER CONTEXTUAL VARIABLES				
Education (prop > HS)	−0.053	(0.065)	−0.060	(0.071)
Mobility (prop, 5yrs)	0.004	(0.027)	0.010	(0.030)
Population density	−0.000	(0.002)	−0.000	(0.003)
BASIC DEMOGRAPHICS				
Female	0.055 ***	(0.010)	0.055 ***	(0.011)
Age (30-49)	0.090 ***	(0.013)	0.091 ***	(0.014)
(50-65)	0.182 ***	(0.015)	0.182 ***	(0.016)
(66+)	0.238 ***	(0.016)	0.248 ***	(0.018)
Education (finished HS)	−0.040 ***	(0.014)	−0.044 ***	(0.015)
(started college/univ.)	−0.025	(0.016)	−0.026	(0.018)
(finished college/univ.)	−0.042 ***	(0.013)	−0.047 ***	(0.014)
Religion (Catholic)	−0.013	(0.014)	−0.020	(0.016)
(Protestant)	0.005	(0.015)	−0.003	(0.015)
Immigrant	−0.014	(0.014)	−0.017	(0.015)
Health	−0.014	(0.014)	−0.017	(0.015)
Resource sample	0.037 ***	(0.011)	0.034 **	(0.013)
Constant	0.726 ***	(0.032)	0.687 ***	(0.037)
N(CT/CSDs)	1,542		1,448	
N(individuals)	4,294		3,790	
R^2	0.100		0.100	

NOTE: See note to Table 11.1.

Ethnicity or ethnic context is a factor in support for some programs, but not for all, not with a consistent structure, and only at the margin. Support for public pensions is affected by none of the relevant factors. Language is implicated in support for employment insurance and welfare, but in a highly localized way. Francophones are more supportive than are anglophones, but Quebec residents are less so. Essentially, what the Quebec dummy is doing is switching off the effect for francophones. Strictly speaking, Quebec francophones are more supportive than non-francophones in the same province but not more supportive than anglophones living elsewhere. Only with health care is there a story much worth telling. Visible minority respondents and Quebec dwellers are less supportive than are all others of the equal-access option in health care. The difference is almost identical in each case, about 0.10-0.12 (on a 0,1 scale) less supportive.

Trust is an attitudinal prop for the welfare state. Each form is more important for some parts of the welfare state than for others, and neither is important for all domains. Interpersonal trust is a factor in support for EI/welfare and for health care, but not at all for pensions. In large, this pattern conforms to our expectations, as pensions seem to us to be the least moralized ground in the domain. Why health care should be more affected than is EI/welfare is a mystery, however. Trust in government is important for pensions and health care but not for EI/welfare. This strikes us as a reasonable complementarity to the pattern for interpersonal trust, in that the issue in both domains is more the government's ability to manage than individuals' propensity to abuse. That its impact is greatest in the health care domain also seems intuitively right.

What, then, of trust as a mediator of ethnic impact? The landscape is bound to be thinly populated. First, political trust cannot really be a mediator as it is scarcely affected by ethnicity or ethnic context. On pensions, there is no ethnic covariance to explain. This leaves a modest role for interpersonal trust in the domains of EI/welfare and health care. For EI/welfare, the positive individual-level effect of being francophone remains essentially unchanged, but the negative contextual effect is reduced. For health care, the individual-level effect of being a visible minority is lessened only very slightly; as with EI/welfare, however, the contextual Quebec coefficient is smaller in magnitude. So there is some very mild evidence that the effects of ethnicity – or at least the effects of living in Quebec – are mediated somewhat by interpersonal trust. But this chapter leaves most of the ethnicity–welfare state relationship unexplained.

Discussion and Conclusions

Is ethnic diversity an enemy of the welfare state? Evidence presented here suggests that it is not – at least not a particularly fearsome one. There is a link between ethnic diversity and support for social programs, admittedly, but it does not operate in quite the way – and is certainly not of the magnitude – that previous research on other countries predicts. In short, while most aggregate-level work comparing countries or US states suggests a powerful, direct, and negative link between ethnic diversity and support for social programs, our individual-level evidence indicates that the link is weak at best.

In detail, our analysis seems to vindicate Miller (1995). Ethnicity affects interpersonal trust. As it is measured here, at least, trust in individuals has an important contextual component, and ethnic diversity appears to play a significant role, as we also claim in Chapter 5. And, at the second stage, interpersonal trust has a positive and significant effect on support for most social programs. Miller's argument that social programs present a collective action problem that interpersonal trust helps resolve is strongly supported. Anything that erodes trust, therefore, has the potential to erode support for the redistributive state. In our data, however, this does not add up to a strong, consistent relationship between the ultimate independent variables – ethnicity and ethnic context – and the ultimate dependent variable – support for the welfare state. Evaluating the impact of a move from 100 percent majority to 50 percent majority based on coefficients as shown, for example, in Tables 11.1 and 11.2, the yields decrease in aggregate support for unemployment and welfare by about 0.0025 percent. In fact, the reduced form estimation in that table suggests that the relationship between diversity and welfare support might even be positive, *ceteris paribus*. Only for pensions is there a hint of a contextual story (and it is swamped by the individual-level ethnic difference).

From a policy perspective, this evidence suggests that Canadian governments can maintain expansive immigration programs and promote multiculturalism without necessarily eroding national support for social welfare programs. Existing policies suggest that Canadian governments have assumed this to be true. This conclusion is by no means obvious, however. It runs counter to the growing body of literature that describes the link between increased immigration and decreased support for social welfare in Western Europe (e.g., Carens 1988; Kitschelt 1995, discussed above). It runs counter to the experience of many other countries, including the United Kingdom and Australia, where residency periods for social benefits have been lengthened.

And it runs counter to the role of social diversity in the politics of social policy in the United States.

Are Canadians exceptional in their ability to accept both diversity and an expansive welfare state? There exist no sufficiently similar individual-level studies in other countries with which to compare our results. From what we can infer from aggregate-level studies, however, Canadians do seem to react differently – or at least react less – to increasing levels of ethnic diversity. Why is this the case? Our results point toward no clear answer, but a number of possible factors suggest themselves. One possibility is the high level of geographic concentration of immigrant minorities in certain regions and, especially, certain urban areas. The crucial question may be: if Canadian neighbourhoods were more ethnically diverse, would Canada reflect the same apparent acceptance of both diversity and a redistributive welfare state? We suspect that the answer is still "yes." There appears to be no direct impact of ethnic diversity on support for social welfare programs. To the extent that there is any impact at all, it is through interpersonal trust, and, although the impact of diversity on support for the welfare state is in the same direction as it is in other countries, the magnitude of that impact in Canada is decidedly small.

Other possible explanations present themselves. One is the structure of the Canadian welfare state itself. In comparison with continental Europe, social spending represents a smaller proportion of Canadian GDP, and the state allocates fewer scarce resources than are allocated in some countries. For example, public housing is a small proportion of the housing market in Canada, and its allocation has not generated the sorts of tensions that have emerged in cities in northern England and elsewhere. Moreover, in comparison with countries such as Australia and the United States, Canadian social policy relies less on means-tested benefits, for which poor immigrants might qualify immediately on arrival. Another possible factor is the historical pattern of relatively rapid economic integration of immigrants in Canada, with the resulting short periods of dependence on social support. If this has been an important factor, it represents another reason that the poorer economic performance of immigrants during the 1990s is an ominous development. But, perhaps, the most intriguing possibility centres on the role of national identity in Canadian life. Our results do not represent a complete test of Miller's argument, neglecting as they do the extent to which national identity may moderate the divisive potential of social diversity by building trust across culturally distinct groups. In discussing multinational countries such as

Canada and Switzerland, Miller argues that the key issue is whether such countries nurture a common national identity alongside communal ones. There are several possibilities here. Perhaps a national identity that has from its inception encompassed different nationalities may be a critical component in Canadians' relative acceptance of increasing diversity. And perhaps Canadian immigration, naturalization, and multicultural programs are particularly effective in building a sense of identity among new arrivals. We plan to extend our analysis to incorporate the role of national identity in the context of multicultural diversity in the next stage of this research.

The sources of Canadian distinctiveness remain elusive, but understanding them is of more than local significance. The viability of a multicultural welfare state is an international issue, and the implications of the Canadian experience go well beyond the country's borders.

APPENDIX

This appendix lists the details for each variable used in the preceding analysis. Where necessary, question wording is included. Table 11A.1 includes basic descriptives for these variables.

ETHNICITY

Visible minority: dummy variable = 1 if respondent is a visible minority, based on the Census definition (includes all individuals except aboriginals who are non-Caucasian in race or colour).

Visible minority percent: percentage of respondents' CT/CSD who are visible minorities, based on the Census definition (as above).

LANGUAGE

French: dummy variable = 1 if respondent speaks French at home.
Quebec: dummy variable = 1 if respondent lives in Quebec.

TRUST

Trust in individuals: based on the following question: "Say you lost a wallet or purse with $100 in it. How likely is it that the wallet or purse will be returned with the money in it if it was found by a [neighbour]? Would you say it is very likely, likely, or not at all likely?" The question is repeated four times, for a neighbour, a police officer, a clerk at the local grocery store, and a stranger; the variable = 1 for very likely, = .5 for likely, and = 0 for not at all likely. The Cronbach's alpha for the four-item measure is .661; the alpha decreases if any single item is removed.

Trust in government: based on the following questions: (1) "How much do you trust the government in Ottawa [or province] to do what is right?" (2) a 100-point feeling thermometer for the federal government, (3) "How much do you trust the government in [province] to do what is right?" and (4) a 100-point feeling thermometer for the provincial government. The four variables are given equal weighting in a 0 to 1 variable, where 1 is most trusting. The Cronbach's alpha for the four-item measure is .806; the alpha decreases if any single item is removed. Strikingly, the alpha does not change dramatically when calculated by province. The link between trust in federal and provincial governments is weakest in Alberta, but the alpha here is still .715; the Quebec and PEI alphas are second-lowest, at .769; the highest is .866, in Saskatchewan. While the variance in alphas fits with what we might expect across Canadian provinces, the differences are minimal. In short, there is a remarkably strong link between support for federal and provincial governments in all provinces.

POLITICAL VARIABLES

Voted for governing party: dummy variable = 1 if respondent voted for the winning party in the last federal (or provincial) election.

ECONOMIC SITUATION

Economic outlook: based on the following question: "What about the next twelve months? Do you feel your household's economic situation will improve, stay about the same, or get worse?" = 1 if respondent feels their household's economic situation will improve over the next twelve months, = .5 if they feel it will stay about the same, and = 0 if they feel it will get worse.

Household income ($100,000s): household income (or, where appropriate, personal income) as reported by respondent, converted to $100,000s.

Income diversity: proportion of households in respondents' CT/CSD earning less than $10,000 and more than $90,000 (about the ninth and ninetieth percentiles for the majority of census subdivisions).

Median household income ($100,000s): median household income in respondents' CT/CSD, converted to $100,000s.

OTHER CONTEXTUAL VARIABLES

Education: proportion of individuals in respondent's CT/CSD with more than a high school diploma (started, but not necessarily finished, college or university).

Mobility: proportion of individuals in respondent's CT/CSD who moved in the five years previous to the 1996 Census.

Population density: number of individuals divided by the number of square kilometres for individual's CT/CSD. This variable is heavily skewed to the right, so the log values are used.

TABLE 11A.1

Descriptives

Variable	N	Mean	Standard deviation	Minimum	Maximum
Female	5,152	0.538	0.499	0.000	1.000
Age	5,152	1.175	0.968	0.000	3.000
Education	5,036	2.840	1.154	1.000	4.000
Religion	4,657	1.037	0.755	0.000	2.000
French	5,152	0.176	0.381	0.000	1.000
Immigrant	5,093	0.222	0.415	0.000	1.000
Health	5,096	0.552	0.329	0.000	1.000
Visible minority	5,152	0.131	0.337	0.000	1.000
Prop. visible minority	5,142	0.140	0.163	0.000	0.519
Economic outlook	4,976	0.598	0.316	0.000	1.000
Household income ($100,000s)	3,790	0.516	0.495	0.000	8.000
Median h'hold income ($100,000s)	5,142	0.045	0.009	0.000	0.102
Income diversity	5,109	0.182	0.653	0.000	0.618
Education (prop > high school)	5,142	0.510	0.962	0.000	0.910
Mobility	5,142	0.428	0.129	0.000	0.831
Population density (log)	5,143	5.827	2.715	−5.186	9.642
Wallet (all four combined)	4,738	0.630	0.232	0.000	1.000
Political trust (fed. & prov.)	4,683	0.451	0.201	0.000	1.000
Voted for govt party (fed.)	5,152	0.294	0.456	0.000	1.000
Voted for govt party (prov.)	5,152	0.249	0.433	0.000	1.000
EI/Welfare	4,784	0.580	0.208	0.000	1.000
Health	5,136	0.729	0.428	0.000	1.000
Pensions	5,109	0.700	0.333	0.000	1.000

NOTE: Results based on combined first wave, metro oversample, and resource community sample.

BASIC DEMOGRAPHICS

Female: dummy variable = 1 if respondent is female.

Age: dummy variables for 30 to 49, 50 to 65, 66 and over; residual category is < 30 years.

Education: dummy variables for finished high school, started college or university, and finished college or university; residual category is did not finish high school.

Religion: dummy variables for Catholic and Protestant; residual category is "other."

French: dummy variable = 1 if respondent speaks French at home.

Immigrant: dummy variable = 1 if respondent is an immigrant.

Health: self-reported health, based on the following question: "Compared to others your age, would you describe your health as excellent, very good, good, fair, or poor?" rescaled from 0 to 1 where 1 is excellent and 0 is poor.

SOCIAL WELFARE POLICY MEASURES

These measures are described in the text. The Cronbach's alpha for the EI/welfare measure is .540; the alpha decreases if any single item is removed. The alpha for the pensions measure is .309.

ACKNOWLEDGMENTS

Earlier versions of this chapter were presented at the conference on "Social Cohesion and the Policy Agenda: Canada in International Perspective" at Queen's University, Kingston, Ontario, 19-21 August 2002, at the Annual General Meeting of the Canadian Political Science Association, Toronto, 30 May – 2 June 2nd 2002, and at the conference on "Conceptualising Trust: Interdisciplinary Perspectives" at Nuffield College, Oxford, 10 May 2002. We are grateful to conference participants for their comments. Special thanks are due to David Miller and Patti Tamara Lenard. The usual disclaimer applies.

NOTES

1. Aboriginal/non-aboriginal relations constitute yet another dimension of social structure, of course, but our study is not well positioned to capture this line of division.
2. The two forms of trust are represented in no particular order in (1), as the equation is just the generic representation of the fact that each type of trust appears on the right-hand side of the estimation with the other as the dependent variable.
3. As of the 1996 Census, visible minorities constitute just over 11 percent of the Canadian population. Of visible minorities, 27 percent are Chinese, 21 percent are South Asian, and 19 percent are Black; the next largest categories are Filipino and Arab / West Asian (about 7 percent each).
4. Census tracts are small geographic units representing urban or rural neighbourhood-like communities. CT boundaries generally follow permanent physical features; they are created in census metropolitan areas and census agglomerations with an urban core population of at least 50,000; CT populations range from 2,500 to 8,000, with a preferred population of 4,000. A CT, then, is the geographic unit that best matches what we conceive of as a "neighbourhood." About one-third of the Canadian population (and about one-third of our sample) lives in areas without CTs, however; for this group, we use census subdivisions (CSDs). CSD is the general term applying to municipalities (as determined by provincial legislation) or their equivalent (e.g., Indian reserves, Indian settlements, and un-

organized territories). Data are available for 5,260 CSDs in the 1996 Census; the mean population is 5,483 with a variance of 32,432. This mean and variance are somewhat overstated, however, since major cities most often comprise a single, large, CSD, and these cities are always divided into CTs. By relying on a combination of CT and CSD data, then, we come as close as possible to using "neighbourhood-level" contextual data for all urban and rural respondents (see Statistics Canada 1996).

5 Francophones are not a linguistic minority everywhere, of course, but then neither are visible minorities ethnic minorities everywhere.

6 Residence is coded as one in Quebec and zero outside. We also estimated the models with percentage francophone in the CT/CSD with substantially the same result. Of course, in one sense, the critical thing about Quebec is its very preponderance of francophones. But is this preponderance mainly a matter of sociology, of contact frequency and the like, as our model presupposes for visible minorities, or is it, rather, a specifically political fact, where Quebec is not just a place but a *jurisdiction*, the only proto-national one in which francophones constitute the majority? Much of Canadian politics turns on the latter, of course, and this seems especially relevant to political trust. Concern for consistency between estimations for the two forms of trust inclined us to the dummy variable specification of linguistic context. And the dummy-variable setup just has more power, in two senses: it yields a larger R^2 in otherwise identical estimations; and linguistic context deploys no power whatsoever when the sample is split between Quebec and the rest of Canada. It seems pretty clear that the operative context is the province.

7 The literature linking individual and contextual demographics to trust and social capital is large and growing. For work including a large number of independent (individual and contextual) variables, see Alesina and La Ferrara (2000), Glaeser et al. (1999), and Helliwell (2002). For work on specific independent variables, see Robinson and Jackson (2001) on age; Helliwell and Putnam (1999) and Nie et al. (1996) on education; Gee and Veevers (1990), Greeley (1997a, 1997b), and Smidt (1999) on religion; Kawachi et al. (1997) on health.

8 All models are estimated using least squares regression. When the sample size for lower-level variables (individual-level) is much larger than that for higher-level variables (contextual-level), observations for the latter are not independent; standard errors for higher-level variables will tend to be biased downwards, and we are more likely to make Type I errors. Multilevel modelling is inappropriate in this case, since the survey includes 2,746 CT/CSDs, 64 percent of which include only one respondent. Accordingly, we use a regular OLS estimation with "corrected" standard errors, calculated using the number of CT/CSDs rather than the number of individuals. Both the number of respondents and the number of CT/CSDs are listed at the foot of Tables 11.1 and 11.2.

9   Strictly speaking, Table 11.1 does not exhaust the possible contrasts in the ethnolinguistic domain. Omitted are interactions among region, language, and race. We did explore them, at considerable peril of collinearity and with small numbers of observations at some of the intersections. There is a hint that francophones outside Quebec are peculiarly sensitive to racial context. But francophones inside Quebec seem utterly like non-francophones, inside and outside Quebec, in sensitivity. Similarly, patterns among visible-minority respondents seem undifferentiated by language. Making these points in a table would have made interpretation of coefficients unwieldy. That fact combined with the absence of effects dictated presenting the simpler pattern in what is already a complicated table.

10 See Table 11A.1.

11 "Theoretical" is here used in the sense intended by Achen (1977). The rest of the discussion in this paragraph mixes what he describes as "level" and "dispersion" effects.

12 Mobility and education are closely related to the local visible-minority percentage.

13 Details on reliability can be found in the appendix to this chapter.

14 Although the α for this scale is only 0.54, no alternative ordering of items dominates this one, in the sense that the α is always smaller. There is no reason to conclude that the scale should be broken up. Item scale correlations are 0.48 to 0.58 for all items, with the weakest links for the items that mention "welfare" by name. In a factor analysis of the items only one factor carries an eigenvalue greater than 1, all items load similarly on this first factor, and rotation of the axes yields nothing informative.

15 The wording separated by a slash indicates a wording experiment. One half the sample received the first wording and one-half, the second, with assignment to treatment determined by a random number. This randomization was motivated by our sense that the claim for choice might seem stronger if it were motivated by intensity of preference rather than simple ability to pay. As it happens, the reverse seems true, and the difference does not clear the minimum 5 percent threshold.

16 Our questionnaire has two other items about the system, but neither fits well with the one in the text. One question is about confidence in the actual availability of a bed when needed. This may be relevant to response to our core question, but it should be regarded as another variable in the estimation rather than as part of the definition of the dependent variable. We leave it aside here as something of a distraction from what is already a complicated argument. We also ask for perceptions of the system's essential fairness. Response to this question can go either way in its implications for the core issue, so we leave it aside as well.

17 The CPP question embodies a randomization on the wording of who would be better off. Ironically, the benefits are seen to be greater the more remote the beneficiary, and each contrast is statistically significant. Although the error in the

measure is tied to treatment, the administration of the treatment is purely at random relative to all other covariance in the data matrix. Were we to use this item alone as our pension indicator, we would dummy out the randomizations. As we are pooling this item's variance with that from the general pension item, we have elected to treat the randomization as measurement error.

Works Cited

Abraham, S. 2002. "Making a Mark: Voting in the Sri Lankan Tamil and Caribbean Communities in the GTA." Unpublished.

—. 2004. "Standing Up for Their Rights: Sri Lankan Tamils and Black Caribbean Peoples in Toronto." *Wadabagei: A Journal of the Caribbean and Its Diaspora* 7(2): 49-89.

Achen, Christopher. 1977. *Interpreting and Using Regression.* Beverly Hills: Sage.

Ackerloff, G., and R. Kranton. 2000. "Economics and Identity." *Quarterly Journal of Economics* 115(3): 715-53.

Adler, P.S., and S.W. Kwon. 2000. "Social Capital: The Good, the Bad, and the Ugly." In E. Lesser, ed., *Knowledge and Social Capital: Foundations and Applications.* Boston: Butterworth-Heineman, 89-115.

Alba, R., and J. Logan. 1992. "Assimilation and Stratification in the Home Ownership Patterns of Racial and Ethnic Groups." *International Migration Review* 26(1): 314-41.

Alesina, A., and E. La Ferrara. 1999. "Participation in Heterogeneous Communities." *Quarterly Journal of Economics* 115(3): 847-904.

—. 2000. "The Determinants of Trust." NBER Working Paper 7621. Cambridge, MA: National Bureau of Economic Research.

Alesina, Alberto, Reza Baquir, and William Easterly. 1997. "Public Goods and Ethnic Divisions." NBER Working Paper 6009. Cambridge, MA: National Bureau of Economic Research.

Alesina, Alberto, Edward Glaeser, and Bruce Sacerdote. 2001. "Why Doesn't the United States Have a European-Style Welfare State?" Brookings Papers on Economic Activity 2. Washington, DC: Brookings Institution.

Allison, P.D. 1995. *Survival Analysis Using the SAS System: A Practical Guide.* Cary, NC: SAS Institute.

Almond, G.A., and S. Verba. 1963. *The Civic Culture: Political Attitudes and Democracy in Five Nations.* Princeton: Princeton University Press.

Andrews, Frank. 1973. *Multiple Classification Analysis.* 2nd ed. Ann Arbor: University of Michigan Press.

Angelusz, Robert, and Robert Tardos. 1991. "The Strength and Weakness of Weak Ties." In P. Somlai, ed., *Values, Networks and Cultural Reproduction in Hungary*. Budapest: Coordinating Council of Programs, 7-23.

—. 2001. "Change and Stability in Social Network Resources: The Case of Hungary under Transformation." In Nan Lin, Karen Cook, and Ronald S. Burt, eds., *Social Capital: Theory and Research*. New York: Aldine de Gruyter.

Anheier, H.K., J. Gerhards, and F.P. Romo. 1995. "Forms of Social Capital and Social Structure in Cultural Fields: Examining Bourdieu's Social Topography." *American Journal of Sociology* 100: 859-903.

Appadurai, A. 1996. *Modernity at Large: Cultural Dimensions of Globalization*. Minneapolis-St. Paul: University of Minnesota Press.

Aquilino, W.S. 1996. "The Returning Adult Child and Parental Experiences in Midlife." In C.D. Ryff and M.M. Seltzer, eds., *The Parental Experience in Midlife*. Chicago: University of Chicago Press, 999-1010.

Arnold, Bruce L., and Fiona M. Kay. 1995. "Social Capital, Violations of Trust and the Vulnerability of Isolates: The Social Organization of Law Practice and Professional Self-Regulation." *International Journal of the Sociology of Law* 23: 321-46.

Astin, Alexander W. 1993. *What Matters in College?* San Francisco: Jossey-Bass.

Atchley, R. 1983. *Aging: Continuity and Change*. Belmont: Wadsworth Publishers.

—. 1989. "The Continuity Theory of Normal Aging." *The Gerontologist* 29: 183-90.

Babchuk, Nicholas, and Alan Booth. 1969. "Voluntary Association Membership: A Longitudinal Analysis." *American Sociological Review* 34: 31-45.

Baer, Doug, James Curtis, and Edward Grabb. 2001. "Has Voluntary Association Activity Declined? Cross-National Analyses for Fifteen Countries." *Canadian Review of Sociology and Anthropology* 28(3): 249-74.

Baier, Annette. 1986. "Trust and Antitrust." *Ethics* 96: 231-60.

Baker, W. 1990. "Market Networks and Corporate Behavior." *American Journal of Sociology* 96: 589-625.

Bandura, A. 1969. "Social Learning Theory of Identificatory Processes." In D.A. Goslin, ed., *Handbook of Socialization Theory and Research*. Chicago: Rand McNally, 213-62.

Bandura, A., and R.H. Walters. 1963. *Social Learning and Personality Developments*. New York: Holt, Rinehart and Winston.

Banerjee, Sidhartha. 2002. "Kirpan Back in School." *Montreal Gazette*, 18 April.

Banerji, H. 1999. "A Question of Silence: Reflections on Violence against Women in Communities of Colour." In E. Dua and A. Robertson, eds., *Scratching the Surface*, Toronto: Women's Press.

Banfield, Edward. 1958. *The Moral Basis of a Backward Society*. Chicago: Free Press.

Banting, Keith. 1999. "Social Citizenship and the Multicultural Welfare State." In Alan Cairns, John C. Courtney, Peter MacKinnon, Hans J. Michelmann, and David E. Smith, eds., *Citizenship, Diversity and Pluralism: Canadian and Comparative Perspectives*. Montreal: McGill-Queen's University Press.

—. 2000. "Looking in Three Directions: Migration and the European Welfare State in Comparative Perspective." In Michael Bommes and Andrew Geddes, eds., *Immigration and Welfare: Challenging the Borders of the Welfare State*. London: Routledge.

Banting, Keith, and Will Kymlicka. 2003. "Do Multiculturalism Policies Erode the Welfare State?" Paper presented to the Colloquium Franqui 2003, Cultural Diversities Versus Economic Solidarities, Brussels.

Banton, M. 1986. *Racial Theories*. Cambridge: Cambridge University Press.

Barefoot, J.C., K.E. Maynard, J.C. Beckham, B.H. Brummett, K. Hooker, and I.C. Siegler. 1998. "Trust, Health, and Longevity." *Journal of Behavioural Medicine* 21: 517-26.

Baron, James N., and Michael T. Hannan. 1994. "The Impact of Economics on Contemporary Sociology." *Journal of Economic Literature* 32: 1111-46.

Baron, Stephen, John Field, and Tom Schuller, eds. 2000. *Social Capital: Critical Perspectives*. Oxford: Oxford University Press.

Barry, Brian. 2001. *Culture and Equality*. Cambridge: Polity.

Bashevkin, Sylvia B. 1991. "Women's Participation in Political Parties." In K. Megyery, ed., *Women in Canadian Politics: Toward Equity in Representation*. Toronto: Dundurn Press.

Baum, F., R. Bush, C. Modra, C. Murray, E. Cox, K. Alexander, and R. Potter. 2000. "Epidemiology of Participation: An Australian Community Study." *Journal of Epidemiology and Community Health* 54: 414-23.

Beck, Paul A., and M. Kent Jennings. 1982. "Pathways to Participation." *American Political Science Review* 76(1): 94-108.

Becker, Gary S. 1957. *The Economics of Discrimination*. Chicago: University of Chicago Press.

—. 1974. "A Theory of Social Interactions." *Journal of Political Economy* 82: 1063-93.

—. 1996. *Accounting for Tastes*. Cambridge, MA: Harvard University Press.

Beggs, John J., and Jeanne S. Hurlbert. 1997. "The Social Context of Men's and Women's Job Search Ties: Membership in Voluntary Organizations, Social Resources, and Job Search Outcomes." *Sociological Perspectives* 40: 601-22.

Berkman, L., T. Glass, I. Brissette, and T. Seeman. 2000. "From Social Integration to Health: Durkheim in the New Millennium." *Social Science and Medicine* 51: 843-57.

Berkman, Lisa F., and S. Leonard Syme. 1979. "Social Networks, Host Resistance, and Mortality: A Nine Year Follow-Up Study of Alameda County Residents." *American Journal of Epidemiology* 109: 186-284.

Bian, Yanjie. 1997. "Bringing Strong Ties Back In: Indirect Ties, Network Bridges, and Job Searches in China." *American Sociological Review* 62: 366-85.

Bianchi, Suzanne M., and John P. Robinson. 1997. "What Did You Do Today? Children's Use of Time, Family Composition, and the Acquisition of Social Capital." *Journal of Marriage and the Family* 59: 332-44.

Bibby, Reginald W. 1990. "Religion." In Robert Hagedorn, ed., *Sociology*. 5th ed. Toronto: Holt, Rinehart and Winston, 401-34.
Bijleveld, Catrien, and Leo van der Kamp. 1998. *Longitudinal Data Analysis: Designs, Models, and Methods*. London: Sage Publications.
Bissoondath, Neil. 1994. *Selling Illusions: The Cult of Multiculturalism in Canada*. Toronto: Penguin.
Black, J.H. 1982. "Immigrant Political Adaptation in Canada: Some Tentative Findings." *Canadian Journal of Political Science* 15(1): 3-27.
—. 1987. "The Practice of Politics in Two Settings: Political Transferability among Recent Immigrants to Canada." *Canadian Journal of Political Science* 22: 731-53.
Blau, Peter. 1994. "Social Structure and Life Chances." Current Perspectives in Social Theory 1: 177-90.
Blau, P., T.C. Blum, and J.E. Schwarts. 1982. "Heterogeneity and Intermarriage." *American Sociological Review* 47: 45-62.
Boissevain, J. 1974. *Friends of Friends: Networks, Manipulators, and Coalitions*. New York: St. Martin's Press.
Booth, Alan. 1972. "Sex and Social Participation." *American Sociological Review* 37: 183-92.
Booth, A., A.C. Crouter, and M.J. Shanahan. 1999. *Transitions to Adulthood in a Changing Economy: No Work, No Family, No Future?* Westport, CT: Praeger.
Bourdieu, Pierre. 1980a. "The Aristocracy of Culture." *Media, Culture, and Society* 2: 225-54.
—. 1980b. "Le capital social notes provisoires." *Actes de la Recherche en Sciences Sociales* 31: 2-3.
—. 1983. "The Field of Cultural Production, or: The Economic World Reversed." *Poetics* 12: 311-56
—. 1985. "The Social Space and the Genesis of Groups." *Theory and Society* 14: 723-44.
—. 1986. "The Forms of Capital." In John G. Richardson, ed., *Handbook of Theory and Research for the Sociology of Education*. New York: Greenwood Press, 241-58.
—. 1990. *The Logic of Practice*. Stanford, CA: Stanford University Press.
Bourdieu, P., and L. Boltanski. 1978. "Changes in Social Structure and Changes in the Demand for Education." In S. Giner and M. Archer, eds., *Contemporary Europe, Social Structures and Cultural Patterns*. London: Routledge and Kegan Paul.
Boyd, M. 1988. "Birds of a Feather: Ethnic Variations in Young Adults Living at Home." Paper presented at the Population Association of America Annual Meeting, Chicago, April.
—. 2000. "Ethnic Variations in Young Adults Living at Home." *Canadian Studies in Population* 27(1): 135-58.
Boyd, M., and D. Norris. 1998. "Changes in the Nest: Young Canadian Adults Living with Parents, 1981-1996." Paper presented at the Canadian Population Society Annual Meeting, Ottawa, June.

—. 2000. "Demographic Change and Young Adults Living with Parent, 1981-1996." *Canadian Studies in Population* 27(2): 267-81.

Brehm, J., and W. Rahn. 1997. "Individual-Level Evidence for the Causes and Consequences of Social Capital." *American Journal of Political Science* 41: 999-1023.

Brodie, Janine. 1991. "Women and the Electoral Process in Canada." In K. Megyery, ed., *Women in Canadian Politics: Toward Equity in Representation*. Toronto: Dundurn Press.

Burns, Nancy, Kay L. Schlozman, and Sidney Verba. 2001. *The Private Roots of Public Action: Gender, Equality, and Political Participation*. Cambridge: Harvard University Press.

Burt, Ronald S. 1987. "Social Contagion and Innovation: Cohesion versus Structural Equivalence." *American Journal of Sociology* 92: 1287-335.

—. 1992. *Structural Holes: The Social Structure of Competition*. Cambridge, MA: Harvard University Press.

—. 1993. "The Social Structure of Competition." In Richard Swedberg, ed., *Explorations in Economic Sociology*. New York: Russell Sage Foundation, 65-103.

—. 1995. "Le capital social, les trous structuraux, et l'entrepreneur." In Emmanuel Lazega, trans., *Revue Française de Sociologie* 36: 599-628.

—. 1997a. "The Contingent Value of Social Capital." *Administrative Science Quarterly* 42: 339-65.

—. 1997b. "A Note on Social Capital and Network Content." *Social Networks* 19: 355-73.

—. 1998. "The Gender of Social Capital." *Rationality and Society* 10: 5-46.

—. 2001. "Structural Holes versus Network Closure as Social Capital." In Nan Lin, Karen Cook, and Ronald S. Burt, eds., *Social Capital: Theory and Research*. New York: Aldine de Gruyter, 31-56.

—. 2004. "Structural Holes and Good Ideas." *American Journal of Sociology* 110: 349-99.

—. 2005. *Brokerage and Closure: An Introduction to Social Capital*. Oxford: Oxford University Press.

Burt, Ronald S., and Holly J. Raider. 1996. "Boundaryless Careers and Social Capital." In Michael B. Arthur and Denise M. Rousseau, eds., *The Boundaryless Career: A New Employment Principle for a New Organizational Era*. New York: Oxford University Press, 187-200.

Calliste, A. 1996. "Anti-Racism Organizing and Resistance: Blacks in Urban Canada, 1940s-1970s." In J. Caulfield and L. Peake eds., *City Lives and City Forms*. Toronto: University of Toronto Press.

—. 2000. "Nurses and Porters: Racism, Sexism and Resistance in Segmented Labour Markets." In A. Calliste and G. Dei, eds., *Anti-Racist Feminism*. Halifax: Fernwood Publishing, 143-64.

Campbell, Angus, Philip E. Converse, Warren E. Miller, and Donald E. Stokes. 1960. *The American Voter*. New York: John Wiley.

Campbell, Catherine. 2000. "Social Capital and Health: Contextualizing Health Promotion within Local Community Networks." In Stephen Baron, John Field, and

Tom Schuller, eds., *Social Capital: Critical Perspectives*. Oxford: Oxford University Press, 182-96.

Canadian Council for Refugees. 1998. *Best Settlement Practices: Settlement Services for Refugees and Immigrants in Canada*. http://www.web.net/~ccr/bpfina1.htm.

Canadian Tamil Congress. 2002. *National Convention Program*. 2002: http://www.ctconline.ca.

Carens, Joseph H. 1988. "Immigration and the Welfare State." In Amy Gutmann, ed., *Democracy and the Welfare State*. Princeton, NJ: Princeton University Press, 207-30.

Carlin, J.E. 1994. *Lawyers on Their Own: The Solo Practitioner in an Urban Setting*. San Francisco: Austin and Winfield Publishers.

—. 1996. *Lawyers' Ethics: A Survey of the New York City Bar*. New York, NY: Russell Sage Foundation.

Cheran, R. 2001. "The Sixth Genre: Memory, History and the Tamil Diaspora Imagination." Marga Monograph Series on Ethnic Reconciliation, 7. Colombo, Sri Lanka: Marga Institute.

Chui, Tina, James Curtis, and Edward Grabb. 1993. "Who Participates in Community Organizations and Politics?" In James Curtis, Edward Grabb, and Neil Guppy, eds., *Social Inequality in Canada: Patterns, Problems, and Policies*. 2nd ed. Scarborough: Prentice-Hall, 524-38.

Coburn, D. 2000. "Income Inequality, Social Cohesion and the Health Status of Populations: The Role of Neo-liberalism." *Social Science and Medicine* 51: 135-46.

Cohen, C. 1999. *The Boundaries of Blackness: AIDS and the Breakdown of Black Politics*. Chicago: University of Chicago Press.

Cohen, C., K. Jones, and J. Tronto, eds. 1997. *Women Transforming Politics*. New York: New York University Press.

Coleman, James S. 1988. "Social Capital in the Creation of Human Capital." *American Journal of Sociology* 94: S95-S120.

—. 1990a. "The Emergence of Norms." In Michael Hechter, Karl-Dieter Opp, and Reinhard Wippler, eds., *Social Institutions: Their Emergence, Maintenance and Effects*. New York: Aldine de Gruyter, 35-39.

—. 1990b. *Foundations of Social Theory*. Cambridge, MA: The Belknap Press of Harvard University.

—. 1990c. "Norm Generating Structures." In Karen Schweers Cook and Margaret Levi, eds., *The Limits of Rationality*. Chicago: University of Chicago Press, 250-73.

—. 1993. "The Rational Reconstruction of Society: 1992 Presidential Address." *American Sociological Review* 58: 1-15.

Cook, Karen S., and Russell Hardin. 2001. "Norms of Cooperativeness and Networks of Trust." In Michael Hecter and Karl-Dieter Opp, eds., *Social Norms*. New York: Russell Sage, 327-47.

Cornish, J. 1992. "Australia's Experience with Census Questions on Ethnicity." Paper presented at the joint Canada/United States conference on the measurement of ethnicity. Ottawa, 1992.

Côté, J.E., and A.L. Allahar. 1994. *Generation on Hold: Coming of Age in the Twentieth Century*. Toronto: Stoddart.

Cox, E. 1995. *A Truly Civil Society: 1995 Boyer Lectures*. Sydney: Australian Broadcasting Corporation.

Creese, G. 1999. *Contracting Masculinity: Gender, Class, and Race in a White-Collar Union, 1944-1994*. Toronto: Oxford University Press.

Crester, G., and J. Leon, eds. 1982. *Intermarriage in the US: An Overview of Theory and Research*. New York: Haworth Press.

Csikszentmihalyi, M. 1997. "Activity, Experience, and Personal Growth." In J.E. Curtis and S.J. Russell, eds., *Physical Activity in Human Experience: Interdisciplinary Perspectives*. Champaign, IL: Human Kinetics.

Curtis, James. 1971. "Voluntary Association Joining: A Cross-National Comparison." *American Sociological Review* 36: 872-80.

Curtis, James, Doug Baer, and Edward Grabb. 2001. "Nations of Joiners: Explaining Voluntary Association Membership in Democratic Societies." *American Sociological Review* 66: 783-805.

Curtis, James, Doug Baer, Edward Grabb, and Thomas Perks. 2003. "Estimating Trends in Voluntary Association Activity in Quebec and English Canada." *Sociologie et sociétés* 35(1): 115-42.

Curtis, James, Edward Grabb, and Doug Baer. 1992. "Voluntary Association Membership in Fifteen Countries: A Comparative Analysis." *American Sociological Review* 57: 139-52.

Curtis, James, and Ronald Lambert. 1976. "Voting, Political Interest, and Age: National Survey Findings for French and English Canadians." *Canadian Journal of Political Science* 9: 293-307.

Curtis, James, William McTeer, and Philip White. 1999. "Exploring Effects of School Sport Experiences on Sport Participation in Later Life." *Sociology of Sport Journal* 16: 348-65.

Curtis, James, Philip White, and Barry McPherson. 2000. "Age and Physical Activity among Canadian Women and Men: Findings from Longitudinal National Survey Data." *Journal of Aging and Physical Activity* 8: 1-19.

Cutler, Stephen J., and Jon Hendricks. 2000. "Age Differences in Voluntary Association Memberships: Fact or Artifact." *Journal of Gerontology* 55: S98-S107.

Damico, Alfonso, Sandra Damico, and M. Margaret Conway. 1998. "The Democratic Education of Women: High School and Beyond." *Women in Politics* 19: 1-31.

Dasgupta, Partha. 2000. "Economic Development and the Idea of Social Capital." In Ismail Serageldin and Partha Dasgupta, eds., *Social Capital: A Multifaceted Perspective*. Washington, DC: World Bank.

Davis, M. 2000. *Magical Urbanism: Latinos Reinvent the US City*. London: Verso.
DeGraff, Nan Dirk, and Hendrick Derk Flap. 1988. "With a Little Help from My Friends." *Social Forces* 67(2): 452-72.
Deroy-Pineau, François, et Paul Bernard. 2001. "Projet mystique, réseaux sociaux et mobilizations des resources: le passage en Nouvelle France de Marie de l'Incarnation en 1639." *Archives de sciences socials des religions* 113: 61-91.
Desmarais, Serge, and James Curtis. 1999. "Gender Differences in Employment and Income Experiences among Young People." In J. Barling and E.K. Kelloway, eds., *Young Workers: Varieties of Experience*. Washington, DC: American Psychological Association, 59-88.
Deverell, John. 2003. "Sri Lanka Looks to Canada as a Political Role Model." *Toronto Star*, 19 January.
Diani, Mario. 1997. "Social Movements and Social Capital: A Network Perspective on Movement Outcomes." *Mobilization: An International Journal* 2(2): 129-47.
Easterly, William, and R. Levine. 1997. "Africa's Growth Tragedy: Policies and Ethnic Divisions." *Quarterly Journal of Economics* 112: 1203-50.
Eastis, Carla M. 1998. "Organizational Diversity and the Production of Social Capital: One of These Groups Is Not Like the Other." *American Behavioral Scientist* 42(1): 66-77.
Edwards, Bob, and Michael W. Foley. 1998. "Civil Society and Social Capital beyond Putnam." *American Behavioral Scientist* 42(1): 124-39.
—. 2001. "Much Ado about Social Capital: Review Article." *Contemporary Sociology* 30(3): 227-30.
Edwards, B., M.W. Foley, and M. Diani. 2001. "Social Capital Reconsidered." In B. Edwards, M.W. Foley, and M. Diani, eds., *Beyond Toqueville: Civil Society and the Social Capital Debate in Comparative Perspective*. Hanover, NH: University Press of New England, 266-80.
Edwards, Patricia K., John N. Edwards, and Ann D. Watts. 1984. "Women, Work, and Social Participation." *Journal of Voluntary Action Research* 13: 7-22.
Elder, G.H., Jr. 1978. "Approaches to Social Change and the Family." *American Journal of Sociology* 84: S1-S38.
—. 1985. *Life Course Dynamics, Trajectories and Transitions, 1968-1980*. Ithaca, NY: Cornell University Press.
—. 1992. "Life Course." In E.F. Borgatta and M.L. Borgatta, eds., *Encyclopedia of Sociology*. Vol. 3. Toronto: Macmillan Publishing Company, 1120-30.
Ellaway, A., and S. Macintyre. 2000. "Social Capital and Self-rated Health: Support for a Contextual Mechanism." *American Journal of Public Health* 90: 988.
Ellison, G. 1999. "Income Inequality, Social Trust, and Self-reported Health Status in High-Income Countries." *Annals of the New York Academy of Sciences* 896: 325-28.
Erickson, Bonnie H. 1996. "Culture, Class, and Connections." *American Journal of Sociology* 102(1): 217-51.

—. 2001. "Good Networks and Good Jobs: The Value of Social Capital to Employers and Employees." In Nan Lin, Karen Cook, and Ronald S. Burt, eds., *Social Capital: Theory and Research*. New York: Aldine de Gruyter, 127-58.

Esping-Andersen, Gosta. 1990. *The Three Worlds of Welfare Capitalism*. Princeton, NJ: Princeton University Press.

Etzioni, Amitai. 2001. "Is Bowling Together Sociologically Lite?" *Contemporary Sociology* 30(3): 223-24.

Evans, P. 1996. "Government Action, Social Capital and Development: Reviewing the Evidence on Synergy." *World Development* 24(6): 1119.

Evans, Robert G., Morris Barer, and Theodore R. Marmor, eds. 1994. *Why Are Some People Healthy and Others Not? The Determinants of Health in Populations*. New York: A. de Gruyter.

Fernandez, Roberto M., and Emilio J. Castilla. 2001. "How Much Is the Network Worth? Social Capital in Employee Referral Networks." In Nan Lin, Karen Cook, and Ronald S. Burt, eds., *Social Capital: Theory and Research*. New York: Aldine de Gruyter, 85-104.

Fernandez, Roberto M., Emilio J. Castilla, and Paul Moore. 2000. "Social Capital at Work: Networks and Hiring at a Phone Center." *American Sociological Review* 62: 883-902.

Fernandez-Kelly, M.P. 1995. "Social and Cultural Capital in the Urban Ghetto: Implications for the Economic Sociology of Immigration." In A. Portes, ed., *The Economic Sociology of Immigration*. New York: Russell Sage.

Field, John. 2003. *Social Capital*. London: Routledge.

Fischer, C.S. 1982. *To Dwell among Friends: Personal Networks in Town and City*. Chicago: University of Chicago Press.

Flanagan, Constance A., Jennifer M. Bowes, Britta Jonson, Ben Csapo, and Elena Sheblanova. 1998. "Ties that Bind: Correlates of Adolescents' Civic Commitments in Seven Countries." *Journal of Social Issues* 54: 457-75.

Flap, Henk. 1987. "De Theorie Van Het Sociale Kapitaal" [The Theory of Social Capital]. *Antropologische Verkenningen* 6: 14-27.

—. 1991. "Social Capital in the Reproduction of Inequality." *Comparative Sociology of Family, Health and Education* 20: 6179-202.

—. 1997. "Conflicting Loyalties Theory." *L'Année sociologique* 47: 183-216.

—. 1999. "Creation and Returns of Social Capital a New Research Program." *La Revue Tocqueville* 20(1): 5-26.

Flap, Henk, and Ed Boxman. 2001. "Getting Started: The Influence of Social Capital on the Start of the Occupational Career." In Nan Lin, Karen Cook, and Ronald S. Burt, eds., *Social Capital: Theory and Research*. New York: Aldine de Gruyter, 159-81.

Flora, Jan L. 1998. "Social Capital and Communities of Place." *Rural Sociology* 63(4): 481-506.

Foley, Michael W., and Bob Edwards. 1997. "Escape from Politics? Social Theory and the Social Capital Debate." *American Behavioral Scientist* 24(6): 550-61.

—. 1998. "Beyond Tocqueville: Civil Society and Social Capital in Comparative Perspective." *American Behavioral Scientist* 42(1): 5-20.

—. 1999. "Is It Time to Disinvest in Social Capital?" *Journal of Public Policy* 19(2): 141-73.

Forbes, H.D. 1997. *Ethnic Conflict: Commerce, Culture, and the Contact Hypothesis*. New Haven and London: Yale University Press.

Forrest, R., and Kearns, A. 2001. "Social Cohesion, Social Capital and the Neighbourhood." *Urban Studies* 38(12): 2125-43.

Forsé, Michel. 1999. "Social Capital and Status Attainment in Contemporary France." *La Revue Tocqueville* 20(1): 59-81.

Fox, Jonathan. 1997. "The World Bank and Social Capital: Contesting the Concept in Practice." *Journal of International Development* 9(7): 963-71.

Francois, Patrick. 2002. *Social Capital and Economic Development*. New York: Routledge.

Frank, K.A., and Yasumoto, J. 1998. "Linking Action to Social Structure within a System: Social Capital within and between Subgroups." *American Journal of Sociology* 104(3): 642-86.

Fraser, Nancy. 1997. *Justice Interruptus: Critical Reflections on the "Postsocialist" Condition*. New York and London: Routledge.

Fratoe, Frank A. 1988. "Social Capital of Black Business Owners." *Review of Black Political Economy* 16(4): 33-50.

Friedman, Raymond A., and David Krackhardt. 1997. "Social Capital and Career Mobility: A Structural Theory of Lower Returns to Education for Asian Employees." *Journal of Applied Behavioral Science* 33(3): 316-34.

Fukuyama, Francis. 1989. "End of History?" *The National Interest* (Summer): 3-18.

—. 1995a. "Social Capital and the Global Economy." *Foreign Affairs* 74: 89-103.

—. 1995b. *Trust: The Social Virtues and the Creation of Prosperity*. New York: Free Press.

Fullinwider, Robert K. 1988. "Citizenship and Welfare." In Amy Gutmann, ed., *Democracy and the Welfare State*. Princeton, NJ: Princeton University Press, 261-78.

Gabbay, Shaul M., and Ezra W. Zuckerman. 1998. "Social Capital and Opportunity in Corporate R and D: The Contingent Effect of Contact Density on Mobility Expectations." *Social Science Research* 27: 189-217.

Gambetta, Diego. 1988. "Can We Trust Trust?" In Diego Gambetta, ed., *Trust: Making and Breaking Cooperative Relations*. New York: Basil Blackwell, 213-37.

Gee, E.M., B.A. Mitchell, and A.V. Wister. 1995. "Returning to the Parental 'Nest': Exploring a Changing Canadian Life Course." *Canadian Studies in Population* 22(2): 121-44.

Gee, E.M., B.A. Mitchell, A.V. Wister, and D. Lai. 1999/2000. "Culture and Co-residence: A Comparative Analysis of Ethnicity, Living Arrangements, Intergenerational Relations, and Support in Canadian Families." Department of Sociology/Anthropology, Simon Fraser University.

Gee, E.M., and J.E. Veevers. 1990. "Religious Involvement and Life Satisfaction in Canada." *Sociological Analysis* 51(4): 387-94.

George, L.K. 1993. "Sociological Perspectives on Life Transitions." *Annual Review of Sociology* 19: 353-73.

Germain, Annick. 2000. *Immigrants and Cities: Does Neighbourhood Matter?* Montreal: INRS-Urbanisation.

Giele, J.Z., and G.H. Elder, Jr. 1998. *Methods of Life Course Research: Qualitative and Quantitative Approaches*. Thousand Oaks, CA: Sage Publications.

Gilens, Martin. 1996. "'Race Coding' and White Opposition to Welfare." *American Political Science Review* 90: 593-604.

—. 1999. *Why Americans Hate Welfare: Race, Media, and the Politics of Antipoverty Policy*. Chicago: University of Chicago Press.

Gitlin, T. 1995. *The Twilight of Common Dreams: Why America Is Wracked by the Culture Wars*. New York: Henry Holt.

Gittell, Ross, and Avis Vidal. 1998. *Community Organizing: Building Social Capital as a Development Strategy*. Thousand Oaks, CA: Sage Press.

Glaeser, Edward L., David Laibson, Jose A. Scheinkman, and Christine L. Soutter. 1999. "What Is Social Capital? The Determinants of Trust and Trustworthiness." NBER Working Paper 7216. Cambridge, MA: National Bureau of Economic Research.

—. 2000. "Measuring Trust." *Quarterly Journal of Economics* 65(3): 811-46

Gold, S.J. 1995. "Gender and Social Capital among Israeli Immigrants in Los Angeles." *Diaspora* 4: 267-301.

Goldmann, G. 1992. "Canadian Data on Ethnic Origin: Who Needs It and Why?" Paper prepared for the joint Canada/United States conference on the measurement of ethnicity, Ottawa.

Goldscheider, F.K., and C. Goldscheider. 1993. *Leaving Home before Marriage: Ethnicity, Familism, and Generational Relationships*. Madison, WI: University of Wisconsin Press.

—. 1999. *The Changing Transition to Adulthood: Leaving and Returning Home*. Thousand Oaks, CA: Sage Publications.

Goodin, Robert E. 1988. *Reasons for Welfare: The Political Theory of the Welfare State*. Princeton, NJ: Princeton University Press.

—. 1996. "Inclusion et exclusion." *Archives européannes de sociologie* 37(2): 343-71.

Gould, S., and John Palmer. 1988. "Outcomes, Interpretations and Policy." In John Palmer, Tim Smeeding, and B. Torrey, eds., *The Vulnerable*. Washington: Urban Institute Press.

Granfield, Robert, and Thomas Koenig. 1992a. "The Fate of Elite Idealism: Accommodation and Ideological Work at Harvard Law School." *Social Problems* 39: 315-31.

—. 1992b. "Learning Collective Eminence: Harvard Law School and the Social Production of Elite Lawyers." *Sociological Quarterly* 38: 503-20.

Granovetter, Mark S. 1973. "The Strength of Weak Ties." *American Journal of Sociology* 78: 1360-80.
—. 1974. *Getting a Job: A Study of Contacts and Careers*. Cambridge, MA: Harvard University Press.
—. 1985. "Economic Action and Social Structure: The Problem of Embeddedness." *American Journal of Sociology* 91(3): 481-510.
—. 1986. "Labor Mobility, Internal Markets, and Job Matching: A Comparison of the Sociological and Economic Approaches." *Research in Social Stratification and Mobility* 5: 3-39.
—. 1995. *Getting a Job: A Study of Contacts and Careers*. 2nd ed. Chicago: University of Chicago Press.
Greeley, Andrew. 1997a. "Coleman Revisited: Religious Structures as a Source of Social Capital." *American Behavioral Scientist* 40: 587-94.
—. 1997b. "The Other Civic America: Religion and Social Capital." *American Prospect* 32: 68-73.
Greene, William H. 2000. *Econometric Analysis*. 4th ed. London: Prentice Hall.
Greenstein, T. 1995. "Gender Ideology, Marital Disruption, and the Employment of Married Women." *Journal of Marriage and the Family* 57(1): 31-42.
Guerin-Gonzales, Camille, and Carl Strikwerda, eds. 1998. *The Politics of Immigrant Workers: Labor Activism and Migration in the World Economy since 1830*. New York: Holmes & Meier.
Guest, A., and R.S. Oropesa. 1986. "Informal Social Ties and Political Activity in the Metropolis." *Urban Affairs Quarterly* 21(4): 550-74.
Guest A., and S.K. Wierzbicki. 1999. "Ties at the Neighbourhood Level: Two Decades of GSS Evidence." *Urban Affairs Review* 35(1): 92-111.
Gummer, Burton. 1998. "Social Relations in an Organizational Context: Social Capital, Real Work, and Structural Holes." *Administration in Social Work* 22(3): 87-195.
Gwyn, Richard. 1995. *Nationalism without Walls*. Toronto: McClelland and Stewart.
Hagan, John. 1993. "The Social Embeddedness of Crime and Unemployment." *Criminology* 31(4): 465-91.
Hagan, J., R. MacMillan, and B. Wheaton. 1996. "New Kid in Town: Social Capital and the Life Course Effects of Family Migration in Children." *American Sociological Review* 61: 368-85.
Hagan, John, and Bill McCarthy. 1997. *Mean Streets: Youth Crime and Homelessness*. Cambridge: Cambridge University Press.
—. 1998. "The Theory of Social Capital and the Renewal of the Paradigm of Tensions and Opportunities in Sociological Criminology." *Sociologie et societés* 30(1): 145-58.
Hagan, J., H. Merkens, and K. Boenhke. 1995. "Delinquency and Disdain: Social Capital and the Control of Right-Wing Extremism among East and West Berlin Youth." *American Journal of Sociology* 100: 1028-52.

Hagestad, G.O. 1990. "Social Perspectives on the Life Course." In R. Binstock and L. George, eds., *Handbook of Aging and the Social Sciences*. New York: Academic Press, 151-68.

Hagestad, G.O., and B.L. Neugarten. 1985. "Age and the Life Course." In R.H. Binstock and E. Shanas, eds., *Handbook of Aging and the Social Sciences*. New York: Van Nostrand Reinhold Co, 35-61.

Hall, Michael, Tamara Knighton, Paul Reed, Patrick Bussiere, Don McRae, and Paddy Bowen. 1998. "Caring Canadians, Involved Canadians: Highlights from the 1997 National Survey of Giving, Volunteering, and Participating." Ottawa: Statistics Canada.

Hallinan, Maureen T., and Warren N. Kubitschek. 1999. "Conceptualizing and Measuring School Social Networks." *American Sociological Review* 64: 687-93.

Halpern, David. 2005. *Social Capital*. Cambridge, UK: Polity Press.

Hanks, Michael, and Bruce K. Eckland. 1978. "Adult Voluntary Associations and Adolescent Socialization." *Sociological Quarterly* 19: 481-90.

Hardin, Russell. 1992. "The Street-Level Epistemology of Trust." *Analyse und Kritik* 14: 152-76.

—. 1993. "The Steet-Level Epistemology of Trust." *Politics and Society* 21: 505-29.

—. 1998. "Conceptions and Explanations of Trust." Working Paper 129. New York: Russell Sage Foundation.

—. 2000. "The Public Trust." In Susan J. Pharr and Robert D. Putnam, eds., *Disaffected Democracies: What's Troubling the Trilateral Countries?* Princeton: Princeton University Press, 31-51.

—. 2002. *Trust and Trustworthiness*. New York: Russell Sage.

Hardy-Fanta, Carol. 1997. "Latina Women and Political Consciousness: La Chispa QuePrende." In C. Cohen, K. Jones, and J. Tronto, eds., *Women Transforming Politics*. New York: New York University Press.

Hareven, T. 1996. *Aging and Generational Relations: Life-Course and Cross-Cultural Perspectives*. New York: Aldine de Gruyter.

Harles, John C. 1997. "Integration before Assimilation: Immigration, Multiculturalism and the Canadian Polity." *Canadian Journal of Political Science* 30: 711-36.

Hawe, P., and A. Shiell. 2000. "Social Capital and Health Promotion: A Review." *Social Science and Medicine* 51: 871-85.

Helliwell, John F. 1996. "Do Borders Matter for Social Capital? Economic Growth and Civic Culture in the U.S. States and Canadian Provinces." NBER Working Paper No. 5863. Cambridge, MA: National Bureau of Economic Research.

—. 2001. "Canada: Life beyond the Looking Glass." *Journal of Economic Perspectives* 15: 107-124.

—. 2002. "How's Life? Combining Individual and National Variables to Explain Subjective Well-Being." NBER Working Paper No. 9065. Cambridge: National Bureau of Economic Research.

—. 2003. "Do Borders Matter for Social Capital? Economic Growth and Civic Culture in the U.S. States and Canadian Provinces." In Lars Osberg, ed., *The Economic Implications of Social Cohesion*. Toronto: University of Toronto Press.

—. 2006. "Well-Being, Social Capital and Public Policy: What's New?" *The Economic Journal* 116 (510): C34-C45.

Helliwell, J.F., and Robert D. Putnam. 1995. "Economic Growth and Social Capital in Italy." *Eastern Economic Journal* 21(3): 295-307.

—. 1999. "Education and Social Capital." NBER Working Paper 7121. Cambridge, MA: National Bureau of Economic Research.

Henry, F. 1994. *The Caribbean Diaspora in Toronto: Learning to Live with Racism*. Toronto: University of Toronto Press.

Hero, Rodney E., and Caroline J. Tolbert. 1996. "A Racial/Ethnic Diversity Interpretation of Politics and Policy in the States of the US." *American Journal of Political Science* 40: 851-71.

Hiebert, D. 1995. "The Social Geography of Toronto in 1931: A Study of Residential Differentiation and Social Structure." *Journal of Historical Geography* 21: 55-74.

Hirdes, J., and W. Forbes. 1992. "The Importance of Social Relationships, Socioeconomic Status and Health Practices with Respect to Mortality among Healthy Ontario Males." *Journal of Clinical Epidemiology* 45: 175-82.

Hirschman, C. 1992. "How to Measure Ethnicity: An Immodest Proposal." Paper presented at the joint Canada/United States conference on the measurement of ethnicity. Ottawa.

Hofferth, Sandra L., and John Iceland. 1998. "Social Capital in Rural and Urban Communities." *Rural Sociology* 63(4): 574-98.

Hooghe, Marc. 2003. "Participation in Voluntary Associations and Value Indicators: The Effect of Current and Previous Participation Experiences." *Nonprofit and Voluntary Sector Quarterly* 32(1): 47-69.

Hooghe, Marc, and Dietlind Stolle. 2003. "Age Matters: Life-Cycle and Cohort Differences in the Socialisation Effect of Voluntary Participation." *European Political Science* 2(3): 49-56.

House, J.S. 1987. "Social Support and Social Structure." *Sociological Forum* 2(1): 135-46.

House, J., K. Landis, and D. Umberson. 1988. "Social Relationships and Health. *Science* 241: 540-44.

House, James, Debra Umberson, and K.R. Landis. 1988. "Structures and Processes of Social Support." *Annual Review of Sociology* 14: 293-318.

Idler, E., and Y. Benyamini. 1997. "Self-Rated Health and Mortality: A Review of Twenty-Seven Community Studies." *Journal of Health and Social Behavior* 38: 21-37.

Inglehart, R. 1988. "The Rennaissance of Political Culture." *American Political Science Review* 82: 1203-30.

—. 1990. *Cultural Shift in Advanced Industrial Society*. Princeton: Princeton University Press.

Jabbra, N.W. 1997. "Politics and Acceptance: The Lebanese in Canada's Maritime Provinces." *Canadian Ethnic Studies* 29(1): 99-119.

Jackman, M., and M. Crane. 1986. "Some of My Best Friends Are Black ... Interracial Friendship and Whites' Racial Attitudes." *Public Opinion Quarterly* 50: 459-86.

James, Estelle. 1987. "The Public/Private Division of Responsibility for Education: An International Comparison." *Economics of Education Review* 6(1): 1-14.

—. 1993. "Why Do Different Countries Choose a Different Public/Private Mix of Education Services?" *Journal of Human Resources* 28(3): 531-92.

James, Sherman A., Amy J. Schulz, and Juliana van Olphen. 2001. "Social Capital, Poverty, and Community Health: An Exploration of Linkages." In Susan Saegert, Phillip Thompson, and Mark Warren, eds., *Social Capital and Poor Communities*. New York, NY: Russell Sage, 165-88.

James, W. 1998. *Holding Aloft the Banner of Ethiopia: Caribbean Radicalism in Early Twentieth-Century America*. New York: Verso.

Janoski, Thomas, and John Wilson. 1995. "Pathways to Voluntarism: Family Socialization and Status Transmission Models." *Social Forces* 74: 271-92.

Jennings, M. Kent, and Richard Niemi. 1981. *Generations and Politics: A Panel Study of Young Adults and Their Parents*. Princeton, NJ: Princeton University Press.

Jennings, M. Kent, and Laura Stoker. 2002. "Generational Change, Life Cycle Processes and Social Capital." Paper presented at the Conference Citizenship on Trial: Interdisciplinary Perspectives on the Political Socialization of Adolescents, Montreal, 20-21 June.

Jenson, Jane. 1998. *Les contours de la cohésion sociale: l'état de la recherche au Canada*. Ottawa: Réseaux canadiens de recherche en politiques publiques.

Johnston, Richard, and Stuart N. Soroka. 2001. "Social Capital in a Multicultural Society: The Case of Canada." In Paul Dekker and Eric M. Uslaner, eds., *Social Capital and Participation in Everyday Life*. London: Routledge, 30-44.

Jones, Frank. 2000. "Community Involvement: The Influence of Early Experience." *Canadian Social Trends* (Summer): 15-19.

Judge, K., J. Mulligan, and M. Benzeval. 1998. "Income Inequality and Population Health." *Social Science and Medicine* 46: 567-79.

Kalbach, W., and M. Richard. 1986. "Ethnic Intermarriage and the Changing Canadian Family." Proceedings of a symposium organized by the Federation of Canadian Demographers and sponsored by the Royal Society of Canada. University of Ottawa.

Kaplan, G., E. Pamuk, J. Lynch, R. Cohen, and J. Balfour. 1996. "Income Inequality and Mortality in the United States." *British Medical Journal* 312: 999-1003.

Kawachi, Ichiro. 1997. "Long Live Community: Social Capital as Public Health." *American Prospect* 35: 56-59.

Kawachi, I., and L.F. Berkman. 2000. "Social Cohesion, Social Capital and Health." In L.F. Berkman and I. Kawachi, eds., *Social Epidemiology.* New York: Oxford University Press, 174-90.

Kawachi, I., B. Kennedy, and R. Glass. 1999. "Social Capital and Self-Rated Health: A Contextual Analysis." *American Journal of Public Health* 89(8): 1187-93.

Kawachi, I., B. Kennedy, K. Lochner, and D. Prothrow-Stith. 1997. "Social Capital, Income Inequality, and Mortality." *American Journal of Public Health* 87: 1491-98.

Kay, Fiona M. 1997. "Flight from Law: A Competing Risks Model of Departures from Law Firms." *Law and Society Review* 31: 301-35.

Kay, Fiona M., and John Hagan. 1995. "The Persistent Glass Ceiling: Gendered Inequalities in the Earnings of Lawyers." *British Journal of Sociology* 46: 279-310.

—. 1998. "Raising the Bar: The Gender Stratification of Law Firm Capitalization." *American Sociological Review* 63(5): 728-43.

Kennedy, B., I. Kawachi, and D. Prothrow-Stith. 1996. "Income Distribution and Mortality: Cross-Sectional Ecological Study of the Robin Hood Index in the United States." *British Medical Journal* 213: 1004-07.

Kennedy, B., I. Kawachi, D. Prothrow-Stith, K. Lochner, and V. Gupta. 1998. "Social Capital, Income Inequality, and Firearm Violent Crime." *Social Science and Medicine* 47: 7-17.

Kenworthy, L. 1997. "Civic Engagement, Social Capital, and Economic Cooperation." *American Behavioral Scientist* 40(5): 645.

Kitschelt, Herbert. 1995. *The Radical Right in Western Europe: A Comparative Analysis.* Ann Arbor: University of Michigan Press.

Knack, Stephen. 2001. "Trust, Associational Life, and Economic Performance." In John F. Helliwell and Aneta Bonikowska, eds., *The Contribution of Human and Social Capital to Sustained Economic Growth and Well-Being,* 172-202, Ottawa: HRDC and OECD. Available at www.hrdc-drhc.gc.ca/arb.

Knack, Stephen, and Philip Keefer. 1995. "Institutions and Economic Performance: Cross-Country Tests Using Alternative Institutional Measures." *Economics and Politics* 7: 207-27.

—. 1997. "Does Social Capital Have an Economic Payoff? A Cross-Country Investigation." *Quarterly Journal of Economics* 112: 1251-88.

Knoke, David. 1986. "Associations and Interest Groups." *Annual Review of Sociology* 12: 1-22.

Knoke, David, and Randall Thompson. 1977. "Voluntary Association Memberships and the Family Life Cycle." *Social Forces* 56: 48-65.

Knox, Paul. 2002. "Sri Lankan Peace Deal Forged on Canada's Federal Model." *Globe and Mail,* 6 December, A1.

Kralt, J. 1990. "Ethnic Origins in the Canadian Census, 1871-1986." In S. Hali, F. Trovato, and L. Driedger, eds., *Ethnic Demography: Canadian Immigrant, Racial and Cultural Variations.* Ottawa: Carleton University Press.

Kurthen, Hermann. 1997. "The Canadian Experience with Multiculturalism and Employment Equity: Lessons for Europe." *New Community* 23: 249-70.

Kymlicka, Will. 1995. *Multicultural Citizenship*. Oxford, UK: Oxford University Press.

—. 1998. *Finding our Way: Rethinking Ethnocultural Relations in Canada*. Toronto: Oxford University Press.

—. 2001. *Contemporary Political Philosophy*. 2nd ed. Oxford, UK: Oxford University Press.

Langton, Nancy, and Jeffrey Pfeffer. 1993. "The Effect of Wage Dispersion on Satisfaction, Productivity, and Working Collaboratively: Evidence from College and University Faculty." *Administrative Science Quarterly* 38: 382-407.

—. 1994. "Paying the Professor: Sources of Salary Variation in Academic Labor Markets." *American Sociological Review* 59: 236-56.

Lapp, M. 1999. "Ethnic Group Leaders and the Mobilization of Voter Turnout: Evidence from Five Montreal Communities." *Canadian Ethnic Studies* 31(2): 17-42.

Laumann, E.O., and D. Knoke. 1987. *The Organizational State: Social Choice in National Policy Domains*. Madison: University of Wisconsin Press.

Lavis, J., and G. Stoddart. 1999. "Social Cohesion and Health." CHEPA Working Papers Series 99-09. Hamilton, ON: McMaster University.

Lehning, P.B. 1998. "Towards a Multicultural Civil Society: The Role of Social Capital and Democratic Citizenship." *Government and Opposition* 33: 221.

Lemelle, S., and R.D.G. Kelley, eds. 1994. *Imagining Home: Class, Culture and Nationalism in the African Diaspora*. London: Verso.

Lesser, Eric L. 2000. "Leveraging Social Capital in Organizations." In Eric L. Lesser, ed., *Knowledge and Social Capital: Foundations and Applications*. Boston: Butterworth-Heinemann, 3-16.

Lévesque, Maurice, and Deena White. 1999. "Le Concept de capital social et ses usages." *Lien social et politiques* 41: 23-33.

Levi, Margaret. 1996. "Social and Unsocial Capital: A Review Essay of Robert Putnam's *Making Democracy Work*." *Politics and Society* 24(1): 45-55.

—. 1998. "A State of Trust." In Margaret Levi and Valerie Braithwaite, eds., *Trust and Governance*. New York: Russell Sage.

Li, Peter. 1998. *The Chinese in Canada*. Toronto: Oxford University Press.

—. 2003. "Deconstructing Canada's Discourse of Immigrant Integration." PCERII Working Paper Series, No. WP04-03. University of Saskatchewan.

Liang, Zai. 1994. "Social Contact, Social Capital, and the Naturalization Process: Evidence from Six Immigrant Groups." *Social Science Research* 23: 407-37.

Liem, P., and E. Montague, eds. 1985. "Toward a Marxist Theory of Racism: Two Essays by Harry Chang." *Review of Radical Political Economics* 17(3): 34-45.

Light, I. and E. Bonacich. 1988. *Immigrant Entrepreneurs: Koreans in Los Angeles 1965-1982*. Berkeley: University of California Press.

Lin, Nan. 1982. "Social Resources and Instrumental Action." In Peter V. Marsden and Nan Lin, eds., *Social Structure and Network Analysis*. Beverly Hills, CA: Sage, 131-45.

—. 1989. "Chinese Family Structure and Chinese Society." *Bulletin of the Institute of Ethnology*, Academia Sinica 65: 59-129.

—. 1995. "Les resources sociales: une théorie du capital social." *Revue française de sociologie* 36(4): 685-704.

—. 1999. "Social Networks and Status Attainment." *Annual Review of Sociology* 25: 467-87.

—. 2000. "Inequality in Social Capital." *Contemporary Sociology* 29(6): 785-95.

—. 2001a. "Building a Network Theory of Social Capital." In Nan Lin, Karen Cook, and Ronald S. Burt, eds., *Social Capital: Theory and Research*. New York: Aldine de Gruyter, 3-29.

—. 2001b. *Social Capital: A Theory of Social Structure and Action*. Cambridge: Cambridge University Press, 2001.

Lin, N., K. Cook, and R.S. Burt. 2001a. *Social Capital: A Theory of Social Structure and Action*. New York: Cambridge University Press.

—, eds. 2001b. "Preface." *Social Capital: Theory and Research*. New York: Aldine de Gruyter.

—, eds. 2001c. *Social Capital: Theory and Research*. New York: Aldine de Gruyter.

Lin, Nan, Walter M. Ensel, and John C. Vaughn. 1981. "Social Resources and Strength of Ties: Structural Factors in Occupational Status Attainment." *American Sociological Review* 46(4): 393-405.

Lin, Nan, Yang-Chih Fu, and Ray-May Hsung. 2001. "The Position Generator: Measurement Techniques for Investigations of Social Capital." In Nan Lin, Karen Cook, and Ronald S. Burt, eds., *Social Capital: Theory and Research*. New York: Aldine de Gruyter, 57-84.

Loizos, P. 2000. "Are Refugees Social Capitalists?" In Stephen Baron, John Field, and Tom Schuller, eds., *Social Capital: Critical Perspectives*. Cambridge: Oxford University Press.

Lopez, M. Lisette, and Carol B. Stack. 2001. "Social Capital and the Culture of Power: Lessons from the Field." In Susan Saegert, J. Phillip Thompson, and Mark R. Warren, eds., *Social Capital and Poor Communities*. New York: Russell Sage Foundation, 3-59.

Loughlin, Catherine, and Julian Barling. 1999. "The Nature of Youth Employment." In J. Barling and E.K. Kelloway, eds., *Young Workers; Varieties of Experience*. Washington, DC: American Psychological Association, 17-36.

Lowndes, V. 2000. "Women and Social Capital: A Comment on Hall's 'Social Capital in Britain.'" *British Journal of Political Science* 30: 533-40.

Lynch, J., and G. Kaplan. 1997. "Understanding How Inequality in the Distribution of Income Affects Health." *Journal of Health Psychology* 2: 297-314.

Lynch, John, George A. Kaplan, Elsie R. Pamuk, Richard D. Cohen, Katherine E. Heck, Jennifer L. Balfour, and Irene H. Yen. 1998. "Income Inequality and Mortality in Metropolitan Areas of the United States." *American Journal of Public Health* 88: 1074-79.

Works Cited

Lynch, J., G. Davey Smith, M. Hillemeier, M. Shaw, T. Raghunathan, and G. Kaplan. 2001. "Income Inequality, the Psycho-Social Environment and Health: Comparisons of Wealthy Nations." *Lancet* 358(9277): 194-200.

Macmillan, Ross. 1995. "Changes in the Structure of Life Courses and the Decline of Social Capital in Canadian Society: A Time Series Analysis of Property Crime Rates." *Canadian Journal of Sociology* 20(1): 51-79.

Macy, Michael W. 1991. "Chains of Cooperation: Thresholds Effects in Collective Action." *American Sociological Review* 56: 730-47.

Mansbridge, Jane. 1999. "Altruistic Trust." In Mark Warren, ed., *Democracy and Trust*. New York: Cambridge University Press.

Marjoribanks, Kevin. 1991. "Family Human and Social Capital and Young Adults' Educational Attainment and Occupational Aspirations." *Psychological Reports* 69: 237-38.

Marschall, Melissa, and Dietlind Stolle. 2004. "Race in the City: Neighbourhood Context and the Development of Generalized Trust." *Political Behavior* 26: 125-53.

Marsden, Peter V. 2001. "Interpersonal Ties, Social Capital, and Employer Staffing Practices." In Nan Lin, Karen Cook, and Ronald S. Burt, eds., *Social Capital: Theory and Research*. New York: Aldine de Gruyter, 105-25.

Marshall, T.H. 1992 [1950]. "Citizenship and Social Class." In T.H. Marshall and T. Bottomore, eds., *Citizenship and Social Class*. London: Pluto Press.

McCarthy, Bill, and John Hagan. 2001. "When Crime Pays: Capital, Competence, and Criminal Success." *Social Forces* 79(3): 1035-59.

McCarty, T.A. 1993. "Demographic Diversity and the Size of the Public Sector." *Kyklos* 46: 225-40.

McInnes, C. 2002. "Welfare Reform: A Trial." *Vancouver Sun*, 19 January, A4.

McLanahan, Sara, and Gary Sandefur. 1994. *Growing Up with a Single Parent: What Hurts, What Helps*. Cambridge: Harvard University Press.

McNeal, Ralph B., Jr. 1999. "Parental Involvement as Social Capital: Differential Effectiveness on Science Achievement, Truancy, and Dropping Out." *Social Forces* 78(1): 117-44.

McPherson, Barry D. 1983. *Aging as a Social Process: An Introduction to Individual and Population Aging*. Toronto: Butterworth.

McPherson, J.M., and W.G. Lockwood. 1980. "The Longitudinal Study of Voluntary Association Membership: A Multivariate Analysis." *Journal of Voluntary Action Research* 9: 61-79.

Meyer, J.W. 1986. "The Self and the Life Course: Institutionalization and Its Effects." In B. Sorenson, F.E. Weinert, and L.R. Sherrod, eds., *Human Development and the Life Course: Multidisciplinary Perspectives*. Hillsdale, NJ: Lawrence Erlbaum, 199-206.

Meyerson, Eva M. 1994. "Human Capital, Social Capital and Compensation: The Relative Contribution of Social Contacts to Managers' Incomes." *Acta Sociologica* 37: 383-99.

Milbrath, Lester W., and M.L. Goel. 1977. *Political Participation*. 2nd ed. Chicago: Rand McNally.

Miller, David. 1995. *On Nationality*. Oxford: Oxford University Press.

—. 1998. "The Left, the Nation-State, and European Citizenship." *Dissent* 48: 47-51.

Minkoff, Debra C. 1997. "Producing Social Capital: National Social Movements and Civil Society." *American Behavioral Scientist* 40: 606-19.

Mishler, William, and Richard Rose. 1997. "Trust, Distrust and Skepticism: Popular Evaluations of Civil and Political Institutions in Post-Communist Societies." *Journal of Politics* 59: 418-51.

Mitchell, B.A. 1994. "Family Structure and Leaving the Nest: A Social Resource Perspective." *Sociological Perspectives* 37(4): 651-71.

—. 2000a. "Conceptual and Methodological Developments in Homeleaving Research." Web-site version of paper presentation at the Max Planck Institute for Demographic Research workshop titled, "Leaving Home: A European Focus," Rostock, Germany, 6-8 September.

—. 2000b. "The Refilled Nest: Debunking the Myth of Families in Crisis." In E.M. Gee and G. Gutman, eds., *The Overselling of Population Aging: Apocalyptic Demography, Intergenerational Challenges and Social Policy*. Toronto: Oxford University Press, 80-99.

—. 2003. "Life Course Theory." In J.J. Ponzetti, ed., *The International Encyclopedia of Marriage and Family Relationships*. 2nd ed. New York: Macmillan Reference USA, 1051-55.

—. 2004. "Making the Move: Cultural and Parental Influences on Young Adults' Departures from Home." *Journal of Comparative Family Studies* 35(3): 423-43.

Mitchell, B.A., and E.M. Gee. 1996. "Young Adults Returning Home: Implications for Social Policy." In J. Hudson and B. Galaway, eds., *Youth in Transition: Perspectives on Research and Practice*. Toronto: Thompson Educational Publishing, 61-71.

Mitchell, B.A., A.V. Wister, and E.M. Gee. 2000. "Culture and Coresidence: An Exploration of Variation in Home-Returning among Canadian Young Adults." *Canadian Review of Sociology and Anthropology* 37(2): 197-222.

—. 2004. "The Ethnic and Family Nexus of Homeleaving and Home Returning among Canadian Young Adults." *Canadian Journal of Sociology* 29(4): 543-75.

Morgan, Stephen L., and Aage B. Sørensen. 1999. "Parental Networks, Social Closure, and Mathematical Learning: A Test of Coleman's Social Capital Explanation of School Effects." *American Sociological Review* 64: 661-681.

Muller, Edward N., and Mitchell A. Seligson. 1994. "Civic Culture and Democracy: The Question of Causal Relationships." *American Political Science Review* 88: 635-53.

Nagin, Daniel, and Raymond Paternoster. 1994. "Personal Capital and Social Control: The Deterrence Implications of a Theory of Individual Differences in Criminal Offending." *Criminology* 32(4): 581-606.

Newton, Kenneth. 1999. "Social and Political Trust in Established Democracies." In Pippa Norris, ed., *Critical Citizens: Global Support for Democratic Governance*. Oxford: Oxford University Press, 169-87.

Newton, Kenneth, and Pippa Norris. 2000. "Confidence in Public Institutions: Faith, Culture, or Performance?" In Susan J. Pharr and Robert D. Putnam, eds., *Disaffected Democracies: What's Troubling the Trilateral Countries?* Princeton: Princeton University Press, 52-73.

Nie, N.H., J. Junn, and K. Stehlik-Barry. 1996. *Education and Democratic Citizenship in America*. Chicago: University of Chicago Press.

Norusis, Marija. 1993. *SPSS for Windows: Users' Guide Release 6.0*. Chicago: SPSS Inc.

O'Rand, A.M. 1996. "The Precious and the Precocious: Understanding Cumulative Disadvantage and Cumulative Advantage over the Life Course." *The Gerontologist* 36: 230-38.

Offe, Claus. 1999. "Trust and Knowledge, Rules and Decisions." In Mark Warren, ed., *Democracy and Trust*. Cambridge: Cambridge University Press.

Omi, M., and H. Winant. 1986. *Race in America*. Berkeley: University of California Press.

Organisation for Economic Co-operation and Development (OECD). 2001. *The Well-Being of Nations: The Role of Human and Social Capital*. Paris: OECD.

Orren, Gary. 1997. "Fall From Grace: the Public's Loss of Faith in Government." In Joseph S. Nye, Philip D. Zelikow, and David C. King, eds., *Why People Don't Trust Government*. Cambridge, MA: Harvard University Press, 66-107.

Orth-Gomer, K., and J. Johnson. 1987. "Social Network Interaction and Mortality." *Journal of Chronic Disease* 40: 949-57.

Pal, Les A. 1989. "Identity, Citizenship and Mobilization: The Nationalities Branch and World War Two." *Canadian Public Administration* 32: 407-26.

Palloni, Alberto, Douglas S. Massey, Miguel Ceballus, Kristin Espinosa, and Michael Spittel. 2001. "Social Capital and International Migration: A Test Using Information on Family Networks." *American Journal of Sociology* 106(5): 1262-98.

Papillon, M. 2002. *Immigration, Diversity and Social Inclusion in Canada's Cities*. Discussion paper Canadian Policy Research Networks. http://www.cprn.com/en/doc.cfm?doc=160.

Parcel, Toby L., and Laura E. Geschwender. 1995. "Explaining Southern Disadvantage in Verbal Facility among Young Children." *Social Forces* 73(3): 841-72.

Passeron, Jean-Claude. 1979. "Democratization of Higher Education in Europe." *Prospects: Quarterly Review of Education* 9(1): 45-53.

Pateman, Carole. 1988. *The Sexual Contract*. Stanford, CA: Stanford University Press.

Paterson, Lindsay. 2000. "Civic Society and Democratic Renewal." In Stephen Baron, John Field, and Tom Schuller, eds., *Social Capital: Critical Perspectives*. Oxford: Oxford University Press, 39-55.

Paxton, Pamela. 1997. "Women in National Legislatures: A Cross-National Analysis." *Social Science Research* 26: 442-64.

—. 1998. "Capitalizing on Community: Social Capital and the Democratic Society." PhD dissertation, Department of Sociology, University of North Carolina at Chapel Hill.

—. 1999. "Is Social Capital Declining in the United States? A Multiple Indicator Assessment." *American Journal of Sociology* 105(1): 88-127.

Peabody, D. 1961. "Attitude Content and Agreement Set in Scales of Authoritarianism, Dogmatism, Anti-Semitism, and Economic Conservatism." *Journal of Abnormal and Social Psychology* 63: 1-11.

Peterson, Trond, Ishak Saporta, and Marc-David L. Seidel. 2000. "Offering a Job: Meritocracy and Social Networks." *American Journal of Sociology* 106(3): 763-816.

Pfeffer, Jeffrey, and Nancy Langton. 1993. "The Effect of Wage Dispersion on Satisfaction, Productivity, and Working Collaboratively: Evidence from College and University Faculty." *Administrative Science Quarterly* 38: 382-407.

Plotnick, Robert D., and Richard F. Winters. 1985. "A Politico-Economic Theory of Income Redistribution." *American Political Science Review* 79: 458-73.

Plutzer, Eric. 2002. "Becoming a Habitual Voter: Inertia, Resources and Growth in Young Adulthood." *American Political Science Review* 96(1): 41-56.

Popielarz, Pamela A. 1999. "Organizational Constraints on Personal Network Formation." *Research in the Sociology of Organizations* 16: 263-81.

Portes, Alejandro. 1987. "The Social Origins of the Cuban Enclave Economy of Miami." *Sociological Perspective* 30: 340-72.

—. 1998. "Social Capital: Its Origins and Applications in Modern Sociology." *Annual Review of Sociology* 24: 1-24.

—. 2000a. "Social Capital: Its Origins and Applications in Modern Sociology." In Eric L. Lesser, ed., *Knowledge and Social Capital: Foundations and Applications*. Boston: Butterworth-Heinemann, 43-67.

—. 2000b. "The Two Meanings of Social Capital." *Sociological Forum* 15(1): 1-12.

—. 2002. "English-Only Triumphs, but the Costs Are High." *Contexts* 1(1): 10-15.

Portes, A., and A. Stepick. 1993. *City on the Edge: The Transformation of Miami*. Berkeley: University of California Press.

Portes, Alejandro, and P. Landolt. 1996a. "The Downside of Social Capital." *The American Prospect* 16: 18-21.

—. 1996b. "Unsolved Mysteries: The Tocqueville Files II – The Downside of Social Capital." *The American Prospect* 7: 26.

Portes, Alejandro, and J. Sensenbrenner. 1993. "Embeddedness and Immigration: Notes on Social Determinants of Economic Action." *American Journal of Sociology* 98(6): 1320-50.

Putnam, Robert D. [with R. Leonardi and R.Y. Nanetti] 1993a. *Making Democracy Work: Civic Traditions in Modern Italy*. Princeton, NJ: Princeton University Press.

—. 1993b. "The Prosperous Community: Social Capital in Public Life." *The American Prospect* 4: http://www.prospect.org/print/V4/13/putnam-r.html.
—. 1995a. "Bowling Alone: America's Declining Social Capital." *Journal of Democracy* 6(1): 65-78.
—. 1995b. "Tuning In, Tuning Out: The Strange Disappearance of Social Capital in America." *PS, Political Science and Politics* 28: 664-83.
—. 1996. "The Strange Disappearance of Civic America." *The American Prospect* 24: 34-48.
—. 2000. *Bowling Alone: The Collapse and Revival of American Community.* New York: Simon and Schuster.
—. 2001. "Social Capital: Measurement and Consequences." *Isuma: Canadian Journal of Policy Research* 2: 41-51.
—. 2002. "Bowling Together." *The American Prospect* 13: http://www.prospect.org/print/V13/3/putnam-r.html.
Reitz, J.G., and R. Breton. 1994. *The Illusion of Difference: Realities of Ethnicity in Canada and the United States.* Toronto: C.D. Howe Institute.
Rex, J. 1986. *Race and Ethnicity.* Stoney Stratford, UK: Open University Press.
Rice, T., and J. Feldman. 1997. "Civic Culture and Democracy from Europe to America." *Journal of Politics* 59(4): 1143-72.
Rice, T., and A. Sumberg. 1997. "Civic Culture and Government Performance in the American States." *Publius* 27: 99-114.
Robinson, R.V., and E.F. Jackson. 2001. "Is Trust in Others Declining in America? An Age-Period-Cohort Analysis." *Social Science Research* 30: 117-45.
Roediger, D. 1991. *The Wages of Whiteness: Race and the Making of the American Working Class.* New York: Verso.
Rose, R. 2000. "How Much Does Social Capital Add to Individual Health? A Survey Study of Russians." *Social Science and Medicine* 51: 1421-35.
Rothstein, Bo. 1998. *Just Institutions Matter: The Moral and Political Logic of the Universal Welfare State.* Cambridge, UK: Cambridge University Press.
Rothstein, Bo, and Dietlind Stolle. 2002. "How Political Institutions Create and Destroy Social Capital: An Institutional Theory of Generalized Trust." Paper presented at the 98th Meeting of the American Political Science Association in Boston, 29 August-2 September.
Rotolo, Thomas. 2000. "A Time to Join, a Time to Quit: The Influence of Life Cycle Transitions on Voluntary Association Membership." *Social Forces* 78: 1133-61.
—. 1999. "Trends in Voluntary Association Participation." *Nonprofit and Voluntary Sector Quarterly* 28: 199-212.
Saegert, Susan, Phillip Thompson, and Mark Warren, eds. 2001. *Social Capital and Poor Communities.* New York: Russell Sage.
Saguaro Seminar. 2000. *Social Capital Community Benchmark Survey: Executive Summary.* Cambridge, MA: John F. Kennedy School of Government.

Sampson, Robert J. 2001. "How do Communities Undergird or Undermine Human Development? Relevant Contexts and Social Mechanisms." In Alan Booth and Nan Crouter, eds., *Does It Take a Village? Community Effects on Children, Adolescents, and Families*. Mahwah, NJ: Lawrence Erlbaum Associates, Publishers.

Sampson, Robert, and John Laub. 1993. *Crime in the Making: Pathways and Turning Points through Life*. Cambridge, MA: Harvard University Press.

Sandefur, Rebecca L., and Edward O. Laumann. 1998. "A Paradigm for Social Capital." *Rationality and Society* 10(4): 481-501.

Sandomirsky, Sharon, and John Wilson. 1990. "Processes of Disaffiliation: Religious Mobility among Men and Women." *Social Forces* 68: 1211-29.

Sassen, S. 1995. "Immigration and Local Labor Markets." In A. Portes, ed., *The Economic Sociology of Immigration*. New York, NY: Russell Sage.

Schlesinger, A.M., Jr. 1992. *The Disuniting of America*. New York: W.W. Norton.

Scholz, J.T., and M. Lubell. 1998. "Trust and Taxpaying: Testing the Heuristic Approach to Collective Action." *American Journal of Political Science* 42: 398-417.

Schulman, Michael D., and Cynthia Anderson. 1999. "The Dark Side of the Force: A Case Study of Restructuring and Social Capital." *Rural Sociology* 64(3): 351-72.

Schuman, Howard, and Stanley Presser. 1996. *Questions and Answers in Attitude Surveys: Experiments on Question Form, Wording, and Context*. Thousand Oaks: Sage.

Seligman, Adam. 1997. *The Problem of Trust*. Princeton, NJ: Princeton University Press.

Seron, Carroll, and Kerry Ferris. 1995. "Negotiating Professionalism: The Gendered Social Capital of Flexible Time." *Work and Occupations* 22(1): 22-47.

Shapiro, Susan. 1987. "The Social Control of Impersonal Trust." *American Journal of Sociology* 93(3): 623-58.

Simons, R., and L. Whitbeck. 1991. "Running Away during Adolescence as a Precursor to Adult Homelessness." *Social Science Review* 65(2): 224-47.

Simpson, G., and M. Yinger. 1965. *Racial and Cultural Minorities: An Analysis of Prejudice and Discrimination*. 4th ed. New York: Harper and Row.

Skocpol, T. 1996. "Unsolved Mysteries: The Tocqueville Files – Unravelling from Above." *The American Prospect* 7(25): 20-25.

Smidt, Corwin. 1999. "Religion and Civic Engagement: A Comparative Analysis." *Annals of the American Academy of Political and Social Science* 565: 176-92.

Smith, David Horton. 1975. "Voluntary Action and Voluntary Groups." *Annual Review of Sociology* 1: 247-70.

Smith, David Horton, and Burt R. Baldwin. 1974. "Parental Socialization, Socioeconomic Status, and Volunteer Organization Participation." *Journal of Voluntary Action Research* 3(3-4): 59-66.

Smith, Elizabeth. 1999. "The Effects of Investments in the Social Capital of Youth on Political and Civic Behaviour in Young Adulthood: A Longitudinal Analysis." *Political Psychology* 20(3): 553-580.

Smith, Jackie. 1998. "Global Civil Society? Transnational Social Movement Organizations and Social Capital." *American Behavioral Scientist* 42(1): 93-107.

Smith, Sandra Susan. 2005. "'Don't Put My Name On It': Social Capital Activation and Job-Finding Assistance among the Black Urban Poor." *American Journal of Sociology* 111(1): 1-57.

Smith, Tom W. 1997. "Factors Relating to Misanthropy in Contemporary American Society." *Social Science Research* 26: 170-96.

Sniderman, P., M. Hagen, P. Tetlock, and H. Brady. 1991. "Reasoning Chains." In P. Sniderman, R. Brody, and P. Tetlock, eds., *Reasoning and Choice: Explorations in Political Psychology*. Cambridge, MA: Cambridge University Press, 70-92.

Snijders, Chris. 1997. "Review of *Trust in Modern Societies: The Search for the Bases of Social Order* by Barbara A. Misztal." *American Journal of Sociology* 102(6): 1724-25.

Snijders, Tom A.B. 1999. "Prologue to the Measurement of Social Capital." *La revue Tocqueville/The Tocqueville Review* 20: 27-44.

Snyder, Eldon E. 1970. "Longitudinal Analysis of Social Participation in High School and Early Adulthood Voluntary Associational Participation." *Adolescence* 17: 79-88.

Stanton-Salazar, D. Ricardo, and Sanford M. Dornbusch. 1995. "Social Capital and the Reproduction of Inequality: Information Networks among Mexican-Origin High School Students." *Sociology of Education* 68: 116-35.

Stasiulis, D. 1980. "The Political Structuring of Ethnic Community Action: A Reformulation." *Canadian Ethnic Studies* 12(3): 19-44.

—. 1982. "Race, Ethnicity and the State: The Political Structuring of South Asian and West Indian Communal Action in Combating Racism." PhD dissertation, Department of Sociology, University of Toronto.

Stasiulis, D., and Y. Abu-Laban. 1991. "The House that Parties Built: Reconstructing Ethnic Representation in Canadian Politics." In K. Megyery, ed., *Ethno-Cultural Groups and Visible Minorities in Canadian Politics: The Question of Access*. Toronto: Dundurn Press.

StataCorp. 1999. *Stata Statistical Software: Release 6.0*. College Station, Texas: Stata Corporation.

Statistics Canada. 1996. *Census of Canada*. CD-ROM. Ottawa: Statistics Canada [producer and distributor].

—. 1997. *The 1997 National Survey of Giving, Volunteering and Participating (NSGVP) Public Use Microdata File*. Ottawa: Statistics Canada.

—. 2003. *Families and Households Profile: Provinces and Territories*. http://www.12statcan.ca/english/census01/products/.

—. 2005. *Population Urban and Rural, by Province and Territory (Canada)*. http://www40.statcan.ca/l01/cst01/demo62a.htm?sdi=rural.

Stein, R., S.S. Post, and A. Rinden. 2000. "Reconciling Context and Contact Effects on Racial Attitudes." *Political Research Quarterly* 52: 285-303.

Stephens, John D. 1979. *The Transition from Capitalism to Socialism.* London, UK: Macmillan.
Stepick, A. 1989. "Miami's Two Informal Sectors." In A. Portes, M. Castells, and L.A. Benton, eds., *The Informal Economy: Studies in Advanced and Less Developed Countries.* Baltimore, MD: Johns Hopkins University Press, 111-34.
Stolle, Deitlind 1998. "Bowling Together, Bowling Alone: The Development of Generalized Trust in Voluntary Associations." *Political Psychology* 19(3): 497-525.
—. 2002. "Trusting Strangers: The Concept of Generalized Trust in Perspective." In G.S. Schaal, ed., *Österreichische Zeitschrift für Politikwissenschaft; Schwerpunktheft 4, 2/4. Vertrauen,* 397-412.
—. 2003. "The Sources of Social Capital." In Dietlind Stolle and Mark Hooghe, eds., *Generating Social Capital: Civil Society in Comparative Perspective.* New York: Palgrave Macmillan, 19-42.
Stolle, Dietlind, and Mark Hooghe, eds. 2003. *Generating Social Capital: Civil Society in Comparative Perspective.* New York: Palgrave Macmillan.
Stolle, Dietlind, and Thomas R. Rochon. 1998. "Are All Associations Alike? Member Diversity, Associational Type, and the Creation of Social Capital." *American Behavioral Scientist* 42(1): 47-65.
Sudbury, J. 1998. *Other Kinds of Dreams: Black Women's Organizations and the Politics of Transformation.* London, UK: Routledge.
Sullivan, M.L. 1989. *Getting Paid: Youth Crime and Work in the Inner City.* Ithaca, NY: Cornell University Press.
Sundeen, Richard A., and Sally A. Raskoff. 1994. "Volunteering among Teenagers in the United States." *Nonprofit and Voluntary Sector Quarterly* 23: 383-403.
Sztompka, Piotr. 1996. "Trust and Emerging Democracy." *International Sociology* 11: 37-62.
Tarrow, Sidney. 1996. "States and Opportunities: The Political Structuring of Social Movements." In Doug McAdam, John D. McCarthy, and Mayer N. Zald, eds., *Comparative Perspectives on Social Movements: Political Opportunities, Mobilizing Structures, and Cultural Framings.* New York: Cambridge University Press.
Taylor, S. 1994. "Darkening the Complexion of Canadian Society: Black Activism, Policy-Making and Black Immigrants from the Caribbean to Canada, 1940s to 1960s." PhD thesis, Department of History, University of Toronto.
Teachman, J.D., and M.D. Hayward. 1993. "Interpreting Hazard Rate Models." *Sociological Methods and Research* 21(3): 340-71.
Teachman, J.D., K. Paasch, and Karen Carver. 1997. "Social Capital and the Generation of Human Capital." *Social Forces* 75(4): 1343-59.
Tilly, Charles. 1998. *Durable Inequality.* Berkeley: University of California Press.
Uehara, Edwina. 1990. "Dual Exchange Theory, Social Networks, and Informal Social Support." *American Journal of Sociology* 96(3):521-57.
UNESCO. *Four Statements on the Race Question.* Paris: UNESCO, 1969.

Uslaner, Eric M. 2001a. "Trust and Consequences." In Paul Dekker and Eric M. Uslaner, eds., *Social Capital and Participation in Everyday Life*. London and New York: Routledge.

—. 2001b. "Trust as a Moral Value." Presented at the conference Social Capital: Interdisciplinary Perspectives. University of Exeter, September.

—. 2001c. "Volunteering and Social Capital: How Trust and Religion Shape Civic Participation in the United States." In Paul Dekker and Eric M. Uslaner, eds., *Social Capital and Participation in Everyday Life*. London and New York: Routledge.

—. 2002. *The Moral Foundations of Trust*. Cambridge, UK: Cambridge University Press.

—. 2003. "Trust, Democracy and Governance: Canadian Government Policies Influence Generalized Trust." In Dietlind Stolle and Mark Hooghe, eds., *Generating Social Capital: Civil Society in Comparative Perspective*. New York: Palgrave Macmillan, 171-90.

van Roosmalen, Erica, and Harvey Krahn. 1996. "Boundaries of Youth." *Youth and Society* 28: 3-38.

Varshney, A. 2002. *Civic Life and Ethnic Conflict: Hindus and Muslims in India*. New Haven, CT: Yale University Press.

Veenstra, G. 2000. "Social Capital and Health: An Individual-Level Analysis." *Social Science and Medicine* 50: 619-29.

—. 2001. "Social Capital and Health." *Canadian Journal of Policy Research* 2(1): 72-81.

—. 2002a. "Explicating Social Capital: Trust and Participation in the Civil Space." *Canadian Journal of Sociology* 27(4): 547-72.

—. 2002b. "Social Capital and Health (Plus Wealth, Income Inequality, and Regional Health Governance)." *Social Science and Medicine* 54: 849-58.

Veenstra, G., and J. Lomas. 1999. "Home Is Where the Governing Is: Social Capital and Regional Health Governance." *Health and Place* 5: 1-12.

Verba, Sidney, Kay L. Schlozman, and Henry E. Brady. 1995. *Voice and Equality: Civic Voluntarism in American Politics*. Cambridge, MA: Harvard University Press.

Voss, K. 1993. *The Making of American Exceptionalism: The Knights of Labor and Class Formation in the Nineteenth Century*. Ithaca, NY: Cornell University Press.

Wacquant, L.J.D., and W.J. Wilson. 1989. "The Cost of Racial and Class Exclusion in the Inner City." *Annals of the American Academy of Political and Social Science* 50(1): 8-26.

Walcott, R. 2000. *Rude: Contemporary Black Canadian Cultural Criticism*. Toronto: Insomniac Press.

Waldinger, R. 1996. *Still the Promised City? African-Americans and New Immigrants in Post-Industrial New York*. Cambridge, MA: Harvard University Press.

Walker, G., B. Kogut, and W. Shan. 1997. "Social Capital, Structural Holes and the Formation of an Industry Network." *Organization Science* 8(2): 109-25.

Wall, Ellen, Gabriele Ferrazzi, and Frans Schryer. 1998. "Getting the Goods on Social Capital." *Rural Sociology* 63(2): 300-22.

Waters, M. 1994. "West Indian Immigrants, African-Americans, and Whites in the Workplace: Different Perspectives on American Race Relations." Paper presented at the Meeting of the American Sociological Association, Los Angeles, CA.

Watkins, Peter E. 1984. "Culture, Cultural Resources, and the Labour Market: A Study of a Christian Brothers College." *Australian Journal of Education* 28: 66-77.

Wegener, Bernd. 1991. "Job Mobility and Social Ties: Social Resources, Prior Job, and Status Attainment." *American Sociological Review* 56: 60-71.

Weinstock, Daniel. 1999. "Building Trust in Divided Societies." *Journal of Political Philosophy* 7(3): 287-307.

Weitzman, E., and I. Kawachi. 2000. "Giving Means Receiving: The Protective Effect of Social Capital on Binge Drinking on College Campuses." *American Journal of Public Health* 90(2): 1936-39.

Wellman, Barry. 1992. "Which Types of Ties and Networks Give What Kind of Social Support?" *Advances in Group Processes* 9: 207-35.

—. 1999a. "The Network Community." In Barry Wellman, ed., *Networks in the Global Village*. Boulder, CO: Westview, 1-48.

—, ed. 1999b. *Networks in the Global Village: Life in Contemporary Communities*. Boulder, CO: Westview.

Wellman, Barry, and Kenneth Frank. 2001. "Network Capital in a Multilevel World: Getting Support from Personal Communities." In Nan Lin, Karen Cook, and Ronald S. Burt, eds. *Social Capital: Theory and Research*. New York: Aldine de Gruyter, 233-73.

Whitbeck, L.B., and D.R. Hoyt. 1999. *Nowhere to Grow: Homeless and Runaway Adolescents and Their Families*. New York: Aldine de Gruyter, 1999.

White, Michael J., and Gayle Kaufman. 1997. "Language Usage, Social Capital, and School Completion among Immigrants and Native-Born Ethnic Groups." *Social Science Quarterly* 78(2): 385-98.

Whiteley, P. 2000. "Economic Growth and Social Capital." *Political Studies* 48(3): 443-66.

Whittington, L.A., and H.E. Peters. 1996. "Economic Incentives and Financial and Residential Independence." *Demography* 33(1): 82-97.

Wilensky, H. 1975. *The Welfare State and Equality: Structural and Ideological Roots of Public Expenditures*. Berkeley: University of California Press.

Wilkinson R. 1992. "Income Distribution and Life Expectancy." *British Medical Journal* 304: 165-68.

—. 1996. *Unhealthy Societies: The Afflictions of Inequality*. London: Routledge.

Willms, J. Douglas. 2001. "Hypotheses about Community Effects on Social Outcomes." *Isuma: Canadian Journal of Policy Research* 2(1): 53-62.

Wilson, John. 2000. "Volunteering." *Annual Review of Sociology* 26: 215-40.

Wilson, John, and Marc Musick. 1997. "Who Cares? Toward an Integrated Theory of Volunteer Work." *American Sociological Review* 62: 694-713.

Wilson, Patricia A. 1995. "Embracing Locality in Local Economic Development." *Urban Studies* 32(4-5): 645-58.

—. 1997. "Building Social Capital: A Learning Agenda for the Twenty-first Century." *Urban Studies* 34(5-6): 745-60.
Wilson, W.J. 1987. *The Truly Disadvantaged: The Inner-City, the Underclass, and Public Policy*. Chicago: University of Chicago Press.
—. 1996. *When Work Disappears: The World of the New Urban Poor*. New York: Knopf.
Wilton, R.D. 1998. "The Constitution of Difference: Space and Psyche in Landscapes of Exclusion." *Geoforum* 29(2): 173-85.
Wolfinger, R., and S. Rosenstone. 1980. *Who Votes?* New Haven, CT: Yale University Press.
Woolcock, Michael. 1998. "Social Capital and Economic Development: Toward a Theoretical Synthesis and Policy Framework." *Theory and Society* 27: 151-208.
—. 2001. "The Place of Social Capital in Understanding Social and Economic Outcomes." *Isuma: Canadian Journal of Policy Research* 2(1): 11-17.
Woolley, Frances. 1998. "Social Cohesion and Voluntary Activity: Making Connections." Paper presented at Centre for the Study of Living Standards Conference, Ottawa.
Wuthnow, Robert. 1994. *Sharing the Journey: Support Groups and America's New Quest for Community*. New York, NY: Free Press.
—. 1997. *The Crisis in the Churches: Spiritual Malaise, Fiscal Woe*. Oxford: Oxford University Press.
Yamaguchi, Y. 1991. "Event History Analysis." *Applied Social Research Methods Series* 28. Newbury Park, CA: Sage.
Yamigishi, T., and M. Yamigishi. 1994. "Trust and Commitment in the United States and Japan." *Motivation and Emotion* 18: 129-66.
Yates, Miranda, and James Youniss. 1998. "Community Service and Political Identity Development in Adolescence." *Journal of Social Issues* 54(3): 495-512.
Young, Iris Marion. 1990. *Justice and the Politics of Difference*. Princeton, NJ: Princeton University Press.
Youniss, James, Jeffrey A. McLellan, and Miranda Yates. 1997. "What We Know about Engendering Civic Identity." *American Behavioral Scientist* 40(5): 620-31.
Zak, Paul J., and Stephen Knack. 1998. *Trust and Growth*. Working Paper 219. IRIS Center, University of Maryland.
Zhou, M. 1992. *New York's Chinatown: The Socioeconomic Potential of an Urban Enclave*. Philadelphia, PA: Temple University Press.
Zucker, Lynne G. 1986. "Production of Trust: Institutional Sources of Economic Structure, 1840-1920." *Research in Organizational Behaviour* 8: 53-111.
Zukin, S., and P. DiMaggio. 1990. *Structures of Social Capital: The Social Organization of the Economy*. Cambridge, UK: Cambridge University Press.

Contributors

SARA ABRAHAM is assistant professor of sociology at the University of Toronto-Mississauga, teaching in the area of race and politics. Her past research has included a study of party politics and opportunities for multi-racial politics in the Caribbean. Her research focus at present is in the political opportunities and political space of immigrants in Canada, and she is part of the Political Participation Research Network of the Metropolis Project.

AMANDA AIZLEWOOD is a senior researcher in the Knowledge and Research Directorate of Human Resources and Social Development Canada. Her research for the Government of Canada has focused on the qualitative and quantitative measurement of social inclusion, social capital, social cohesion, and public attitudes and values, as well as the critical examination of citizenship and identity. She is a graduate of political science from McGill University in Montreal and from Carleton University in Ottawa.

KEITH BANTING is the holder of the Stauffer-Dunning Chair in Policy Studies and director of the School of Policy Studies at Queen's University. He earned his BA (Hon.) from Queen's University and a doctorate from Oxford University. He taught for thirteen years in the Department of Political Science at the University of British Columbia and has been associated with Queen's since 1986. In addition, he has been a visiting scholar at a number of institutions, including the London School of Economics, the Brookings Institution, and Harvard University. In 2005, he was appointed an Officer in the Order of Canada. His research interests focus on social policy in Canada and other western nations. He is the author of *Poverty, Politics and Policy* and *The Welfare State and Canadian Federalism*. In addition, he is an editor and co-author of a dozen books dealing with public policy, including most recently: *Federalism and Health Policy: A Comparative Perspective on Multi-Level Governance;* and *Towards a Social Understanding of Productivity*. He has also contributed many articles to professional journals and other books.

PAUL BERNARD is professor of sociology at the Université de Montréal. He completed a PhD in sociology at Harvard University. He conducts both research and teaching on social inequality and life course and on epistemology and methods. His recent work contributes to the study of contingent work, job quality, living arrangements of young people, family unemployment, social cohesion, social capital, welfare regimes and gender regimes, social inequalities of health, and indicators of social development. Professor Bernard is a member of the National Statistics Council of Canada, the Board of the Social Research and Development Corporation, and the Board of Governors of the Canadian Academies of Science. He is Founding Chair of the Research Data Centres National Coordination Committee, and leader, with the Institut de la statistique du Québec, of the ESSIL/SHILS project for the construction of a household panel survey.

JAMES CURTIS (deceased May 2005) was professor of sociology at the University of Waterloo. He served as editor of the *Canadian Review of Sociology and Anthropology* and was a member of Statistics Canada's Advisory Committee on Social Conditions. He had recently received the Outstanding Contributions Award from the Canadian Sociology and Anthropology Association for research contributions to the fields. Among his publications are: *Exploring Myths about Canada and the United States: Four Regional Societies, Past and Present* (with Edward Grabb); *Social Inequality in Canada*, 4th edition (with Edward Grabb and Neil Guppy); *The Vertical Mosaic Revisited* (with Rick Helmes-Hayes); *Images of Canada* (with Lorne Tepperman); *The Social Significance of Sport* (with Barry McPherson and John Loy); and *Social Problems: A Canadian Perspective* (with Lorne Tepperman). As suggested by these titles, Curtis's primary areas of research interest were social inequality, Canadian society in comparative perspective, sport, and social problems. His two collaborators, Edward Grabb and Douglas Baer, are continuing a study on voluntary association activity in Canada and several other nations, and are preparing a book on historical and contemporary comparisons of the United States and English Canada and French Canada.

AVIGAIL EISENBERG is associate professor of political science at the University of Victoria. Her research focuses on democratic politics and minority rights. She is the author of *Reconstructing Political Pluralism*, co-editor of *Minorities within Minorities*, and editor of *Diversity and Equality: The Changing Framework of Freedom in Canada*. She serves as associate editor of the journal *Contemporary Political Theory*. She is currently writing a book entitled *Reasons of Identity: A Normative Guide to the Political and Legal Assessment of Identity*, which explores how political institutions apprehend minority identities.

CONTRIBUTORS

JOHN F. HELLIWELL is professor emeritus of economics at the University of British Columbia, member of the National Statistics Council, research fellow of the National Bureau of Economic Research, board member of the Institute for Research in Public Policy, and co-director of a new research program of the Canadian Institute of Advanced Research titled "Social Interactions, Identity and Well-Being." He was Mackenzie King Visiting Professor of Canadian Studies at Harvard University from 1991 to 1994, Christensen Visiting Fellow of St. Catherine's College, Oxford, in 2001, Visiting Research Fellow at Merton College Oxford in 2003, Visiting Special Adviser at the Bank of Canada 2003-2004, and Killam Visiting Scholar at the University of Calgary, 2005. He holds a DPhil in Economics from Oxford University, and honorary doctorates from McMaster University and the Universities of Guelph and New Brunswick. He was appointed a Fellow of the Royal Society of Canada in 1976 and an Officer of the Order of Canada in 1987. His books include *How Much Do National Borders Matter?*, *The Contribution of Human and Social Capital to Sustained Economic Growth and Well-Being*, and *Globalization and Well-Being*.

RICHARD JOHNSTON is Professor of Political Science and Research Director of the National Annenberg Election Survey at the University of Pennsylvania. He taught for several years at the University of British Columbia, where he was Head of the Political Science department and Distinguished University Scholar. He has also taught at the University of Toronto, the California Institute of Technology, Harvard University (Mackenzie King Chair, 1994-95), has been the Official Visitor in Politics and an Associate Member of Nuffield College, Oxford. He holds a BA (Hon) from UBC and an AM and PhD from Stanford. He is author or co-author of *Public and Opinion* and *Public Policy in Canada: Questions of Confidence*, *Letting the People Decide: Dynamics of a Canadian Election* (winner of Harold Adams Innis Prize for the best book in the social sciences published in English in Canada), *The Challenge of Direct Democracy: The 1992 Canadian Referendum*, *The 2000 Presidential Campaign and the Foundations of Party Politics*, and *The End of Southern Exceptionalism: Class, Race, and Partisan Change in the Postwar South*. He is co-editor of *Strengthening Canadian Democracy* and *Capturing Campaign Effects*. In addition, he has written more than fifty book chapters and refereed journal articles.

FIONA M. KAY is associate professor of sociology at Queen's University in Kingston, Ontario. Her research interests focus on the sociology of law; comparative analyses of civil and common law jurisdictions of law practice; gender, ethnicity, and career mobility; and life course transitions and career patterns. She is currently engaged in a study of social capital and professional careers with a focus on cultural diversity, professional mentorship, clientele relations, and legal tactics among lawyers. She is author of *Gender in Practice: A Study of Lawyers' Lives*, co-authored with John Hagan. She has also published extensively in sociology and law journals, including *American Sociological Review*, *Law and Society Review*, *Law and Social Inquiry*, *British Journal of Sociology*, *International Journal of the Sociology of Law*, *McGill Law Review*, *Osgoode Hall Law Journal*, *Feminist Legal Studies*, and *Canadian Review of Sociology and Anthropology*.

BARBARA A. MITCHELL is associate professor of sociology and gerontology at Simon Fraser University in Burnaby, BC. She received her degrees from the University of Waterloo (Hon. BA and MA, sociology) and McMaster University (PhD, sociology). Her current areas of research interest include ethnicity, generational support, and health; family related transitions to adulthood in comparative perspective; mid-life and later-life parenting; and social policy issues. She is author of *The Boomerang Age: Transitions to Adulthood in Families* and *Canadian Families in Social Context*. She has produced numerous articles, book chapters, and reports. Her work has appeared in such journals as *Canadian Journal of Sociology*, *Canadian Review of Sociology and Anthropology*, *Sociological Perspectives*, *Journal of Marriage and the Family*, *Family Relations*, *International Journal of Aging and Human Development*, and *Canadian Journal on Aging*.

RAVI PENDAKUR is assistant director of research in the Knowledge and Research Directorate of Human Resources and Social Development Canada in Ottawa. He has managed to work on issues of diversity through to the present despite two major government reorganizations, both of which saw his department (and work unit) dissolved and entailed four job changes. His most recent work (written with his economist brother) looks at the degree to which Canadian-born minorities face earnings gaps. His other work has examined the labour force contribution of immigrants to the Canadian economy. This is his first foray into the world of social capital.

THOMAS PERKS is an assistant professor in the Department of Sociology at the University of Lethbridge. His areas of research interest include studies in social capital, social inequality, sport, and research methodology. Recent research includes collaboration with Jim Curtis and colleagues on trends in voluntary association activity over recent decades in Quebec and English Canada, and on patterns of public protest. Also, he is a co-author of a chapter on inequality in political and community participation in *Dimensions of Inequality in Canada*, edited by Jonathan R. Kesselman and David A. Green.

CONTRIBUTORS

STUART N. SOROKA is associate professor and William Dawson Scholar in the Department of Political Science at McGill University. His is co-director of the Observatory on Media and Public Policy at the McGill Institute for the Study of Canada. From 2000 to 2002, he was the Gwilym Gibbon Postdoctoral Research Fellow at Nuffield College, Oxford. He is author of *Agenda-Setting Dynamics in Canada*, and author or co-author of a wide range of book chapters and journal articles; recent articles have been published in the *Journal of Politics*, *British Journal of Political Science*, *Canadian Journal of Political Science* (winner of the John McMenemy Prize for best paper of that year), and *Policy Studies Journal*.

GERRY VEENSTRA is assistant professor of sociology at the University of British Columbia. He has published articles on trust and participation in the civil space, social capital and health, social status and health, and health-care regionalization in such journals as the *Canadian Journal of Sociology*, *Social Science and Medicine*, *Health and Place*, the *Canadian Medical Association Journal*, and the *Canadian Journal of Public Health*. Current research areas include social class, social status and health; space, place, and health; and capital, cultural knowledge, and social space.

Index

9/11, and social trust, 81

Aboriginal people. *See* First Nations
Additive model, of social capital. *See* Coalescence
Adolescents. *See* Youth
African Liberation Support Committee, 205
Age
  at home-leaving, and survival time, 238, 242
  and trust
    generalized trust, 102, 109, 288
    political trust, 184, 288
    specific trust, 112, 114
  youth volunteer activities, and current community participation, 166-67
Asians. *See also* Chinese; Indians (Indo/South Asians)
  employees, low returns to education (US), 57
  social capital measures, 191
Association. *See* Bonding; Bridging; Inclusion; Social activity; Volunteer activity

Blacks
  American
    business owners, disenfranchisement of, 58
    job search, and networks, 57
  Canadian (Caribbean origins)
    community programs, 200
    education projects, 200, 204
    employment as working class, 202
    immigration pattern, 202
    immigration to Canada, 202
    inter-group relations with Canadian Tamils in Toronto, 200
    Pan-Africanism, 9, 203-7
    political organizations, 202, 203-7, 212-13
    social capital, 191, 210-12
    social movement organizations, 201
    women's organizations, 206
    youth activism, 205-6
Bonding. *See also* Bridging; Community; Ethnic groups; Families; Ghettoization; Immigrant groups; Minority groups; Networks
  characteristics, 24-25
  and coalescence, 54
  definition, 72
  as exclusion, 2, 7, 33, 72, 73
  and formal associations, 108
  and insularity, 72-74, 79
  and multiculturalism, 72-79
  and negative aspects of social capital, 33
  as possible barrier to social cohesion, 62
  and social capital, 253

theoretical and empirical bases of analysis, 5
"Boomerang" effect, of home-leaving, 8, 219, 222, 226
Bourdieu, Pierre
  definition of social capital, 17, 50
  on social capital
    as credit, 45
    as membership in communities, 222-23
Bowling Alone: The Collapse and Revival of American Community (Putnam), 10, 19, 84, 160
Bridging. *See also* Bonding; Community; Ethnic groups; Families; Immigrant groups; Minority groups; Networks; Trust
  characteristics, 24-25
  and coalescence, 54
  definition, 72, 108
  importance to democracy, 72
  as inclusion, 2, 7, 46
  and multiculturalism, 72-79
  networks, and interpersonal trust, 108, 109
  theoretical and empirical bases of analysis, 5
British
  intergenerational coresidence patterns, 221, 224-25, 226, 227, 231, 232, 234, 235, 237, 239
  young adult patterns of home-leaving, 221, 224-25
British Columbia Resource Community Sample, 4
Burt, Ronald S., 23, 28-29, 51-52

Campbell, Horace, 206
Canada. *See also* First Nations; Francophones; Multiculturalism; names of ethnic groups

ethnic diversity
  cultural, 3, 6, 7-8
  and support for social programs, 192, 295-97
  and trust, 173, 175
  and urbanization, 175-76
ethnic groups
  and social capital, as different from US, 192
  survey samples, 3-4
  trust, variance with community size, 192-93
  health, and social capital, 266-70
Canadian Council of Tamils, 207
Canadian Tamil Congress (CTC), 208, 210
Canadian Tamil Youth Development (CanTYD), 208, 210
Caribbeans. *See* Blacks
Chinatown (New York), 60
Chinese
  intergenerational coresidence patterns, 221, 224, 226, 227, 231, 232, 235, 237, 239, 241
  social capital measures, 191
  trust
    interpersonal trust, 188
    social trust, and economic system, 21
Church attendance, by gender, 145, 146, 148, 149
Civic involvement. *See* Voluntary activity
Coalescence
  benefits of, 54-56
  definition, 61
Coleman, James
  on coalescence, 54
  on social capital
    on benefits of civic engagement, 29
    and cultural heritage, 223
    definition, 45
    elements of, 30
    and networks, 61

research, 39
and resources, 49
theory of rational action, 51
on trust, 26-27
Community. *See also* Ethnic groups; Immigrant groups; minority groups; Networks
community enhancement
  definition, 61
  multiplicative benefits, 58-59
ghettoization, 54, 59-61
resource communities, and specific trust, 112, 114-15
rural, and coalescence, 55
size
  associated with variance in trust levels in Canada, 170-71, 192-93
  as contextual variable in measuring social capital, 183, 185, 186, 188, 189
  and interpersonal trust, 119, 175, 178, 183, 185, 189
  and social capital measures, 182, 192-93
  and social capital, 18, 19, 20-22, 172, 182, 184, 185, 186, 188, 189, 192-93
  and social networks, 175, 193, 223, 245
support for social programs, 280-81
"Continuity theory" of activity, 157-58
Coresidence, intergenerational
analysis
  home-leavers, 232, 233-37, 241-42, 247-48
  home-returners, 231, 237-40, 247-48
  home-stayers, 227, 231, 235-36
  "boomerang" effect, for young adults, 219, 222, 226
ethnic groups
  with highest rates, 219
  living arrangements, 231

females, compared with males, 220, 224, 235, 237, 239, 242
and life-course theory, 221-22, 225-26, 243-44
patterns by ethnic origins
  British, 221, 224-25, 226, 227, 231, 232, 234, 235, 237, 239
  Chinese, 221, 224, 226, 227, 231, 232, 235, 237, 239, 241
  Indian (Indo/East Asian), 221, 224
  Southern European, 221, 224, 226, 227, 231, 232, 235, 239
probablility factors, for young adults, 219-20
and quality of parent-child relationships, 225, 235, 237-38, 239, 241-42, 243-44
reasons for leaving home, 232, 238, 240, 242, 248
as social capital, for young adults, 221
study variables, 226-30
Criminal groups, as negative aspect of social capital, 33-34, 48, 53, 56
Culture and Coresidence Study, 8, 226. *See also* Coresidence, intergenerational
Current affairs tracking
  by gender, 145, 146, 148, 149
  and health, 271, 272

Democracy. *See also* Welfare state
and social capital, 19, 20, 52, 72
and trust, 85
Disassociation. *See* disenfranchisement; exclusion
Disenfranchisement
  definition, 61
  as exclusionary dynamic of social capital, 56
  results of, 57-58
Dispersion (distribution variance), of social capital, 25

Donations, by gender, 145, 146, 147
Douglas, Rosie, 206

Economics
  economic capital, compared with social capital, 253
  and social capital, 3, 21-22, 53
Education
  and association memberships, 131
  and formal participation, 184
  and home-leaving, 219, 237, 242, 245
  minority groups, and "bridging," 204
  and participation, 193
  private, in ethnically diverse states, 280
  and trust
    general trust, 102, 104-5, 118
    interpersonal trust, 184, 193
    specific trust, 112, 115
Egocentric social networks, 50
Employment
  minority groups, disenfranchisement, 57-58
  networks
    importance of "weak ties," 28, 46-47, 50
    and job mobility, 28, 55
    and promotion opportunities, 51-52
  young adults, home-leaving patterns, 220, 237, 238, 242
  youth, part-time jobs, 138
Employment insurance, support for, 288-89, 291, 294
Equality. *See also* inequality
  and health, 256
  and multiculturalism, 67, 84
  and trust, 80, 81-85, 88, 256
Equality, Security, and Community (ESC) survey, 3-4, 67-68, 97-100, 170, 176, 179, 263
Ethnic diversity. *See also* ethnic groups; immigrant groups; multiculturalism
  and multiculturalism, 67, 68-71
  and social capital, 169-70, 171, 184
  and social inequality, 7-8
  and social trust, 89, 115-16, 173-75, 284-85
  and support for social programs, 279, 295
Ethnic Diversity survey, 109
Ethnic groups. *See also* Bonding; Bridging; Coresidence, intergenerational; Ethnic diversity; Immigrant groups; Minority groups; Multiculturalism; Names of specific groups; Networks
  integration, and decline in protest movements, 211-12
  inter-group relations, 199-201, 211
  as networks, 18
  and social capital
    based on exclusion, 171
    contributions to, 90
  social movements, construed as "social conflict," 201
  social solidarity, and insularity, 33, 72-79, 90
  trust
    generalized, 102, 108-9, 118
    "imported trust," 117-18
    interpersonal trust, 181, 188, 190, 191, 295
    and majority group, 115-17, 119, 172
    in national community, 87
    "national trust," 116, 119
    "parental trust," 117
    of police, 115-16
    political trust, 188, 190, 191, 192
    and social capital measures, 188, 190-91
    specific trust, 115, 119
  young adults, intergenerational coresidence study, 219-48
  youth, and activist organizations, 203

INDEX

Exclusion. *See also* Bonding; Networks
   definition, 46
   disenfranchisement, 56-58
   as distribution process, 48-49

Families. *See also* Coresidence, intergenerational; networks
   inclusion, advantages of, 55
   quality of parent-child relationships, 55, 225, 235, 237-38, 239, 241, 243-44
   and social capital, "family socialization" model, 135-36
   socializing, by gender, 145, 146, 148, 149
   young adults, patterns of home-leaving, 219-48
First Nations
   as "national minority," 8, 70, 76
   social capital measures, 182, 191
Formal participation. *See* Social activity; volunteer activity
France
   ethnic diversity, less accommodating than Canada, 71
   trust assessments, 106
Francophones (Canada)
   and association memberships, 130
   and individual variables in measuring social capital, 187, 190, 192
   as "national minority," 8, 70, 76
   and social capital measures, 185, 187, 190, 192
   support for social programs, 294
   and trust
     generalized trust, 102, 106, 286
     political trust, 288
     regression modelling of trust, 284, 285-88
Free-riders, 82, 83
Fungibility
   definition, 23
   and kinds of capital, 9-10, 23-24
   theoretical and empirical bases of analysis, 5

Gender. *See also* Men; Women; Young adults; Youth
   and adolescent extracurricular activities, 136-39
   participation in community activities, 154-56
   and trust
     generalized trust, 102, 109
     specific trust, 112, 114
Ghettoization
   bonding, as divisive, 54, 59
   definition, 61
   and poverty, 60-61
Granovetter, Mark
   on coalescence, 54
   on networks, as generators of trust, 27
   "weak" vs. "strong" ties, in job searches, 46-47

Health
   and civic activity, 270, 271
   health care programs, support for, 289-90, 292, 294
   and social capital, 11, 251-73
   and social engagement, 269-70, 271
   status, sociodemographic predictors, 267-68
   survey variables, 273-77
   theoretical and empirical bases of analysis, 5, 256-57, 260-61, 264
   and trust
     generalized trust, 102, 105, 265
     political trust, 270, 271
     social trust, 265, 268-69
     specific trust, 110, 112
Human capital, 2, 22-23, 45

Immigrant groups. *See also* Ethnic groups; Minority groups; Multiculturalism
Canada
acculturation, and multiculturalism, 74-75
historical pattern of economic integration, 296
multicultural policies, 70
inclusion, benefits of, 55-56
and social capital
contributions to, 75-76
measures, 181, 182, 190-91
and social cohesion, 199
and trust
general trust, 102, 106
"imported trust," 106, 107, 113, 114
"national trust," 106, 113, 116-17
"parental trust," 107, 113
political trust, 192
specific trust, 112, 114
Inclusion. *See also* Bridging; Networks
and availability of resources, 55
definition, 46
as distribution process, 46-48
"weak" vs. "strong" ties, 46-47
Income
inequality
and crime rate, 259
and health, 258, 262
and trust, 83, 109
and political trust, 184
and social capital, 184, 193
"Incomplete launch," of home-leaving. *See* "Boomerang effect," of home-leaving
Indians (Indo/East Asian)
intergenerational coresidence patterns, 221, 224, 226, 227, 231, 232, 235, 239
social capital measures, 191

Inequality. *See also* Equality; Welfare state
and ethnic diversity, 7-8
income
and crime rate, 259
and health, 258, 262
and trust, 83, 109
and social capital, 25, 62, 63
and social networks, 57, 63
Italy
community participation levels, and performance of regional government, 259
social capital, and regional government, 20, 30, 107

Japan, social trust, and economic system, 21
Jobs. *See* Employment
Jordan, June, 206

Koreatown (Los Angeles), 18, 60

Lawyers, and social capital, 56
Liberation Tigers of Tamil Eelam (LITE), 207, 209
Life-course theory, and social capital
effect of parental resources during transition to adulthood, 221-22
and patterns of home-leaving heterogeneity, 222-25, 242-43
"ripple effect," 222, 225-26, 242, 243-44
Little Havana (Miami), 18, 60

Majority group. *See also* Ethnic groups; Minority groups
benefits of multiculturalism, 79
distrust of minority groups, 115-16, 172, 285-86
insularity of, 78, 90
social capital measures, 182, 190

Index

and view of welfare state, 69, 71, 72, 80
Marriage, and home-leaving of young adults, 238
Men
  adolescent activity participation
    increase over time, 145
    paid part-time jobs, 138
    sports, 136, 142, 143, 145, 159
    volunteer activities, 136, 139, 142, 143
  adult activity participation
    measures, 141
    political involvement, 136, 146
    relative effects of participation as youth, 152, 153-54, 155-56
    types of activities, 146
  interpersonal trust, decrease with age, 184
Minority groups. *See also* Ethnic groups; Immigrant groups; Majority group; Multiculturalism; Names of specific groups
  association memberships, 130
  and bonding, 8-9
  and bridging, 8-9
  employment disenfranchisement, in US job market, 57-58
  and social capital
    measures, 181, 182, 190-91
    use of, 48-49
  and trust
    interpersonal trust, 68, 286
    and social participation, 68
    specific trust, 115-16
Multiculturalism. *See also* Ethnic groups; Immigrant groups; Minority groups
  Canada
    accommodation of cultural differences, 77
    integration of immigrant groups, 107, 296-97

    policies, 69-71, 77
  and purpose of acculturation, 74-75
  and trust levels, 119-20
  and welfare state, 281-82
  definition, 69
  as distinct from ethnic diversity, 69, 71, 90
  as distinct from ethnic insularity, 72-74, 79
  and equality, 84
  and ethnic diversity, 67-71
  objections to, 67
  trust, and equality, 79-81, 84-85
  viewed as threat to social capital by majority group, 172
  and welfare state, 67-68, 69, 71, 72, 80, 279-97

National Education Longitudinal Study (US), 136
National Survey of Giving, Volunteering and Participating (NSGVP), 10, 140
Networks. *See also* Bonding; Bridging; Community; Ethnic groups; Exclusion; Families; Immigrant groups; Inclusion; Social networks
  activation, 50-51
  density, 28-29
  dysfunctional, 33, 53
  and health, 254, 255-58
  processes
    distribution, 46-49
    operating, 47, 49-51
    reproduction, 47, 51-53
    structuring, 28-29, 47, 51-53
  and social capital
    critique of, 42-43, 44
    individual, 17-18
    negative aspects of, 33-34
    social participation patterns, 133-65

"strong ties," 172
"structural holes," 28-29, 52
theoretical and empirical bases of analysis, 5
and trust
  centrality of, 4, 6-7
  general trust, 102, 107-9, 118
  social trust, 20
  specific trust, 113, 118
as viewed by social science disciplines, 3
"weak ties," advantages of, 28, 29, 46-47, 50, 52
Norms, as social capital, 52

OECD report (2001), on social capital, 62
Operating processes, 51. *See also* Networks

Pan-Africanism, 203-7
Pensions, support for, 290, 293, 294
Personality characteristics, and community involvement, 158-59
Physical capital, 45
Police, trust of, 114, 115, 116
Political science, and social capital, 3, 19-21, 52. *See also* Political trust
Population density, and trust, 109, 112, 114-150. *See also* community
poverty, and ghettoization, 60-61
Putnam, Robert
  on bonding, 24, 108
  on bridging, 24, 72, 108
  contradiction of theory of voluntary activity decline, 161-62
  on social capital and community, 19, 20-21, 161-62
  on trust, 27, 81-82, 87

Québécois. *See* francophones (Canada)

Racialization, as negative social capital, 202, 210-11
Redistributive programs. *See* Social programs; Welfare state
Religion
  and bonding, 108
  church attendance, by gender, 145, 146, 148, 149
  decline in participation, 144
  and group membership, 130
  as individual variable in measuring social capital, 185, 187, 188, 190
  and interpersonal trust, 185
  youth participation in, 142, 143, 144
Restorative justice, and social capital, 76
"Ripple effect," and life-course theory, 222, 225-26, 242, 243-44

Sir George Williams University, 205, 206
Social activity. *See also* volunteer activity
  association memberships, 107-8, 124-31
  and health, 269-70
  and social capital, 108, 181, 182, 183, 184
  socializing, by gender, 145, 146, 148, 149
Social capital. *See also* Bonding; Bridging; Coresidence, intergenerational; Fungibility; Trust
  acquisition, theories of, 26, 133-36, 157
  benefits, 36
  causation, and circular reasoning, 32-33, 38, 42, 43-44
  compared with other forms of capital, 2, 22-23, 45, 253
  as concept, 1-2, 17, 41
  as credit, 30, 45
  critiques of, 41-43
  definitions, 3, 17, 30, 31, 42, 43, 50, 61, 133, 171, 221, 252-53

as depreciating, if not renewed, 51
distribution of, 25
ethnic group aggregations, 179
and health, 251-73
indicators
　formal participation, 22, 177, 182
　interpersonal trust, 177, 182
　political trust, 177, 182
　social interaction, 177, 182
and life-course theory, 221-22
negative aspects of
　conformity, 34
　deviant social groups, 33-34, 48, 53, 56
　exclusion, 48, 49
　racialization, 202, 210
as "private good," 51
as "public good," 33-34, 43, 44, 53, 56, 169, 253, 254
and social cohesion, 53, 58
and social networks, 42-44, 49-51, 55, 59, 157, 222, 253
in social science disciplines, 2-3, 17-22
structure *versus* content, 29-30
theory and research, 5, 34-39
typology, dynamics
　distribution, exclusion, 47, 48-49, 53
　distribution, inclusion, 46-48, 47, 53
　reproduction, operating, 47, 49-51, 54
　reproduction, structuring, 47, 51-53, 54
typology, process applications
　coalescence, 54-56
　community enhancement, 54, 58-59
　disenfranchisement, 54, 56-58
　ghettoization, 54, 59-61
variables
　community-level, 194-95
　definitions, 193-97
　dependent, 177

independent, contextual level, 177-78, 183
independent, individual level, 27, 28, 178-79, 183, 195-97
measurement issues, 30-31, 32, 35-36, 38, 42
Social Capital Community Benchmark project, 173
Social cohesion
　bonding, as possible barrier to, 62
　and immigrant groups, 199
　and social capital, 53, 58
　and social networks, 171
　structuring processes, 46, 47
Social networks. *See also* Networks
　and community, 175, 193, 223, 245
　dysfunctional, 33, 53
　egocentric, 50
　importance of, 1, 23
　processes
　　reproduction, 46
　　structuring, 46, 47
　and social capital, 42-44, 49-51, 55, 57, 59, 157, 222, 253
　and social cohesion, 171
　and social inequality, 57, 63
　and social structure, 50, 251-52
　sociocentric, 50
　use of, 28
Social programs. *See also* Welfare state
　difference between Canada and US, 295, 296
　and welfare state, 288-97
Sociology, and social capital, 3, 17-18, 21
Southern Europeans, intergenerational coresidence patterns, 221, 224, 226, 227, 231, 232, 235, 239
Sri Lanka. *See* Tamils, Sri Lankan
"Strong ties," as social capital, 172
"Structural holes," in networks, 28-29, 52

Structuring processes, 51. *See also* Networks
Subtractive model, of social capital. *See* Disenfranchisement
Survey of Labour and Income Dynamics, 4

Tamil Eelam Society (TESOC), 207, 208
Tamils, Sri Lankan
  community programs, 200
  contribution to democracy in Canada and Sri Lanka, 76
  employment as working class, 202
  ideology, 208-9
  immigration pattern, 202-3
  nationalist movement, 9, 200, 201, 207-210
  negative media portrayal, 209-210
  political organizations, 202-3, 207-210, 214
  and social capital, 210-12
  social movement organizations, 201
  in Toronto, inter-group relations with Caribbean Blacks, 200
  youth activist groups, 209
Trust. *See also* Social capital
  "aversion to heterogeneity" hypothesis, 173-74
  importance, to social capital, 4, 6-7, 18, 26-27, 253
  interpersonal trust
    and community size, 170-71
    and ethnic groups, 284-85, 295
    indicators, 9
    and minority groups, 285-88, 290-94
    and participation in voluntary associations, 21, 107-8
    and public policies, 19
    and satisfaction with regional government, 53, 107
    as social capital measure, 180, 181, 183

  and support for social programs, 288-94, 295-96
  measurement
    issues, 95-101
    variables, 120-31
  modelling
    generalized trust, 90, 97-100, 101-9, 118-20, 265
    specific trust, 109-18
  personal
    as distinct from social trust, 72-73, 80, 85-86, 87, 89
    "strategic," 96-97, 98, 100
  political
    and health, 271
    indicators, 9
    and interpersonal trust, 282-88
    measurement, 87-88, 89, 265
    and public policies, 11-12, 19, 21
    as social capital measure, 181, 182, 183, 184, 186-87, 189-91
  social
    associated with lower mortality rate, 262
    as distinct from personal (particularized), 72-73, 80, 85-86, 87, 89
    and equality, 80, 81-85, 89, 90
    ethnicity, and trust, 284-88
    as extension of personal trust, 86-87
    and free-rider problem, 82, 83
    and health, 268-69
    "imported," 106-7
    measurement, 90, 97-100, 265
    modelling, 101-9
    moralistic, 72-73, 86-87, 88, 89, 96, 97, 100, 285
    and multiculturalism, 79-80
    "national," 106-7
    "parental," 107
    and political participation, 258-59

Index

specific, and lost wallet experiment,
    109-18
and welfare state, 81
theoretical and empirical bases of
    analysis, 5
as viewed by social science disciplines, 3

United States
    ethnic diversity and support for social
        programs, 295, 296
    trust, and ethnic diversity, 173
Uslaner, Eric M.
    "moralistic" vs. "strategic" (particular-
        ized) trust, 72-73, 86, 96-97, 100
    trust, and economic inequality, 83

Valence, and social capital, 48
Villipu (Tamil women's group), 208
Voluntary associations. *See* Volunteer
    activity, participation study
Volunteer activity, participation study
    adults, gender and community
        involvement, 145-46, 147, 149
    "continuity theory" of activity over
        lifetime, 157-58
    design and procedures
        data source and method, 140-42
        measures used, 162-65
        research questions, 139
    and health, 262
    personality characteristics, and
        participation, 158-59
    political participation, 20, 22, 59, 259
    and social capital, 52-53
    youth
        gender, and community involvement,
            142-45
        increase in volunteer activity, 161
        participation, and later adult
            activities, 146-60, 266
Voting, by gender, 145, 146, 147, 149

"Weak ties"
    advantages of, 46-47, 50, 52, 55
    ethnic groups, inter-group relations,
        200
Welfare state. *See also* Social programs
    and equality, 85
    and ethnically diverse societies, 67-68
    modelling, 288-94
    and multiculturalism, 67, 279-97
    social capital, and public policy, 11
    and social trust, 67-68, 80-81, 88-89,
        280-81
Women
    activist groups, 201, 206, 208
    adolescent activity participation
        high school clubs, 136, 142
        higher involvement than males, 138,
            142, 145
        increase over time, 145
        paid part-time jobs, 138
        sports, 141, 142, 145, 159
        types of volunteer activities, 136, 142,
            143
    adult activity participation
        greater volunteer activities than men,
            139, 145
        measures, 141
        more hindered than males by social
            background, 160
        and personality characteristics, 159
        political involvement, 136, 146
        relative effects of participation as
            youth, 151, 153, 155-56
        types of volunteer activities, 143,
            146
    marriage, as reason for home-leaving,
        224
    parental home-leaving, compared with
        men, 220, 224, 235, 237; 239, 244
World Tamil Movement (WTM), 207
World Values Survey (WVS), 96, 173

Young adults
 home-leaving, social policy and
  program recommendations, 244-45
 "incomplete launch/boomerang," of
  home-leaving, 219, 222, 226
 intergenerational coresidence, among
  ethnic groups, 219-48

Youth
 Black Caribbean, activist groups, 205-6
 volunteer activities, and adult participation levels, 146-60, 266
 Youth Activity Indexes, 141, 142, 144,
  154, 159, 162-63

Printed and bound in Canada by Friesens
Set in Giovanni and Scala Sans by Artegraphica Design Co. Ltd.
Text designer: Irma Rodriguez
Copy editor: Larry MacDonald
Proofreader: Dianne Tiefensee
Indexer: Annette Lorek